VISUAL QUICKSTART GUIDE

PINNACLE STUDIO 9

FOR WINDOWS

Jan Ozer

Peachpit Press

Visual QuickStart Guide
Pinnacle Studio 9 for Windows
Jan Ozer

Peachpit Press
1249 Eighth Street
Berkeley, CA 94710
510/524-2178
800/283-9444
510/524-2221 (fax)

Find us on the World Wide Web at: http://www.peachpit.com
To report errors, please send a note to errata@peachpit.com

Peachpit Press is a division of Pearson Education.

Copyright © 2004 by Jan Ozer

Editor: Jill Marts Lodwig
Copy Editor: Judy Ziajka
Tech Editor: Stephen Nathans
Production Editor: Lupe Edgar
Composition: Owen Wolfson
Cover Design: The Visual Group
Cover Production: George Mattingly
Indexer: Emily Glossbrenner

Notice of rights
All rights reserved. No part of this book may be reproduced or transmitted in any form by any means, electronic, mechanical, photocopying, recording, or otherwise, without the prior written permission of the publisher. For information on getting permission for reprints and excerpts, contact permissions@peachpit.com.

Notice of liability
The information in this book is distributed on an "As Is" basis, without warranty. While every precaution has been taken in the preparation of the book, neither the author nor Peachpit Press shall have any liability to any person or entity with respect to any loss or damage caused or alleged to be caused directly or indirectly by the instructions contained in this book or by the computer software and hardware products described in it.

Trademarks
Visual QuickStart Guide is a registered trademark of Peachpit Press, a division of Pearson Education.

Many of the designations used by manufacturers and sellers to distinguish their products are claimed as trademarks. Where those designations appear in this book, and Peachpit Press was aware of a trademark claim, the designations appear as requested by the owner of the trademark. All other product names and services identified throughout this book are used in editorial fashion only and for the benefit of such companies with no intention of infringement of the trademark. No such use, or the use of any trade name, is intended to convey endorsement or other affiliation with this book.

ISBN 0-321-24749-3

9 8 7 6 5 4 3 2 1

Printed and bound in the United States of America

*For the three girlies in my life:
Barb, Whatley, and Rose.*

Acknowledgements

This book, pulled together largely during the 2003 holiday season, owes a huge debt to those who gave up large chunks of their holidays and vacation to get it done, including Stephen Nathans (technical editor), Judy Ziajka (copy editor), Jill Marts Lodwig (developmental editor), production editor Lupe Edgar, and compositor Owen Wolfson. Thank you all for your efforts.

Special thanks to the Pinnacle folks for answering my frantic inquiries during the final stages of product testing.

As always, thanks to Pat Tracy for technical and other assistance.

Table of Contents

	Introduction	ix
Part I:	**Getting Started**	**1**
Chapter 1:	**Creating Watchable Video**	**3**

What Is Watchable Video? 4
Watchable Video Guidelines 5
Using a Feature-Rich Video Editor 7
Developing Strong Nonlinear Editing Skills 8
Choosing the Right Camera Settings 10
Applying Basic Shot Composition 17
Applying Advanced Shot Composition 24

Chapter 2: Introduction to Studio 9   **29**

Taking the Guided Tour 30
Using Edit Mode 31
Using Capture Mode 37
Using Make Movie Mode 40
Using Undo and Redo 41
Saving Your Projects 43
Using Online Help 46
Selecting Your Capture Drive 48
Defragmenting Your Capture Drive 51
Testing Your Capture Drive 53
Setting Default Durations 55
Setting the Auxiliary File Location 57

Part II:	**Gathering Your Assets**	**61**
Chapter 3:	**Capturing DV**	**63**

The DV Capture Interface 64
Connecting for DV Capture 68
Entering DV Capture Mode 70
Capturing DV Video 73
Choosing Your Capture Format 76
Capturing DV Video to MPEG Format 77

Table of Contents

        Customizing Album Views.................... 81
        Adding Scene Comments..................... 82
        Viewing Your Captured Video................ 83

Chapter 4: Capturing Analog Video   85
        The Analog Capture Interface................ 86
        Connecting for Analog Capture 89
        Choosing Your Analog Capture Parameters..... 92
        Tuning the Incoming Video Signal............ 96
        Adjusting the Incoming Audio Volume......... 98
        Capturing Analog Video..................... 100
        Customizing Album Views................... 103
        Adding Scene Comments.................... 104
        Viewing Your Captured Video................ 105

Chapter 5: Working with Still Images   107
        Capturing Still Images...................... 108
        Editing Still Images 115

Chapter 6: Collecting Assets in the Album   119
        Opening the Album to Video Scenes.......... 120
        Loading Video Files 121
        Playing Videos............................. 123
        Combining Scenes 125
        Splitting Scenes............................ 127
        Working with the Album's Views and Tools.... 131
        Working with Scene Comments.............. 135
        Working with the Still Images Tab 137
        Working with the Sound Effects Tab.......... 140

PART III: EDITING   143

Chapter 7: Producing Videos in the Movie Window   145
        Looking at Movie Window Views............. 146
        Working on the Storyboard 148
        Getting Video Clips to the Timeline 155
        Customizing Your Timeline View............. 162
        Common Tasks 164
        Trimming with the Clip Properties Tool....... 170
        Trimming a Clip on the Timeline............. 175
        Trimming Multiple Clips on the Timeline 176
        Advanced Timeline Editing 179
        Working with Still Images 190
        Working with Audio Files.................... 193

Chapter 8: Using Transitions — 197
- Looking in the Box — 198
- Understanding Transitions — 200
- Using Transitions — 202
- Customizing Transitions — 209
- Working with Hollywood FX Transitions — 212
- Ripple Transitions for Slide Shows — 217
- Hollywood FX Exposed — 219

Chapter 9: Applying Special Effects — 225
- What's in the Box? — 226
- Before Getting Started — 228
- Learning the Special Effects Interface — 229
- Studio's Cleaning Effects — 235
- Varying Playback Speed — 243
- Adding Motion to Still Images — 248
- Creating Music Videos Automatically — 253

Chapter 10: Designing Titles and Menus — 257
- Opening the Title Editor — 258
- Looking at the Title Editor — 262
- Adding and Editing Text — 264
- Using Studio's Styles — 268
- Resizing and Justifying Text — 274
- Kerning and Leading Text — 276
- Rotating and Skewing Text — 277
- Using Full-Screen Titles — 278
- Adding Logos to Video — 282
- Creating and Editing Title Objects — 287
- Working with Buttons — 288
- Working with Multiple Objects — 292
- Creating DVD Menu Templates — 299
- Creating Rolls and Crawls — 301

Chapter 11: Working with Audio — 303
- About Audio Tracks and Workflow — 304
- Setting Recording Options — 306
- Ripping CD Audio — 309
- Creating Background Tracks Using SmartSound — 312
- Recording Narrations — 314
- Using Studio's Sound Effects — 317
- Editing Audio Clips — 318
- Using the Volume Tool — 320
- Adjusting Volume, Balance and Fade on the Timeline — 332

Table of Contents

Using Studio's Audio Effects 336
Cleaning Your Audio 341

Chapter 12: DVD Authoring   **343**
About DVD Authoring 344
Using Menu Templates 350
Using Custom Menus 363
Previewing Your DVD 372
Creating Audio Menus 375
Creating Video Menus..................... 377
Burning a DVD Title 380
Creating P-i-P Effects with Video Thumbnails . 386

PART IV:	OTHER OUTPUT	391

Chapter 13: Writing to Tape   **393**
Setting Up Your Hardware 394
Writing to Tape............................ 395
Writing Disk Files to Tape 400

Chapter 14: Creating Digital Output   **403**
Decoding Your Compression Parameters...... 405
Compressing to AVI Format 407
Producing MPEG Files..................... 413
Creating RealVideo Files................... 416
Creating Windows Media Files 422

Chapter 15: Using StudioOnline   **425**
Uploading Videos to StudioOnline........... 426
Sending Videos from StudioOnline 431
Managing Videos in StudioOnline 435

PART V:	REFERENCE	437

Appendix A: Keyboard Shortcuts   **439**

Appendix B: Troubleshooting   **441**
Optimizing Your Capture Computer 442
Troubleshooting Common Problems......... 445

Index   **455**

INTRODUCTION

When I started working with digital video in 1991, the sheer ability to play video on a computer was a technical marvel. If you showed it to the average consumer, however, the typical response was, "Gee, why doesn't it look as good as my TV?" Tough to explain when the computer cost $3,000 and the TV cost $300.

Thus began my search for "apology-free video"—video I could show my wife, children, and friends without apologizing for poor sound or image quality.

As interest in digital video grew, friends and family asked with increasing frequency for a video editor they could both afford and quickly learn to use. Wary of the unspoken technical-support obligation that comes with recommending just any software program, I began my search for a product I could recommend without getting an unlisted phone number.

As you've probably guessed, I found that product in Pinnacle Systems' Studio.

Studio 9 delivers apology-free video courtesy of its MPEG-2 encoding engine, which is the same format used on DVDs coming from Hollywood. Hey, if it's good enough for *The Matrix* and *When Harry Met Sally*, it's good enough for me.

After working on software-review teams that awarded Studio several *PC Magazine* Editor's Choice awards, I knew that even newcomers to digital video could quickly master Studio's interface. Studio offers an unprecedented range of movie creation options. Want to quickly convert your 60-minute digital videotape to DVD and send it to the in-laws? It's a simple two-step process—no muss, no fuss. Want to invest hours to produce a polished, Hollywood-style video? Studio can do that too, with distribution options ranging from the Internet to DVD and all points in between.

It's a program that can easily be mastered by beginners and also satisfy intermediate or even advanced users with its breadth of features.

Using This Book

If you bought Studio 9 through a retail channel, you already have a manual that explains how to use the various components of the Studio interface. This book complements the manual in two ways.

First, like all *Visual QuickStart Guides*, this one is task oriented, describing and showing you how to perform most common video production tasks. The descriptions are precise and exhaustive, identifying with screen shots and text the best ways to get the job done.

In addition, having worked with digital video for many years, I know that video editing can be an incredible time sink, probably the main reason most folks simply don't edit their camcorder tapes. Thus many sections and tips focus on how to avoid problems and work as efficiently as possible. Sidebars address technical topics to help you make decisions.

Making Movies with Studio

Within its uniquely unified video-editing/DVD-authoring interface, Studio gives you an unparalleled range of production activities. Depending on your equipment, you can capture footage from a digital or analog camcorder, edit the footage, integrate video from other sources, and output the results for streaming on the Internet, playing back on your desktop, or delivering via DVD or CD.

However, all good movies, regardless how they are delivered, must start with an appreciation of how to create movies worth watching. Chapter 1 explores the notion of creating *watchable* video, a primer aimed at teaching you the proper settings for your video camera and sound shooting techniques. Chapter 2 introduces you to the Studio interface and gets your computer ready for video production.

Editing and production

After you've shot your source videos using the proper camera settings and solid shooting techniques, the process of editing and production begins. It involves the following four steps:

◆ **Gathering assets.** This is where you capture your video, import still images, or grab them from your camcorder or captured video, and import any background audio files. These activities in covered in Chapters 3, 4, and 5.

- **Trimming and organizing.** In most instances, you won't want to include every minute that you shot in the final production. Accordingly, you trim unwanted sections, then place your video clips and still images in the desired order. Chapter 7 describes how to get this done.

- **Garnishing.** Here's where the true editing comes in. During this stage, you add transitions between clips, title tracks, still image overlays, and any special effects. You can also input a narration track, add music ripped from a CD, or create your own custom background track using SmartSound (a utility included with Studio). Chapters 8 through 11 cover these activities.

- **Rendering.** This is where you produce your final output. Though "encoding into a streaming format" may sound complicated, Studio includes easy-to-follow templates that simplify the task, making this stage the most mechanical of all. Chapter 14 describes how to output your videos as digital files for posting to a Web site, sending via email, or copying to CD-ROM.

If you're outputting to DVD there's another stage, of course, typically called *authoring*. This is when you create your menus, link videos and still image assets, and preview to ensure that your project flows as desired. Then you burn your disc. DVD production is covered in Chapter 12.

You can also write your production back to your camcorder, where you can dub copies for VHS or other analog players. I describe how to do this in Chapter 13.

Finally, Pinnacle provides a free service for posting your video files online, appropriately called StudioOnline. I discuss how you can best utilize this service in Chapter 15.

System Requirements

Most products ship with two sets of requirements, minimum and recommended. Here are Studio 9's minimum and recommended requirements:

- Intel Pentium or AMD Athlon 800 MHz or higher (1.5 GHz or higher recommended)
- 256 MB RAM (512 MB recommended)
- Windows 98SE, "Millennium", 2000, or XP (Windows XP recommended)
- DirectX 9 compatible graphics card (ATI Radeon or Nvidia Geforce 2 or higher recommended)
- DirectX 9 compatible sound card (Creative Labs Audigy recommended)
- 500 MB of disk space to install software
- CD-ROM drive
- 4.5 GB of hard disk space for every 20 minutes of video captured at best quality
- Hard disk capable of sustained throughput of at least 4 MB per second. All SCSI and most ultra direct memory access (UDMA) drives are fast enough; dedicated hard drive recommended. (Studio will automatically test your hard drive for sufficient speed for real-time video capture when you first enter Capture mode.)
- CD-Recordable or CD-Rewritable drive for creating VideoCDs or Super VideoCDs that will play on most living room DVD players
- DVD-Recordable, DVD-Rewritable, or DVD+RW drive for creating DVDs

Disk requirements

A faster processor and more RAM are certainly better when it comes to video production, but the most significant area of potential trouble relates to disk requirements. Here's a quick example that illustrates how to estimate how much disk space you'll need for your projects.

Assume that you've shot 60 minutes of video that you want to edit down to a 30-minute production. You plan on including both a narration and background audio track, and will burn the result to DVD.

Table i.1, which presents a worst-case estimate of required disk space, assumes that you'll be applying edits to every single frame in the production footage. If you edit more sparingly, you'll need less space.

In 1994, the required 22 GB would have cost close to $30,000, and your electrical bill would jump significantly. Today, you can buy an 80 GB drive for well under $100, a great investment if you plan on pursuing multiple editing projects.

Table i.1

Calculating Disk Requirements			
ITEM	DURATION	MB/MINUTE	TOTAL
Capture footage	60 minutes	216	12.96 GB
Production footage	30 minutes	216	6.48 GB
Narration track	30 minutes	10.5	315 MB
Background audio	30 minutes	10.5	315 MB
DVD files	30 minutes	60	1.8 GB

Total disk space required: 21.87 GB

Part I: Getting Started

Chapter 1 Creating Watchable Video 3

Chapter 2 Introduction to Studio 9 29

CREATING WATCHABLE VIDEO

A video editor is like a hammer. Knowing how to hammer nails, straight and true, is a noble skill, but it doesn't guarantee you can build a sturdy house. Similarly, knowing how to capture your video and add transitions and titles and perhaps a special effect or two doesn't guarantee your video is *watchable*—that family and friends will be able to watch it for more than two or three minutes without squirming in their chairs.

My goal with this book is not only to show you the capabilities of Studio, our metaphorical hammer, but to help you create watchable videos. This involves a range of skills, such as using the proper camcorder settings; framing your shots correctly; shooting the right shots; and capturing, trimming, and weaving your scenes into a polished video production.

Don't fret. I'm not talking Hollywood movies, MTV videos, or 60-second commercials here. If you're like me, you probably shoot most, if not all, of your videos of friends and family for viewing by that same group and have minimal or no commercial aspirations.

So this chapter doesn't throw a lot of advanced theory your way—just a small set of fundamentals that will change the way you shoot and edit, and hopefully increase your enjoyment of the process. It should also greatly improve the perceived quality of your video.

What *Is* Watchable Video?

For better or for worse, what's on television today defines what's "watchable." Next time you're watching television, pay attention to the following elements.

First, in most shows, note the relative lack of camera motion. Specifically, while the show shifts from camera to camera, there is very little *panning* (moving the camera from side to side) or *fast zooming* (changing the zoom magnification either into or away from the subject). You'll almost never see the shaking that evidences a hand-held camera.

Second, note how transitions are used as the behind-the-scenes producer shifts from camera to camera. *Transitions* are visual effects that help smooth the change from shot to shot. Inside of a scene, or within a series of shots from a single location during a single time period, most directors simply *cut* between the various clips. One camera angle stops, and the other starts.

When television shows use a transition to alert the viewer that the time or location is about to change, it's almost always a simple *dissolve* (an effect that briefly merges the current clip with the next clip and then displays the second) or *fade to black*. On kids' shows and "zany" sitcoms, you may see more "artistic" transitions, but they're not random. Typically, the effect relates to the subject matter of the show—for instance, a crocodile dragging the first clip over the second in *Crocodile Hunter*.

Finally, note the pace of change. Few, if any, shows (or movies) display a static screen for longer than 10 or 15 seconds. News and sports shows use multiple text streams to keep viewers' eyes occupied, along with frequent background updates and cuts to reporters in the field, while sitcoms and other shows change cameras and camera angles frequently.

So here's the bar: videos worth watching use stable shots filmed from multiple angles and don't introduce random special effects, but they still manage to introduce some element of change every 5 to 15 seconds. If you want to produce watchable video, that's your target.

You really can't produce watchable video without shooting well and capturing well. For the most part, this chapter discusses how to shoot well, while the remainder of the book covers the editing side.

Watchable Video Guidelines

The good news is the building blocks of TV-quality video are very accessible. You simply need to follow a few guidelines (see the sidebar on the left).

Shooting for success

A key point to keep in mind in creating watchable video is the goal of your movie. Let's start with one proposition: that not all occasions demand the same level of attention in either shooting or editing. Sometimes you bring the camera just to capture the day or the event and really just want to have fun without the pressure of creating a masterpiece. Still, you want the video you shoot to look as good as possible, so you definitely want to use the proper camera settings and compose your shots carefully.

Other times, for weddings, significant birthdays and anniversaries, graduations and other events, you want to weave in advanced shot combinations that captivate and impress your viewers. You may even want to develop a short list of shots so that your video can follow a definite storyline. This takes a bit more planning up front and more editing time at the back.

So you don't need to concern yourself with advanced shot composition each time you dust off your camera. You should gain a fundamental knowledge of the basics that will improve all of your videos. Then you should learn some more advanced techniques, for those special occasions where you want to spread your creative wings.

Let's start at the top of the guidelines and then work our way through the other elements.

Guidelines for Creating Watchable Video

- Use a feature-rich video editor
- Develop strong nonlinear editing skills
- Choose the right camera settings
- Apply basic shot composition
- Apply advanced shot composition

Definitions 101

Here are some terms that are critical to video production. I'll try to stick with the following definitions in this chapter and throughout the book to ensure that we're speaking a common language.

Shot composition: Composition is the arrangement of the primary subjects on the screen. The goal is to present the most aesthetically pleasing image possible without exceeding the ambitions and time constraints of your project.

Shooting, taping, or videotaping: These terms all refer to the process of pointing your camera, pressing the red Record button, and recording on tape. I may slip up sometimes and use the term *filming*, a definite faux pas since we're using a DV or other tape-based camcorder that doesn't have film, but the process meant is the same.

Scene (during shooting): During shooting, the scene is the key area where the action takes place. In a crime drama, the murder scene takes place in the bedroom or boardroom or library. In a football movie, you'll have locker room scenes (tasteful, of course), scenes on the field, and finally the tickertape parade scene, in the center of town.

Shot: A shot typically is described in terms of what you're doing with the camera when you're shooting a particular scene. So in a long shot, the camera is very far from the subject (unless you're at the race track, of course), while in a close-up shot, the camera is close to the subject. An establishing or wide shot typically shows the entire scene so that the viewer understands the environment relevant to that footage. You'll learn more about the different types of shots later in this chapter.

Scene (during editing): During editing, a scene is a discrete chunk of video composed of one or more shots. Typically, during editing, you identify the scenes you want to use in the final project and then assemble them with your video editor.

Clip: A clip is a generic term for a chunk of audio or video that you're editing in Studio's Movie window. It is often used interchangeably with *scene*.

Sequence: A sequence is a group of scenes pieced together. In a wedding video, for instance, you might have a sequence for the rehearsal dinner, a sequence for the ceremony, and a sequence for the reception. You piece these sequences together into a finished movie.

Movie: A movie is the end product of your shooting and editing—what you end up with after you've pieced together the various scenes and added all the transitions, titles, and special effects; it's the creative fruit you serve up to your audience.

Video: Typically refers to what's transferred from your camcorder to your computer. Video is also used interchangeably with the term *movie*.

Using a Feature-Rich Video Editor

The video editor serves two primary functions in the creation of watchable video. First, it provides an accessible workspace for cutting up your raw footage into the most watchable segments and then piecing them together into a compelling movie. As you'll see in Chapter 7, Studio excels in this regard.

Second, the video editor provides a multitude of elements for introducing change into your videos to satisfy the MTV-nurtured attention spans of viewers. Studio excels here, too. For example, Studio's between-scenes transitions are the best in the industry, as are its background-music features, and its titling tool makes creating attractive, professional-looking titles easy. In Studio 9, special effects have been bolstered, so you can pan in and around an image (using a third-party utility discussed in "Adding Motion to Still Images" in Chapter 9. Studio 9 also introduces Smart Movie, which can automatically create a music video for you (see "Creating a Music Video with Smart Movie" in Chapter 9).

Developing Strong Nonlinear Editing Skills

A great tool, like our metaphorical hammer, does little good if you don't know how to use it. The rest of this book will give you the details. Even while you're shooting, however, you should understand Studio's most valuable capability so that you can make the best use of this tool.

Simply stated, Studio, like all computer-based video editors, is a nonlinear tool, which means that you can move video scenes around freely, like checkers on a checkerboard. Consider **Figure 1.1**. At the upper left is the Video Album, which contains the scenes in the order that I shot them and later captured them on my hard disk. At the bottom is the Storyboard, where I can assemble all the scenes that I want in the final movie. (I'm jumping ahead a bit here on the interface side; if you want to bone up on Studio's interface elements, you can take a quick look at "Using Edit Mode" in Chapter 2.)

This is the beginning of a video I'm creating with footage shot at the Fiddler's Convention here in Galax, where I live. This is the opening sequence that introduces the viewer to the yearly, world-famous gathering. Later sequences will highlight individual bands and music and instrument types, like bluegrass and mandolins, and some of the country dancing I shot at the event.

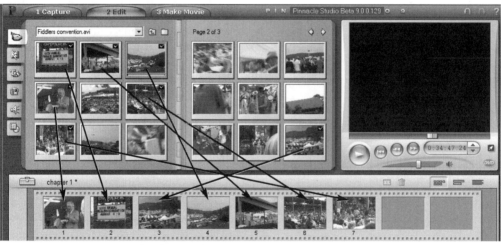

Figure 1.1 One of Studio's best features is that it's nonlinear, so you can cut and paste videos from anywhere to anywhere.

As you can see in the Studio Storyboard, Scene 1 shows an announcer introducing a band on stage. The next scene is the sign at the entrance to the Fiddler's Convention, which I shot first on the way in, so that the viewer instantly knows what the video is about.

Next, using the song from the background music in the first scene, I display several other scenes that visually illustrate the magnitude of the festival: the hundreds of parked trailers and tents spread over about 20 acres, the thousands of people in the stands and milling about. (To make everything work together seamlessly, I use the Continuity system, described later in this chapter.).

Going to the Fiddler's Convention, I knew that I would need these shots to complete the video, but it wasn't convenient to shoot them all immediately upon my entrance. Hey, I was being dragged around by two little girls who didn't give a hoot about continuity. No problem, though, because whenever I get the shots—later that night or even the next day—I can cut and paste them in Studio wherever and whenever I need them.

If you've never edited video before, you will find this is a huge paradigm shift that really unleashes significant creative potential. As you'll discover throughout this chapter and later in the book, Studio's nonlinear nature is absolutely key to creating watchable videos.

That said, it all starts with the camera. So let's focus on that aspect of creating watchable video.

Choosing the Right Camera Settings

If you produced camcorders and sold them to untrained consumers, your primary goal, if you wanted to sell a lot of them, would probably be to allow your customers to produce the best possible videos right out of the box—no tweaking of controls required. Camcorder manufacturers are a bright group, and this is pretty much what they've attempted to do.

Still, in certain instances, you can improve the quality of your video if you tune the controls to match your surroundings and the goals of the shot. In addition, there are certain camera features you should always use, and some to avoid at all costs.

Finally, two realities of consumer camcorders—lighting and audio—have their own sets of challenges, which you should know about up front. This section briefly addresses these issues, and then we move on to shot composition.

It's all about exposure

No, this isn't a section about Madonna or Justin Timberlake; it's about the exposure setting on your camera, which controls how much light gets to the charged coupled device (CCD) that captures the image. Virtually all consumer camcorders have automatic exposure settings that work well most of the time.

However, they also feature special *programmed auto-exposure (AE)* modes that can improve video quality in well-defined shooting conditions. For example, most Sony camcorders have the following programmed AE modes for specific shooting conditions:

- **Spotlight** prevents faces from being excessively white.
- **Portrait** sharpens close-up images and softens the background.
- **Sports** captures crisp images of fast-moving subjects.
- **Beach & Ski** prevents faces from appearing dark against the generally lighter background.
- **Sunset Moon** optimizes shooting controls for low-light conditions.
- **Landscape** focuses solely on far-away objects, softening any objects in the foreground.

Many DV cameras also have settings for backlit conditions, which, like the Beach and Ski mode, can prevent faces from appearing overly dark. In my experience, these modes work very well in their defined roles, improving image quality over fully automatic settings. For this reason, you should definitely identify the modes available on your camera and learn how to switch to them for the defined conditions.

The skinny on night-shot modes

Most DV cameras offer one or two low-light modes, which fall into two categories. The first is an infrared-assisted mode that creates a greenish "night vision goggles" effect. This is very effective for capturing sleeping children or nocturnal animals, but you lose all the color in the shot—the image's colors consist of shades of green.

The other mode doesn't use infrared, but slows the shutter speed dramatically to ensure that sufficient light gets to the CCD. This preserves color, but even minimal motion produces extreme blurriness that usually makes the video unusable.

Depending upon your goal, either or both modes work just fine. However, don't confuse either as a mechanism for boosting light under low-light conditions. That is, if you're shooting video at a quiet dinner party or dark restaurant, neither mode will improve your results. You need to either boost the ambient light in the room by turning on some lights or get a light for your video camera.

The white balance issue

White balance is kind of like bad cholesterol. It's not something you think about often, but whenever it comes up, it's generally negative news.

White balance is a problem because cameras perceive the color white differently based upon the light source, whether florescent or incandescent light or sunlight. All cameras perform white balancing automatically, but under some circumstances, such as shooting in sunlight, under florescent lights, or under rapidly changing lighting conditions, the auto-sensing mechanisms may not be accurate, so you run a pretty significant risk that the colors will be off.

For example, I once forgot to white balance my camera during a trip to Zoo Atlanta, and all of the video had a blue tone. Or when I switched from outdoor shooting to indoor shooting at a wedding without white balancing, all whites appeared slightly pinkish, including the bride's wedding dress, which was a big hit, let me tell you.

Both problems could have been prevented with proper white balancing, and fortunately I was able to fix both problems using color correction, like that added to Studio 9 and discussed in "Applying Color Correction" in Chapter 9. Still, it's always better to avoid these issues by white balancing before you start shooting.

The procedure is similar for most cameras: you zoom the camera into a white object like a wall, wedding dress, or piece of paper and press the white-balance button. Alternatively, many cameras have white-balance presets for indoor and outdoor shoots. Check your camera's documentation for details.

If this all sounds overly technical, you can also simply stay in automatic white-balance mode and point the camera at a white object for about 10 seconds or so whenever lighting conditions change, such as when you move into direct sunlight from the shade or move indoors from outside. This will give the automatic white-balance mechanism the best chance of operating correctly.

Automatic versus manual focus

Automatic focus is generally effective for keeping the video image sharp and in focus. Under certain conditions such as the following, however, manual focus produces superior results:

- Shooting a stationary subject from a tripod (where focus can inadvertently drift if the subject momentarily moves out of the picture).

- Shooting under low-light conditions (where the camera can lose focus and repeatedly adjust the focus back and forth to find it).

- Shooting through a window (where the camera may focus on the glass, rather than the objects behind the glass).

Check your camera's documentation to learn how to disable automatic focus and how to operate the manual focus controls.

When to use image stabilization

Image stabilization is a feature that minimizes minor hand shaking and other camera motion such as might occur while walking or riding in a car. While not a panacea, image stabilization provides some benefit and should be used whenever you're not shooting from a tripod. When shooting from a tripod, however, most camera vendors recommend disabling this feature. Check your camera's documentation for the recommendations regarding image stabilization and to learn how to enable and disable this mode.

Other settings

Here are other controls to consider before shooting, along with some suggestions for using the best setting.

- **Date:** DV cameras imprint the date and time of each shot in the video, and Studio uses this information to detect scenes in the video. It's a great feature that makes setting the time and date on your camera a priority.

- **12-bit audio versus 16-bit audio:** Use 16-bit audio; 12-bit audio was created so that you could lay down two tracks of audio simultaneously while shooting, a capability that most cameras don't offer. The 16-bit audio setting creates larger files, so it requires more space on your hard disk. However, the additional data delivers better quality.

- **Digital zoom:** Unlike optical zoom, which uses the camera's lens to produce additional detail when zooming in, digital zoom simply zooms into the digital image, which creates obvious pixilation (jaggies) at extreme settings. Most pros disable digital zoom, and you should, too.

- **Standard play (SP) versus long play (LP):** With DV camcorders, you can record up to 90 minutes of video on a 60-minute tape using LP mode, which uses a slower tape recording speed (12.56 mm per second compared to 18.812 mm per second for standard play) to pack more video onto the same tape. The same video signal is stored in each mode; it's just that LP mode stores the same video on less tape, which is theoretically less safe. For example, if an inch of tape is damaged in LP mode, you'd lose 50 percent more video than you would in SP mode. Some pundits state that the slower tape speed actually decreases your chances for error, but also that LP modes are implemented slightly differently on different camcorders and shouldn't be used if the tape may later be played back on a different camera. For me, this was much more of an issue when DV tapes cost $25; now that they're under $4 in bulk, SP is probably a safer choice.

- **16:9 aspect ratio versus 4:3 aspect ratio:** Use 16:9 only if you have a widescreen television that can play it without distortion. Note that 16:9 video played on a normal TV will appear squashed.

- **Digital effects:** Many cameras offer digital effects such as sepia, mosaic, fade from black, and fade to black, plus primitive titling capabilities. You can produce these with much greater precision using Studio, so disable these effects on your camcorder.

The realities of shooting with consumer camcorders

There are two realities about shooting with DV camcorders, particularly inexpensive consumer models. First, most camcorders produce suboptimal quality in anything other than extremely bright conditions. Second, it's very difficult to capture clear, crisp audio using solely the camcorder's microphone unless you're very close to the subject. Fortunately, you can minimize or resolve both problems with some advance planning and/or some inexpensive accessories.

Figure 1.2 Unless you're shooting participants in the witness protection program, poor lighting like this produces unacceptable images.

Let's look at the lighting problem first. This is a particular issue for me because my wife favors cozy, intimate family celebrations with minimal lighting, preferably candlelight. Unfortunately, under these conditions, it's impossible to shoot video that looks even remotely good. For example, **Figure 1.2** was taken at a wedding reception without ancillary lighting, and the subject's faces are very indistinct because of the low light.

Of course, under candlelight, the problem is obvious. The low-light issue is much more insidious under normal room lighting, which generally is still too dark for high-quality images. Here, however, the image on your LCD panel may look fine, and you won't discover that your images are too dark until you've captured your video on disk or viewed it on a television screen. Either way, it's too late to address the problem.

Creating Watchable Video

Figure 1.3 Lights like this one from Sony can go a long way toward reducing low-light quality issues.

Basically, there are two ways to solve the lighting problem. First, you can turn on every light in the room, sacrificing short-term intimacy for the long-term quality of your memories of the event. This generally works well in most homes, where lighting is plentiful, so long as you can get your spouse to agree.

In darker reception halls, restaurants, and similar venues, where you can't control the lighting, your best option is to purchase a video light like the Sony HVL-20DW2 shown in **Figure 1.3** (assuming your camcorder doesn't have a light, of course). This particular model attaches to the accessory shoe on top of the camera and draws power from the camcorder's battery. Alternatively, you can get a light that uses separate batteries.

Note that capturing good-quality video under low-light conditions is a serious, serious issue, probably mentioned more in most camcorder reviews than any other deficit. Unfortunately, short of spending $3,000 for a camcorder that takes pictures in low light, there is no simple solution. Ignore it, and it will repeatedly degrade the quality of your indoor shots; take the steps discussed here, and you can minimize this problem.

Improving audio quality

As you would expect, the problem with camcorder-based audio starts with the microphone. First, since it's located on the camera body, it can easily pick up a host of operator noises such as the clicking of the zoom controls. More serious is the pickup pattern of the microphone, which defines the area from which the microphone gathers sound.

Figure 1.4 Microphones like this one from Sony help capture better audio when the audio source is distant from the camera.

Typically, DV camcorders use microphones that prioritize all sounds in front of the camera equally. This pattern works well if you're shooting a group of people equidistant from the camera, but is useless if you're shooting a lecturer or speaker at the front of the room or anyone far away from the camera.

Here, you also have two options: either get closer to the speaker or purchase a separate microphone. For the latter, the options are almost limitless, but the easiest and cheapest alternatives are microphones that sit on the camera body itself, like the Sony ECM-MSD1 (**Figure 1.4**).

The MSD1 offers a narrower, front-focused pickup pattern that ignores ambient noise and captures audio primarily from the direction in which the camera is pointing. These types of microphones are also called shotgun or gun microphones.

These types of microphones probably won't help if you are shooting a lecturer from the back of the room. However, at a birthday party or wedding, you can shoot someone 10 to 15 feet away and clearly hear what the person is saying, which is almost impossible using solely the microphone on the camera body.

Creating Watchable Video

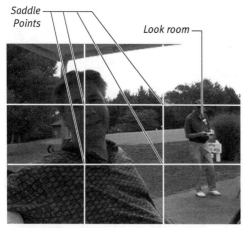

Figure 1.5 The rule of thirds. My golf buddy's head is located at the upper-left saddle point in the video frame, providing the necessary look room.

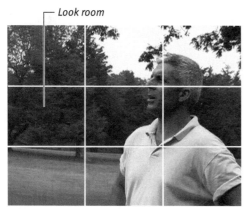

Figure 1.6 My other buddy is facing the opposite direction, so I placed him at the upper-right saddle point. Note how the eyes are above the top third of the frame.

Applying Basic Shot Composition

Once you get the camera settings down and deal with audio and lighting, it's time to start thinking about shot composition, which is the art of placing your subjects in the frame to create the most aesthetically pleasing image.

Here are four basic techniques to keep in mind while shooting. After you read this section, watch for them on TV and in the movies. Once you see how consistently the pros use these techniques, you'll be surprised that you never noticed them before.

The rule of thirds

According to the rule of thirds, you should divide each image into a tic-tac-toe grid, like that shown in **Figure 1.5,** and place the primary subject of the frame at one of the four saddle points, or intersections of the four lines. This rule has its roots in Greek architecture and Renaissance art and is based on the belief that certain shapes and proportions are more pleasing to the eye than others.

When you are shooting a subject that isn't moving, the image looks best when the open space is located in front of where the subject is facing, as shown in Figure 1.5 and **Figure 1.6**. This is called providing look room or nose room.

When your primary subject is moving, place your subject in the back third of the frame, leaving lead room in the front. In **Figure 1.7**, my daughter is skating from left to right, so the lead room is on the viewer's right. Similarly, in **Figure 1.8**, my other daughter is moving from right to left, so the lead room is on the viewer's left.

A corollary to the rule of thirds is that the eyes should always be at or above the top third of the video. This holds true regardless if the shot is taken from close up and includes the face only, or from farther back, as in Figures 1.5 to 1.8.

Like all rules of aesthetics, the rule of thirds isn't fixed in stone; sometimes you simply have to shoot what looks appropriate at the time. For example, if the background is direction-neutral, I find it hard to apply the rule of thirds when shooting a subject looking straight at me, as in **Figure 1.9**.

That said, it's clear that the "center the image in the camera" instruction we learned back with our first Instamatic is not universally appropriate. Though it's impossible to apply the rule of thirds to every frame in your video, especially with moving subjects, use it as a guide, and you'll find your videos more aesthetically pleasing.

Motion techniques

One of the most striking differences between professional and amateur video is the amount and quality of the motion in the video. When you watch most television shows or movies, you'll notice two facts related to motion. First, most shots are either totally stable or have only slight, virtually unnoticeable motion. Second, if there is significant motion, it's very smooth.

Figure 1.7 Whatley is skating from left to right, so I try to keep her in the back left of the frame, to provide lead room.

Figure 1.8 Rose is skating (well, shuffling, actually) from right to left, so the lead room is on the other side.

Creating Watchable Video

Figure 1.9 I find it hard to apply the rule of thirds on a subject facing directly at me, unless there's another object in the background that dictates it. Here the background is neutral, so this buddy is framed in the middle.

In contrast, most amateur videos are shot from unstable platforms that shake continuously, with fast zooms (using the camera's zoom controls to zoom into or out of the image), pans (moving the camera from side to side), and tilts (moving the camera up and down).

Obviously, the pros have multiple cameras and better equipment, making their jobs a lot easier. Still, if you follow these five rules, you can produce very similar results.

◆ Shoot from a stable platform. I'm not going to tell you to shoot with a tripod because I know it's impractical most of the time. However, you can buy an inexpensive monopod (a one-legged tripod) at Wal-Mart for under $20 that will hold your camera at a steady height, making it much simpler to reduce the shake in the video. Folded up, it's only slightly longer than an umbrella, so it's easy to carry around. Even with a monopod, you should lean against something solid, like a wall, tree, or fence, whenever possible.

If you're shooting without a tripod or monopod, find the most comfortable sustainable position for the camera; usually this is about chest high, holding the camera with both hands and sighting with the viewfinder. If your camera has a shoulder strap, see if you can use this strap to support the weight of the camcorder when you're shooting. One of the best approaches is to simply lay the camera on a fixed object, like a desk, table, or shelf.

continues on next page

APPLYING BASIC SHOT COMPOSITION

- Zoom, pan, or tilt only to follow the action, not for dramatic effect. Don't try to slowly zoom into your wife's face as she watches your daughter's gymnastics meet; frame the close-up shot and then start shooting. Don't pan from skyscraper to skyscraper in downtown Manhattan; shoot one building, stop, reframe the next building, and start shooting again (or cut the panning sequences between buildings during editing).

- Whenever possible, rehearse the necessary camera motion beforehand. This approach works exceptionally well at sporting events like baseball games or gymnastics meets, where the athlete has to follow a designated path, whether to first base or to the vault spring. While you're waiting for your child, practice with other children. Not only does this promote the smoothness of your camera motion, but it also helps ensure that obstacles don't obscure your line of sight during that critical moment.

- For all shots that have motion, start at a stable position for a few seconds whenever possible, and hold the final shot for a few seconds to ensure that you have sufficient footage for editing.

- Use your waist for panning and tilting shots, not your hands or your feet. That is, to pan across a scene, hold the camera steady and swivel at the waist across the scene. To tilt up and down, hold the camera steady and bend forward and backward at the waist.

The Continuity system

Briefly, the Continuity system is a style of editing whose goal is to present a scene so that the cuts from scene to scene are unnoticeable to the viewer—that is, the progression of shots within the scene is logical, without any discontinuities that jar the viewer. It's a pretty complex system with lots of rules, so for our purposes here we'll focus on its absolutely critical points.

Most importantly, you need to start each sequence with an establishing shot that presents the watcher with a complete view of the setting. Then you can move into medium shots and close-ups, with periodic reestablishing shots to keep the viewer grounded. (See the sidebar "Taxonomy of Shots" later in this chapter for definitions of these types of shots.)

This sequence of shots is shown in **Figure 1.10**, taken from a television interview I participated in several years ago at a trade show. This was a two-camera shoot, so it's unlike what most of us do day to day, but the technique is instructive.

The first shot is the establishing shot: two guys talking with the stage and people walking around behind us clear to the viewer. This gives the viewer a feel for the environment. This is Camera 1. Next is a medium shot of me with a title, on Camera 2. Then Camera 1 tightens the framing to a medium two-shot of the friendly interviewer and me (note the adherence to the rule of thirds in the medium shot of me, but not in either the wide shot or the medium two-shot).

What's particularly instructive is the difference between the establishing shot and the medium two-shot. They look very similar, but in the establishing shot, you can clearly tell what's going on in the background—folks walking around with bags; must be a trade show. In the medium two-shot, you see only body parts walking around, and the environment is much less comprehensible to the viewer. That's okay, since the establishing shot already clued the viewer to what's going on. In addition, the camera person periodically shifted back to a wider shot with this camera so that viewers entering in midstream would understand the context.

The clear lesson is this: Start every sequence with an establishing shot, or series of shots, that presents the environment to the viewer. Then shoot progressively closer so that you get scenes that present the detail you want without confusing the viewer. Next time you watch ESPN Sports Center or the evening news, notice how the video follows this progression.

continues on next page

Establishing shot   Medium shot   Medium Two shot

Figure 1.10 The continuity system in action. The first shot is an establishing shot that clearly shows we're at a trade show. The next is a cut to a medium shot and then to a medium two-shot.

Let's apply this theory to our typical one-camera shoot, using the Fiddler's Convention video mentioned earlier. As shown in **Figure 1.11**, I start with a medium shot of the announcer, breaking the rules, but only for a second. Call this my nod to the *Tom Jones Show*, which always started with Tom's hand on the microphone before he broke into "It's Not Unusual." Always liked that dramatic effect.

However, the first shot is on the screen for only a moment or two, primarily to introduce the audio background track of the announcer and the band playing on the stage. Then I cut to the Fiddler's Convention sign, so the viewer immediately knows what's going on; then several wide shots showing the stage from the background, the acres of trailers and tents, and the thousands of folks in the stands; and then the stage.

After this, I can start adding medium shots and close-ups of the band members and interesting attendees because I've set the stage with the wide shot. Let's apply this approach to some common situations.

- **Birthday party:** Start with exterior shots of the house and interior shots of the party room showing all participants and decorations. Then move to medium shots of guests and the birthday celebrant.

- **Soccer game:** Set the stage with wide shots of the field, showing both goals, the location of both teams, and the grandstands. Then start working in views of your star forward, the team, the coach, and other participants.

- **Dance recital or play:** Use exterior shots of the gymnasium or theater to set the stage; then shoot the entire gym or stage to show the complete environment. Then add medium shots of the participants and, later, close-ups.

Figure 1.11 In my first video of the Fiddler's Convention, I used a series of wide shots to introduce the spectacle to the viewer before transitioning to medium shots of the band.

Remember to shoot an establishing shot each time you change the physical location of the scene. For example, if you're shooting a family wedding, you shouldn't shift from a scene in the chapel to a scene in the reception hall without an establishing shot of the reception hall. It also helps to shoot closing wide shots that you can fade to black during editing so that the viewer understands one sequence is ending and another is starting.

Once again, the lovely aspect of digital video is the nonlinear nature of the editing process. You don't have to shoot the establishing shots first; you can shoot them later and cut and paste them in at the proper location.

The Continuity system for audio

The Continuity rule for audio is a bit cerebral, but it's exceptionally important so bear with me for a moment. I'll use an example to illustrate the point.

Assume that you're at a wedding reception. You want to show people dancing and having a good time, so you shoot a bunch of shots of everyone dancing—say 10 minutes worth taken over a 30-minute period.

You start editing and quickly realize that no one will watch 10 minutes of dancing, so you start trimming away footage to get down to a more palatable 4 minutes. Here's the problem: Since the band or DJ didn't play the same song all night, most shots of the revelers have different songs playing in the background. Though your viewers can accept visual cuts from person to person without a sense of discontinuity, audio cuts are a different matter—that is, cutting from 5 seconds of one song to 5 seconds of another song is a big red flag that signals a discontinuity.

To avoid this, when shooting, make sure that you capture at least one complete song that you can use as background for the entire finished dance sequence. Then, as described in "Insert Editing" in Chapter 7, you can use that song as the background for the entire 4 minutes and cut and paste bits of other shots to complete the sequence.

In essence, you're fooling the audience into thinking that you took all of the shots during one song, simulating a multiple camera shoot with one camera, which is incredibly effective. Sure, problems can arise—for example, if you choose a disco song and have footage of people slow dancing—but overall, this is a very powerful technique, with broad application.

For example, in the Fiddler's Convention video, I used the audio from the first scene as the background for the entire first sequence. In addition to the wide shots, I came back to medium and close-up shots of the band and pasted in other bits of people listening, dancing, and generally having a good time. These are all the shots I would use to convey the atmosphere of the event, and provide the visual context for later sequences. But because I captured one entire song on tape and used it to create essentially a music video, the presentation is much more polished than if I had pasted the same scenes together with disparate audio tracks, revealing to my viewers that the scenes aren't really continuous.

At a recent wedding, I kept the camera running during both the entry and exit processionals, which took about 10 minutes each. Then, using one song from each processional as the background, I condensed each sequence to about 2 minutes, which was much more palatable to viewers.

Chapter 1

Applying Advanced Shot Composition

Advanced shot compositions typically involve different types of shots and shot combinations. You've seen them hundreds of times on TV; they're easy to implement and look very polished. Here's how to use some in your own movies.

Medium shot, point-of-view shot, reaction shot

Figure 11.12 starts with a medium shot of my wife and daughter, obviously staring at something. What is it, you find yourself asking. Then I cut to a point-of-view shot, which shows the action in the eyes of my daughter: her point of view. Then, as the horse draws nearer to her, she smiles in delight; that's the reaction shot.

As with all of the shots we're discussing, it's important to recognize that these shots were filmed out of order. I shot about 2 minutes of video before a horse carriage ride and pieced together these 15 or 20 seconds before we got on the carriage to show how Whatley was enjoying the day.

I used the background audio from the first and third shots for the entire sequence to preserve audio continuity. Then I pasted a shot of the horse, taken later, into the middle to show Whatley's point of view. It looks like I have two cameras to most untrained eyes, which was the effect I was seeking, but I had only my trusty Sony DCR-PC1.

Think, for a moment, about the unlimited potential for these types of shots. You're at a softball game and your daughter gets a hit. You catch the line drive on video and then want to switch to the crowd cheering and your spouse smiling like a fool.

But you can't physically move the camera fast enough to catch all this action. Thinking in advance, while other kids were at bat, you took several shots of the crowd cheering and your spouse smiling. You also took several shots of your spouse pensively watching the action, just to use when piecing together this video.

During editing, you start with the pensive shots of the spouse, then the line drive, and then the crowd and proud spouse shots. If you use the audio from the actual line drive for the whole sequence, it will look like you had multiple cameras working the entire game. It's not hard, it's not time consuming; you just need to plan ahead.

Medium shot   *Point-of-view shot*   *Reaction shot*

Figure 1.12 What's Whatley staring at? A horse? How delightful.

Over-the-shoulder shot, point-of-view shot

An over-the-shoulder shot is what you see on the left in **Figure 1.13**, a shot that includes the back of one of the subjects and the focus of the subject's attention. It's also an establishing shot, because it shows the elephant's environment at Zoo Atlanta.

Then you switch to a point-of-view shot that shows in detail what your subject is looking at. This is a great combination for involving your primary subject in your sequence while following the rules of continuity discussed earlier.

Over-the-shoulder shot *Point-of-view shot*

Figure 1.13 Using the over-the-shoulder shot as an establishing shot; then cutting to a point-of-view shot of the elephant.

Cutaways

A cutaway is a shot that relates to the primary subject of the video, but isn't the primary subject. For example, when ESPN interviews the winning coach after a football game, the coach might attribute the win to a goal-line stand late in the fourth quarter. During the interview, while the coach is still talking, ESPN switches to a view of the play and then cuts back to the coach once the play is done.

Or maybe it's the weatherperson describing the wonderful spring-like weather that just descended in mid December. The shot starts with the weatherperson, and then cutaways show joggers running in shorts, couples sunning on the grass, and babies crawling on blankets. Then back to the weatherperson for tomorrow's forecast.

Here's what I like about cutaways. Number one, they allow you to show the flavor of the entire event. Rather than simply keeping the camera on little Sally during the softball game, you shoot the coaches cajoling, the parents praising, the shortstop shuffling, an uproar from the umpire—all the shots that make baseball such a compelling game.

Second, cutaways can serve as patches for badly shot video that you can't cut from your sequence, as may occur when you're capturing an entire song, speech, or sermon to use as the background track for your audio as described earlier.

For example, **Figure 1.14** shows six images of a shot from the Fiddler's Convention. Much of the fun action occurs away from the stage, and this dynamic duo had generated an amazing amount of dancing, shuffling, and stomping. The main subjects of the video sequence were the two performers; all other shots not directly of them were cutaways.

Figure 1.14 Using cutaways. The primary subject here is the two person band; the cutaways are the folks dancing.

Following the audio continuity system described previously, I filmed one entire song, moving from one side of the scene to the other while recording, and catching some of the dancing action as I went. Then I hung around for two other songs, shooting different, additional dance sequences.

Because I was moving around while filming the one background song, there was an awful lot of unusable footage, camera motion that was too violent, and bad framing. Wherever necessary, however, I just pasted in a dance sequence to hide the bad footage, allowing me to produce one fairly cohesive 4-minute song.

Similarly, for a wedding video, you might want pictures of the proud parents watching the ceremonial first dance. So you shoot the entire ceremonial dance and later shoot the proud parents beaming at something else; you can then use these shots of the parents as cutaways to patch into the dance sequence.

My rule for cutaways is that you can never get enough of them. If your goal is advanced shot composition, spend a lot of time shooting subjects other than your primary ones.

Taxonomy of Shots

Here's a list of shots and some suggestions for when to use them.

- **Establishing shot:** Any shot that provides the viewer with a visual overview of the environment of the shot.

- **Long shot:** Any shot that doesn't cut out any body part of the primary subject. For example, **Figure 1.15** is a long shot that shows a lovely straight left arm but a disturbing hint of a reverse pivot. This is about the shortest long shot you'll see; shots from farther away are also called medium or extreme long shots. Long shots are good for showing action and as establishing shots and are also called wide shots.

Figure 1.15 Here's a long shot that adheres to the rule of thirds. For those who care about such things, I parred this short par-three hole (that's my story and I'm sticking to it).

- **Medium shot:** Any shot that cuts away a portion of the primary subject, up to a close-up, which shows only the upper shoulders and face. These shots are also called mid-shots. Medium shots are good for introducing the viewer to the character and should be used before a close-up.

- **Close-up shot:** Any shot that shows only the shoulders and head, or closer in. These shots are good primarily for reaction shots. Use close-ups sparingly, for effect only; during most shoots, a medium shot is a much better choice to show people talking.

- **Over-the-shoulder shot:** Shows the upper shoulder of a subject and the primary subject of the video.

- **Point-of-view shot:** Shows the point of view of the immediately preceding subject on the screen.

- **Reaction shot:** Shows a subject's reaction to the immediately preceding shot.

Introduction to Studio 9

Though generally straightforward, Pinnacle Systems' Studio 9 has a few nooks and crannies that aren't obvious at first glance. Fortunately, Studio includes a comprehensive guided tour to get you familiar with the landscape fast. This chapter starts by showing you how to take the tour and then quickly introduces you to Studio's primary modes: Capture, Edit, and Make Movie. It also shows you how to undo or redo your work; use online help; and name and save your project files.

Studio 9 is a very accessible program, so it's tempting to just jump in and get started. Still, for each project, a few options should be set beforehand. For example, you must choose the location for your captured video and auxiliary files, and you should perform a disk performance test to see if your system is up to the rigors of video editing. Most of these options are "set 'em and forget 'em": Studio will maintain them from project to project until you manually change them.

Just a quick note: Studio displays housekeeping options, such as file location settings, in the same dialog boxes that display configuration options such as capturing and transition rendering. This chapter focuses mainly on the housekeeping options; other options are covered later in this book.

Chapter 2

Taking the Guided Tour

Studio 9 includes a guided tour that's a great first step toward familiarity with the program's interface.

To take the guided tour:

◆ Choose Help > Guided Tour (**Figure 2.1**). The Pinnacle Studio Guided Tour starts (**Figure 2.2**). Use the controls at the bottom of the tour window to control the experience.

✔ Tip

■ The first time you run Pinnacle Studio, the program displays a window asking whether you want to either view the guided tour or launch the program (**Figure 2.3**). You can click the Don't Ask Me This Again check box in the bottom-left corner, and Studio will stop showing this window when you launch the application. Until you're comfortable with the program, however, it's a good idea to keep this window readily available.

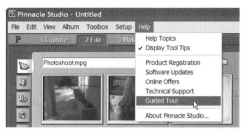

Figure 2.1 Pinnacle Studio's guided tour will familiarize you with the program components.

Figure 2.2 Use the controls at the bottom of the screen to control your tour experience.

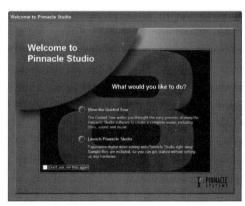

Figure 2.3 Until you disable this screen, whenever you launch Studio, you'll see a prompt for the guided tour.

Introduction to Studio 9

Using Edit Mode

When you first enter Studio, you're in Edit mode (**Figure 2.4**), where you'll spend the bulk of your time. Capture mode and Make Movie mode, accessible via tabs at the upper left of the screen, enable their namesake activities.

The Edit mode interface is composed of three windows: the Album, the Player, and the Movie window. While in Edit mode, you have access to Undo, Redo, and Help buttons at the upper right of the screen.

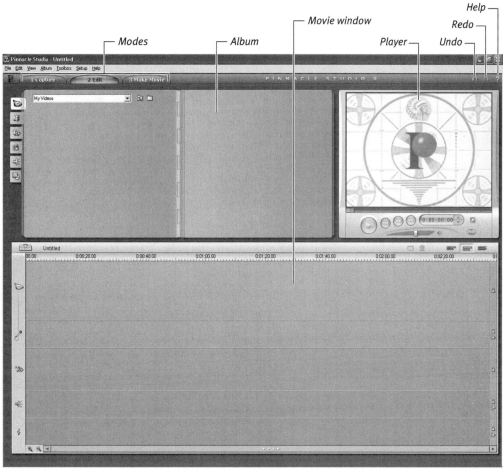

Figure 2.4 When you first run Studio, you're in Edit mode, where you'll spend most of your time.

The Album

The Album consists of six windows, which you can select using the icons on the left panel (**Figure 2.5**). Three of these windows are for collecting video, audio, and still image files so that you can include them in a project (for details on how to do this, see Chapter 6).

The other three windows contain libraries of effects supplied by Pinnacle, offering transitions, titles, and disc menus. For information on how to apply and customize these, see Chapters 8, 10, and 12, respectively.

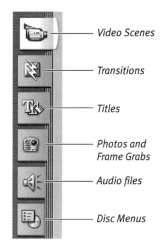

Figure 2.5 Use the tabs on the left side of the Album to navigate among the various content types.

The Player

The Player is where you preview content and effects contained in the various albums, as well as your editing progress in the Movie window (**Figure 2.6**). Click the DVD icon at the lower left, and you convert the Player into a DVD playback remote control for previewing your DVD titles.

In Studio 9, you can toggle to full screen preview by clicking the arrow key at the upper-right corner of the toolbar. You return to the program by pressing Esc on your keyboard or by using right-click commands detailed in the section "Viewing Your Captured Video" in Chapter 3. The Player also features volume controls and a Mute button.

Note that you can't detach or enlarge the Player, because like all interface components, it's fixed, for simplicity. Since the Player is integral to virtually all editing operations, its use is discussed in most of the chapters in this book.

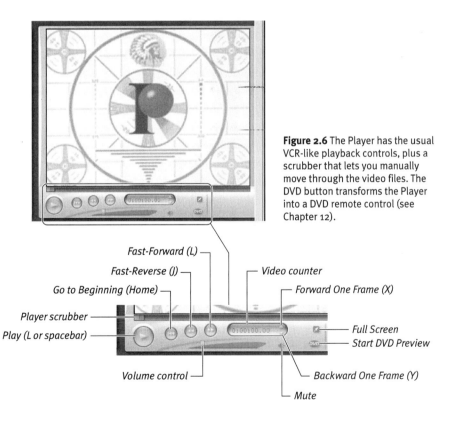

Figure 2.6 The Player has the usual VCR-like playback controls, plus a scrubber that lets you manually move through the video files. The DVD button transforms the Player into a DVD remote control (see Chapter 12).

The Movie window

The Movie window has three views—Timeline (shown in **Figure 2.7**), Storyboard, and Text (called Edit List view in the Studio menu)—that you toggle using controls in the upper-right corner of the Movie window (see Figure 2.7). See Chapter 7 to learn how and when to use these modes. Two icons, the Razorblade (for splitting clips) and the Trash Can (for deleting clips), are available in all three modes.

Video toolbox. In the upper-left corner of the Movie window is a Toolbox icon, which reveals a Camcorder icon when you hover the cursor over the left side of the toolbox (**Figure 2.8**). Click the Camcorder icon and the Video toolbox opens (**Figure 2.9**), revealing six editing functions.

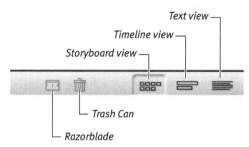

Figure 2.7 You can easily switch among the Timeline, Storyboard, and Text views of the Movie window. Note the omnipresent Razorblade, for splitting your videos, and the Trash Can, for deleting them.

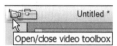

Figure 2.8 The Camcorder icon opens and closes the Video toolbox.

The Video toolbox offers the following functions:

- *Clip Properties*. Use this tool, shown in Figure 2.9, to trim your videos to the desired length (see Chapter 7).

- *Add Full Screen Title or Title Overlay.* Use this tool to edit the name and duration of images and to access title-editing screens (see Chapter 10).

- *Create or Edit a Disc Menu.* Use this tool to link menus to content and customize the DVD menus (see Chapter 12).

- *Grab a Frame of Video from Video Input.* Use this tool to grab still-frame images from your camcorder or disk-based video files (see Chapter 5).

- *Create a Music Video Automatically.* Use this tool to access the Studio 9 feature for converting footage to a music video (see Chapter 9).

- *Add an Effect to a Video Clip.* Use this tool to access Studio's color correction facilities and other special effects, expanded dramatically in Studio 9 (see Chapter 9).

You can click through the various options at will; click the Camcorder icon again to close the Video toolbox.

continues on next page

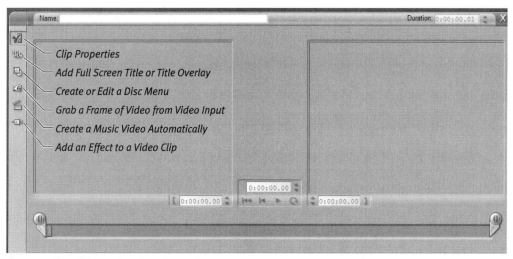

Figure 2.9 The editing tools in the Video toolbox.

Audio toolbox. If you hover the cursor over the right side of the toolbox, Studio reveals a Speaker icon in the upper-left corner of the Movie window (**Figure 2.10**). You can click this icon to open the Audio toolbox, which contains its own set of unique tools (**Figure 2.11**).

The Audio toolbox provides the following functions (see Chapter 11 for more information):

- *Audio Clip Properties.* Use this tool, which is open in Figure 2.11, to trim audio files to the desired length.

- *Change the Volume of the Three Audio Tracks.* Use this tool to adjust the volumes of the three audio tracks.

- *Record a Voice Over Narration.* Use this tool to record your voice-over track.

- *Add Background Music from an Audio CD.* Use this tool to rip CD-Audio tracks to include in your projects.

- *Create Background Music Automatically.* Use this tool to create custom background music of any length.

- *Add an Effect to an Audio Clip.* Studio 9 introduces a range of audio effects, which you can use this tool to add (see "Adding Effects to Audio Clips" in Chapter 11).

✔ **Tip**

■ Double-clicking any icon in the Video or Audio toolbox returns you to the main Movie window.

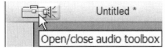

Figure 2.10 The Speaker icon opens and closes the Audio toolbox.

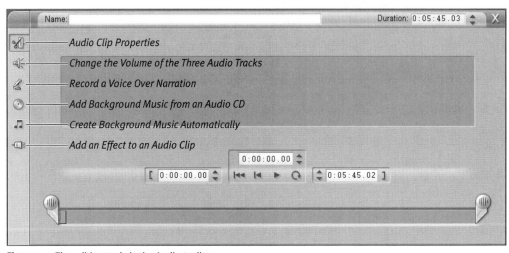

Figure 2.11 The editing tools in the Audio toolbox.

Introduction to Studio 9

Using Capture Mode

You enter Capture mode by selecting the Capture tab at the upper left of the Studio interface (Figure 2.4). Here you transfer video from a camcorder or another source to your computer. Studio has two interfaces for capturing: one for digital video (DV) and MicroMV devices and one for analog camcorders and decks.

Studio includes a Frame Grab feature for capturing still images from your camcorder or captured video (see Figure 2.5). This feature is covered in more detail in "Capturing Still Images" in Chapter 5.

Capturing from DV source devices

Figure 2.12 shows the four basic windows in Capture mode: the Album, the Player, the Camcorder Controller, and the Diskometer.

The **Album** holds the captured video files, which are added dynamically during capture when Studio detects additional scenes in your source video. After capture, you can change the comments associated with each scene (see Chapters 3 and 4) and thus search for scenes while in Edit mode. However, you can't play back your videos in Capture mode; you must switch to Edit mode.

continues on next page

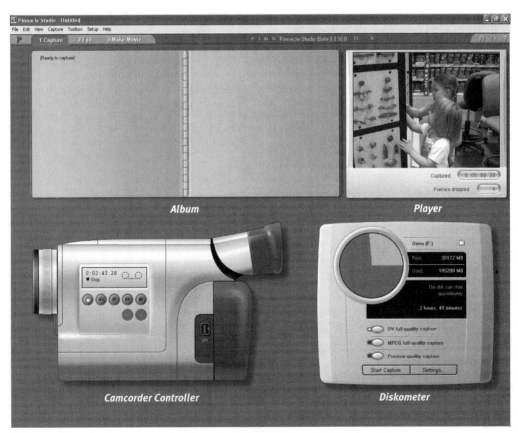

Figure 2.12 Meet the Capture screen, configured to capture DV video. Note the four major components: the Album, the Player, the Camcorder Controller, and the Diskometer.

37

The **Player** previews the captured video, providing information on capture duration and the number of frames dropped during capture, if any. As you can see, there are no playback controls, so you have to switch to Edit mode to play your captured video.

The **Camcorder Controller** lets you control your DV or MicroMV camcorder. Briefly, one of the key advantages of these digital formats is the ability to control your camcorder over the same FireWire connection that transfers video from the camcorder to the computer (see the sidebar "FireWire to the Rescue" in Chapter 3). This ability makes capture from these sources much easier than when you use analog capture.

The **Diskometer** contains the controls for starting and stopping capture. It also provides features to let you select your capture drive and see how much disk space remains on your capture drive (in megabytes) and the amount of time remaining for the selected capture format. You can select several capture options on the face of the Diskometer; to choose all other relevant options, you click the Settings button.

Capturing from analog sources

Figure 2.13 shows Studio's interface for capturing analog video. As you can see, the Album and Player remain unchanged from DV capture, but two additional panels appear to the left and right of the Diskometer for adjusting the brightness and color of the captured video and for adjusting the incoming audio volume. These are unnecessary with DV or MicroMV source video, as you're simply transferring the digital video from camera to computer.

Capturing from an analog source, however, usually involves some fine-tuning, especially for audio, and Studio provides a strong toolset for doing so. Also, when capturing analog video, you have to select the format for storing your video and, often, the quality options associated with that format—hence, the additional controls adjacent to the Diskometer.

If all this capturing business sounds scary, don't sweat. Capturing analog video is more meticulous than mysterious, and the process is spelled out in Chapter 4.

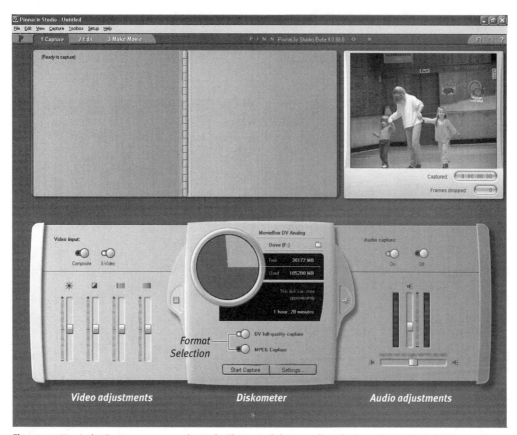

Figure 2.13 Here's the Capture screen, analog style. The controls let you adjust the incoming audio and video.

Using Make Movie Mode

You enter Make Movie mode (**Figure 2.14**) by selecting the Make Movie tab at the upper left of the Studio interface (see Figure 2.4). This takes you to the controls for outputting your work.

Note that Studio customizes the Make Movie interface based on output type. In the example in Figure 2.14, I'm about to produce a DVD of a wedding where my eldest daughter served as flower girl. As you can see, Studio shows a Diskometer-like view of the amount of space available on the DVD, and clicking the Settings button launches a screen with options specific to your output medium of choice. Select Make Disc from the tabs at the top of the Settings window (this tab will be selected automatically if you chose Disc from the left panel of the Make Movie tab), and you'll see choices for output to VideoCD, S-VCD (Super VideoCD), and DVD (**Figure 2.15**).

As indicated on the vertical panel on the left of the Make Movie tab (see Figure 2.14), you can also output to tape (see Chapter 13); produce AVI, MPEG, and streaming media files (see Chapter 14); and share your file by uploading it to Pinnacle's StudioOnline Web site (see Chapter 15).

Figure 2.14 The Make Movie screen is your last stop in the production process. Note the tabs at the upper left that let you select the output type.

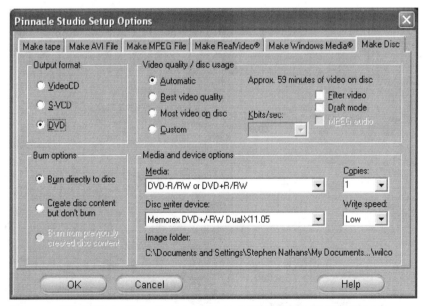

Figure 2.15 Click Settings and choose an output type, in this case from the Make Disc tab.

Figure 2.16 Video requires lots of experimentation, so Studio gives you several options if you change your mind, such as an Undo icon.

Figure 2.17 Studio also provides a menu control and a keyboard shortcut (Ctrl+Z) that you can use to undo a previous edit.

Using Undo and Redo

Experimentation is a major part of the video creation process, which means trying and discarding lots of options. Studio makes this process painless with an exhaustive Undo/Redo feature that saves all edit decisions made since the project was loaded for the current editing session. You can even save your file and then undo previous edit decisions (a rare option in my experience) and, of course, redo them all if you change your mind again.

To undo an edit:

- To undo the immediately preceding edit that you've made, do *one of the following*:
  - ▲ Click the Undo icon in the upper-right corner of the Studio interface (**Figure 2.16**).
  - ▲ Select Edit > Undo (**Figure 2.17**).
  - ▲ Press Ctrl+Z on your keyboard to activate the Undo keyboard shortcut.

  Studio will undo the last edit—in this case, a trim end.

  Note that Studio stores edits sequentially, so if you want to undo the third previous edit, you must first undo the two most recent edits.

To redo an edit:

◆ To redo an edit, do *one of the following*:

▲ Click the Redo icon in the upper-right corner of the Studio interface (**Figure 2.18**).

▲ Select Edit > Redo (**Figure 2.19**).

▲ Press Ctrl+Y on your keyboard to activate the Redo keyboard shortcut.

Studio will redo the last edit—in this case, a trim end.

As with edits, Studio stores Undo commands sequentially, so you must apply Redo commands sequentially if you want to reverse previously applied Undo commands.

Figure 2.18 Changed your mind again? Simply click the Redo icon.

Figure 2.19 You can also use the menu control or the keyboard shortcut (Ctrl+Y) to redo an action.

Saving Your Projects

Like most design products, Studio lets you save a project at any time, preserving your careful editing so that you can return later and continue working. Unlike many other programs, however, Studio doesn't have a true "bin" that saves assets captured or imported into the project.

Rather, the Album merely displays the assets available in the currently selected directory. If all you've done is capture files, there's no reason to save the project file, and Studio won't prompt you to do so when you exit the program. As long as you don't change the directories for your captured files (see "Loading Video Files" in Chapter 6), the files will appear in the Album next time you load Studio.

Once you drag an asset into the Movie window and start editing, however, the project has officially begun. If you try to close the program or start a new project, Studio ensures you don't lose your work—or you can be proactive and save the file yourself. Instructions for both options follow.

I typically create a separate folder for each project, using an obvious name like "Fiddler's Convention" so that I know exactly what's in the folder. Then I save all relevant video, still image, and auxiliary files, as well as the project file, in that folder. This approach makes everything easier to find and clean up later. Studio sets up a Pinnacle Studio folder with a My Projects subfolder in the My Documents folder on your hard drive. If you don't specify a file path, that's where your project files will reside.

To save a project for the first time:

1. Do *one of the following*:
   ▲ Choose File > Save Project.
   ▲ Choose File > Save Project As.
   ▲ Press Ctrl+S.
   The Save As dialog box opens (**Figure 2.20**).

2. Find the desired folder and type the desired name; then click Save.
   Studio saves the project as a .stu file (**Figure 2.21**).

✔ Tip

■ Note the asterisk next to the name wedding.stu in the top line of Figure 2.20. This is Studio's way of telling you that the file has changes that need to be saved. Once you save the file, the asterisk disappears, reappearing, of course, after your next edit.

To save a project after naming it:

◆ Choose File > Save Project, or press Ctrl+S.

To save a project to a new name or location:

1. Choose File > Save Project As.
   The Save As dialog box opens.

2. Find the desired folder, type the desired name, and click Save.
   Studio saves the project file.

Figure 2.20 Here's the familiar dialog box for choosing a name for your file and a location to save it. I usually save my files in the same directory I use to capture my files.

Figure 2.21 Nothing is more irritating than losing the fruits of your editing. Saving your file early is a great way to prevent this from happening.

Introduction to Studio 9

Figure 2.22 Try to exit the program by using the menu command.

Figure 2.23 Or exit via the icon.

Figure 2.24 Either way, Studio prompts you to save your project file. Studio can also automatically save your file at periodic intervals.

To respond to Studio's automatic save functions:

1. Attempt to exit Studio by doing *one of the following*:
   ▲ Choose File > Exit (**Figure 2.22**).
   ▲ Click the X icon in the upper-right corner of the screen (**Figure 2.23**).
   The dialog box shown in **Figure 2.24** appears.

2. Do *one of the following*:
   ▲ Click No.
   Studio exits.
   ▲ Click Cancel.
   You return to Studio.
   ▲ Click Yes.
   The Save As dialog box opens.

3. Find the desired folder and type the desired name.

4. Click Save.
   Studio saves the project file.

✔ Tip

■ Studio can automatically save your file at selectable periods—a good insurance policy to protect against system crashes. The default Autosave interval is 180 seconds. For details on how to enable and configure this option, see "Setting Default Durations" in Chapter 2.

SAVING YOUR PROJECTS

Chapter 2

Using Online Help

Studio includes extensive online help—essentially a digital version of the product manual. Studio also provides tooltips, those little flags that explain an icon's function when you hover over the icon with your cursor for a moment or two. If you find these irritating, Studio lets you disable them.

Figure 2.25 Here's how you open Studio's online Help screen.

In addition, Studio provides keyboard shortcuts for many common activities. In this book, I present the keyboard shortcuts that I find most useful; a list of all keyboard shortcuts can be found in Appendix A. Studio also offers an online list of shortcuts, which you can access as described in the following tasks.

To open Studio's Help screen:

◆ Do *one of the following*:
  ▲ Press the F1 key.
  ▲ Click the Question Mark icon in the upper-right corner of the screen (see Figure 2.14).
  ▲ Choose Help > Help Topics (**Figure 2.25**).
  Studio's Help screen appears (**Figure 2.26**).

Figure 2.26 What you get is essentially an online version of the manual.

46

Introduction to Studio 9

Figure 2.27 If you find tooltips irritating, you can disable them.

Figure 2.28 Tooltips are disabled when the check mark is gone from the side of the menu item.

Figure 2.29 If you're a fan of keyboard shortcuts, Pinnacle makes them easy to learn by posting them online.

To disable Studio's tooltips:

◆ Choose Help > Display Tool Tips (**Figure 2.27**).

When you select Display Tool Tips, the check mark beside the Display Tool Tips menu item is removed (**Figure 2.28**). You can re-enable tooltips by selecting Display Tool Tips in the Help menu again.

To view Studio's keyboard shortcuts:

◆ With Studio Help open, select Keyboard Shortcuts at the bottom of the Contents menu.

A list of keyboard shortcuts appears in the display window (**Figure 2.29**).

Now let's take a look at the steps you should take before starting your initial project.

USING ONLINE HELP

Chapter 2

Selecting Your Capture Drive

Most video old-timers use systems with two or more hard disk drives: one for the operating system and applications and one for captured video and project files. This model arose in the days of underpowered computers and cranky disk drives that were barely up to the task of capturing video. To capture effectively, you needed a separate, high-powered SCSI drive that cost thousands of dollars, required frequent defragmenting, and had to be dedicated to video capture.

Things have changed since then. Most computers purchased since 2000 are more than capable of video capture and editing. Still, with 80-gigabyte (GB) drives costing well under $100, most video producers should consider purchasing a separate drive, especially for long projects or DVD production.

Even if you use only one drive, you may want to create a separate folder for captured video and auxiliary files so that they're easier to find during production and easier to delete when your project is done.

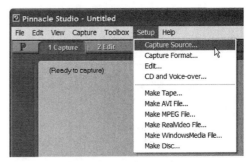

Figure 2.30 Choose Setup > Capture Source to access disk selection and test settings.

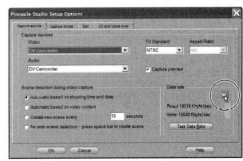

Figure 2.31 Click the yellow Folder icon to select your capture drive and folder.

To select your capture drive:

1. From the Studio menu, choose Setup > Capture Source (**Figure 2.30**).

   The Pinnacle Studio Setup Options dialog box appears, set to the Capture Source tab.

2. In the Data Rate box (at the lower right of the Pinnacle Studio Setup Options dialog box), click the yellow Folder icon (**Figure 2.31**).

   The Select Folder and Default Name for Captured Video dialog box appears.

Introduction to Studio 9

Figure 2.32 Click the Save In list box to change capture drives.

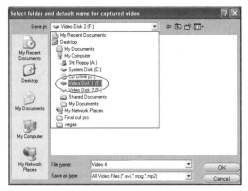

Figure 2.33 Select the target drive for your captured video.

3. To change drives, click the Save In list box at the top of the screen (**Figure 2.32**). The list of available drives drops down.

4. Click to select the target drive (**Figure 2.33**).

✔ Tips

- Even if you're running a fast network at home, don't select a network drive as your capture disk. Performance is best with a local drive.

- If you have multiple drives, sometimes it's helpful to label your capture drive "Video Disk."

To create a new folder and name your clips:

1. At the top of the Select Folder and Default Name for Captured Video dialog box, click the yellow Folder icon to the right of the selected disk drive.

   When you hover the mouse over the icon, the Create New Folder tooltip appears (**Figure 2.34**).

2. Studio creates a new folder, which you can name at will (**Figure 2.35**).

3. If desired, type the name of the captured file in the File Name box.

   If you capture sequential files, Studio simply updates the file from Video 1 to Video 2, and so on.

✔ Tips

- Don't stress about what to name your files at this point, as you'll revisit this topic during the capture process.

- Try to make your folder names descriptive; otherwise, six months from now you'll have trouble figuring out what's in them.

Figure 2.34 Click the Create New Folder icon to create a new folder.

Figure 2.35 Give your folders descriptive names so that you can remember what's in them.

Defragmenting Your Capture Drive

Although most current computers (that is, those manufactured from 2000 onward) have enough power to handle digital video capture and editing, Studio includes a performance test so that you can be sure your computer has what it takes. Run this test as soon as you install Studio to identify any problems that may prevent smooth operation.

If you're using a disk that contains lots of data for your capture and edit drive, you should defragment the drive before performing this test. During normal disk operation, Windows copies and deletes files all over the drive, sometimes splitting up longer files when writing them to disk. *Defragmenting* the drive reunites all file components and packs the files efficiently together on the drive, opening up large contiguous spaces for the performance test and video editing projects.

The Windows Disk Defragmenter has a tool that lets you analyze the drive to see if it needs defragmenting. We'll skip that test and defragment anyway, just to be sure your disk is in the optimal condition to take the performance test.

To defragment your capture drive:

1. From the Windows desktop, choose Start > Accessories > System Tools > Disk Defragmenter (**Figure 2.36**).

   The Disk Defragmenter application window appears.

   continues on next page

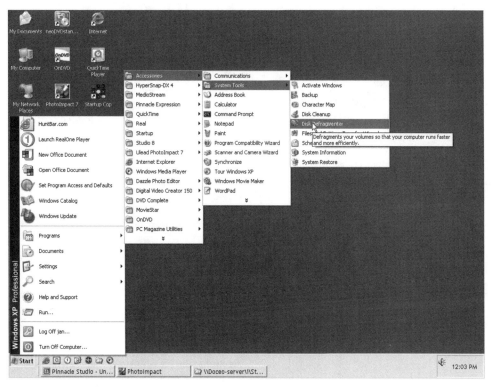

Figure 2.36 The long and winding road to the Disk Defragmenter utility, a hard drive's best friend.

2. Choose the video capture disk by selecting it in the application window; then click the Defragment button (**Figure 2.37**).

While you're waiting, go get a cup of coffee. You're pretty much done, but if you care to watch, here's what you should be seeing:

The program analyzes disk usage before defragmenting. Although you can't see it in the black-and-white screen shots, most of the small lines surrounded by white spaces are fragmented files that will be consolidated during the defragmentation process (**Figure 2.38**).

In the defragmented disk, which is ready for testing, all files are consolidated and efficiently packed, leaving plenty of contiguous disk space (**Figure 2.39**).

✔ **Tips**

- Depending on the size of the drive and how much data is on the disk, defragmenting can take anywhere from 30 seconds to several hours. Keep this in mind before starting this operation.

- Turn off all background programs and don't use the computer when you're defragmenting the drive. If any program writes data to disk while the system is defragmenting, the Disk Defragmenter may stop and then restart, extending the completion time significantly.

- Large files slow the disk defragmentation process. If you have large video files or other files on the capture drive that you don't need, delete them and any other extraneous files before defragmenting.

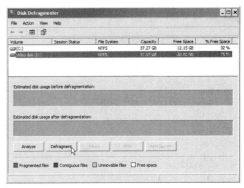

Figure 2.37 Select your target drive and click the Defragment button to get started.

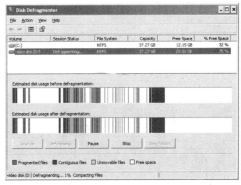

Figure 2.38 The Disk Defragmenter first analyzes your file and then starts to consolidate files, compacting them to the inner tracks of the drive.

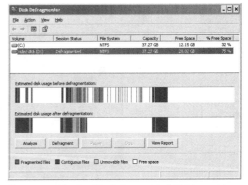

Figure 2.39 The freshly defragmented disk has wide open spaces, perfect for efficient video capture.

Testing Your Capture Drive

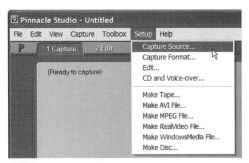

Figure 2.40 Choose Setup > Capture Source to access Studio's disk test utility.

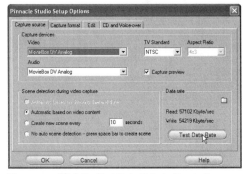

Figure 2.41 Click the Test Data Rate button in the lower-right corner to check disk performance.

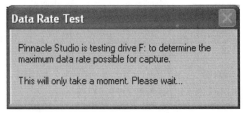

Figure 2.42 You should see this dialog box for 10 to 15 seconds.

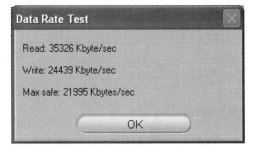

Figure 2.43 Voilà! I passed the test and am almost ready to get started.

Now that your drive is freshly defragmented, let's see how it performs in the Pinnacle drive test.

For perspective, keep in mind that DV streams from a camera at about 3.6 megabytes (MB) of video data per second. To successfully capture DV, a disk must be able to write, or store, at least 3.6 MB of data per second. To successfully transfer DV back to the camera, the disk must be able to read at least 3.6 MB of data per second.

As you'll see, the video disk on my HP xw4100 workstation can far exceed these requirements. In all likelihood, your computer will also pass this test with flying colors, but it's better to test early to identify any problems than to experience balky operation during capture and editing.

To test your capture drive:

1. From the Studio menu, choose Setup > Capture Source (**Figure 2.40**).

    The Pinnacle Studio Setup Options dialog box appears, set to the Capture Source tab.

2. Click the Test Data Rate button in the lower-right corner of the Capture Source tab (**Figure 2.41**).

    Studio starts the test, and the Data Rate Test dialog box appears (**Figure 2.42**). The test should take no longer than about 10 seconds, and then a Data Rate Test results screen appears (**Figure 2.43**). I passed!

    continues on next page

Studio lists these results on the Capture Source tab (**Figure 2.44**). You can retest at any time. For example, if you start experiencing dropped frames during capture or you can't write video back to the camera, retest and make sure that performance is up to par.

Figure 2.44 Studio notes the results in the Capture Source tab's Data Rate section.

✔ Tip

- I've noticed big ranges in test rates when I test several times in sequence. So don't sweat it—expect some variance, and recognize that any score over 10,000 kilobytes per second (Kbyte/sec) should be fine.

Optimizing System Disk Performance

Is your computer's performance not up to snuff? Assuming that the Disk Defragmenter doesn't indicate that your hardware is faulty, two conditions could be the cause of poor disk performance. First, if you're running Windows 98, direct memory access (DMA) may not be enabled for your capture disk. Enable DMA in the System Properties control by selecting the properties window for your disk drive. DMA is automatically enabled in all operating systems after Windows 98, so this shouldn't be a problem in Windows 2000, Windows Millennium Edition, or Windows XP.

The other possible cause of poor disk performance is too many programs loaded into background memory. You'll know this is the culprit if your Windows taskbar on the bottom right has more icons than a NASCAR racer. You can attack this problem in two ways. First, click each icon, thus loading each corresponding program. In the properties or similar window, you should find a control for disabling the background process. For example, to disable QuickTime, choose Edit > Preferences and make sure that QuickTime System Tray Icon is not selected. While you wouldn't want to disable your virus checker, you probably don't need RealPlayer, QuickTime Player, the Microsoft Office taskbar, and other items running all the time.

The other alternative is to use a program called a startup manager, which lets you control which programs load in the background and when. *PC Magazine* offers a utility called Startup Cop that provides basic functionality (www.pcmag.com). The program I've used most extensively is Shensoft Power Launcher Plus, but it doesn't appear to have been updated since 2000 (www.shensoft.com). Most recently, *PC Magazine* recommended Startup Manager by Kissco (www.startupmgr.com). If none of these suits you, search under *startup manager* in your favorite search engine for other options.

Introduction to Studio 9

Figure 2.45 Choose Setup > Edit to access basic editing default settings.

Setting Default Durations

When you insert transitions, titles, still images, and audio fades into your video projects, Studio assigns default durations to these assets. You can modify these defaults for each asset or effect during editing, but here's how you set the default values.

To set default durations:

1. From the Studio menu, choose Setup > Edit (**Figure 2.45**).

   The Pinnacle Studio Setup Options dialog box appears (**Figure 2.46**).

2. To change the default duration for transitions, titles, still images, or volume fades, do *one of the following*:

   ▲ Click the number you want to change and enter a new number (**Figure 2.47**).

   ▲ Use the arrow controls beside each duration to adjust the numbers manually (**Figure 2.48**).

Figure 2.46 Default durations for transitions, titles, still images, and audio volume fades are at the upper left of the screen.

Figure 2.47 To change the duration, you can click the current number and enter a new one.

Figure 2.48 You can also use the arrow controls next to each value to change the settings.

To enable Autosave and set the duration:

1. Click the Save Project Automatically Every check box to add a check mark (see Figure 2.46).

   Autosave is enabled.

2. To modify the default duration of 180 seconds, select the number; then enter another value (**Figure 2.49**).

   The Autosave function saves your project periodically, so if your computer crashes or you lose power, most of your work will be preserved. The only downside is a momentary loss of responsiveness as the system freezes slightly during the save process. Unless you're in the middle of an edit, you probably won't notice a thing, leaving little reason to disable this helpful process. The default duration is probably fine for most users.

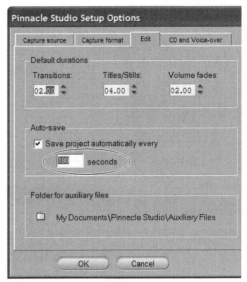

Figure 2.49 Modify the default Autosave value by clicking the number and typing another one.

Setting the Auxiliary File Location

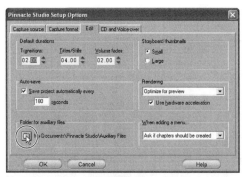

Figure 2.50 Click the yellow folder at the bottom left to change the auxiliary file location.

I don't know about you, but it drives me crazy when I don't know the location of all the files associated with a project. These can include background audio files, narration tracks, DVD image files, and the other file detritus associated with project development.

Fortunately, Studio makes it simple to keep track of these auxiliary files by letting you set their location. This makes finding them easy when you want to reuse them, or when you want to delete them en masse once your project is complete.

Generally, I like to place my auxiliary files on the same drive and in the same folder as my captured files so that they're easy to find. The only reason to select another location is if you're running out of space on your capture drive; then you can use another location with more space. When you're writing a DVD, you may need close to 5 GB of storage space for the DVD image file; most other auxiliary files, however, are much, much smaller.

The Edit dialog box contains several other presets, but leave these at their default settings for now; they're covered in detail later in the book.

To set the auxiliary file location:

1. From the Studio menu, choose Setup > Edit (see Figure 2.45).

    The Pinnacle Studio Setup Options dialog box appears (**Figure 2.50**).

    The Folder for Auxiliary Files section of the dialog box at the lower left contains a yellow Folder icon.

continues on next page

Chapter 2

2. Click the yellow folder to open the Browse for Folder dialog box (**Figure 2.51**).

3. Click the desired drive and folder for your auxiliary files.

   Studio creates a separate directory structure off the selected drive and folder (**Figure 2.52**) and doesn't mix the files with your captured files.

✔ Tip

- According to the technical-support discussion forums at Pinnacle's Web site, some users have experienced problems when changing the auxiliary file location in mid-project. At the very least, you'll end up copying all auxiliary files from the old to the new location, which could be time consuming. At worst—and this appears to be rare—you'll corrupt your project file and have to start over. So make sure you have enough space before selecting the auxiliary file location.

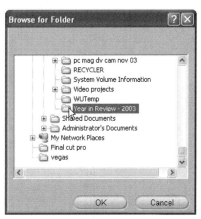

Figure 2.51 Scroll down to choose the drive and folder for the auxiliary files.

Figure 2.52 Studio creates an entirely new folder for the auxiliary files and doesn't intermingle these files with those containing your captured video clips.

About 16:9 Mode

The designation 16:9 is what's called an *aspect ratio*, which defines the relationship between horizontal and vertical display units in a display technology such as a television set. For example, all camcorders sold in the United States shoot in an aspect ratio of 4:3, because that's the aspect ratio most domestic television sets use to display video.

In addition to supporting 4:3, most new DV camcorders also support the 16:9 aspect ratio. The 16:9 mode captures video in a widescreen format like that used in Hollywood movies, making it ideal if you have a widescreen television or high-definition television (HDTV) that supports widescreen footage. Check the documentation that came with your camcorder to learn how to enable and disable this shooting mode.

Studio and 16:9

Studio can't mix 16:9 and 4:3 video in a single project, and it assumes that the aspect ratio of the first video inserted into the project is the default mode. So if you capture in 16:9 mode in DV format, Studio should detect this and enter 16:9 mode automatically.

However, if you capture in 16:9 mode using analog capture, or if you import 16:9 video into a project, Studio may not be able to recognize it as 16:9 footage. In these instances, you can trigger 16:9 mode by switching to 16:9 display mode in either the Capture Album or Edit Album. (For more information on switching to 16:9 views in the Capture Albums, see Chapters 3 and 4, Customizing Album Views. For more information on the Edit Album, see "Working with the Albums' Views and Tools" in Chapter 6.)

Note that Studio notifies you if you try to insert 4:3 footage into a 16:9 project, and vice versa, by displaying a status message like that in **Figure 2.53**. If Studio fails to produce this message and accepts the footage, the video using the mode that was loaded last will be distorted. For example, if you mistakenly loaded video using the 4:3 display mode into a 16:9 project and Studio accepts it, the 4:3 video will be distorted during rendering.

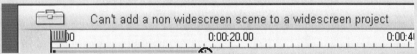

Figure 2.53 Studio shouldn't load non-widescreen (4:3) videos into a widescreen (16:9) project.

If you're using 16:9 footage, whether captured or imported, it's good practice to use 16:9 display mode in the Edit Album. See Chapter 6, "Working with the Albums' Views and Tools."

continues on next page

Chapter 2

> **About 16:9 Mode** *continued*
>
> **When's the Right Time for 16:9?**
>
> Before shooting in 16:9 format, consider where you and others will view your project. This format works best with older widescreen televisions and newer HDTVs. In addition, most software DVD players like Sonic Solutions' CinePlayer and Intervideo's WinDVD can play both 16:9 and 4:3 video.
>
> However, most standard TV sets (neither widescreen nor HDTV) will stretch the video vertically to full screen, distorting its appearance. You'll likely get similar results if you output your video to analog tape such as VHS. So while 16:9 may look great in your own living room, it might not look so great on grandma's older TV set, a definite factor to consider when choosing your shooting format. If you're unsure of the capabilities of the television or other device that will play your upcoming project, the best course is to test before shooting a major production. Shoot some video in 16:9 format and then capture and render to DVD, to tape, or to whatever format you intend to distribute. Make sure that the video is displayed correctly on your target device. Otherwise, you may be in for a nasty surprise when you show your video masterpiece.

Part II: Gathering Your Assets

Chapter 3   Capturing DV 63

Chapter 4   Capturing Analog Video 85

Chapter 5   Working with Still Images 107

Chapter 6   Collecting Assets in
the Album 119

3

CAPTURING DV

DV offers better video quality than most analog camcorders, and since DV camcorders record the time and date of each shot, Studio 9 can divide captured video into scenes, making it easier to find the clips you want.

Since DV is a digital format, *capturing* from a DV camcorder is more like a file transfer; some even refer to the process as a file import. Call it what you will, getting DV video from your camcorder to your computer is a snap. No video resolution to set or audio volume to adjust—just press Start and Stop.

The same cable that carries the DV video to your computer lets you control the camera, so you can start, stop, rewind, and fast-forward your DV camera within Studio—a useful capability unavailable with most analog camcorders. All of these factors make DV capture quick, painless, and highly functional.

Note that capture operation is identical whether you shot your footage in 16:9 or 4:3 mode. However, the first video you insert into the project determines the aspect ratio that Studio uses for that project. In addition, Studio won't let you capture 16:9 and 4:3 footage from the same tape into the same project. Studio's Capture Album does have the ability to display 16:9 and 4:3 footage at the proper aspect ratios, an option we'll explore in this chapter.

Chapter 3

The DV Capture Interface

Let's have a quick look at the tools you'll use to control and monitor DV capture. Note that the interface is different when you're capturing from a DV camcorder than it is when you're capturing from an analog camcorder. (See Chapter 4 for the scoop on analog capture.)

You access the main capture window by clicking the Capture tab at the upper left of the Studio interface (**Figure 3.1**). In Capture mode, Studio has four main components: the Album, where Studio displays the captured clips; the Player, which displays video during capture; the Camcorder Controller; and the Diskometer.

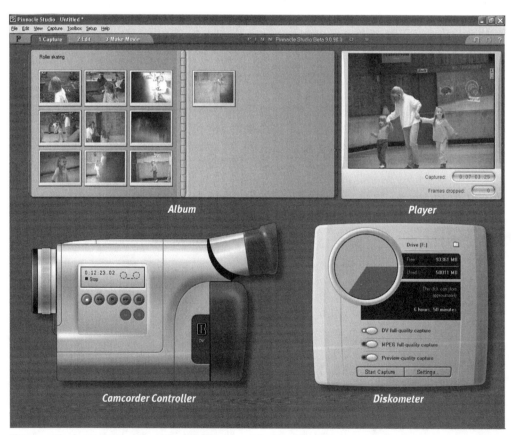

Figure 3.1 The four main windows of Studio's DV capture interface.

Capturing DV

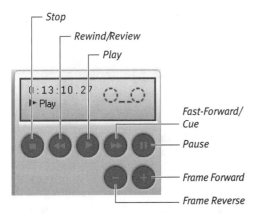

Figure 3.2 The Camcorder Controller lets you control the playback of your DV camcorder.

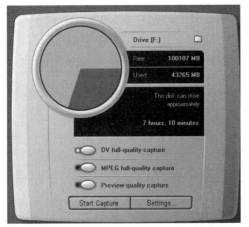

Figure 3.3 The Diskometer tells you how much video you can store on your capture drive, lets you choose among the three capture options, and contains the Start Capture button.

The Album. The Album contains your captured clips, though you can't play them back while in Capture mode. If you enable scene detection (see the sidebar "Making the Scene with Scene Detection" later in this chapter), each scene from that file appears in the Album, thus accounting for the multiple scenes in the Album in Figure 3.1. Had you captured more scenes than could fit on the two pages in the Album, you would see a little white arrow at the upper-right of the second page of the Album, indicating more scenes are stored on subsequent pages.

Studio stores captured files either during capture or, in the case of MPEG files, immediately after capture. Either way, no user intervention is needed to store the files. Once you start to capture another file, your previously captured files disappear from the Album—but don't worry; they are safely stored and accessible in Edit mode.

The Player. Note the lack of playback controls in the Player window. The Player's role during capture is to let you preview the incoming video and give you information about dropped frames. To play the captured files, you have to switch to Edit mode.

The Camcorder Controller. The controls in the Camcorder Controller mimic those on your camcorder (**Figure 3.2**). Use these to navigate through the tape to find the scenes you want to include in your project.

The Diskometer. The Diskometer serves multiple purposes. First, the wheel and associated text describe how much additional video you can store on the capture drive at the selected format and capture quality. For example, **Figure 3.3** shows about 100 GB of space left on the capture drive, which means the drive has enough available space to hold seven hours (at 13 GB per hour) of video recorded in DV format.

continues on next page

Chapter 3

In the middle of the Diskometer are controls for toggling among DV, MPEG, and preview-quality capture—options discussed later in this chapter (see "Choosing Your Capture Format"). You also control capture from the Diskometer, clicking Start Capture to start. After you start capture, this button changes to Stop Capture, which you click to stop the capture (**Figure 3.4**).

Click the Settings button in the lower-right corner to open the Pinnacle Studio Setup Options dialog box. The Capture Format tab is where you choose your capture parameters if you capture in a format other than DV (**Figure 3.5**).

The Capture Source tab is where you select your capture device and scene-detection options (**Figure 3.6**). This is also where you choose and test the capture drive (see "Testing Your Capture Drive" in Chapter 2).

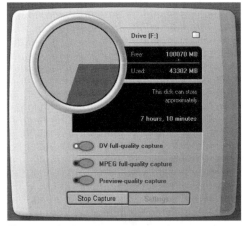

Figure 3.4 The Start Capture button changes to Stop Capture during capture. You can also press the Esc key on your keyboard to end capture.

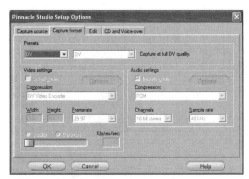

Figure 3.5 The Capture Format tab. Since DV is a standard format, there are no options, but you'll have to select options here when capturing in MPEG or preview format.

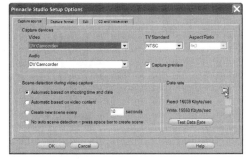

Figure 3.6 Here's the Capture Source screen again. Chapter 2 explained how to select and test the capture drive from this screen; this chapter explores the scene-detection options and how to choose among various capture devices.

Making the Scene with Scene Detection

Sifting through your scenes and finding the ones to include in your final project can be extraordinarily time consuming. Fortunately, Studio automates much of the process with its comprehensive scene-detection feature.

Studio offers four scene-detection modes (Figure 3.6), accessed via the Capture Source tab in the Pinnacle Studio Setup Options dialog box (click Settings on the Diskometer or choose Setup > Capture Source). The mode I've found most useful is Automatic Based on Shooting Time and Date, an option that analyzes time codes embedded on the DV tape to identify new scenes.

Here's how it works: I chronicle family events with my DV camcorder continuously, usually taking two or three months to complete a 60-minute tape of holidays, school events, and other camera-worthy moments. When it's time to produce a video, I have Studio use the Automatic Based on Shooting Time and Date scene-detection mode to scan the tape, examine the time codes, and break the captured video into multiple scenes that appear in the Album. Without scene detection, I'd have to view the video and perform that work manually, which is time consuming and tedious. Although the scenes are all part of a single video file, during editing they look and act like discrete files, so I can easily pull one or more scenes into the Timeline for editing. For many productions, the amount of time saved is enormous.

The Automatic Based on Video Content option analyzes the video frame by frame, identifying a scene change when the amount of interframe change is significant. This mode is useful for DV cameras when the source video contains one long scene with no breaks—for instance, when you're dubbing a tape from analog to DV or using a single camera to film one long event.

You can also have Studio break a scene into regular intervals of 1 second or more, by choosing the Create New Scene Every *x* Seconds option, or you can eschew automated scene detection and manually create scenes by pressing the spacebar, by choosing No Auto Scene Detection.

Chapter 3

Connecting for DV Capture

Before setting up for DV capture, quickly review the sections "Selecting Your Capture Drive," "Defragmenting Your Capture Drive," and "Testing Your Capture Drive" in Chapter 2.

I'm assuming that you have a FireWire connector or card installed in your computer. If you don't, start there, and make sure it's up and running. Don't spend too much on the connector; for your purposes, virtually all cards will serve equally well, from the $19 variety on up, and they all plug into an available PCI card slot inside your PC. Choosing one with at least two ports will allow you to connect both your camcorder and a FireWire hard drive, as needed, for additional storage space for your captured video.

FireWire to the Rescue

FireWire technology was invented by Apple Computer and then standardized by the Institute of Electrical and Electronic Engineers as IEEE 1394. Sony's name for FireWire is iLink, and companies refer to the connectors as FireWire, DV, or IEEE 1394. Whatever the name, they should all work together seamlessly.

Some newer DV cameras, like the Canon GL2, have Universal Serial Bus (USB) ports to transfer still images from camera to computer, but it doesn't work for DV video. To capture DV, ignore this connector (and the traditional analog connectors) and find the FireWire plug.

While most computers use a six-pin port, some computers (like my Dell Latitude D800 laptop) use a four-pin connector identical to that in most cameras. Identify which connector you have before buying a cable; cables come in three varieties: four-pin to six-pin, four-pin to four-pin, and six-pin to six-pin.

Capturing DV

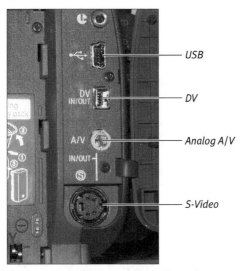

Figure 3.7 The DV port on my loaner Canon GL2 camera. Note the single analog A/V connector for composite video and both audio channels.

Figure 3.8 A four-pin (on the left) to six-pin DV cable. DV cables also come with dual four-pin and dual six-pin connectors.

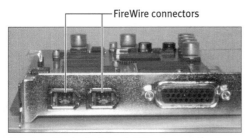

Figure 3.9 The typical six-pin DV connectors (on the left) are found on most—but not all—computers.

To connect your camera and computer for DV capture:

1. Plug in your DV camcorder to AC power. Battery power should work, but it doesn't work with all cameras.

2. Make sure that the camcorder is in VCR, VTR, or Play mode.

3. Connect your FireWire cable to the camera's DV connector (**Figure 3.7**).
   Virtually all cameras use a tiny four-pin connector like that on the left side of **Figure 3.8**.

4. Connect the FireWire cable to your computer using one of the two slots shown on the left in **Figure 3.9** and the larger six-pin connector shown on the right in Figure 3.8.
   You're now ready to run Studio and enter Capture mode.

✔ Tip

- Speaking of buying a cable, basic FireWire cables are priced between $12 and $50, depending on brand and store. If you're buying, check out www.cables.com, which offers a complete line of FireWire cables at very reasonable prices.

Entering DV Capture Mode

As the name suggests, Capture mode is where Studio manages all video capture activities. Entering Capture mode isn't as simple as it sounds.

As soon as you click the Capture tab, Studio checks to ensure that your DV capture device is running properly and your camera is connected, turned on, and in the proper mode.

If everything is configured and connected properly, the process will be invisible to you—you'll simply be ready to capture. If there are problems, however, this section can help you tackle them.

To enter DV Capture mode:

1. Run Studio, and at the upper left, click the Capture tab (Figure 3.1).

   You are in Capture mode. If this is the first time you've entered Capture mode, Studio runs a quick diagnostic test on your system disk to determine if it's fast enough to capture video (**Figure 3.10**).

   If Studio reports that your drive is too slow to capture video, defragment your drive as detailed in "Defragmenting Your Capture Drive" in Chapter 2, and test again. If the drive can't meet these minimum requirements, you need to diagnose and fix the problem, or get a new computer or drive.

   You can scan through the Troubleshooting appendix (Appendix B) for some tips, but you may need some additional assistance not provided in this book. When the check is completed, Studio attempts to load the DV capture driver and find the DV camera.

   If Studio finds the driver and the camera, the LCD panel in the Camcorder Controller will show the time code position of the tape in the DV camera and indicate that playback is stopped (**Figure 3.11**). You are clean, green, and ready for takeoff. Proceed to Step 2.

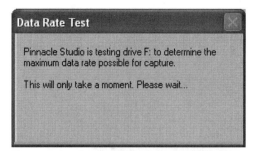

Figure 3.10 Studio runs a quick test on your system disk the first time you enter Capture mode. To read about selecting and testing your capture disk, see "Testing Your Capture Drive" in Chapter 2.

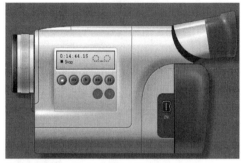

Figure 3.11 Your best clue that Studio recognizes your DV capture board and DV camera is the time code displayed in the Movie window.

Capturing DV

Figure 3.12 Ruh-roh, Scooby Doo, rumpring's rong... This is what you see when Studio can't find the driver or camera.

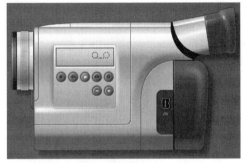

Figure 3.13 The blank camera LCD means you're in Capture mode, but Studio can't "see" your DV camcorder.

Figure 3.14 When you see video in the Player, your setup is working and you're ready to capture.

If Studio doesn't find either the driver or the camera, an error message appears (**Figure 3.12**). If you click OK, you enter Capture mode, but the camera LCD is completely blank and you can't capture (**Figure 3.13**). Take the steps recommended in the error message:

▲ Turn the DV camera off and on.

▲ Disconnect and reconnect the 1394 cable.

▲ Restart Windows and try again.

After each step, see if you can enter Capture mode without error. If so, proceed to Step 2; if not, check Appendix B for troubleshooting information.

2. Click the Play control button, the middle button on the top row (Figure 3.11).

Video should appear in the Player window, signifying that you're ready to capture (**Figure 3.14**). Pause the video and turn to the next section for instructions on capturing.

If you can't see video in the Player window, check Appendix B for troubleshooting information.

✔ **Tip**

■ Studio doesn't pass audio through the system during DV capture, so don't sweat it if you don't hear audio during capture. Besides, unlike when you capture from an analog device, it's virtually impossible to transfer the DV video without the audio: it's stored in the same file in the camera.

ENTERING DV CAPTURE MODE

Time Code: What You Need to Know

As you shoot, your DV camcorder stamps each frame with a sequential time code that looks like this:

`01:02:03:04`

Here's what it stands for:

`Hours:minutes:seconds:frames`

Time code gives your DV camcorder and programs like Studio the ability to locate and access any particular frame on the DV tape.

Note that DV tapes don't come with time code embedded; these codes are stored on the tape by the camera as you shoot. Ideally, time code is consecutive from start to finish, so each frame is unique. If there is a break in time code, the camera starts counting again at 00:00:00:01, which means duplicate time codes and potential confusion.

Duplications can occur, for example, when you watch video that you've recorded and play past the end point of the recorded video. If you start recording anew from that subsequent point, the camera restarts the time code from the beginning.

Studio handles time code breaks fairly well, but other programs don't—especially higher-end programs that use continuous time code for features like batch capture. For this reason, it's good practice to maintain a continuous time code on each recorded tape. You can accomplish this in two ways:

- Put each tape in your DV camcorder with the lens cap on and record from start to finish. Then rewind and start your normal shooting, which will overwrite the previously recorded frames but maintain the time code structure.

- Whenever you film with your DV camcorder, be sure you don't start beyond the last previously written time code segment. You've gone beyond the time if you see nothing but lines in the time code field.

Don't confuse time code with the time and date stamp the DV format uses to produce scene changes, which are stored on a different part of the tape. On many camcorders, including most Sony DV camcorders, you can see time and date stamps by pressing the data code control.

Capturing DV Video

There are several capture options and other settings that you could mess with, but let's capture some video using Studio's default settings and return to the key capture options later in the chapter.

Begin by working your way through the steps in the last two tasks. Once you enter Capture mode, the Camcorder Controller should appear, with live time code information. If it doesn't, run through the steps in the previous two tasks again.

Note that it doesn't matter whether you're capturing 16:9 or 4:3 video; Studio will automatically adjust accordingly. You don't need to set any switches or controls to make this happen.

To capture DV video:

1. Click the Capture tab to enter Capture mode.

2. Use the Camcorder Controller to move the DV tape in the camera to the desired starting point.

3. Click the Start Capture button on the Diskometer (**Figure 3.15**).

    The Capture Video dialog box opens (**Figure 3.16**), and the Start Capture button changes to Stop Capture (**Figure 3.17**).

4. For this test, enter a duration of 1 minute and 00 seconds in the Capture Video dialog box as shown in Figure 3.16.

    When the Capture Video dialog box first appears, it displays the maximum duration of video your disk can store, which is limited by either the file size or the version of Windows you're running. (For more information, see the sidebar, "Windows File Size Limitations," later in this chapter.)

    continues on next page

Figure 3.15 Click the Start Capture button on the Diskometer.

Figure 3.16 You can name your file before capture and elect to capture for a specified interval. This is useful, for example, when you want to capture a 60-minute tape while you're away from the computer.

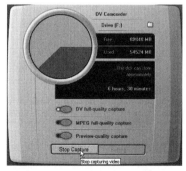

Figure 3.17 To stop capture, click Stop Capture on the Diskometer or press the Esc key on your keyboard.

Chapter 3

If the duration shown in your program is *less than* one minute, either your capture disk is almost full or you're pointing toward the wrong disk. See "Selecting Your Capture Drive" in Chapter 2.

5. Click Start Capture in the Capture Video dialog box to start capturing.

6. If an error message appears (**Figure 3.18**), you've already captured some video using the same file name. Do *one of the following*:

   ▲ Click Yes to overwrite the file and start the capture.

   ▲ Click No to return to the Capture Video dialog box and rename the file. Then click Start Capture to start capturing.

   Your DV camera starts playing, and capture begins.

7. Studio should capture one minute of video. To stop capture before then, do *one of the following*:

   ▲ Click Stop Capture on the Diskometer.

   ▲ Press the Esc key on your keyboard.

   After the capture stops, a file labeled Video 1 (or whatever name you may have chosen) appears in the Album (**Figure 3.19**). You'll see multiple files if any scene changes occurred in the source video during the one-minute capture. (See the sidebar "Making the Scene with Scene Detection" earlier in this chapter for scene-detection options.)

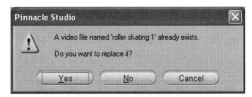

Figure 3.18 Studio won't automatically overwrite previously captured files—a nice feature.

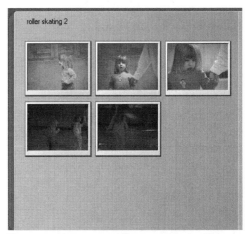

Figure 3.19 Your captured file appears in the Album, with a separate icon for each scene identified by Studio during capture.

Capturing DV

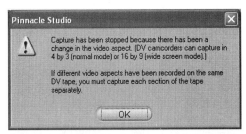

Figure 3.20 Studio won't capture 4:3 and 16:9 footage from the same tape during the same capture session.

Windows File Size Limitations

A consistent thorn in the side of video developers has been file size limitations inherent to Windows. Depending on a bunch of arcane rules, such as which version of Windows you're running and how you formatted your drives, the maximum file size your system can store may be 2 GB (about 9 minutes of video) or 4 GB (about 19 minutes of video). In these instances, you'll have to divide your capture into 2-GB or 4-GB chunks to capture an entire 60-minute DV tape.

Fortunately, Windows XP and Windows 2000 have no file size limitations as long as you format your drives using the Windows NT file system. That's why most video developers have moved to these versions.

If you're running Windows 98 or Me, however, you're probably using a fairly old computer with lots of out-of-date drivers and other code bits and fragments. Upgrading to Windows XP and reformatting your capture drive will allow you to capture files of any size and will provide a cleaner starting point for your programs.

Whichever version of Windows you're running, Studio should automatically list the maximum duration you can capture in the Capture Video dialog box (Figure 3.16).

✔ Tips

- If you attempt to capture 4:3 and 16:9 footage from the same tape during the same capture session, you'll see the error message displayed in **Figure 3.20**.

- You can't view your captured video in Edit mode. To play back your captured file, see the section "Viewing Your Captured Video," later in this chapter.

- Note the Frames Dropped counter at the bottom of the Player in Figure 3.14. Dropped frames are frames that the computer couldn't capture, usually because the disk wasn't fast enough to keep up with the incoming video. This counter updates in real time during capture. If you drop more than one or two frames, stop capturing and check Appendix B to diagnose and fix your problem. Often, running other applications while capturing will cause Studio to drop frames, which should be reason enough not to do so.

- The first several hundred times I used Studio, I would start the video rolling, click the Start Capture button, and get frustrated when Studio asked me for a file name before starting capture, since the video I wanted to capture would be speeding by while I named the file. Then the nickel dropped in my brain, and I realized that I should simply move the video to the desired spot and let Studio do the rest by following the procedures in the preceding task.

- When you capture DV video, Studio's default scene-detection mode automatically detects scenes based on time code. If you desire, change this option on the Capture Source tab, accessible from the Studio menu by choosing Setup > Capture Source.

Choosing Your Capture Format

The previous exercise explained how to capture in DV format, which is appropriate for the vast majority of users and projects. However, when you are capturing DV video from a DV camcorder, Studio gives you two other options: preview-quality capture and MPEG full-quality capture.

Preview-Quality Capture. You select this option on the Diskometer or on the Capture Format tab of the Pinnacle Studio Setup Options dialog box. Preview-quality capture relates to Studio's SmartCapture feature, which stores the DV footage in a reduced-quality format that saves disk space but retains the original DV time code information. You edit using the preview-quality video, and then Studio captures the footage at full DV quality before rendering.

SmartCapture was wonderful when it was introduced because disk drives were pricey and workspace critical. Today, however, an 80-GB hard drive costs under $100. And although SmartCapture works well, it adds both time and complexity to the production process. For this reason, I won't discuss SmartCapture further; see Studio's manual or Help files for assistance.

MPEG Full-Quality Capture. Capturing in MPEG format is a slightly different story with a similar ending. Capturing using the MPEG option saves file space and production time if you're producing a DVD, VideoCD (VCD), or Super VideoCD (SVCD) project with MPEG video.

However, the algorithm that Studio uses to encode MPEG during capture is optimized for speed, not quality, so Studio can store the video to disk in as near to real time as possible. In contrast, when Studio outputs to MPEG format during final project rendering, say for DVD production, the algorithm is optimized for quality, not speed.

Note also that when you insert effects such as transitions, titles, or color correction into captured MPEG video, Studio implements the effects and then re-renders the affected portions of the video into MPEG format. So if your edits affect substantial portions of the video, your production-time savings will be minimal. In addition, the edited sections are encoded in MPEG format twice—once during capture and once during rendering—the digital equivalent of photocopying a photocopy.

So unless you're producing a disk-based project and your edits will be minimal—and production time is absolutely critical—you should capture in DV format and then render in MPEG format after editing. This approach will maximize production quality, though production time may be extended.

This leaves DV video as the best capture format for virtually all projects.

To choose your capture format:

- On the Diskometer, click the button for the desired capture format (Figure 3.15). The light to the left of the button lights up.

  If you choose DV Full-Quality Capture, you're all set; there are no other options to select.

  If you choose MPEG Full-Quality Capture, you need to set several options before capture. (See the following section for more information.)

  If you choose Preview-Quality Capture, check Pinnacle's Studio 9 manual for additional help.

Capturing DV Video to MPEG Format

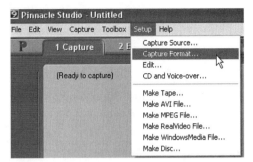

Figure 3.21 Access the Capture format tab to change your capture format to MPEG.

The most obvious time to capture directly into MPEG format is when you're creating projects using MPEG-formatted video, such as in DVDs, VCDs, and SVCDs. Studio simplifies these captures with presets that deliver the properly formatted video for each project.

However, remember that during MPEG capture, Studio defaults to an encoding algorithm optimized for encoding speed rather than quality, so quality will be optimized if you capture with DV and encode in MPEG format during final rendering.

Also note that all versions of Studio before 8.6 re-encode all MPEG footage during final rendering. Version 8.6 introduced smart rendering for MPEG, so that only the segments of video affected during editing are re-encoded before production. This makes the upgrade to version 8.6 essential to all producers who capture MPEG video.

Finally, remember that if your edits affect significant portions of the video in the project, you will have to re-render these anyway before producing your disc. If this is the case, capturing in DV format will produce better overall quality with minimal increase in production time.

Knowing all of these caveats, if you still want to capture in MPEG format, here's how.

To capture DV video in MPEG format:

1. Open the Pinnacle Studio Setup Options dialog box to the Capture Format tab by doing *one of the following*:
   - ▲ From the Studio menu, choose Setup > Capture Format (**Figure 3.21**).
   - ▲ In Capture mode, click the Settings button on the Diskometer.

continues on next page

Chapter 3

2. Click the text in the first list box in the Presets section and select MPEG (**Figure 3.22**).

   This also changes your selection on the Diskometer, so you don't have to change it there separately.

3. In the second list box in the Presets section, choose *one of the following options:*

   ▲ If encoding for a DVD project, choose High Quality.

   ▲ If encoding for an SVCD project, choose Medium Quality.

   ▲ If encoding for a VCD project, choose Low Quality.

   ▲ If you want to customize your encoding settings, choose Custom (but be sure to read the following tips first).

4. Click OK to close the Pinnacle Studio Setup Options dialog box.

5. If you're not in Capture mode, click the Capture tab.

6. Use the Camcorder Controller to move the DV tape in the camera to the desired starting point.

7. Click the Start Capture button on the Diskometer.

   The Capture Video dialog box opens, and the Start Capture button changes to Stop Capture.

8. If you desire, change the duration of the video capture and/or change the name of the captured file.

9. Click the Start Capture button in the Capture Video dialog box to start capturing.

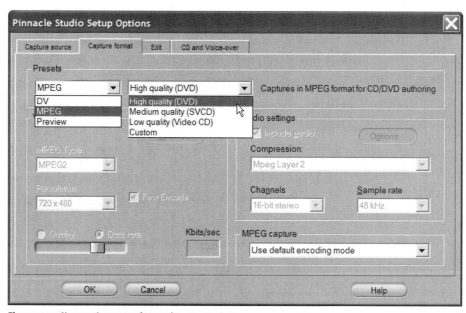

Figure 3.22 Choose the preset format for your project.

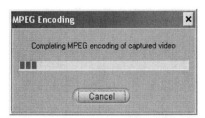

Figure 3.23 On all but the fastest computers, Studio requires a few moments to finish encoding after you stop the tape.

10. If the error message appears (refer to Figure 3.18), do *one of the following*:
    ▲ Click Yes to overwrite the file and start the capture.
    ▲ Click No to return to the Capture Video dialog box and rename the file. Then click Start Capture.

    Your DV camera starts playing, and capture begins.

11. Allow capture to proceed through the specified duration or, to stop capture before then, do *one of the following*:
    ▲ Click Stop Capture on the Diskometer.
    ▲ Press the Esc key on your keyboard.

    Unless you have an extraordinarily fast computer, it may take Studio a while to compress the DV footage into MPEG format, and you'll see a message like the one shown in **Figure 3.23**.

    After encoding stops, a file labeled Video 1 (or whatever name you may have chosen) appears in the Album. You'll see multiple files if any scene changes occurred in the source video during the capture.

continues on next page

MicroMV Capture

Camcorders using Sony's new MicroMV format have a compelling vision: DV quality at about half the data rate, enabling smaller cassettes and less storage space on the computer.

Technically, MicroMV captures in MPEG-2 format, the same high-quality format used in DVD production, and MicroMV camcorders connect to the computer via the FireWire port. According to the Studio manual, the capture interface for MicroMV is identical to that for DV, but many features are disabled, such as the ability to capture to DV format.

Unfortunately, we did not have access to a MicroMV camera while producing this book and have performed no tests on this format. Judging from comments on the Pinnacle support forums, it appears that there have been some settling-in issues relating to this format, so before starting your work, be sure you have the latest Studio release.

✓ Tips

- The Custom option mentioned in Step 3 should be used only by advanced users, since it presents additional encoding controls unfamiliar to most users (**Figure 3.24**).

  Don't modify the MPEG capture parameters at the lower right of the screen (**Figure 3.25**). Do so could lead to dropped frames during capture (**Figure 3.26**).

- If you're capturing video to include on DVD, VCD, or SVCD, stick to the presets and avoid the custom settings. These optical formats define video parameters very tightly, and custom settings could render your video files unusable in these projects.

- If you're using the same captured video in different types of projects—for instance, to create both a DVD and VCD—use the lowest-common-denominator format. For instance, DVDs can incorporate video encoded for VCD and SVCD, but VCDs can't integrate video encoded for SVCD or DVD.

- If you're capturing video in MPEG format simply to distribute it on CD-ROM or via the Internet, note that virtually every computer on the planet can now play back MPEG-1 files, since MPEG-1 decoders have been standard on Windows and Macintosh computers for years. However, MPEG-2 decoder capabilities are much less prevalent and generally not available for free. Thus, MPEG-1 is a much better format for general sharing.

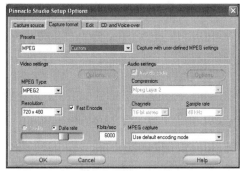

Figure 3.24 Studio lets you customize MPEG capture settings, but most users should stick with the presets whenever possible.

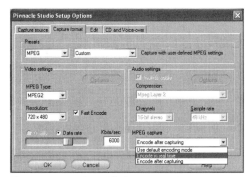

Figure 3.25 Messing with the MPEG capture settings almost always causes a severe problem with dropped frames.

Figure 3.26 Studio will be the first to tell you that what you're about to do may cause a problem.

Customizing Album Views

While your time spent using the Capture Album is usually brief, Studio helps you get as comfortable as possible by providing options for customizing the view.

I've captured some 16:9 footage to illustrate 16:9 views in the Album. **Figure 3.27** shows the Album post-capture in the default mode, which is Scene View with 4:3 images.

Figure 3.27 The default Album view: Scene view in 4:3 mode.

To switch between Scene and Comment views:

◆ Right-click anywhere in the Album and choose Comment View (**Figure 3.28**).
The Album switches to Comment view. See the next section, "Adding Scene Comments," to learn how to add comments to your scenes.
Note that if you touch the Album in a gray area, and not on a picture, you get only the options shown in Figure 3.27. To get the complete list of options shown in **Figure 3.29**, you must right-click a picture.
To switch back to Scene view, right-click and choose Scene view.

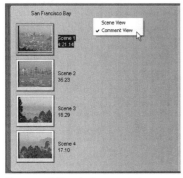

Figure 3.28 Now in Comment view, where you can annotate your scenes.

To switch between 4:3 and 16:9 views:

◆ Right-click a picture in the Album and choose Aspect Ratio 16x9 (Figure 3.29).
The Album switches to 16:9 view. To switch back, right-click and choose Aspect Ratio 4x3.

✔ Tip

■ Note that changing views does absolutely nothing to the captured file; it just changes the way that Studio displays it. It does not convert the file from 4:3 to 16:9 or vice versa.

Figure 3.29 Now in 16:9 mode, converting your project to the 16:9 aspect ratio.

Adding Scene Comments

Immediately after capture, you can annotate your captured scenes in the Album while in Capture mode. This is useful for flagging a specific scene that you want to recall later when you're actually editing.

If you intend to add comments to your scenes, note that Studio updates the Album each time you capture, so if you start another capture before changing the scene comments, Studio stores the captured file and associated comments and clears the Capture Album to make room for the next capture. Don't worry; you can easily find your captured files and comments in the Album in Edit mode and edit your comments there (see "Working with Scene Comments" in Chapter 6).

Figure 3.30 To add or change scene comments, slowly double-click the text to make it editable.

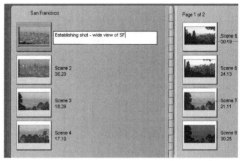

Figure 3.31 Then type your description.

To add scene comments to your captured video:

1. In the Album, slowly double-click the text immediately to the right of the Video icon to make it editable (**Figure 3.30**).
2. Type the desired comment (**Figure 3.31**).
3. Save your comment by doing *one of the following*:
   ▲ Press Enter.
   ▲ Click anywhere outside the comment box on the Studio interface to set the comments.

✔ Tips

- You're not actually changing the file name; you're merely editing text that can be seen only inside Studio.
- If you plan to combine your scenes on the Edit tab of the Album, note that Studio blows away all screen comments when you combine scenes. You might want to look at "Combining Scenes" in Chapter 6 before you invest much time in naming your captured scenes.

Viewing Your Captured Video

If you're like me, the first thing you want to do after capture is watch the video. To do this, switch to Edit mode and use the Player there.

To view your captured video:

1. Select the Edit tab at the upper left of the Studio interface.

   Studio enters Edit mode.

2. In the Album, double-click the video you want to play (**Figure 3.32**).

   The video starts playing in the Player.

3. Use the controls beneath the Player to stop, rewind, fast-forward, go to the beginning of the video, and move through your video frame by frame.

✔ Tip

- If you captured using scene detection and the Album contains multiple scenes, the Player automatically plays from one scene to the next without breaks.

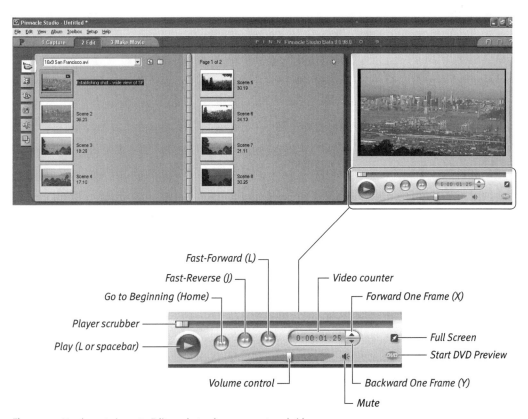

Figure 3.32 You have to jump to Edit mode to play your captured videos.

Capturing Analog Video

While DV capture is a simple file transfer with few settings to worry about, analog capture involves a plethora of controls, including resolution, quality, brightness, volume, and much, much more. To paraphrase Zorba the Greek, the sheer number of options can easily turn analog capture into "the whole catastrophe."

Fortunately, Studio simplifies the process with some well-designed presets and an excellent interface for making all the choices and adjustments necessary to capture analog video at top quality. With some care and frequent checking of your captured files, you should be in great shape.

Note that while DV capture interfaces are relatively standard among different cameras and FireWire devices, analog capture devices and their software interfaces can be as different as snowflakes. Although Pinnacle attempts to present a standard approach for analog capture in Studio, differences among the various devices abound. The best approach is to use this chapter as a guide and then consult the manual or Help files that came with your analog capture card for fine-tuning.

Because 16:9 is primarily a DV-enabled format, you most likely won't want to capture 16:9 video in analog mode. But if you do, Studio can definitely handle it, as you'll discover near the end of this chapter.

The Analog Capture Interface

As you would expect, Studio's analog capture interface (**Figure 4.1**) contains various controls for adjusting your analog capture. Its three main components perform the following roles:

The Album. Your captured clips go directly into the Album, though you can't play them back while in Capture mode. Only one captured file appears in the Album at a time. If you enable scene detection, however (see the sidebar "Scene Detection with Analog Video" later in this chapter), each scene from that file appears in the Album, thus accounting for the multiple scenes (**Figure 4.2**). Had you captured more scenes than could fit on the two pages in the Album, you would see a little white arrow on the upper right corner of the Album, which lets you know more scenes are stored on subsequent pages.

Studio may store captured files during capture, or it may store them immediately after capture, as in the case of MPEG files, which must be converted before storage. Either way, no user intervention is needed to store the files. Once you start to capture another file, your previously captured files disappear from the Album—but don't worry; they are safely stored and accessible in Edit mode.

The Player. Note the lack of playback controls in the Player window. The Player's sole role during capture is to preview the incoming video and provide information about dropped frames; you have to switch to Edit mode to actually play the captured files.

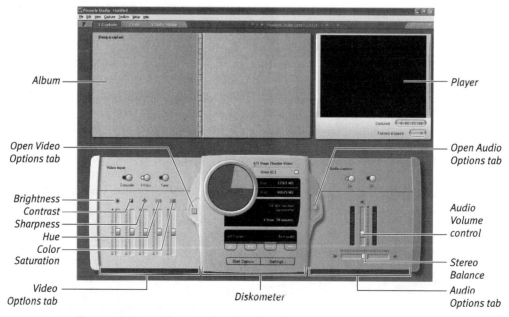

Figure 4.1 In the analog capture interface, the Diskometer has sprouted wings, enabling you to fine-tune the incoming video and control audio volume.

Capturing Analog Video

Figure 4.2 The Album, with scene detection enabled.

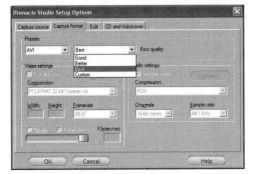

Figure 4.3 Here's where you set your analog capture options.

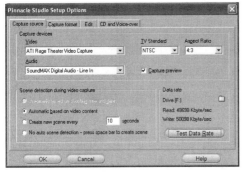

Figure 4.4 Here's where you select your analog video and audio capture devices, as well as scene detection.

The Diskometer. If you study the analog capture interface in Figure 4.1, you'll see that the Camcorder Controller, present in the DV interface, is missing in action. That's because the lack of a FireWire or similar connection for analog capture prevents Studio from controlling the camcorder.

The Diskometer for analog capture looks vaguely similar to the DV-capture version, at least on top, where it displays the space remaining on the capture drive. However, the DV, MPEG, and preview capture options are replaced with Good, Better, Best, and Custom quality settings.

In addition, the Diskometer has sprouted wings, with controls for selecting and customizing analog video source and input on the left, and controls for enabling audio capture and setting volume on the right. You open and close these wings by clicking the TV and Speaker icons on the sides of the Diskometer (video on the left and audio on the right). You'll learn how to operate these controls later in this chapter.

Click the Settings button at the lower right of the screen to open the Setup Options dialog box. It will open to the default Capture Format tab (**Figure 4.3**), where you select your analog capture parameters. The tab to the left is the Capture Source tab (**Figure 4.4**), where you choose your capture device and scene-detection options.

Chapter 4

Scene Detection with Analog Video

With analog footage, sifting through and finding the scenes to include in your project can be extraordinarily time consuming. When you're using DV footage, on the other hand, you can set Studio to analyze the time and date codes on the tape and identify scene changes by noting when you stop and start the camera. This makes choosing the scenes to include in your final project a lot easier.

Because analog consumer camcorders don't store time code, you don't have this option (that's why the option Automatic Based on Shooting Time and Date is dimmed in Figure 4.4). Fortunately, Studio provides three analog options that can help you find the scenes you want:

- If you choose the first available option, Automatic Based on Video Content, Studio identifies scene changes based on significant changes between frames. For example, if one second you're filming the birthday cake and the next your child's delighted face, Studio breaks the two Kodak moments into separate scenes.

- If you choose the next option, Create New Scene Every x Seconds, you can break the scene into regular intervals of one second or more.

- Finally, when all else fails, you can watch the video and manually create scenes by pressing the spacebar at the appropriate moments during capture. (Choose the option No Auto Scene Detection.) Though this is obviously the most time-consuming method, you get reacquainted with all the best moments of your video—helpful when you're editing several months (or years) after filming.

Capturing Analog Video

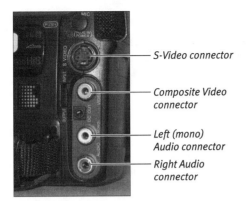

- S-Video connector
- Composite Video connector
- Left (mono) Audio connector
- Right Audio connector

Figure 4.5 The business end of my venerable Sony Hi-8 recorder has separate outputs for S-Video and composite analog video as well as stereo audio.

Figure 4.6 An S-Video cable. Use S-Video whenever it's available, because you'll definitely get higher quality than with composite video.

Connecting for Analog Capture

Although not quite as simple as setting up for DV capture, connecting for analog capture is pretty easy if you can follow color codes and fit square pegs into square holes (metaphorically speaking).

Before taking the steps that follow, make sure that your analog capture card is installed and running. In addition, quickly review the sections "Selecting Your Capture Drive," "Defragmenting Your Capture Drive," and "Testing Your Capture Drive" in Chapter 2.

To connect the camera and computer for analog capture:

1. Plug in your analog camcorder to AC power.

   Battery power should work, but it doesn't always with some cameras.

2. Make sure that the camcorder is in VCR, VTR, or Play mode.

3. Connect your video cables to the camera (**Figure 4.5**) by doing *one of the following*:

   ▲ If both your camera and analog capture device have S-Video connectors and you have the necessary cable (**Figure 4.6**), use the S-Video connector.

   continues on next page

▲ If S-Video is not available and your analog camera or deck has a separate composite video port (Figure 4.5), use the composite video connectors with a cable like the one shown in **Figure 4.7**. In most instances, composite video connectors are yellow, and most three-headed cables are coded yellow (composite video), red (right audio), and white (left audio and mono audio). Follow the color coding at both ends and you'll speed your installation.

Figure 4.7 The typical three-headed analog cable with separate RCA connectors, for composite video and left and right audio. Fortunately, most cables are color-coded to help you make the right connections.

▲ If S-Video is not available and your camera has a specialty A/V port, use the composite video connectors with a specialty cable. You should have received a specialty cable that looks like that shown in **Figure 4.8**. Plug the single end into your camera.

4. Connect your audio cables to the camera by doing *one of the following*:

▲ If your camera has separate audio connectors (Figure 4.5), connect a cable like that shown in Figure 4.7, being careful to match the colors of the connectors and output ports when applicable.

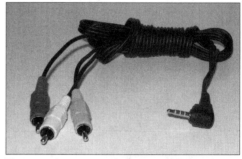

Figure 4.8 If your camcorder has a specialty AV plug, you'll need a specialty cable. Note the three rings on the single connector: one for each of the three outputs.

▲ If your camera has a specialty A/V port, you should have a specialty cable that looks like the one in Figure 4.8. Plug the single end into your camera.

Capturing Analog Video

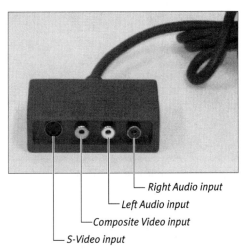

— Right Audio input
— Left Audio input
— Composite Video input
— S-Video input

Figure 4.9 The breakout box for ATI's All-in-Wonder graphics card. This box accepts analog inputs.

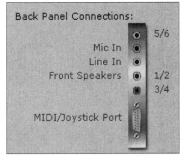

Figure 4.10 A representation of the bracket on my sound card. Use the line-in connector, not the mic-in (microphone), for your analog input.

Figure 4.11
Use a Y-connector to convert the two RCA-type analog connectors to one stereo connector compatible with your sound card.

5. Connect your video cable to the capture card in your computer.

   Most capture cards have input ports and output ports. For example, the ATI All-in-Wonder 9000 PRO card installed in my HP Workstation xw4100 uses a separate breakout box for analog input, with ports for S-Video and composite video and right and left audio (**Figure 4.9**) but a different, port and cable for outputting productions back to analog tape. If you see two sets of analog connectors, either in a break-out box like the All-in-Wonder or on the bracket of the internal card itself, check the product's documentation to determine which connector is input and which is output.

6. Connect your audio cables to the computer by doing *one of the following:*

   ▲ If your analog capture card has separate audio inputs, use the audio input on your capture card.

   ▲ If your analog capture card doesn't have separate audio inputs, use your sound card's Line-in connector (**Figure 4.10**).

   Most computers have single pin stereo audio inputs (Figure 4.10) rather than separate RCA connectors (Figures 4.7 and 4.8). To convert RCA inputs into stereo audio inputs, you'll need a Y-connector like the one shown in **Figure 4.11**, or a similar adapter. You can find these at Radio Shack or on the Web at www.cables.com.

   You're now ready to run Studio, set the appropriate software options, and start capturing.

Chapter 4

Choosing Your Analog Capture Parameters

Now that the hardware side is squared away, it's time to start working on the software side by first selecting your capture source and then setting and adjusting your capture parameters.

To select your capture source:

1. Run Studio and enter Capture mode by selecting the Capture tab at the upper left of the screen (Figure 4.1).

2. From the menu bar, choose Setup > Capture Source (**Figure 4.12**).
   The Pinnacle Studio Setup Options dialog box appears.

3. In the Video Capture Devices drop-down menu, select your analog video capture device (**Figure 4.13**).

4. In the Audio Capture Devices drop-down menu, select your analog audio capture device (**Figure 4.14**).

5. Select the desired scene-detection option.
   Remember that the option Automatic Based on Shooting Time and Date is unavailable because analog tapes don't store this information.

6. Click OK to return to Capture mode.
   If your analog capture card has audio input, it should be one of the listed options. Since in this example the system's sound card is used, Line In is selected on the SoundMax sound card.
   At this point, you should be in analog Capture mode, and your screen should look identical to Figure 4.1.

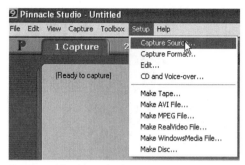

Figure 4.12 Getting to the Capture Source screen.

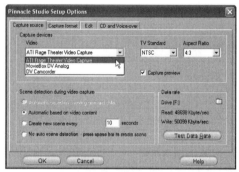

Figure 4.13 Choosing your analog video capture device.

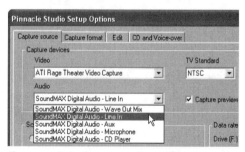

Figure 4.14 Selecting your analog audio capture device. Remember to use Line-in!

Capturing Analog Video

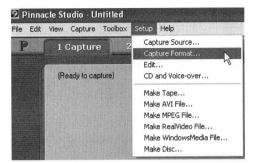

Figure 4.15 Getting to the Capture Format screen.

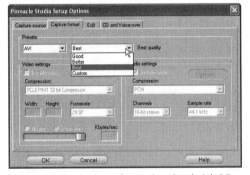

Figure 4.16 Best is always better than Good, right? For more information on these settings, read the sidebar "Navigating Your Analog Capture Format Options."

✔ Tips

- If the video and audio capture controls are not open, open them by clicking the icons on the sides of the Diskometer (Figure 4.1).

- If you see the Camcorder Controller, you're in DV Capture mode. Go back and reselect your capture source (Step 3 in the preceding task).

- If your analog capture source appears in the drop-down menu, it's properly loaded and running under Windows. If it's not listed, it's not properly installed, and you have some work to do before you can start capturing. Go back to "Connecting for Analog Capture" earlier in this chapter and try again.

To configure your capture parameters:

1. Open the Studio Setup Options dialog box set to the Capture Format tab by doing *one of the following:*

   ▲ Click the Settings button on the Diskometer.

   ▲ From the Studio menu, choose Setup > Capture Format (**Figure 4.15**).

   The Capture Format tab appears (**Figure 4.16**).

2. Choose the appropriate preset—Good, Better, or Best—for your project.

   Studio also offers a Custom option that lets you customize capture options at will. See the sidebar "Navigating Your Analog Capture Format Options" for assistance with selecting the best preset or customized parameters.

3. Click OK to return to the capture interface.

Navigating Your Analog Capture Format Options

The most critical options to consider during analog capture are the video resolution, or the width and height of the captured video in pixels, and the frame rate, or number of frames per second (fps) captured. For example, when you capture at a resolution of 320 x 240 pixels, you produce a captured file that's 320 pixels wide and 240 pixels high. Similarly, when producing an MPEG-1 file that requires 29.97 fps, you must capture at this frame rate.

When determining the best resolution to use during capture, the most important factor is your intended output resolution. For example, suppose you intend to create a DVD using MPEG-2. This high-quality format generally outputs at a resolution of 720 x 480. In contrast, MPEG-1 files, typically used for posting to the Web or sharing on CD-ROM, generally have a resolution of 320 x 240. If you're creating a RealVideo file to post for streaming at modem speeds, the resolution may be as low as 176 x 120.

The general rule for selecting capture resolution is always to capture at the exact output resolution whenever possible. If not, capture at the next available *higher* resolution. Similarly, for frame rate, the general rule is to capture at the exact output frame rate.

Although all capture devices use different Good, Better, and Best presets (and sometimes name them slightly differently), those in ATI's All-in-Wonder capture card provide an example.

- **Good:** 176 x 120 at just under 14.985 fps. Use this preset for all streaming output.
- **Better:** 352 x 240 at 14.985 fps. This preset has little use, primarily because it captures at 14.985 fps, which is insufficient for the 30 fps used by MPEG-1. To capture for AVI video or for MPEG-1 video displayed on a computer (as opposed to a television set via Video CD), I would customize the capture parameters to 320 x 240 at 30 fps. To produce VideoCD discs for display on TV sets, I would use 354 x 240.
- **Best:** 720 x 480 at 29.997. Use this for MPEG-2 and DVD projects.

To capture audio and configure video input:

1. At the top of the Video Options tab (Figure 4.1), select the icon that corresponds to your physical cable connection (in this case, S-Video).

2. At the top of the Audio Options tab, choose the On button to enable audio capture, to make sure that the audio is up and running.

   Once you know it's working, you can disable it if you want by choosing the Off button.

3. The moment of truth has arrived. Press Play on your camcorder.

   You should see video in the Player and hear audio over your speakers. If you do, try not to jump up and down if people are around. You've crossed a significant hurdle. Now you're ready for analog capture.

   If you don't get video and audio right away, take heart. I've installed hundreds of capture cards and rarely get it right the first time. Run through the steps in this and the previous task one more time. If you still have no signal, check your capture card installation first and then the troubleshooting tips in Appendix B.

Adjustments Defined

Here are definitions for the analog capture adjustments that Studio provides.

- **Hue:** This is the visual property that allows you to distinguish colors. The slider biases all the colors in a clip toward red (left) or green (right). This can be especially useful for correcting flesh tones.

- **Saturation:** This is the quantity of pure color, ranging from zero (no color at all, or gray scale) to fully saturated (the maximum color intensity your output system can deliver). Move the slider to the left for a tonally reduced, washed-out look, or to the right for extra vibrancy.

- **Brightness:** This is the relative intensity of light, without regard to color. Try adjusting both brightness and contrast to correct video that is underexposed or overexposed.

- **Contrast:** This is the range of light and dark values in a picture or the ratio between the maximum and minimum brightness values. Moving the slider to the left lowers contrast, forcing all areas of the image toward medium brightness values. Moving the slider to the right increases contrast, making dark areas darker and bright areas brighter.

- **Sharpness:** Increases the contrast of edges in the image, making them appear sharper.

Tuning the Incoming Video Signal

Because DV video is digitized by the camera, digital video capture is a simple file transfer from camera to computer. In contrast, analog capture involves an analog-to-digital conversion, which is something like a negotiation between two parties speaking a common language with slightly different accents.

This is how it works: The analog camera outputs an analog signal that it perceives represents reality, adjusting the brightness, color, and contrast accordingly. Then, using factory preset values, the analog capture card looks for and captures a signal that it perceives represents reality. Seldom do the two realities match.

This is a long way of saying that if you're going to capture analog video, most of the time you will have to mess with the analog input controls to get the video looking right. Compare the image in **Figure 4.17**, which used the default settings, with the image in **Figure 4.18**, which used optimized settings; as you can see, the differences can be dramatic.

As Figure 4.1 shows, Studio provides the adjustments for brightness, contrast, sharpness, hue, and color saturation, but these technical terms don't tell the story (see the sidebar "Adjustments Defined"). The only way to become skilled at capturing analog video that looks as it should is to play with the controls during each capture and fine-tune as you go along.

Figure 4.17 My mom insisted that I have at least one picture of me in this book. With brightness and contrast at their default settings, here I am speaking at a trade show. Pretty dark, eh?

Figure 4.18 Here's the new me, with enhanced brightness and contrast. These controls make a huge difference in the ultimate quality of your video projects.

To adjust incoming video:

1. On your camcorder, press Play to start the video playing. Try to find frames that contain objects with known color and brightness values, such as faces or clothing.

2. Using the video options tab, adjust the various sliders up and down until the picture quality is where you want it (Figure 4.1).

3. Note the adjusted values used during capture so that you can re-create your results if necessary.

   These adjustments would be easier if Studio offered numerical presets, but it doesn't. Instead, you need to note the relationship of the slider to the midline. For example, the adjustments in Figure 4.18 would have a brightness value of approximately +14 and a contrast value of +5.

✔ Tips

- Studio lets you modify these same video options settings during editing. However, adjusting color and brightness during editing can degrade quality and takes time, so it's better done while tweaking parameters before capturing your video files.

- If your tape contains radically different scenes, you should adjust the video options for each scene.

- Encoding often darkens video slightly. To make sure that your video is bright enough after encoding, encode a short segment in the final format as early as possible. If you'll be viewing the video on a range of output devices, say laptops or projectors, you might test playback on these as well.

Adjusting the Incoming Audio Volume

Pop quiz: You've just captured some analog video and you play it back to check the volume. Unfortunately, it's way too low. But why? Some of the possibilities follow:

a) Your speaker system is too low.

b) Your Windows volume control is too low.

c) You didn't boost audio volume sufficiently during capture.

d) All of the above.

Hmmm. Tough one. The answer is, unless you checked your speakers and playback volume before capture, you don't really know. So don't roll your eyes as you walk through the following steps; it's all about the process.

To adjust incoming audio volume:

1. Make sure that your system sound speakers are set at an appropriate playback volume. Disable any treble, bass, or similar boosts, since your ultimate viewer may not have the same tools.

2. Open your computer's volume control by doing *one of the following:*
   ▲ Click the Speaker icon in the Windows taskbar (**Figure 4.19**).
   ▲ From the Windows Start menu, choose Programs > Accessories > Entertainment > Volume Control (**Figure 4.20**).

   The Volume Control dialog box opens (**Figure 4.21**).

3. Make sure that the Volume Control slider, at the far left of the screen, is not muted and is set somewhere near mid-volume.

Figure 4.19 Click the Speaker icon to open the Volume Control dialog box.

Figure 4.20 Or take the long route to the volume controls.

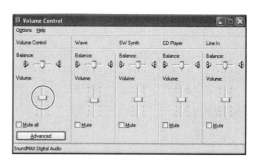

Figure 4.21 Whichever way you get here, make sure that the Volume Control slider at the far left of the Volume Control dialog box is set at approximately mid-level during capture.

4. Make sure the slider that controls your capture source (typically, Line In) is not muted. Studio will adjust the Line In volume as described in Step 8 of this exercise, but you may not hear (or capture) any audio if the control is muted here.

5. Make sure that the Wave slider is not muted and is set somewhere near mid-volume.

   This is the slider that controls the playback volume of the Wave audio captured with the video file.

   Settings for all other sliders are irrelevant. I typically don't mute them because when I later try to play a CD-ROM or MIDI music, I forget I turned them off and spend 20 minutes trying to figure out why there's no sound.

6. Close the Volume Control dialog box and return to Studio.

7. Press Play on your camcorder.

8. Use the Audio Volume control (on the Audio Options tab; see Figure 4.1) to adjust the volume during capture so that the lights occasionally reach into the yellow bar but never into the red (**Figure 4.22**). Be sure to test both high- and low-volume regions of the clip.

9. After capture, periodically play back your captured files to check the audio volume level.

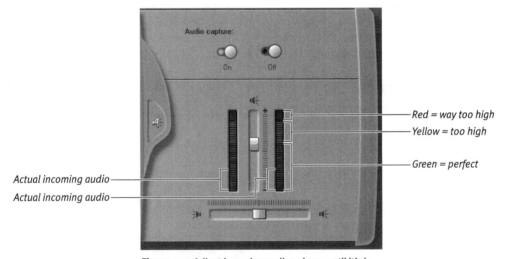

Figure 4.22 Adjust incoming audio volume until it's in the middle to upper regions of the green zone.

Chapter 4

Capturing Analog Video

The big moment is finally here. It's time to capture some analog video.

To capture analog video:

1. Using your camcorder controls, position your tape about 30 seconds before the initial frame you want to capture.

2. Click the Start Capture button on the Diskometer (**Figure 4.23**).

   The Capture Video dialog box opens (**Figure 4.24**), and the Start Capture button changes to Stop Capture (**Figure 4.25**).

3. For this test, enter a duration of 1 minute and 00 seconds in the Capture Video dialog box as shown in Figure 4.24.

   When the Capture Video dialog box first appears, it displays the maximum duration of video your disk can store, which is limited by either the file size or the version of Windows you're running (for more information, see the "Windows File Size Limitations" sidebar that follows).

   If the duration shown in your program is less than 1 minute, either your capture disk is almost full or you're pointing toward the wrong disk. (See "Selecting Your Capture Drive" in Chapter 2 for more information.)

4. Press Play on your camcorder to start the video rolling.

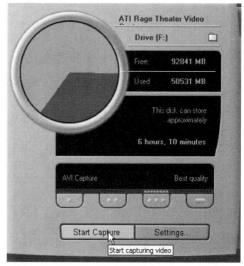

Figure 4.23 Click the Start Capture button on the Diskometer to start capture.

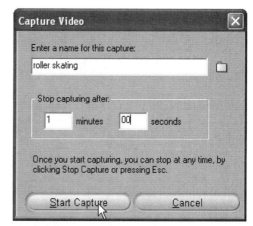

Figure 4.24 You can name your file before capture and elect to capture for a specified interval. Capturing for a particular interval is useful, for example, when you want to capture a 60-minute tape while you're away from the computer.

Capturing Analog Video

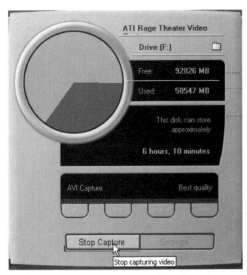

Figure 4.25 Click the Stop Capture button on the Diskometer to stop capture, or press the Esc key on your keyboard.

Figure 4.26 After analog capture, Studio takes a moment to check the accuracy of the scene-detection settings.

5. Watch the video in the Player and click Start approximately 10 to 15 seconds before you actually want capture to begin.

   Some capture devices take a few seconds to start capturing; starting early ensures that you capture the desired frames and provides additional frames for fade-in and fade-out or for inter-scene transitions during editing.

6. Studio will capture one minute of video. To stop capture before then, do *one of the following*:

   ▲ Click the Stop Capture button on the Diskometer.

   ▲ Press the Esc key on your keyboard.

   Assuming that you enabled scene detection by video content, Studio takes a moment after capture stops to rescan the file for scene changes (**Figure 4.26**). Then your captured scenes appear in the Album (**Figure 4.27**).

   Note that this footage was shot in 16:9 mode. However, it appears in Figure 4.27 in 4:3 mode because the default view in the Album is Scene view in 4:3 mode. To ensure that Studio recognizes that this footage is actually 16:9 video, we'll change to 16:9 view in the next section.

   continues on next page

Figure 4.27 Then your scenes appear in the Album in all their glory. Note that the scenes are in default Scene view in 4:3 mode.

✓ Tips

- You may not always hear audio during capture (I didn't using All-in-Wonder). Even if you do, there's no guarantee that the audio was properly captured in the file. For this reason, check the presence, quality, and volume of audio frequently during the capture process.

- If you attempt to capture 4:3 and 16:9 footage from the same tape during the same capture session, you'll see the error message displayed in **Figure 4.28**.

- Note the Frames Dropped counter under the Player in Figure 4.27. Dropped frames are frames that the computer couldn't capture, usually because the disk wasn't fast enough to keep up with the incoming video. This counter updates in real time during capture; if you drop more than one or two frames during capture, stop capturing and check Appendix B to diagnose and fix your problem.

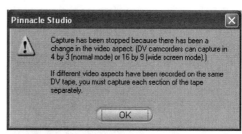

Figure 4.28 Studio won't capture 4:3 and 16:9 footage from the same tape during the same capture session.

Customizing Album Views

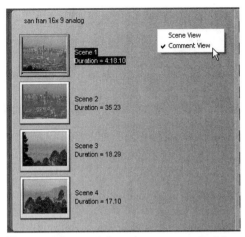

Figure 4.29 Comment view, where you can annotate your scenes.

Figure 4.30 Now in 16:9 mode, converting the project to the 16:9 aspect ratio.

While time spent using the Capture Album is usually brief, Studio helps you get as comfortable as possible by providing options for customizing the view.

I've captured some 16:9 footage to illustrate 16:9 views in the Album. Figure 4.27 shows the Album post-capture in the default mode, which is Scene view with 4:3 images.

To switch between Scene and Comment views:

◆ Right-click anywhere in the Album and choose Comment View (**Figure 4.29**).

The Album switches to Comment view. See the following section, "Adding Scene Comments," to learn how to add comments to your scenes.

Note that if you click the Album in a gray area rather than on a picture, you get only the options shown in Figure 4.29. To get the complete list of options shown in **Figure 4.30**, you must click a picture.

To switch back to Scene view, right-click and choose Scene View.

To switch between 4:3 and 16:9 views:

◆ Right-click a picture in the Album and choose Aspect Ratio 16x9 (Figure 4.30).

The Album switches to 16:9 view. To switch back, right-click and choose Aspect Ratio 4x3.

✔ Tip

- Changing views does absolutely nothing to the captured file; it just changes the way that Studio displays it. It does not convert the file from 4:3 to 16:9 or vice versa.

Adding Scene Comments

If you want to rename or annotate your captured scenes to make them easier to find and use in your final production, go to the Album in Capture mode.

If you intend to add comments to your scenes, note that Studio updates the Album each time you capture, so if you start another capture before changing the scene comments, Studio stores the captured file and associated comments and clears the Capture Album to make room for the next capture. Don't worry; you can easily find your captured files and comments in the Album in Edit mode and edit your scene comments there (see "Working with Scene Comments" in Chapter 6).

Figure 4.31 To add or change scene comments, click the text twice slowly.

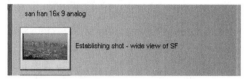

Figure 4.32 Then type in your description.

To add scene comments to your captured video:

1. In the Album, slowly double-click the text immediately to the right of the Video icon to make it editable (**Figure 4.31**).

2. Type the desired comment.

3. Save your comment by doing *one of the following* (**Figure 4.32**):
    ▲ Press the Enter key on your keyboard.
    ▲ Click anywhere outside the comment box on the Studio interface to set the comments.

✔ Tips

- You're not actually changing the file name; you're merely editing text that can be seen only inside Studio.

- If you plan to combine your scenes on the Edit tab of the Album, note that Studio blows away all screen comments when you combine scenes. You might want to look at "Combining Scenes" in Chapter 6 before you invest much time in naming your captured scenes.

Viewing Your Captured Video

If you're like me, the first thing you want to do after capture is watch the video. To do this, switch to Edit mode and use the Player.

To view your captured video:

1. Select the Edit tab at the upper left of the Studio interface (Figure 4.1).
   Studio enters Edit mode.

2. In the Album, double-click the video you want to play (**Figure 4.33**).
   The video starts playing in the Player.

3. Controls beneath the Player let you stop, rewind, fast-forward, go to the beginning of the video, and move through each frame of your video.

✔ Tip

- If you capture using scene detection and the Album contains multiple scenes, the Player automatically plays from one scene to the next without breaks.

Figure 4.33 Once you're in Edit mode, you can play your captured videos by clicking the icons in the Album.

Working with Still Images

I absolutely adore capturing still images from my digital videotapes, especially when shooting videos of the young 'uns. Why? Because although my Kodak DC4800 takes much higher-quality, 3.2-megapixel images, it can shoot only about once every six seconds. When you've got DV tape rolling, this gives you about 180 chances to get the shot you really want, compared to one shot with the Kodak.

On the other hand, some days I just don't want to mess with my camcorder, and I grab the Kodak instead. With my 1-GB flash memory card, I can take pictures all day long and usually find many nuggets worth keeping. Of course, these are huge images that often need to be cropped, cut, or reduced in resolution to work optimally in Studio.

This chapter covers two topics: grabbing images from your camcorder or movie files and prepping images from your still camera. As you'll see in Chapter 7, you can combine these images on the Timeline, with background music and/or narration, to produce the perfect slide show.

Capturing Still Images

To capture images from your camcorder, you need to have everything connected, tested, and turned on (see Chapters 3 and 4). Operation is similar for digital video (DV) and analog camcorders, so this section covers both. Studio can also grab still images from movie files on disk, whether previously captured within Studio or sourced from another location.

When it comes to capturing still images, DV cameras have one killer feature: the ability to pause on a single frame for multiple seconds without distortion. This makes frame capture from your DV camera frame-accurate. In contrast, most analog camcorders can't pause for more than a moment or two without some image distortion, making it difficult to capture the precise frame you're seeking. For this reason, when you have images you'd like to grab on DV tape, go ahead and grab them from the camera.

On the other hand, if you have images on analog tape that you'd like to capture, the easier, faster, and more accurate approach is to capture the video to disk first and then grab the frame from the captured file.

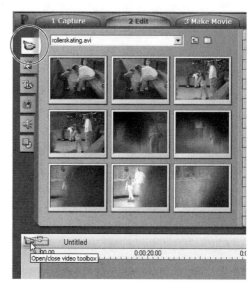

Figure 5.1 Click the Camcorder icon to open the Video toolbox.

To capture still images from your camcorder:

1. Click the Edit tab at the upper left of the Studio interface.

   Studio switches to Edit mode.

2. At the top left of the Movie window, click the Camcorder icon to open the Video toolbox (**Figure 5.1**).

   The Video toolbox opens.

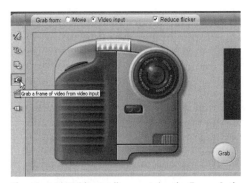

Figure 5.2 The Video toolbox contains the Frame Grab tool. Note that when you're using an analog camcorder, there are no camcorder controls.

3. Click the Frame Grab icon to open the Frame Grab tool (**Figure 5.2**).

4. Click the Video Input radio button, located at the top of the window, to capture from your camcorder.

5. Use the Camcorder Controller controls to start your DV camcorder, or press Play on your analog camcorder to start the video rolling. Watch the video in the Player window; then do *one of the following*:

   ▲ If you have a DV camcorder, you can pause (not stop) at the exact frame you want to capture (**Figure 5.3**).

   ▲ If you have an analog camcorder, try pausing at the desired capture frame using camcorder controls. If the frame is clear and undistorted, you can move to Step 6. However, many analog devices can't pause on a frame without distortion, so you'll have to capture by playing the video in real time, and then pressing the Grab button as the desired frame passes by, which is obviously less accurate.

continues on next page

Figure 5.3 When you're using a DV camcorder, Studio provides software controls for getting to the desired frame.

Chapter 5

6. Click the Grab button to capture the frame visible in the Player.

   The frame appears in the Frame Grab window (**Figure 5.4**).

7. Do *one or both of the following*:

   ▲ Click the Add to Movie button to add the frame to a movie.

   Studio adds the movie to the Video track at the first blank location (**Figure 5.5**).

   ▲ Click the Save to Disk button to save the still image.

   Studio opens the standard Save As dialog box, which is configured to store the frames on your default capture drive (**Figure 5.6**).

8. In the Save as Type drop-down box, choose Bitmap Files. (For more information on choosing formats, see the tips that follow.)

9. In the Save Grabbed Frame in This Size drop-down box, choose Original Size. (See the tips that follow for more information about choosing resolutions.)

10. Name the file and click Save (or press Alt+S).

11. At the top left of the Movie window, click the Camcorder icon to close the Video toolbox (Figure 5.1).

Figure 5.4 Click the Grab button, and Studio grabs the image.

Figure 5.5 Click the Add to Movie button, and Studio places it in the Video track.

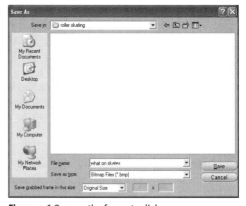

Figure 5.6 Or save the frame to disk.

Working with Still Images

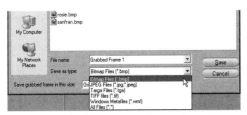

Figure 5.7 Among Studio's many format choices, your best bet usually is Bitmap Files (*.bmp); choose this option unless you have a strong need to use another.

Figure 5.8 You can scale your image up or down at will, but Studio scales it anyway, if necessary, once the image is loaded on the Timeline. To avoid potential distortion, save your image in its original size.

✔ Tips

- If you're capturing still images from an analog camcorder and the camera won't pause without distorting the image, you're better off capturing the video to disk and then grabbing your still image from the captured file, as detailed in the next task.

- Most camcorders don't include frame-advance controls on the camcorder body, but do on the camcorder remote, usually with other nice controls such as slow motion.

- Studio lets you save a still image in a number of formats (**Figure 5.7**). Generally, if you plan on using the image in your video production, choose bitmap (BMP), Targa, TIFF, or Windows Metafile format, which are all uncompressed. I like BMP because it's the format most widely recognized by other programs, giving me more flexibility if I decide to use the image again. If you're capturing an image to send via email, you might want to go with JPEG, since it produces a smaller, compressed file (though Studio doesn't have the optimization tools offered by most still-image editors).

- Studio also lets you save your still images at a number of different resolutions (**Figure 5.8**). Generally, if you plan on using the image in your video production, your best choice is Original Size, which stores the image at its actual capture resolution.

To capture still images from a file on disk:

1. Click the Edit tab at the upper left of the Studio interface.

   Studio switches to Edit mode.

2. Drag the video containing the target frames from the Album to the Movie window (**Figure 5.9**).

   If you're in the Timeline view, drag the video to the Video track. In the other two views, it doesn't matter where you drag the file, so long as it's in the Movie window.

3. At the top left of the Movie window, click the Camcorder icon to open the Video toolbox.

   The Video toolbox opens, most likely to the Clip Properties tool.

Figure 5.9 To capture a frame from a video on disk, load the video into the Movie window.

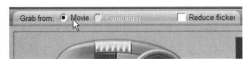

Figure 5.10 Select the Movie button to capture frames from the selected movie.

4. Click the Frame Grab icon at the left to open the Frame Grab tool.
5. Select the Movie radio button at the top of the screen to grab frames from the Movie window (**Figure 5.10**).
6. Use the Player controls or the Timeline scrubber (**Figure 5.11**) to move to the target frame.

   You can use the Jog controls to the right of the Player counter (up and down arrows) to move one frame at a time. If the Player controls aren't active, you didn't select the Movie radio button in Step 5.

continues on next page

Timeline scrubber

Player controls

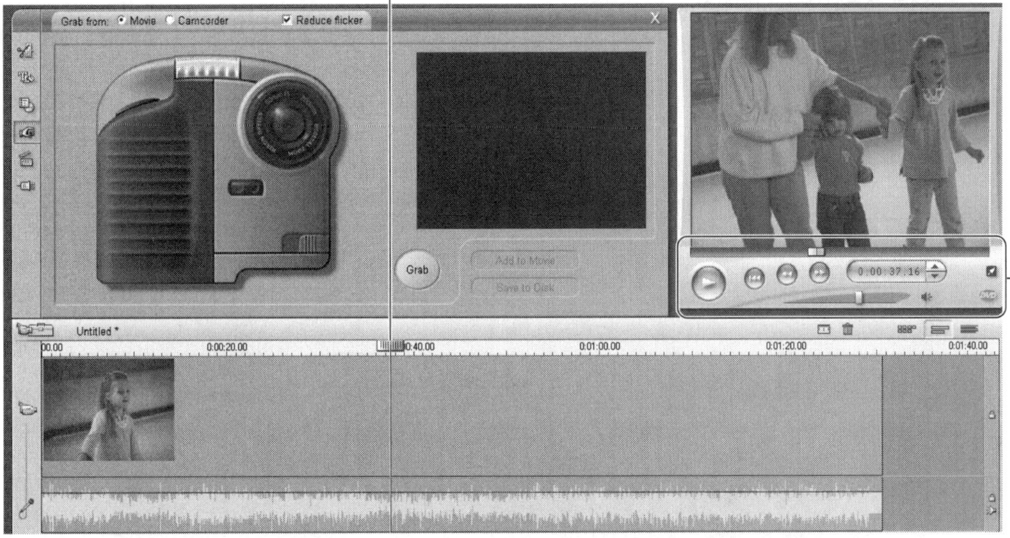

Figure 5.11 Use the Timeline scrubber or the Player controls to move to the desired frame, or the Jog controls to move one frame at a time.

CAPTURING STILL IMAGES

7. Click the Grab button to capture the frame visible in the Player.

   The frame appears in the Frame Grab window (**Figure 5.12**).

8. Do *one or both of the following*:
   - ▲ Click the Add to Movie button to add the frame to the movie.

     Studio adds the movie to the Video track at the first blank location.
   - ▲ Click the Save to Disk button to save the still image.

   Studio opens the standard Save As dialog box, which is set to store the frames on your default capture drive.

9. In the Save as Type drop-down box, choose Bitmap Files (Figure 5.6). For more information on choosing formats, see the tips from the previous task.

10. In the Save Grabbed Frame in This Size" drop-down box, choose Original Size. (See the tips from the previous task for more information on choosing resolutions.)

11. Name the file and click Save (or press Alt+S).

12. At the top left of the Movie window, click the Camcorder icon to close the Video toolbox.

✔ **Tips**

- Still-image capture in 16:9 mode works just fine for disk-based files and when grabbing the frames from your DV camcorder via DV or analog connectors, with 16:9 images stored at 853 x 480 resolution.

- Note the flicker reduction option on the right of Figure 5.8. I tested this feature with multiple frame grabs, storing the files at number of different resolutions and formats. I found that flicker reduction helped slightly when capturing from a DV camcorder or a DV file, but hurt image quality significantly when capturing via an analog connection. However, this testing falls far short of a scientific study, and your results may vary. When you're grabbing still frames for your productions, try toggling the Reduce Flicker button on and off, and use whichever setting produces the best possible quality.

Figure 5.12 Once again, click Grab, and you've got your frame.

Editing Still Images

Okay, the question on the table is this: Your digital camera takes shots at a princely resolution of, say, 2160 x 1440 pixels. The maximum DVD video resolution is 720 x 480. How do you resolve the difference?

To answer this question, let's first get a bird's-eye view of how Studio works with still images and then explore the different ways you can crop your images so that you can present them most effectively in Studio.

How Studio works with images

Studio takes an admirably laissez-faire approach to images, basically displaying them as you place them in the movie. It doesn't try to fill the screen with your image, stretching it horizontally or vertically, or trim your image to fit; it simply makes your image larger or smaller to fit the screen without changing the aspect ratio. If this means that your image doesn't completely fill the 720 x 480–pixel DVD frame, so be it. At least there's no distortion.

Studio also provides excellent visual cues about what your image will look like when it's finally produced. Let's take a look at **Figure 5.13** to get a sense of how this works.

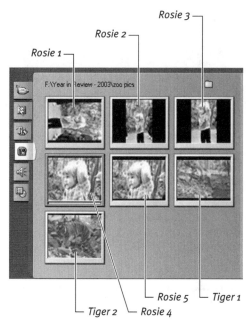

Figure 5.13 The black bars beside Rosie 2 and Rosie 3 are Studio's way of telling you that the image resolution isn't optimal.

Rosie 1 is the original 2160 x 1440–pixel image, shot by turning the camera to the side to capture Rosie's full 36-inch height. Rosie 2 is the same image rotated 90 degrees to the left, so that she's standing straight up.

If you click Rosie 2 to preview her in the Player, you see large areas of black to her left and right, which is precisely the way the image would appear in the final DVD or video (**Figure 5.14**). This is Studio's way of telling you that the image doesn't match the final resolution of your project, and Studio is not going to squish or otherwise distort the video to make it appear full screen. Note that these same black areas show up on the Still Images tab of the Album, providing the same message.

Figure 5.14 Here's the big view of Rosie 2. Surely you can show more of this beautiful girl!

Optimizing Rosie

The Rosie picture presents two opportunities. To go with the original impulse of the photographer and display her height, you can crop away as much extraneous material as you want from the top, as shown in Rosie 3 (**Figure 5.15**). She's a bit more prominent in the screen, but you still have those black areas on the sides. The other alternative is the full-screen, fetching face shot. Here the image has been cropped so that Rosie fills the entire screen, making all involved thankful that she takes after her mother, not her father (**Figure 5.16**).

Figure 5.15 Rosie 3. The top has been cropped off the image, making Rosie slightly bigger.

The obvious question is, what image resolution must you use to totally fill the Player window and eliminate those black bars? Since picture resolutions vary immensely among different cameras, the answer isn't a particular resolution, but a specific aspect ratio, which must be 4:3.

What this means is that for every 4 horizontal pixels, you must grab 3 vertical pixels. To grab the image of Rosie, the capture resolution was 1120 pixels across and 840 pixels high. If you divide 1120 by 4, you get 280. Multiply 280 by 3 and you get 840.

Figure 5.16 Rosie 4. Full-screen Rosie, providing a much closer look and filling the screen.

Working with Still Images

Figure 5.17 The secret's in the tool: Ulead's PhotoImpact lets you constrain an image to a 4:3 aspect ratio, so that you can easily grab the best image.

Figure 5.18 Your brain says 720 x 480 resolution, but those black bars above and below the image say no, no, no.

It's a pain, but keep a calculator open on your desktop when you're grabbing still images. Once you find the optimal horizontal resolution for your images, divide by 4, multiply by 3, and you've calculated the ideal height. Or find an image editor like Ulead Systems' excellent PhotoImpact 8, which does the math for you (**Figure 5.17**). The little Lock icon in the top tool panel constrains the crop tool to the selected shape, Digital Camera (4:3).

The other obvious question is, why can't you capture at an aspect ratio of 4:2.66, which is the aspect ratio for 720 x 480 pixels—the ultimate resolution at which you'll be displaying the video? The complete answer is long, confusing, and involves arcane differences between how computers and televisions display video data.

The quick, empirical answer is this: If you capture at the 4:2.66 aspect ratio and enter the result, Studio tells you via black bars at the top and bottom of the screen that you're not totally filling the screen (**Figure 5.18**). These bars aren't present when the 4:3 aspect ratio is used, so 4:3 must be the optimal setting (Figure 5.16).

Seeing the eyes of the tiger

Now it should be easy to tackle the problem in the second example: the picture of the tiger taken from a distance. You took a great shot of the tiger, but wished you'd had a better telephoto lens, since the noble animal is a mere speck in the Player (**Figure 5.19**).

To enlarge the tiger in the screen, crop your image to an aspect ratio of 4:3, or 720 x 540 pixels. This dramatically increases the size, and now you can actually see the eyes of the tiger (**Figure 5.20**).

✔ Tip

- When fine-tuning your images, always crop to a resolution that matches the desired aspect ratio. Never change the aspect ratio of an image or resize an image to make it fit a specific area.

Figure 5.19 The tiger favored us with a close walk-by that day, but I forgot to zoom.

Figure 5.20 The benefit of working with megapixel images is that I can zoom in without distortion. Once again the screen is filled by cropping the photo to create an aspect ratio of 4:3.

Collecting Assets in the Album

The Album is an integral component of Studio's interface: a place for loading video, still images, and audio files—the basic assets that comprise your project—into separate, tab-selected folders before integrating them into your projects. The Album also contains transitions, titles, and menus—effects discussed in subsequent chapters.

The Album isn't a true bin or library, like those found in many programs, that stores the imported assets in a project file. Rather, the Album simply displays the files in the currently selected directory.

One Album feature in version 9 is critical to users working with 16:9 video. Although Studio should detect 16:9 video during capture, it may not if you load 16:9 video from another source, such as a previously captured file. In such instances, you can now switch the Album to 16:9 viewing mode, directing Studio to process the video in 16:9 mode.

Otherwise, the Album's features—compared with the flexible Storyboard, bountiful transitions, and other rich features that lie beyond—are not Studio's most impressive. However, the Album is unquestionably one of Studio's most valuable tools. You could easily spend the bulk of your time just finding the assets to put into your project; working efficiently in the Album cuts this time considerably.

Chapter 6

Opening the Album to Video Scenes

Few things in life are easier than getting to the Video Scenes component of the Album. So let's get right to it ourselves.

To open the Album to Video Scenes:

◆ Do *one of the following*:
  ▲ If you're not running Studio, load the program. Once Studio loads, you're in Edit mode, and the Album opens to the Video Scenes tab. Click a scene to select it (**Figure 6.1**).
  ▲ If you're running Studio and you're in Capture or Make Movie mode, select the Edit tab in the three-tab menu at the top of the Album. Once you're in Edit mode, the Album opens to the video scenes you've accessed or captured most recently.
  ▲ If you're in Edit mode and working on any Album tab other than Video Scenes, click the Camcorder icon at the top of the column of icons along the left side of the Album window (**Figure 6.2**). The Album switches to Video Scenes.

Figure 6.1 Here's Studio in Edit mode, with the Album containing about an hour's worth of video shot at the annual Fiddler's Convention here in Galax.

Figure 6.2 If you're on any other Album tab in Edit mode, click the Camcorder icon to get to the Video Scenes tab.

Collecting Assets in the Album

Figure 6.3 Click here to move up one level, and see other video files in this folder.

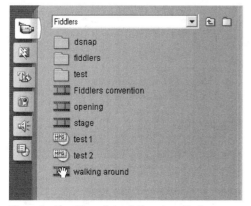

Figure 6.4 The Album lists all files stored in the selected folder, making it easy to switch among captured files. Double-click the video that you want displayed.

Loading Video Files

Before you can split, combine, or annotate your video files, you have to load them into the Album. Here's how.

To load captured files into the Album:

◆ If you just finished capturing video files, select the Edit tab to enter Edit mode.

The most recently captured video file appears in the Album.

To display other captured files in the Album:

1. Click the Move Up One Level folder icon (**Figure 6.3**).

   Studio displays a list of other files captured in that folder.

2. Double-click the file you want to display (**Figure 6.4**).

   The selected file appears on the Video Scenes tab (**Figure 6.5**). Note that if it hasn't already done so, Studio performs scene detection on the new clip using whatever option is currently selected on the Capture Source tab (see Figure 3.6 in Chapter 3).

Figure 6.5 Presto—there's the video you want.

To display other videos in the Album:

1. Click the Directory icon to the right of the Album list box (**Figure 6.6**).

   A standard Open dialog box appears (**Figure 6.7**).

2. Navigate to the folder that contains the target file (**Figure 6.8**).

3. Do *one of the following:*
   ▲ Double-click the target file.
   ▲ Select the target file with the pointer and click Open (**Figure 6.9**).

   If it hasn't already done so, Studio performs scene detection on the selected clip using whatever option is currently chosen on the Capture Source tab.

   If Studio can't display all of the scenes from that video on one page, it creates multiple pages. Move through the pages by clicking the arrows at the upper right and upper left of the Album pages.

✔ Tips

- Studio imports only AVI, MPEG-1, and MPEG-2 video files. Studio cannot import RealVideo, Windows Media, or QuickTime files or files saved in animated formats such as Autodesk's FLC format.

- The Album can display only one video at a time. Although the Album can display multiple scenes from one video, you cannot import, combine, or otherwise display scenes in the Album from more than one video at a time.

- You can't delete scenes or change their order in the Album. However, Studio provides a great tool for choosing and rearranging the order of your videos: the Storyboard view in the Movie window, which is discussed in Chapter 7.

Figure 6.6 To select files in other folders, click the Directory icon to the right of the drop-down box.

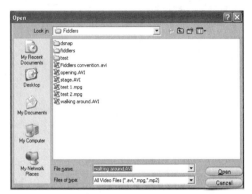

Figure 6.7 A standard Open dialog box appears.

Figure 6.8 Navigate to the folder that contains the new files.

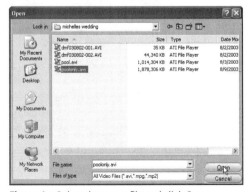

Figure 6.9 Select the target file and click Open.

Playing Videos

It's tough to select the right scenes for your project without playing the video. For this reason, the Album works closely with the Player to let you view and move through your video scenes.

To play your videos:

1. Do *one of the following*:

   ▲ Double-click the scene you want to play.

   The video immediately starts to play in the Player.

   ▲ Click the scene you want to play.

   The border around the video turns from white to blue. If you're in Comment View mode (see "Working with the Album's Views and Tools" later in this chapter), the scene comments immediately to the right of the video are also highlighted. In addition, the initial frame of the scene appears in the Player (Figure 6.10).

   continues on next page

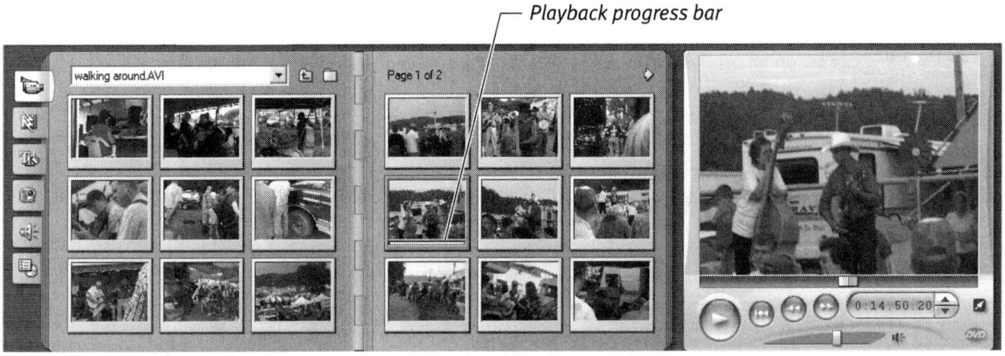

— Playback progress bar

Figure 6.10 To play any video file in the Album, double-click it, or click it once and click Play in the Player.

Chapter 6

2. Under the Player, click Play to start video playback and use the other controls to navigate through the video (**Figure 6.11**). Playback shifts automatically from scene to scene when multiple scenes are present.

   The progress bar, a white line underneath the thumbnail in each scene in the Album that fills as the player progresses through the scene, represents the position of playback within each scene. The Player scrubber represents the position of playback within the entire video.

✔ **Tip**

- Keyboard shortcuts are really helpful for playing back video in the Player from both the Album and the Movie window. Here are the relevant commands:

  ▲ *Spacebar*   Play and stop
  ▲ *J*   Fast-reverse (press multiple times for faster speed)
  ▲ *K*   Stop
  ▲ *L*   Play
  ▲ *L*   Fast-forward (press multiple times for faster speed)

Figure 6.11 To manually move through the scenes, use the familiar VCR playback controls or the Player scrubber.

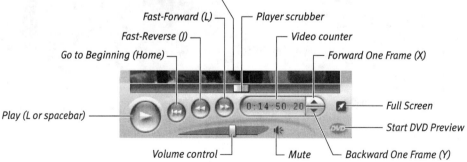

Combining Scenes

Scene detection is a great feature, but often you'll want to combine multiple scenes before moving the composite clip to the Timeline, or perhaps you'll want to consolidate scenes to reduce clutter in the Album. After all, it's always easier to keep track of one asset than five.

Studio's Combine Scenes feature has one, very significant limitation: you can combine only contiguous scenes captured from a single video, preventing serious rearranging. No problem, however; Studio has a great Storyboard feature that's perfect for extensive reorganizing.

To combine scenes:

1. Select the scenes to combine by doing *one of the following*:

   ▲ While holding down the Shift key, use the pointer to select the desired contiguous scenes.

   ▲ Drag to select all scenes under the marquee, starting with the pointer over a gray area (not a scene).

   ▲ While holding down the Shift key, click a scene with the pointer and then press the arrow keys to select the desired scenes.

   ▲ Choose Ctrl+A to select all scenes on all pages of the Album.

   ▲ Choose Edit > Select All to select all scenes on all pages of the Album.

2. Once the scenes are selected, do *one of the following*:

   ▲ From the Studio menu, choose Album > Combine Scenes.

   ▲ Place the pointer over one of the scenes you want to combine; then right-click and choose Combine Scenes (**Figure 6.12**).

   continues on next page

Figure 6.12 To combine multiple scenes into one, you can hold down the Shift key while clicking the desired contiguous scenes. In this example, I'm combining three scenes of one band into a single scene.

Studio combines all selected scenes (**Figure 6.13**). Had you selected any noncontiguous scenes, Studio would have ignored those selections and combined only the contiguous scenes.

In addition, had you left any contiguous scenes unselected, Studio would have combined all selected contiguous scenes on either side of the unselected scenes into separate groups, excluding the unselected scene.

✔ Tips

- If you customize scene comments for a scene (see "Working with Scene Comments" later in this chapter) and later combine the scene with another scene, Studio deletes the customized comments and reverts to the default naming convention: scene number, date and time of shooting, and duration. Similarly, though you can later subdivide clips and re-establish the original scenes, Studio won't recall your custom comments. If you plan on customizing scene comments, do so after combining or splitting your clips (see the next section, "Splitting Scenes").

- After combining scenes, Studio automatically renumbers all scenes that follow the combined scenes. For example, if you combine Scenes 1 through 5, the consolidated scene becomes Scene 1, and the old Scene 6 becomes Scene 2. Keep this in mind if you've been cataloging your scenes-based on automatic names.

- No matter what method you use to select scenes, Studio ignores the order of selection, combining only the selected contiguous scenes in their original order.

- Don't group scenes if you plan to trim frames from scenes (see Chapter 7) or add transitions between them (see Chapter 8), as Studio will simply make you re-split them to access the individual scenes.

Figure 6.13 Now we have one scene we'll later call "Honky Tonk."

Splitting Scenes

In addition to a feature for combining your scenes, Studio gives you three options for dividing up scenes in the Album: splitting, subdividing, and scene detection. Splitting is the manual process of dividing one scene into two or multiple scenes, convenient when automatic scene detection doesn't yield useful results. Subdividing involves cutting your clips into regular intervals, useful when working with long continuous videos with no natural breaks. Finally, automatic scene detection breaks the video into intervals based on scene changes in the content or discontinuities in the shooting time and date of the video.

These three options are available during capture and can be accessed in the Album for scenes captured with scene detection disabled, captured clips with scenes that were manually combined, or videos that were imported. Note that making scene changes based on discontinuities in the shooting date and time requires DV source video, since MPEG and non-DV-source AVI files don't contain the necessary time code.

To split scenes manually:

1. Select the video to split.
2. Use the Player controls to move to the desired initial frame of the second scene (**Figure 6.14**).

continues on next page

Figure 6.14 To create a new scene for this backstage warm-up area, move the Player controls to the desired initial frame of the second scene.

Chapter 6

3. Do *one of the following:*

   ▲ From the Studio menu, choose Album > Split Scene.

   ▲ Place the pointer over the video you want to adjust; then right-click and choose Split Scene (**Figure 6.15**).

   Studio splits the scene into two scenes, with the selected frame as the initial frame of the second scene (**Figure 6.16**).

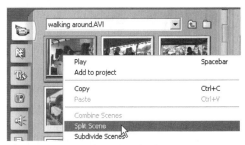

Figure 6.15 Then right-click and select Split Screen.

Figure 6.16 Now we have a new scene of the backstage warm-up area. Momma and Rosie get their new scene.

Collecting Assets in the Album

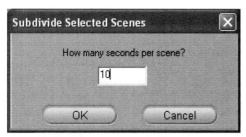

Figure 6.17 Select the desired interval (the minimum is 1 second, default is 5) and click OK.

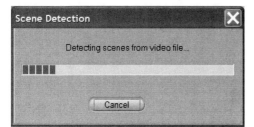

Figure 6.18 When the progress bar appears, Studio is analyzing the clip using the selected scene-detection method.

To subdivide scenes into intervals:

1. Select the video to subdivide.
2. Do *one of the following*:
   ▲ From the Studio menu, choose Album > Subdivide Scenes.
   ▲ Right-click and choose Subdivide Scenes.

   The Subdivide Selected Scenes dialog box appears.
3. Type the desired interval in the dialog box, with the minimum interval being 1 second (**Figure 6.17**).
4. Click OK

   Studio splits the video into scenes of the specified interval, with any remaining time placed in a separate scene. The new scenes are added to the Album.

To detect scenes in your clips:

1. Select the video to be adjusted.
2. Do *one of the following*:
   ▲ In the Studio menu, choose Album > Detect Scenes by Video Content *or* Detect Scenes by Shooting Time and Date.
   ▲ Right-click and choose Detect Scenes by Video Content *or* Detect Scenes by Shooting Time and Date.

   Studio implements the selected scene-detection option. First you see a dialog box with a bar tracking Studio's progress (**Figure 6.18**); then the new scenes appear in the Album.

continues on next page

✔ Tips

- Studio has much more precise tools for *trimming*, or the process of cutting unwanted frames from the beginning and end of each video. Accordingly, use splitting for rough cuts and for making the scenes in the Album easier to manage, and use the tools in the Movie window for fine-tuning.

- If you customize comments for a scene and later split, subdivide, or use scene detection for that scene, Studio deletes the customized scene comments and uses the default naming convention. If you plan on customizing scene comments, do this after splitting or combining your scenes.

- Splitting also updates the order of all Album scenes, so if you split Scene 1 into two scenes, the former Scene 2 becomes Scene 3. Keep this in mind if you've been cataloging your scenes-based upon automatic names.

Working with the Album's Views and Tools

The first time you load Studio, the Album is in Scene view, where each scene is represented by an icon: essentially a thumbnail of the initial frame in the scene. However, the Album lets you customize this view to make your videos more accessible. Here's how.

To change from Scene view to Comment view:

- Do *one of the following*:
   ▲ Hold the pointer over any gray area in the Album; then right-click and choose Comment view (**Figure 6.19**).
   ▲ Hold the pointer over any thumbnail in the Album; then right-click and choose Comment view.
   ▲ From the Studio menu, choose Album > Comment view.

   The Album switches to Comment view (**Figure 6.20**).

The scene comments to the right of each video list the scene number, duration, and date and time the scene was shot. As you'll see in the next section, you can customize these comments so that you can more easily find relevant scenes during production.

(Note that while working with the beta program, we noticed the scene information seemed to change randomly. So if you see different information from what is shown in Figure 6.20, don't be surprised.)

Figure 6.19 To switch to Comment view, hold the pointer over any gray area in the Album, right-click, and choose Comment view.

Figure 6.20 The Album switches to Comment view.

To switch between 4:3 and 16:9 views:

◆ Right-click on a picture in the Album and choose Aspect Ratio 16:9 (**Figure 6.21**).

The Album and Player switch to 16:9 view (**Figure 6.22**). To switch back to 4:3, right click and choose Aspect Ratio 4:3 view.

✔ Tip

■ Note that changing views does nothing to the captured file; it just changes how Studio displays the file and renders the project. Specifically, changing the view will not convert the captured file from 4:3 to 16:9 or vice versa. However, Studio will process the file at the selected aspect ratio. If any video with the incorrect aspect ratio is loaded, it will be distorted during rendering.

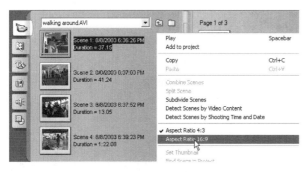

Figure 6.21 Here's how you switch back and forth between 16:9 and 4:3 modes

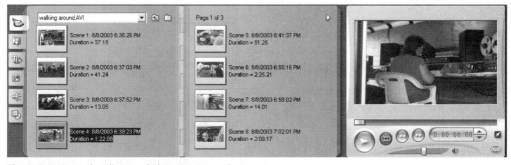

Figure 6.22 Here's the Album and Player in 16:9 mode.

Collecting Assets in the Album

To change the video thumbnail:

1. Click the target video.

   Studio highlights the scene in the Album and displays the initial frame in the Player (**Figure 6.23**).

2. Use the Player controls to move to the frame you want to use as the new thumbnail image (**Figure 6.24**).

3. Do *one of the following*:

   ▲ From the Studio menu, choose Album > Set Thumbnail.

   ▲ Place the pointer over the video you want to adjust; then right-click and choose Set Thumbnail.

   Studio changes the thumbnail image to the new frame (**Figure 6.25**).

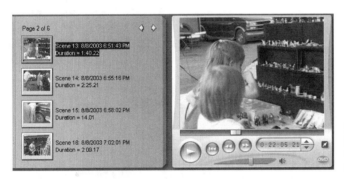

Figure 6.23 Here's the original thumbnail of this scene. Sure wish I had a thumbnail showing the girlies' faces.

Figure 6.24 This one will do just fine.

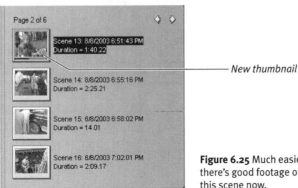

New thumbnail

Figure 6.25 Much easier to tell that there's good footage of the girlies in this scene now.

To locate a clip from the Album in a production:

1. Click any scene with a green check mark in the upper-right corner (**Figure 6.26**).

    The check mark identifies scenes that are included in the production.

2. Do *one of the following:*

    ▲ From the Studio menu, choose Album > Find Scene in Project.

    ▲ Place the pointer over the scene you want to find; then right-click and choose Find Scene in Project.

    Studio highlights the selected scene in the Movie window (**Figure 6.27**).

✔ Tip

■ If you hold the pointer over any scene for a moment, Studio displays the start time and duration of the scene (**Figure 6.28**). Keep in mind that this and other helpful information found by hovering over a scene or other icon works only with the Tooltips feature enabled—be sure the Display Tool Tips option is checked in the Help pull-down menu.

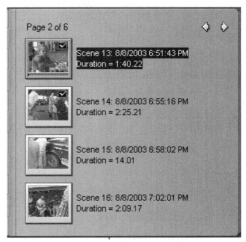

Figure 6.26 The green check mark tells you that you've used the scene somewhere in the production. To find it, select the scene.

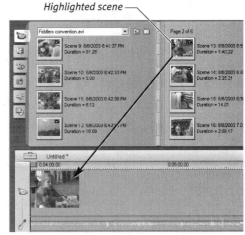

Figure 6.27 Studio shifts the Timeline to make the scene visible in the Movie window (if necessary) and highlights the scene.

Working with Scene Comments

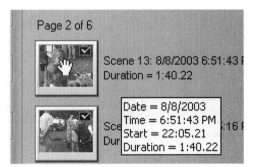

Figure 6.28 The pop-up box that appears when you hold the pointer over a scene's thumbnail identifies the date and time that the scene was shot and the scene's starting time and duration in the video.

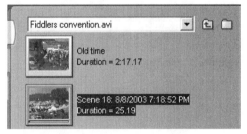

Figure 6.29 Changing scene comments helps you find videos fast. Start by clicking the scene.

Figure 6.30 Then type the desired text.

In smaller productions, it's easy to keep track of videos and scenes, but when you're tracking multiple videos over many months, finding the scenes you want can be harder. This is where the ability to add descriptive comments to scenes and later search for these scenes can be immensely helpful.

To change scene comments:

1. In Comment View mode, click the target video and click again on the comments box.

   The outline around the video turns blue, and the scene comments are highlighted (**Figure 6.29**).

2. Click the comments box again.

   It turns white, signifying that it's ready for editing.

3. Type the desired scene comments (**Figure 6.30**).

4. To save the scene comments, press Enter or click anywhere in the Studio interface outside the comments box.

   Studio saves the scene comments.

✔ Tips

- With a long video like this shoot from the Fiddler's Convention, I take the time to label every clip so that I know both what the content is and how I might use the shot. This way, relevant scenes will be easy to search for, as you'll see in the next section.

- I typically leave the duration information in the description, since this is useful to know when assembling videos.

To select scenes based on keywords:

1. From the Studio menu, choose Album > Select Scenes by Name.

   The Select Scenes by Name dialog box appears (**Figure 6.31**).

2. Enter the keywords you want to search for.

3. Do *one of the following*:

   ▲ Select And to find all scenes containing *all* of the words typed in the Keywords box.

   ▲ Select Or to find all scenes containing *any* of the words typed in the Keywords box.

   ▲ Select Not and And to find any scenes that *don't* contain *all* of the words typed in the Keywords box.

   ▲ Select Not and Or to find any scenes that *don't* contain *any* of the words typed in the Keywords box.

   The Album highlights the scenes that meet the specified criteria (**Figure 6.32**). You'll have to page through the Album to locate the highlighted clips; Studio doesn't move them to a new location.

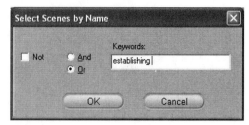

Figure 6.31 Type the words you want to search for and specify the conditions.

Figure 6.32 Studio highlights the conforming clips.

✔ Tips

- Studio's search function searches only scenes in the video currently loaded in the Album, not other videos saved to disk. This somewhat limits its functionality except with extremely large capture files.

- Unlike Windows Explorer, the Album doesn't prevent you from using duplicate names. Your files won't self-destruct; you'll just end up with different scenes with identical names.

Collecting Assets in the Album

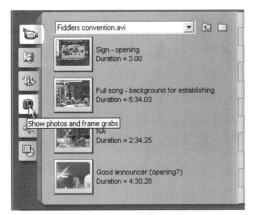

Figure 6.33 Let's throw in some digital photos shot at the aquarium in Gatlinburg, Tennessee.

Working with the Still Images Tab

The Still Images tab is where you load still images from all sources for deployment in your projects. The Album's functions in this area are extremely limited; you can't combine, arrange, or annotate the images in the Album. Don't worry; there's plenty of functionality for that in the Movie window.

To open the Album to the Still Images tab:

1. Open Studio in Edit mode.

   When you first open Studio, Edit mode is the default.

   If you're running Studio and are in Capture or Make Movie mode, select the Edit tab.

2. Click the Camera icon, the fourth icon from the top along the left side of the Album window (**Figure 6.33**).

   The Album switches to the Still Images tab and displays any images in the currently selected folder (**Figure 6.34**). Click any image, and Studio will display it in the Player.

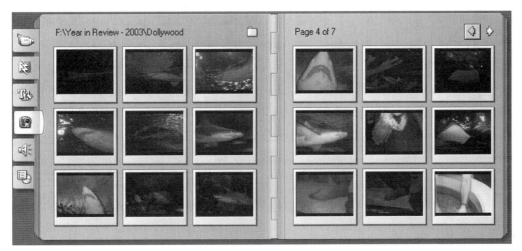

Figure 6.34 Here they are in the Album. Yup, those are sharks, and they looked hungry and hostile, a bad combination.

To display file names:

- Hover the pointer over any image.

    The pointer immediately changes to a hand and then (with Tooltips on) displays the image's file name (**Figure 6.35**).

Figure 6.35 Hover the pointer over an image, and Studio tells you its name.

To load files from a different location:

1. Click the Directory icon to the right of the Album's list box (**Figure 6.36**).

    A standard Open dialog box appears (**Figure 6.37**).

Figure 6.36 To load files from a different directory, click the Folder icon.

2. Navigate to the folder that contains the files to be imported and select any file in the folder; then click the Open button (**Figure 6.38**).

    Studio loads all files in the folder (**Figure 6.39**).

Figure 6.37 Once the Open dialog appears, navigate to the desired location.

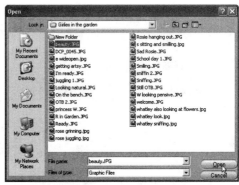

Figure 6.38 Select any file and click Open.

Collecting Assets in the Album

✔ Tips

- If you select a subdirectory with many high-resolution images, it may take several minutes for Studio to create the thumbnails to display in the Album, during which time your hard drive will be chugging like crazy, and your computer will feel extremely sluggish. If your still image folders contain lots of images, consider moving the images you want to incorporate into your production to a separate folder for input into Studio.

- Studio can import files in the following formats: bitmap (BMP), JPEG (JPG, JPEG), Targa (TGA), TIFF (TIF), Windows Metafiles (WMF), and files created by Title Deko, Studio's titling utility. This pretty much covers the majors, but if you want to use a GIF image or Photoshop document (PSD), you have to convert to one of the supported formats in another program first.

Figure 6.39 Studio loads all of the directory's images into the Album. A much less threatening group of pictures, don't you think?

Working with the Sound Effects Tab

The Sound Effects tab is where you load audio files for deployment in your projects. As with the Still Images tab, the Album's functions in this area are extremely limited; you can't combine, arrange, or annotate the audio files in the Album, nor can you adjust volume. All this and more are possible in the Movie window; the Album is here simply to help you collect and deploy.

To open the Album to the Sound Effects tab:

1. Open Studio in Edit mode.

   When you first open Studio, Edit mode is the default.

   If you're running Studio and are in Capture or Make Movie mode, select the Edit tab.

2. Click the Speaker icon, the fifth icon from the top on the left side of the Album window (**Figure 6.40**).

   The Album switches to the Sound Effects tab and displays all supported files in the current folder (**Figure 6.41**).

To display file duration:

♦ Hover the pointer over any audio file.

   The pointer immediately changes to a hand and then, in a moment, displays the file duration (**Figure 6.42**).

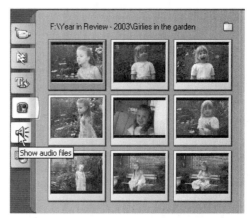

Figure 6.40 Click the Speaker icon to select the Sound Effects tab, where you load audio files into the project.

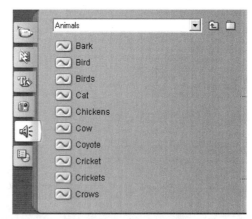

Figure 6.41 The Album defaults to folders containing sound effects that Pinnacle includes with Studio 9.

Figure 6.42 As with still images, the Album features for audio files are light, but (with Tooltips on) you can ascertain file duration by hovering the pointer over the icon.

Collecting Assets in the Album

Figure 6.43 You know the drill by now. To open new audio files, click the Folder icon.

Figure 6.44 Choose any file and click Open.

Figure 6.45 Studio displays all compatible audio files in the Album.

To play any audio file:

◆ Click any file on the Sound Effects tab.

The file immediately plays through to the end. Use the controls in the Player to replay, rewind, or move through the scene.

To load files from a different location:

1. Click the Directory icon to the right of the Album list box (**Figure 6.43**).

   A standard Opendialog box appears.

2. Navigate to the folder containing the files to be imported, select any file in the folder, and click Open (**Figure 6.44**).

   Studio loads all compatible files in the folder into the Album (**Figure 6.45**).

✔ Tip

■ Studio can import WAV files, MP3 files, and audio from AVI files. Notable missing formats include QuickTime, RealAudio, and Windows Media files. The lack of the latter two is a pain given that many folks who collect digital audio files use these formats extensively for their collections.

Part III: Editing

Chapter 7 Producing Videos in the Movie Window 145

Chapter 8 Using Transitions 197

Chapter 9 Applying Special Effects 225

Chapter 10 Designing Titles and Menus..............257

Chapter 11 Working with Audio 303

Chapter 12 DVD Authoring..343

Producing Videos in the Movie Window

7

Once you've captured your video, still image, and audio assets, you will have created a huge collection of files—usually far more than you'll want to include in your final production. The next steps are to cut out the fat and assemble the basic pieces of your project, all of which you do in Studio's Movie window.

The Movie window showcases the most flexible part of Studio's interface, providing three views of your assembled assets: Storyboard, Timeline, and Text view (called Edit List view on the Studio menu). This chapter discusses the strengths of each view and then teaches you how to customize and efficiently work within the Storyboard and Timeline views. Considering how much time you'll be spending in the Movie window—particularly the Timeline—spending a short time on the basics now will save you hours of work later.

Chapter 7

Looking at Movie Window Views

The Movie window offers three views: Storyboard (**Figure 7.1**), Timeline (**Figure 7.2**), and Text (**Figure 7.3**).

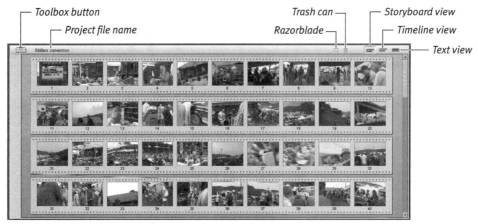

Figure 7.1 The Storyboard view, the best view for initially loading and sequencing your assets.

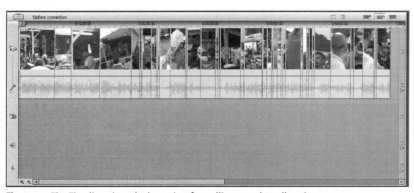

Figure 7.2 The Timeline view, the best view for pulling together all project components.

Figure 7.3 The Text view (also called Edit List), for those who prefer working in text rather than using visual tools.

146

Producing Videos in the Movie Window

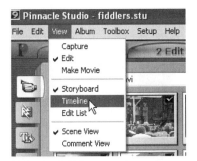

Figure 7.4 Switch among views using the Studio menu or the icons at the top of the Movie window.

Briefly, the Storyboard view uses a thumbnail image to represent each asset in a project. This is a great view for sequencing your assets and inserting transitions between them, but little else, since you can't access tracks for titles, narration, or background music.

The Timeline view is a graphical representation of an entire project, with the length of each clip on the Timeline representing the duration of that clip. Although Timeline view lets you recognize bits and pieces of clips, you won't be able to recognize most of the smaller clips, especially if you've zoomed out to get a bird's eye view. So it's best to sequence your videos in Storyboard view and then switch to Timeline view for serious editing such as adding titles, background music and other elements.

The Text view is appropriate for those who enjoy working with text descriptors rather than visual assets. I don't work that way and have seldom found uses for this view, so I won't elaborate more on it.

To switch among Movie window views:

- Do *one of the following:*
  - ▲ At the upper right of the Movie window, click the appropriate button for the desired view (Figure 7.1).
  - ▲ In the Studio menu, choose View and the desired view (**Figure 7.4**).

Chapter 7

Working on the Storyboard

In traditional video productions, a storyboard is a large chart or series of charts with images representing the various scenes of a project. It's a great tool for conceptualizing the content and flow of your movie, and it's even better in digital form, since you can easily rearrange your assets.

If you're at all unsure of the order of your scenes, Studio's Storyboard is a very convenient place for shuffling them around until you've decided. You can even add transitions and preview your project on the fly to quickly view the rough cut. However, when it's time to trim your videos and perform other more sophisticated editing, you'll need to use the superior tools available only in Timeline view.

Note that by default, Studio maintains audio and video synchronization in all Movie window views by automatically tying the Audio track to the Video track through all edits. Accordingly, if you move, delete, split, or combine scenes in the Video track, the audio automatically follows. (Later in this chapter, you'll learn how to adjust this default, so that you can delete the Audio track or perform advanced editing operations that let you edit the Audio and Video tracks separately.)

Producing Videos in the Movie Window

Figure 7.5 Getting to the Pinnacle Studio Setup Options screen.

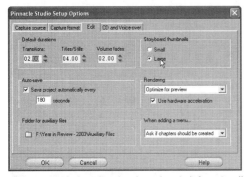

Figure 7.6 With the Edit tab selected, switch from Small (the default setting) to Large Storyboard thumbnails.

To customize the Storyboard view:

1. From the Studio menu, choose Setup > Edit (**Figure 7.5**).

   The Pinnacle Studio Setup Options screen appears, open to the Edit tab (**Figure 7.6**).

2. In the Storyboard Thumbnails section, select the Large radio button to increase the size of the images on the Storyboard.

   Studio increases the size of the individual images and decreases the number of images shown from 27 to 10 (**Figure 7.7**). Use the scroll bar on the right to scroll down to see the additional thumbnails, or use the Page Up and Page Down keys to move through the pages of the Storyboard.

Figure 7.7 Select Large Storyboard Thumbnails to see more detail in your thumbnails. Note the scroll bar on the right, which you'll use to access the rest of your assets.

To drag video clips to the Storyboard:

1. On the Video Scenes tab, hold down the mouse button and select one or more contiguous or noncontiguous scenes.

    The borders turn from white to blue, and a small hand appears over the scenes (**Figure 7.8**).

2. Drag the scenes toward the empty frame at the upper left of the Storyboard.

    A green box appears around the empty frame, and a small plus sign and box appears below the pointer (**Figure 7.9**). (You won't be able to see the green frame in Figure 7.9, but you will when you try this in Studio.)

3. Release the mouse button.

    Studio inserts the scenes in the highlighted Storyboard frame (**Figure 7.10**).

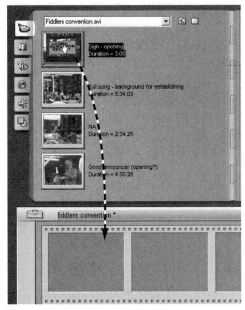

Figure 7.8 Getting videos into the Movie window is as simple as selecting and dragging.

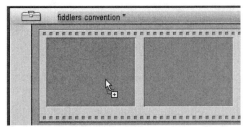

Figure 7.9 The green border and plus sign are your clues that it's safe to drop the asset in the selected frame.

Figure 7.10 Voilà. There's your clip.

Producing Videos in the Movie Window

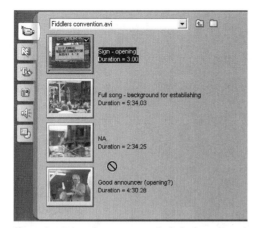

Figure 7.11 Other placement cues include the universal "prohibited" sign, indicating that you can't arrange your clips on the Video Scenes tab.

✔ **Tips**

- Studio provides visual cues regarding where you can drop all assets. As shown in **Figure 7.11**, if you attempt to drop a scene in a prohibited zone, such as another location on the Video Scenes tab, Studio displays the universal "prohibited" sign.

- Studio drops video and still image assets in the first available space at the beginning of a project. Although you can reorder at will once the assets are on the Storyboard, Studio doesn't let you create gaps in your projects in any Movie window view.

- To create a black scene at the start of your video, create a full-screen blank title and drag it to the Video track (see "To create a single-color background" in Chapter 10).

- You can also use the Cut and Paste commands to move videos and still images to and around the Movie window, but dragging and dropping is much more intuitive.

151

To insert a video clip between two scenes in the Storyboard:

1. On the Video Scenes tab, hold down the mouse button and select one or more scenes.

   The borders turn from white to blue, and a small hand appears over the scene.

2. Drag the scenes to the desired location.

   A green line appears between the video scenes, and a small plus sign appears below the pointer (**Figure 7.12**).

3. Release the mouse button.

   Studio inserts the scene between the existing scenes (**Figure 7.13**).

✔ Tip

- Studio inserts the new clip between the selected clips, pushing back all clips after the newly inserted clips. No clips are deleted or otherwise truncated.

Figure 7.12 The green line and a small plus sign tell you that you can drop the assets in that location.

Figure 7.13 The assets, successfully inserted and shifted.

Producing Videos in the Movie Window

Figure 7.14 Decided to reorder the scenes? Select the clip you want to move.

Figure 7.15 When you see that green line and the small box under the arrow, you can drag the clip to the desired location and drop it.

Figure 7.16 Done. This ease of sequencing is why the Storyboard view is great for arranging your assets.

Figure 7.17 Since the Storyboard view doesn't visually convey duration-related information, Studio provides it when you hover your mouse over the asset.

To arrange assets in Storyboard view:

1. On the Storyboard, hold down the mouse button and select one or more scenes.

    Studio highlights the clip in blue, and a small hand appears over the scene (**Figure 7.14**).

2. Drag the scenes to the desired location.

    A green line appears each time you cross an available space to drop the new scenes, and a small box appears below the pointer (**Figure 7.15**).

3. Release the mouse button at the desired location.

    Studio inserts the scene in the specified location (**Figure 7.16**).

To see clip-related information on the Storyboard:

◆ On the Storyboard, hover the pointer over a clip for a moment.

    The scene name and duration appear in a yellow box beneath the scene (**Figure 7.17**). The top duration is the total duration of the clip. The bottom duration is the duration of the clip remaining in the sequence after trimming. (For more information, see "Trimming with the Clip Properties Tool" later in this chapter.)

    (Note that while using the beta product, I found that the appearance of the box varied randomly. So don't be surprised if your box looks different than the one shown in Figure 7.17.)

153

To preview your video clip on the Storyboard:

1. Select the scene you want to play back. Studio highlights the clip in blue.

2. Start playback by doing *one of the following*:
   ▲ In the Player, click Play (**Figure 7.18**). The Play key switches to Pause mode, which you can click to stop playback.
   ▲ Press the spacebar to start playback. Press the spacebar again to stop playback
   ▲ Press the L key to start playback. Press K to stop playback.

Playback shifts automatically from scene to scene when multiple assets are present. During playback, Studio displays a progress bar beneath the scene.

The progress bar represents the position of playback within each scene; the Player scrubber represents the position of playback within the entire video.

✔ Tips

- Here are some keyboard shortcuts:
  Press L for fast-forward (press L multiple times to accelerate the effect).
  Press J for fast-reverse (press J multiple times to accelerate the effect).
- You can always use the Player scrubber to move around in the video file.

Figure 7.18 The Player is your preview window.

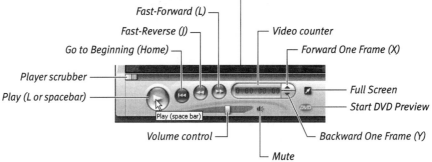

Getting Video Clips to the Timeline

Timeline view is where you'll spend the bulk of your editing time. Although it's not quite as straightforward as Storyboard view, its operational advantages quickly become apparent.

This section identifies the various Timeline tracks and explains how to get video scenes to the Timeline. If your Timeline starts getting cramped or otherwise out of control, skip ahead one section to learn how to customize your Timeline view.

As mentioned earlier, in default mode Studio automatically inserts the audio that was originally captured with the video file on the appropriate track when you transfer the video, so you don't have to worry about manually moving the audio track yourself.

The components of the Timeline and other components of the Studio interface that are important in using the Timeline effectively are summarized here (**Figure 7.19**):

◆ **Timescale:** Shows the absolute time of the assets displayed in Timeline view. You can modify the Timescale to show more or less detail (see "Customizing Your Timeline View" later in this chapter).

continues on next page

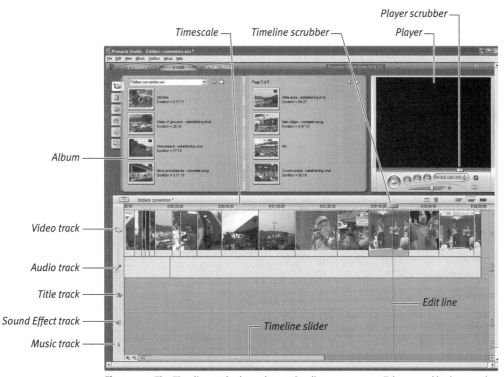

Figure 7.19 The Timeline and other relevant Studio components. Take a good look around; you'll be spending lots of time here.

- **Menu track:** Appears only after you add a DVD menu to the Timeline. (For details on DVD authoring, see Chapter 12.)

- **Video track:** The only track that can display video; it can also display still images.

- **Audio track:** Contains only the audio that was captured with the video clip. Note that Studio 8 referred to the Audio track as the Original Audio track, and still does in the Help files. However, tooltips refer to it as the Audio track. For the purposes of this book I also refer to it as the Audio track, though I may slip and mention Original Audio track occasionally.

- **Title track:** Contains titles and still image overlays (For more information on creating titles, see Chapter 10). Note that in the Studio 8 and the Studio 9 Help files, the Title track is called the Title Overlay track, but the tooltips refer to it as the Title track. For the purposes of this book, I try to be consistent with the tooltips, but if I occasionally refer to it as Title Overlay, you'll know what I mean.

- **Sound Effect track:** Studio places all voice-over recordings on this track, or you can insert audio from any source. For example, to insert only the audio from a captured video file into the production, simply drag it to this track. Once again, the Help files may refer to this as the Sound Effect and Voice Over track, but I'm sticking with the tooltips version. If I happen to refer to it in the same way the Help files do, you'll know I'm talking about the Sound Effect track.

- **Music track:** Studio places background music produced by the SmartSound utility or from any source on this track. To learn how to set audio levels for the three Audio tracks, see "Using the Volume Tool" in Chapter 11. Studio 8 referred to this track as the Background Music track; I'm sticking with Music track, which is the current tooltips designation.

- **Edit line:** The current editing position on the Timeline and the frame currently visible in the Player.

- **Timeline scrubber:** A tool used to drag the edit line to different positions on the Timeline.

- **Player scrubber:** A tool used to move the edit line through the project.

- **Timeline slider:** A tool used to drag the visible area on the Timeline forward and backward through the project.

Producing Videos in the Movie Window

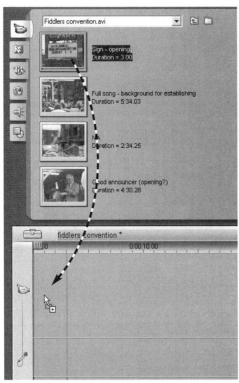

To drag video clips to the Timeline:

1. On the Video Scenes tab, hold down the mouse button and select one or more contiguous or noncontiguous scenes.

   The borders turn from white to blue, and a small hand appears over the scenes.

2. Do *one of the following:*

   ▲ Drag the scenes to the Video track.

   ▲ Drag the scenes to the Sound Effect and Voice-Over track.

   ▲ Drag the scenes to the Music track.

   A green rectangle representing the duration of the clip appears in the first open space on the Timeline, and a small plus sign appears below the pointer (**Figure 7.20**).

3. Release the mouse button.

   Studio inserts the scenes on the selected track (**Figure 7.21**).

   continues on next page

Figure 7.20 More placement cues. A green box defines the duration of the video clip on the Timeline, and the plus sign says it's okay to drop the file here.

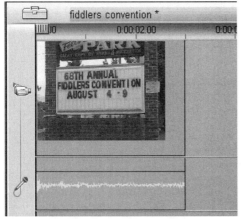

Figure 7.21 There's your scene, ready to go.

157

✓ Tips

- If you drop a video on the Video track, Studio always inserts the associated audio on the Audio track. To delete the Audio track, lock the video track and delete the associated Audio track. See Advanced Timeline editing later in this chapter for details on locking tracks.

- If you drop a video file on either the Sound Effect track or the Music track, only the audio, not the video, is inserted on the track.

- Studio provides the same visual cues on the Timeline to show where you can drop all assets as it does on the Storyboard. If you attempt to drop scenes on prohibited tracks, such as the Title track, you'll see red lines instead of green, a "prohibited" sign, and the error message "Only titles, photos and transitions on title track" above the Timescale (**Figure 7.22**).

- As with the Storyboard, Studio always drops video and still image assets in the first available space at the beginning of a project. Although you can reorder assets at will once they're on the Storyboard, you can't create gaps in your projects in any of the Movie window views.

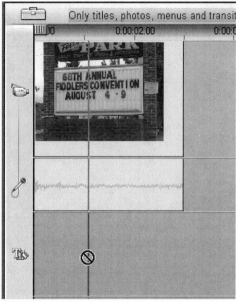

Figure 7.22 Danger, danger, Will Robinson—don't drop your clip there. See the prohibited sign and error message on the top line.

To insert video clips between two clips on the Timeline:

1. On the Video Scenes tab, hold down the mouse button and select one or more scenes.

   The borders turn from white to blue, and a small hand appears over the scenes.

2. Drag the scenes to the desired location.

   Two vertical green lines appear between the two selected video clips, and a small plus sign appears below the pointer (**Figure 7.23**).

3. Release the mouse button.

   Studio inserts the scene between the existing scenes (**Figure 7.24**).

✔ Tips

- Note that Studio inserts the new clip between the selected clips, pushing back all clips after the newly inserted clips (potentially out of your current view of the project). No clips are deleted or otherwise truncated.

- You can normally insert a clip only at the beginning or end of another clip, not in the middle of a clip. Both of the "To perform an insert edit," tasks later in this chapter show you how to insert a clip in the middle of a different clip, a process called insert editing.

Figure 7.23 Studio won't let you drop a clip in the middle of another one. Move the pointer until you see the green lines and plus sign.

Figure 7.24 Release the mouse button, and there you go.

To arrange video clips on the Timeline:

1. On the Video track, hold down the mouse button and select one or more scenes.

    Studio highlights the clip in blue, and a small hand appears over the scene (**Figure 7.25**).

2. Drag the clip to the desired location.

    Studio displays green lines at the beginning and end of the clip that you're arranging, and a small box appears below the pointer (**Figure 7.26**).

3. Release the mouse button.

    Studio inserts the scene in the specified location (**Figure 7.27**).

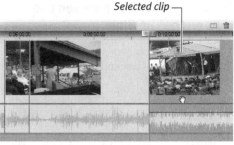

Figure 7.25 You move clips on the Timeline the same way you do on the Storyboard, with slightly different cues. Start by selecting the clip.

Figure 7.26 Move the clip to the desired space, watching for the green lines and plus sign, and then release the mouse button.

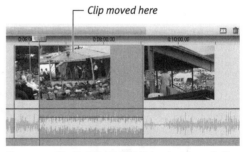

Figure 7.27 Studio inserts the clip and pushes all clips behind it to the back of the line.

Producing Videos in the Movie Window

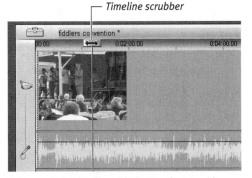

Figure 7.28 Get familiar with the Timeline scrubber, which shifts the edit line and controls the frames viewed in the Player.

To preview your video clip on the Timeline:

1. Do *one of the following:*

   ▲ Select the scene you want to play back.

   Studio highlights the clip in blue and positions the Timeline scrubber at the start of the scene.

   ▲ Drag the Timeline scrubber to the desired start location (**Figure 7.28**).

2. Start playback by doing *one of the following:*

   ▲ In the Player, click Play.

   The Play key switches to Pause mode, which you can click to stop playback.

   ▲ Press the spacebar to start playback. Press the spacebar again to stop playback.

   ▲ Press the L key to start playback (ignore the tooltip). Press K to stop playback.

   Playback shifts automatically from scene to scene when multiple assets are present.

   During playback, the Timeline and Player scrubbers advance with the video.

✔ Tips

- Here are some relevant keyboard shortcuts:

   ▲ Press L for fast-forward (press L multiple times to accelerate the effect)

   ▲ Press J for fast-reverse (press J multiple times to accelerate the effect)

   ▲ Press K to stop playback

- You can always use the Player scrubber to position video playback.

- If your mouse has a wheel, you can use it to scroll through the video. Note that if you press and hold down the Ctrl key as you're doing it, you'll move through the video frame by frame.

161

Chapter 7

Customizing Your Timeline View

As you've probably already noticed, as you place additional videos on the Timeline, it gets increasingly difficult to see the big picture. Fortunately, Studio supplies several tools that help you control your Timeline environment.

First, a slider bar at the bottom of the Timeline makes it easy to move through your production. In addition, Studio can stretch the Timeline so that it represents a longer period (and thus shows more video clips, or longer stretches of a single video clip) to provide a high-level view. Or you can shrink down the Timeline to a frame-by-frame view, which is helpful when synchronizing production elements such as audio and the main video.

To move around on the Timeline:

◆ Do *one of the following:*

  ▲ Drag the Timeline slider at the bottom of the Timeline to the right to reveal the video clip inserted after the last visible track (**Figure 7.29**).

  ▲ Press the Page Down key to move from the beginning to the end of the Timeline, or the Page Up key to move from the end to the beginning.

  ▲ Press the right arrow key to move forward to the next scene on the Timeline, and the left arrow key to move backward from scene to scene.

✔ Tips

- The Timeline slider is not movable until the project assets exceed the space then visible on the Timeline.

- The Timeline slider will shrink as the project gets longer, essentially representing the size of the video visible at that time on the Timeline relative to the entire project.

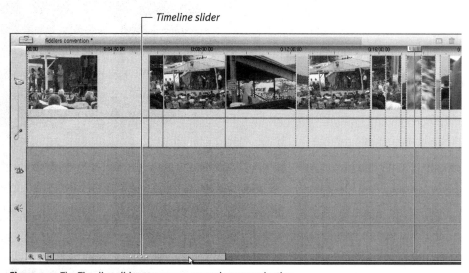

Figure 7.29 The Timeline slider moves you around your production.

Producing Videos in the Movie Window

Figure 7.30 Working on the Timeline requires constant shuffling of the Timescale. Here's one way to adjust the Timescale, giving you control over the duration of the video in the project you can see on the Timeline at one time.

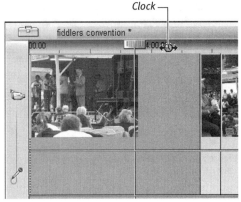

Figure 7.31 Here's another. Just click the yellow Timescale anywhere but on the Timeline scrubber, and the clock appears.

To adjust the Timescale of the Timeline:

◆ Do *one of the following:*

▲ Place your pointer over the yellow Timescale on the Timeline and right-click. Studio opens a menu that lets you select the desired duration visible on the Timeline (**Figure 7.30**).

▲ Press the plus (+) or minus (–) key to make the Timescale larger or smaller.

▲ On the yellow Timescale bar, place the pointer anywhere except directly over the edit line until a small clock with arrows appears (**Figure 7.31**). Drag the clock left to expand the Timescale and show more video clips or right to compress the Timescale and see more detail.

✔ Tips

- If you choose Entire Movie (Figure 7.30), Studio places the entire movie in the visible area of the Timeline. This is the best way to see your whole production fast.

- When you set the Timescale at the highest magnification, each tick mark on the Timescale represents an individual video frame (although Studio shows only the initial frame on the Timeline). When performing precision trims on the Timeline, this level of detail can be extremely useful, though you'll have to view the frames in the Player, not on the Timeline.

163

Common Tasks

As you'd expect, Studio has common commands for many housekeeping tasks you perform in the Storyboard and Timeline views. Here are the major ones, shown in the Timeline view for simplicity.

To delete assets:

1. Select the asset you want to delete. Studio highlights the clip in blue.

2. Do *one of the following:*
   ▲ Press the Delete key.
   ▲ From the Studio menu, choose Edit > Delete (**Figure 7.32**).
   ▲ Right-click and choose Delete (**Figure 7.33**).

   Studio deletes the clip from the Timeline, but not from the Album or your disk.

✔ Tips

- If you delete any video scene, all scenes after the deleted clip automatically shift over to close the gap. This is called a ripple edit (see the section "Trimming Multiple Clips on the Timeline" later in this chapter). The only exception is when you lock the Video track (see the section "Advanced Timeline Editing" later in this chapter).

- In addition to the options of the Edit menu and right-click menu, you can use keyboard commands to cut (Ctrl+X), copy (Ctrl+C), and paste (Ctrl+V) files.

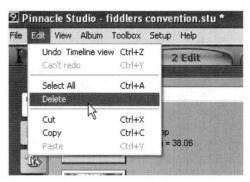

Figure 7.32 One way to delete a clip in the Movie window.

Figure 7.33 Another way to delete, using the right-click command.

Producing Videos in the Movie Window

To split clips:

1. Use Player controls or the Timeline scrubber to move the edit line to the initial frame of the desired second clip (**Figure 7.34**).

2. Split the clip by doing *one of the following*:
   ▲ Click the Razorblade icon at the top the Movie window.
   ▲ Right-click the selected clip and choose Split Clip (**Figure 7.35**).
   ▲ Press the Insert key.

   Studio splits the clips at the edit line (**Figure 7.36**).

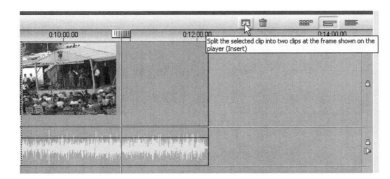

Figure 7.34 To split a clip, move the edit line to the desired location and click the Razorblade icon.

Figure 7.35 Or, for you right-click fans, choose Split clip.

Figure 7.36 Either way, you now have two clips where formerly there were none.

165

To combine scenes:

1. Select the scenes to combine by doing *one of the following:*

   ▲ Hold down the Shift or Ctrl key and select two or more scenes (**Figure 7.37**).

   ▲ Starting with the pointer over a gray area (and not a scene) on the Storyboard or Timeline, drag to select all scenes within the marquee (**Figure 7.38**).

   ▲ From the Studio menu, choose Edit > Select All to select all scenes on the Storyboard or Timeline.

   ▲ Press Ctrl+A to select all scenes on all pages of the Album.

Figure 7.37 To combine scenes, hold down the Shift key while clicking two (or more) clips.

Figure 7.38 You can also drag on the Timeline to include the desired clips.

Producing Videos in the Movie Window

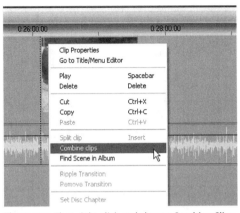

Figure 7.39 Then right-click and choose Combine Clips.

2. Position the pointer over one of the selected scenes; then right-click and choose Combine Clips (**Figure 7.39**). Studio combines all selected scenes (**Figure 7.40**).

✔ Tips

- If you select noncontiguous scenes from the same or different capture file, Studio ignores these selections and combines only the contiguous scenes. To help you in this process, Studio identifies contiguous scenes with a dotted vertical line between them on the Timeline (Figure 7.38).

- You can't combine two scenes if transitions have been inserted between them, even if they are contiguous. To combine them, delete the transition.

- You can't combine scenes if you've trimmed any frames from the beginning or end of either scene. To combine, restore each scene to its original length.

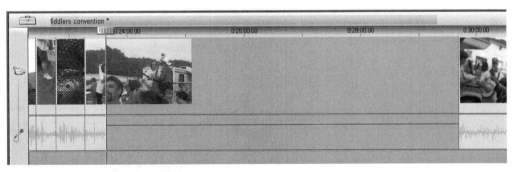

Figure 7.40 Studio combines the clips.

167

Chapter 7

To change the thumbnail image:

1. Use Player controls or the Timeline scrubber to move the edit line to the image you want to use as the thumbnail (**Figure 7.41**).

2. Right-click the selected clip and choose Set Thumbnail (**Figure 7.42**).

   Studio sets the new thumbnail image (**Figure 7.43**).

✔ **Tips**

- Setting a new thumbnail in the Movie window doesn't reset the thumbnail in the Album. It also doesn't set it as the thumbnail for use when making your DVD.

- To reset the thumbnail to the original location, Undo doesn't work, even though it appears as an option in the usual spot, under Edit. You'll need to move the scrubber to the original location and repeat Step 2.

Figure 7.41 A thumbnail should tell you what's in a scene at a glance. If yours doesn't, change it by clicking the clip and moving the Timeline or Player scrubber to a better frame.

Figure 7.42 Then right-click the clip and choose Set Thumbnail.

Figure 7.43 The new thumbnail. No problem telling what's in this video now.

COMMON TASKS

Producing Videos in the Movie Window

Figure 7.44 If you ever need to find the clip you're editing back in the Album, right-click the clip and choose Find Scene in Album.

To find a scene in the Album while in the Movie window:

1. Select the scene you want to locate.

2. Right-click and choose Find Scene in Album (**Figure 7.44**).

   Studio opens the Album to the page containing the scene and highlights the scene and scene comments (**Figure 7.45**). If another video file is loaded, Studio loads the necessary video clip to locate the scene.

Figure 7.45 Studio locates the scene, even if it's in a different video clip.

Trimming with the Clip Properties Tool

Trimming video is the process of removing unwanted frames from the beginning and end of your captured scenes, often referred to as the *heads* and *tails*. Since this is probably the most common editing activity, Studio's Clip Properties tool (**Figure 7.46**), a mechanism for trimming your clips, is accessible in all three Movie window views. See **Table 7.1** for a list of the controls that the Clip Properties tool provides.

You can also trim your videos directly on the Timeline (see "Trimming a Clip on the Timeline," later in this chapter), although generally you have greater precision with the Clip Properties tool.

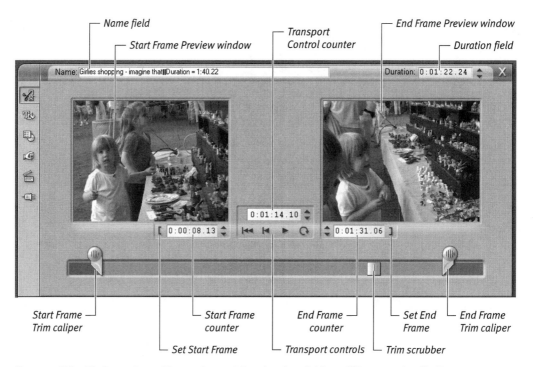

Figure 7.46 The Clip Properties tool is great for precision trimming of video, still image, and audio files.

Table 7.1

Controls in the Clip Properties Tool	
CLIP PROPERTIES	**TOOL CONTROLS**
Name field	Contains the scene name specified in the Album.
Duration field	Displays the video duration with new start and end frames.
Start Frame Preview window	Displays the currently selected start frame.
End Frame Preview window	Displays the currently selected end frame.
Transport controls	Like the Trim scrubber, can be used to move loaded video to any desired frame, or can play back the trimmed clip.
Transport Control counter	Displays the current edit point in the video.
Set Start Frame	Sets the start frame to the current edit point.
Start Frame counter	Displays the current start frame location in standard hours:minutes:seconds:frame format. You can select the desired start frame by entering time code directly or by adjusting the start frame position using the jog controls at the right.
Set End Frame	Sets the end frame to the current edit point.
End Frame counter	Displays the current end frame location in standard hours:minutes:seconds:frame format. You can select the desired end frame by entering time code directly or by adjusting the end frame position using the jog controls at the right.
Start Frame Trim caliper	Shows the location of the currently selected start frame; can be dragged to the desired location.
Trim scrubber	Reflects the edit point of the currently loaded video. You can use the scrubber to drag video to any desired frame to set the frame as the start or end frame using the appropriate icon or keyboard command. As you scrub through the video, frames appear in the Player window to the right of the Clip Properties tool, not in the Start or End Frame Preview window. These displays change only as you move the Start and End Frame Trim calipers or the clocks beneath them.
End Frame Trim caliper	Shows the location of the currently selected end frame; can be dragged to the desired location.

Planning Your Trimming Activities

Before trimming your clips, consider whether you intend to fade into the first scene, fade out of the final scene, and/or use transitions between the scenes. If you use any of these effects, you need to account for them in your trimming.

Briefly, transitions are animated effects inserted between video scenes to either smooth or emphasize the passage from one clip to the next (for details, see Chapter 8). The most commonly used transition is a cut, which is actually the absence of a transition: the video simply jumps from the last frame of the first clip to the first frame of the second clip. Other frequently used transitions are dissolves, wipes, and fades, which you implement using frames that overlap between two clips.

If you were trimming two clips to be joined by a cut, the end frame for your first video clip would be the last frame you want to appear in the production. Similarly, the start frame for the second video clip would be the initial frame you want visible.

continues on next page

Planning Your Trimming Activities *continued*

For example, one fun scene for me in the Fiddler's Convention video shows my daughters looking at some dodo-bird puppets (**Figure 7.47**). The visual is key because of the comment my eldest daughter made at the time: "Daddy, can we take these due-due birds home?" This brought a lot of chuckles from those around us.

Figure 7.47 Two seconds can make a huge difference. If I cut into this clip at 7 seconds, 15 frames in, viewers see DODO BIRDS and get the joke. If I transition in using a 2-second transition, the first complete frame viewers see is O BIRDS, and the context of the joke is lost.

Anyway, if I cut from the previous scene into this scene, the frame shown on the left of Figure 7.47, which is located at 7 seconds and 15 frames into the scene, will be the first one shown, so the viewer will understand the visual context of the remark. In contrast, if I transition from the previous scene using Studio's default 2-second transition, the first completely visible frame will be 2 seconds later, shown on the right of Figure 7.47, located at 9 seconds, 15 frames into the clip. As you can see, "DODO BIRDS" is no longer visible (extinct, so to speak), and though the audio is still there, the visual context is lost.

What this boils down to is that you need to leave sufficient frames at the front of the scene so that the target frame becomes the first visible frame after the transition. If you're using 2-second transitions or fades, this means 2 seconds before the target start frame.

Of course, the same approach applies at the end of the scene if you plan to fade out or transition into another scene. Specifically, if you're using a 2-second transition or fade, leave 2 seconds of video after the last frame to be completely visible before the transition or fade.

A similar approach is a good rule to use when shooting and capturing your video in general. Always start shooting 5 to 10 seconds before you think you actually want to start and let the camera roll for a similar duration after the end of the shot. When capturing, always start the capture a few seconds before the target first frame and continue a few seconds after the target last frame to provide the extra footage needed during editing.

Producing Videos in the Movie Window

Figure 7.48 Click the Camcorder icon to open the Clip Properties tool for video or still images.

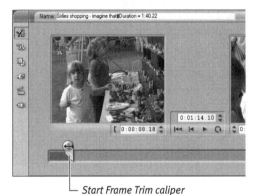

Start Frame Trim caliper

Figure 7.49 The fastest way to set the start frame is with the Start Frame Trim caliper.

Figure 7.50 Or you can use the Transport controls to find the perfect frame and click the Set Start Frame icon.

To open the Clip Properties tool:

◆ Do *one of the following*:
   ▲ Double-click the video you want to trim.
   ▲ Select a clip and click the Camcorder icon at the top left of the Movie window (**Figure 7.48**).

Studio opens the Video toolbox, which contains the Clip Properties tool. If the toolbox doesn't open to the Clip Properties tool, click the Scissors icon at the upper left of the screen to open it.

If you haven't yet trimmed the clips, the tool opens with the start frame time set to 0:00:00.00 and the end frame time set to the final frame of the clip. If you have trimmed the clip, the values will be those set in the previous session.

To set a new start frame:

◆ Do *one of the following*:
   ▲ Click the Start Frame Trim caliper and drag it to the desired start frame (**Figure 7.49**) or enter the desired start frame in the Start Frame counter either manually or via the jog controls.

   Studio immediately sets the new start frame, shifting to the left all videos placed after the edited clip to close any gaps on the Timeline.

   ▲ Move the Trim scrubber to the desired start frame by manually dragging the Trim scrubber to the desired start frame or by using the transport controls located in the center of the Clip Properties tool to play or advance the video until it reaches the frame you want. Then set the new start frame by clicking the Set Start Frame icon to the left of the Start Frame counter (**Figure 7.50**) or pressing the I (for *in*) key.

TRIMMING WITH THE CLIP PROPERTIES TOOL

173

To set a new end frame:

◆ Do *one of the following*:

▲ Drag the End Frame Trim caliper to the desired end frame (**Figure 7.51**), enter the desired end frame in the End Frame counter either manually or via the jog controls, or enter a new duration in the duration field either manually or by using the jog controls.

Studio sets the new end frame, shifting to the left all videos placed after the edited clip to close any gaps on the Timeline.

▲ Move the Trim scrubber to the desired end frame by dragging it or using the Transport controls located in the center of the Clip Properties tool. Then set the new end frame time by clicking the Set End Frame icon to the right of the End Frame counter or pressing the O (for *out*) key.

End Frame Trim caliper

Figure 7.51 To set the end frame, drag the End Frame Trim caliper to the desired shot.

✔ Tips

■ Trimming doesn't affect the actual captured video file in any way. You're not really deleting any frames; you're just telling Studio to use a different start frame and end frame when incorporating the scene into your production. For this reason, you can easily reverse your trims by clicking the Undo icon or using the steps in the preceding tasks to locate new start and end frames.

■ Once you're in the Clip Properties tool, you can select additional clips to trim by clicking them or moving the Timeline scrubber to another clip.

■ If you trim a scene that has many clips after it on the Timeline, Studio has to shift all subsequent clips to the left to eliminate any gaps on the Timeline. Depending on the project length, this process can cause perceptible delays. To avoid this, trim soon after you place individual clips on the Timeline rather than waiting until all clips are in place.

■ The Clip Properties tool edits the original audio along with the video.

Producing Videos in the Movie Window

Figure 7.52 Trimming on the Timeline is much faster than trimming using the Clip Properties tool, but it is a touch more difficult to precisely select the desired start and end frames.

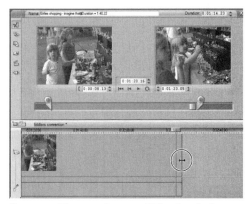

Figure 7.53 The arrow becomes bidirectional when you can edit in both directions.

Trimming a Clip on the Timeline

The Clip Properties tool lets you makes trims with the ultimate in precision. However, trimming on the Timeline is generally much quicker and provides much more interactivity with other project elements (audio, video, and so on). Most producers use both tools extensively when crafting their videos.

Trimming on the Timeline is generally easier when you're zoomed into the project and the Timescale covers a relatively short duration, since grabbing and moving the edge shifts only a few frames at a time. When long stretches of video are showing on the Timeline, grabbing and moving the edge may shift a few seconds at a time, making precise adjustments much more difficult to make. If you're going to trim on the Timeline, be sure to adjust the Timescale to a comfortable view (see "Customizing Your Timeline View" earlier in this chapter).

To trim a single video on the Timeline:

1. Select the clip you want to trim by placing the pointer on the right edge of the clip.

   The pointer becomes an arrow pointing left (**Figure 7.52**), or a bidirectional arrow if you previously trimmed the clip (**Figure 7.53**).

2. While holding down the mouse button and watching the video frames displayed in the Player, drag the arrow to the desired end frame.

3. Release the mouse button to set the trim. Studio sets the end frame to the new location.

   As soon as you shift a single frame to the left, the single arrow becomes bidirectional, signifying that you can now drag the edge both ways.

✔ Tip

- Use the same procedure to trim unwanted frames from the start of a scene. The only difference is that the cursor arrow will initially point to the right.

175

Chapter 7

Trimming Multiple Clips on the Timeline

Studio offers two approaches to trimming when two scenes are adjacent on the Timeline: the ripple edit and the rolling edit.

Performing a ripple edit is very much like trimming a single clip on the Timeline—only that clip's duration is changed. However, the effect of the trimming *ripples* through the remainder of the project to compensate for the change in the trimmed clip. For example, if you trim 2 seconds from a clip, you shorten the entire project by 2 seconds.

In contrast, in a rolling edit you trim two contiguous scenes simultaneously. As a result, the duration changes to both clips offset each other, so the overall project duration doesn't change.

Studio handles ripple editing, the program's default mode, very well, rippling not only the Video track but all other associated tracks. This ensures that titles, overlays, and sound effects remain synchronized with the underlying video.

Sometimes, however, you don't want the project duration to change each time you trim a video. For example, if you create a narration or Music track closely synchronized to a video, a series of ripple edits would likely destroy synchronization. Or if you committed to delivering exactly 2 minutes of video, ripple edits would make this difficult. For this reason, Studio supports both ripple and rolling edits. The following tasks show you how to perform each type.

Producing Videos in the Movie Window

32-minute duration

Figure 7.54 You can also trim clips within the production by dragging the edge of the clip. Note the 32-minute duration.

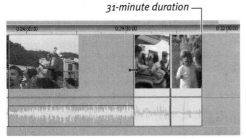

31-minute duration

Figure 7.55 The ripple trim affects all clips behind it on the Timeline, reducing duration from 32 minutes to 31 minutes in this example.

To perform a ripple edit on the Timeline:

1. Select the clip you want to trim and place the pointer over the right edge of the clip.

   The pointer becomes an arrow pointing left or, in this case, a bidirectional arrow because the clip was previously trimmed (**Figure 7.54**). The project duration is approximately 32 minutes.

2. Holding down the mouse button and watching the video frames displayed in the Player, drag the arrow to the left to shorten the clip (**Figure 7.55**) or to the right to lengthen the clip.

3. Release the mouse button.

   Studio shortens the clip. The project duration is now approximately 31 minutes, as Studio shifted all clips to the left.

To perform a rolling edit on the Timeline:

1. Pressing either the Ctrl or Shift key, select two contiguous clips.

2. Position the pointer over the connection point between the two clips.

   The pointer becomes a bidirectional arrow with a vertical line in the middle (**Figure 7.56**).

3. Drag the pointer to the desired location.

4. Release the mouse button.

   Studio shortens the first clip and extends the second clip backward to fill the gap. The overall project duration remains at approximately 30 minutes.

✔ Tips

- Rolling edits are limited to the start and end of the original scene. When Studio reaches this limit, it displays a unidirectional arrow (**Figure 7.57**).

- When performing a rolling edit, Studio displays the start frame of the second video in the Player. Ideally, you would also see the final frame of the first video, but there's no way to display both simultaneously.

- Studio can't perform a rolling edit when there's a transition between the two target clips. To perform a rolling edit, delete the transition, perform the edit, and then reinsert the transition.

Figure 7.56 Avoid messing up synchronization by using the rolling edit tool, which trims without affecting the overall video duration.

Figure 7.57 As with all video trims, your edit can't go beyond the starting or ending point of the original video.

Advanced Timeline Editing

Okay, you've worked through Timeline 101; now it's time for the advanced course. As previously mentioned, in its default state, Studio maintains synchronization of the video file and the original audio file captured with the video, and also uses global ripple edits to maintain the relative position of assets on the Timeline. This setup works well in most common editing situations, but there are times when you will want to undo both defaults. Fortunately, through the use of *locked tracks,* Studio allows just that.

When a track is locked, all assets on the track are locked, and edits that would normally affect these assets have no effect on them. Lock the Video track, for example, and you can delete the Audio track and keep the Video track. Similarly, if you lock the Title track, you can add, trim, or delete video clips, and the titles will stay in place.

Locked tracks enable some interesting edits that can add a professional touch to any production. Let's take a brief look at one of these, the insert edit, before moving on to the nuts and bolts of locking tracks and performing advanced edits.

The insert edit

An insert edit is a technique that lets you insert just the video portion of one clip into another larger clip, while using the background audio from the larger clip. It's a useful technique in a variety of circumstances. You might shoot an entire song, for instance, so that you can create a music video composed of the original video shot with the song, plus video scenes pasted in from earlier or later shots.

A good example of such a project is the first edited sequence of my Fiddler's Convention video, which I touched on in "Applying Basic Shot Composition" in Chapter 1. In this sequence, I introduce viewers to the entire spectacle of the event—from the acres of trailers and tents to the capacious grandstands with thousands of attendees watching, listening, and dancing—using the complete audio from one of the first songs I shot as the background music and video bits I shot later cut and pasted into the composite clip.

Another useful application of the insert edit is to seamlessly shorten the duration of some aspect of an event, such as the opening and closing processionals at a wedding, graduation, or other ceremony. If you use the audio you captured at a wedding ceremony during the closing processional, for example, and then trim out segments when not much is going on or when no one is on camera, you can shorten the sequence dramatically, yet still retain the highlights. And if you do your work well, no one will even notice.

Chapter 7

To lock the Audio track:

1. Drag the clip containing the background audio onto the Timeline (**Figure 7.58**).

2. At the far right of the Timeline, click the Lock the Main Audio Track button (**Figure 7.59**).

   Studio turns the lock red and dims the Audio track (**Figure 7.60**). If you attempt to select this audio track thereafter, Studio posts the error message: "Can not select clip when track is locked" (Figure 7.60).

   At this point, you can freely cut the video above the locked Audio track, and Studio won't snap the remaining video together to fill the gaps. You can paste in other video scenes, and Studio will ignore the audio associated with the pasted clip.

Figure 7.58 Here's the clip containing the Music track I'm going to use for this music video. We'll be cutting out segments of video and replacing them with other scenes shot after this video.

Figure 7.59 Click here to lock the Audio track.

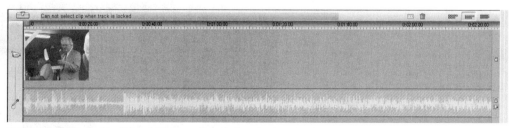

Figure 7.60 The locked audio track is gray, and the lock at the far right shines a bit red.

Producing Videos in the Movie Window

Figure 7.61 Split the clip at the first frame where you want to paste in another video scene.

Figure 7.62 Next, move the edit line to the desired end point, and split the clip again to create a section you can delete.

To insert video scenes into original video and audio:

1. Move the edit line to the target insertion point for the second video clip and split the clip by doing *one of the following*:
   ▲ Click the Razorblade icon at the top of the Movie window (Figure 7.34).
   ▲ Right-click the selected clip and choose Split Clip (Figure 7.35).
   ▲ Press the Insert key.
   Studio splits the clip into two parts (**Figure 7.61**).

2. Move the edit line to the approximate point at which the inserted clip should end and then create another split (**Figure 7.62**).

3. Hover the pointer over the segment to be replaced and delete it by doing *one of the following*:
   ▲ Press the Delete key.
   ▲ From the Studio menu, choose Edit > Delete.
   ▲ Right-click and choose Delete.
   Studio deletes the segment (**Figure 7.63**).

continues on next page

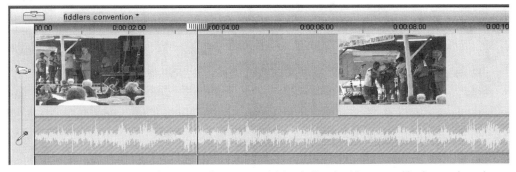

Figure 7.63 Hover the pointer over the unwanted segment and delete it. You should see a gap like the one shown here.

181

4. Drag the segment to be inserted from the Album into the gap created by the deleted segment.

   Studio inserts the segment (**Figure 7.64**).

   If the new segment is too large for the slot you created, Studio fits it into the slot. You can then use the trimming tools discussed earlier to resize all elements of the composite clip.

   If the new segment is too small for the slot you created, manually close the gap by dragging the original clip segments to the edge of the inserted scene.

5. Repeat Steps 1 through 5 until you've inserted all the clips you want in your video. When you're finished, your Timeline will look like **Figure 7.65**.

Figure 7.64 Now drag in the desired segment.

Figure 7.65 Here's my opening music video, which runs for approximately 2 minutes and 10 seconds and contains 17 different scenes, which amounts to a scene change every 8 seconds.

✔ Tips

- I use this insert technique to hide bad camera moments, such as when I'm moving the camera from subject to subject, or zooming in and out to frame a shot. It's generally easiest for me to go through the clip, excise all the bad camera spots, and then fill these gaps with other video scenes.

- If you plan on doing this type of cutting and pasting, it really pays to annotate your clips when you bring them into the Edit window. (see "Working with Scene Comments" in Chapter 6). Annotating allows you to work much more efficiently by allowing you to quickly identify the scenes you want to insert.

- To make your music video look good, all the parts of the original video clip you retain must remain synchronized with the background audio. This isn't really relevant with the dancing and clapping scenes you insert, since there's almost no way to tell if they're synchronized or not, at least with foot stomping country music or most other fast dancing. However, if the singer's lips are moving and the voice isn't playing, you've got a problem.

  Note that once you lock the Audio track, Studio will let you move the video track above it, and if you do, you may lose synchronicity. So be mindful of this when you're cutting, pasting and trimming, and remember never to *move* the original video.

- To insert audio in the Audio track, you follow the same procedure, except that you need to first lock the Video track and then cut the audio track. Of course, you can also drag the intended audio insertion to either of the other tracks and then mute the Audio track (see "Using the Volume Tool" in Chapter 11).

- You can easily insert a still image into a video clip: just drag the image to the Title track and resize it (see "To change the duration of a still image on the Timeline" later in this chapter).

- You can lock any track or combination of tracks except the Menu track, which appears when you're creating DVD menus.

- Get in the habit of unlocking tracks immediately after performing any edits that require locked tracks. Otherwise, when you try to select a clip track later, nothing will happen, and you'll see the error message shown in Figure 7.60.

To shorten a wedding processional:

1. Load the video clip that contains the processional.
2. Lock the Audio track (see "To lock the Audio track" earlier in this section).

   The clip should appear as in **Figure 7.66**.

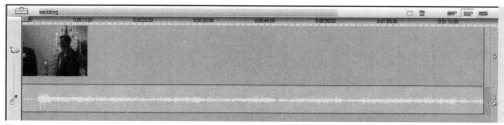

Figure 7.66 Here's the scene containing the entire processional I want to transparently condense. I've already locked the Audio track.

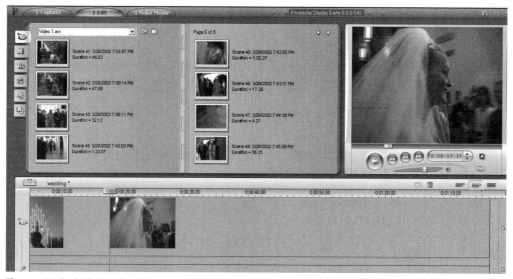

Figure 7.67 The bride has already walked by me, so most likely it's time to delete some video. Start by splitting the clip after the first group has walked by.

3. Move the edit line to the end of the first sequence and split the clip by doing *one of the following*:
   ▲ Click the Razorblade icon at the top of the Movie window (Figure 7.34).
   ▲ Right-click the selected clip and choose Split Clip (Figure 7.35).
   ▲ Press the Insert key.

   Studio splits the clip into two parts (**Figure 7.67**). As you can see in the Player at the upper right, the bride and groom have walked past the camera. Now it's time to find a starting point for the next group to walk back up the aisle.

4. Drag the starting point of the second clip to the first frame of the next group to come down the aisle (**Figure 7.68**).

5. Drag the entire second clip to the left until it abuts the initial clip (**Figure 7.69**).

continues on next page

Figure 7.68 No use watching the ushers walk back down the aisle to retrieve another batch of guests. Delete this footage by clicking the second clip and dragging the clip to the start of the next group to walk back up the aisle.

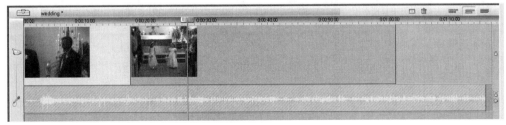

Figure 7.69 Then drag the second clip to abut the first.

Chapter 7

6. Repeat Steps 3, 4, and 5 for each group in the processional. At the end of the exercise, your Timeline should look like **Figure 7.70**.

   This example shaved almost a minute off the sequence, and the trick is totally transparent to the viewer.

7. Unlock the Audio clip.

8. Move the edit line to the end of the video and split the audio clip using one of the techniques discussed in Step 3.

   Studio splits the audio clip (**Figure 7.71**).

9. Select and delete the second (unneeded) audio clip.

   For details, see "To delete assets" earlier in this chapter.

Figure 7.70 Repeat as necessary. Here I shaved almost a minute off the viewing time, and no one in the audience will notice a thing because the audio is continuous.

Figure 7.71 Now split the audio clip and delete the excess.

Producing split edits

Split edits are transitions in which the audio and video start playing at different times. There are two basic types of split edits: L-cuts and J-cuts.

In an *L-cut*, the audio from the first video continues while the second video starts playing. The classic use is in newscasts, when the video switches from the anchor to a reporter on the scene. To make the transition feel seamless, the audio of the anchor asking a question continues to play while the video switches to a field reporter, usually nodding sagely to acknowledge the wisdom of the question. In the task that follows, I've used an L-cut to transition from a sequence where Whatley is talking about her gymnastics meet to the scene where she arrives at the gym. Viewers hear Whatley talking for about 10 seconds while she's walking into the building.

In a *J-cut*, the audio from the second video precedes the appearance of the actual frames. In the J-cut task that follows, I've maintained the camera on my wife while the audio from the grand entrance of the gymnasts starts, to presage the entrance. Though all this may sound complicated, Studio makes short work of both kinds of edits.

Figure 7.72 To create an L-cut, trim the first video back to the last video frame that you want to appear.

To create an L-cut:

1. Load two clips onto the Timeline and select the first clip.

2. Hover the pointer over the connection point between the two clips.

    The pointer becomes an arrow pointing left, or a bidirectional arrow if you previously trimmed the clip.

3. Holding down the mouse button and watching the video frames displayed in the Player, drag the arrow to the left until you reach the last frame to be displayed (**Figure 7.72**).

continues on next page

4. Hover the pointer over the Camcorder icon on the Video track and then click the Camcorder button to lock the Video track.

5. Use the pointer to select the Audio track from the first clip.

6. Hover the pointer over the connection line between the two clips, being careful to avoid the blue horizontal line (which is the Volume control) in the middle of the audio clips.

    Hovering the pointer over the line converts the pointer to a Speaker icon, which will change the volume—something you don't want to do here (**Figure 7.73**).

    The pointer becomes a bidirectional arrow (**Figure 7.74**).

7. Drag the audio file to the right, to the desired starting point from the second clip.

    Studio extends the audio from the first clip under the video to the second clip, forming the namesake *L* appearance (**Figure 7.75**).

✔ Tip

- If, during Step 6, you accidentally click the blue horizontal Volume control, you may inadvertently adjust the track volume. If so, you'll see a small blue dot in the middle of the line. You can undo this volume change by choosing Undo from the Edit menu or by clicking the Undo button at the upper right or by pressing Ctrl+Z.

    If you've already performed some additional edits that you don't want to undo, you can click the blue dot (the pointer becomes a Speaker icon when placed over the Audio track) and drag it straight down, thus deleting the dot.

Figure 7.73 When dragging the audio track, select anywhere but the middle line, which is the Volume control that produces a Speaker icon.

Figure 7.74 To drag the audio to the right, select the audio at the connection line, converting the pointer to a bidirectional arrow.

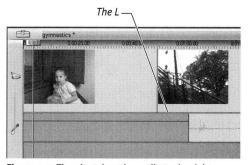

Figure 7.75 Then just drag the audio to the right, creating the *L* pattern.

Producing Videos in the Movie Window

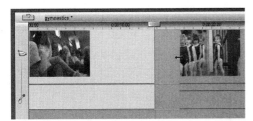

Figure 7.76 Drag the second clip to the first frame to be displayed after the video cut.

Figure 7.77 Lock the main Video track.

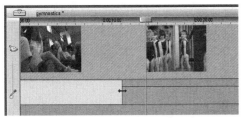

Figure 7.78 Drag the audio from the second clip to the first. Now the audience will hear the prefatory music before they actually see my daughter appear.

To create a J-cut:

1. Load two clips on the Timeline.

2. Click the second scene. While watching the Player window, drag the second clip to the first target frame to be displayed after the cut (**Figure 7.76**).

   In Figure 7.76, the first target frame to be displayed in the second clip is the shot where my daughter first appeared in the gym (she's the girl on the far right who's about to make the turn). Once the tracks are locked, I'll drag the audio I just trimmed under the first clip, a process similar to the one described in Steps 6 and 7 of the previous task.

3. Click the lock at the far right of the Video track to lock the track (**Figure 7.77**).

4. Hover the pointer over the connection line between the two clips.

   The pointer becomes a bidirectional arrow.

5. Drag the audio file to the left, to the desired starting point within the first clip.

   Studio extends the audio from the second clip to the desired position under the video track of the first clip, forming the namesake *J* appearance (**Figure 7.78**).

ADVANCED TIMELINE EDITING

189

Chapter 7

Working with Still Images

Studio handles still images in two completely different ways, depending on where you drop the file. Drop an image in the Title track, and it can serve as the background for a DVD menu or contain a logo or watermark to blend into the Video track. Drop an image into the Video track, and it can serve as the foreground video, usually in the form of a slideshow. We deal with the latter scenario in this section.

When you drop images into the Video track, Studio treats the image files almost the same way as it treats video files, except that there are no duration limits or associated audio files. Accordingly, all the techniques described in the previous sections for getting videos into the Movie window, moving them around, trimming them on the Timeline, and splitting and deleting them apply equally to still images. There are just a couple of differences to note.

First, you set the default duration for all images inserted into your projects in the Pinnacle Studio Setup Options box, using a process described in "Setting Default Durations" in Chapter 2. This section also explains two ways to modify the default duration and how to create a slideshow.

Studio 9 also has two mechanisms for adding motion to still images in what's generally referred to as the Ken Burns effect (a term that surfaced after filmmaker Ken Burns created *The Civil War* and *Baseball* entirely out of still images). This effect is detailed in "Adding Motion to Still Images," in Chapter 9.

190

To change the duration of a still image on the Timeline:

1. Do *one of the following:*

   ▲ Trim the still image on the Timeline using the same techniques as for trimming video files, described in "Trimming a Clip on the Timeline" earlier in this chapter.

   ▲ Launch the Clip Properties tool by selecting the still image with the pointer and clicking the Camcorder icon at the top left of the Movie window (Figure 7.47).

   Studio opens the Video toolbox.

   If you don't see the Clip Properties tool, click the Scissors icon at the upper left of the screen to open it.

2. At the upper right of the tool, adjust the duration by typing a new value in the Duration field or by using the jog controls at the right (**Figure 7.79**).

Figure 7.79 You can change the duration of a still-image file.

To create a slideshow:

1. Start with the Movie window in Storyboard view and the Album window open to the Still Images tab.

2. Do *one of the following:*

   ▲ Drag images one by one onto the Storyboard.

   ▲ To select all images on the Still Images tab and drag them to the Storyboard, choose Edit > Select All from the Studio menu or press Ctrl+A.

   ▲ To select multiple sequential images, click the first image, hold down the Shift key, and click the final image.

   ▲ To load multiple nonsequential images, click the first image, hold down the Ctrl key, and click additional target images (**Figure 7.80**).

   ▲ To select groups of images, click any gray area in the Album and drag over the target images.

   Once your images are on the Storyboard, add, delete, and arrange them as desired via drag and drop (see "To arrange assets in Storyboard view" earlier in this chapter).

✔ Tip

- For the ultimate in professional-looking slideshows, learn how to add motion to your images in "Adding Motion to Still Images" in Chapter 9 and how to insert a ripple transition between images in "Ripple Transitions for Slide Shows" in Chapter 8.

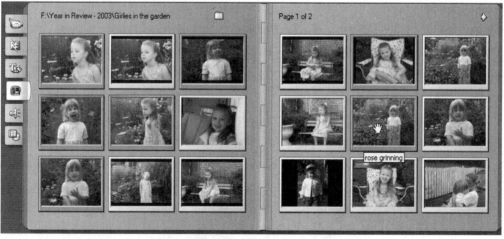

Figure 7.80 Hold down the Ctrl key to select still images that are out of order.

Working with Audio Files

Studio includes many different methods to capture and integrate audio into your production. Whether you're ripping music from a CD, adding a narration track, or creating background music from SmartSound, Studio places the results directly on the Timeline for you—no muss, no fuss. (These activities are covered in Chapter 11.) On the other hand, if you're using audio files you previously produced, you'll have to import them into the Album (see "Working on the Sound Effects Tab" in Chapter 6) and then get them to the Timeline.

Studio treats audio files almost identically to video files and still images, with exceptions noted in the sidebar, "Tracking the Audio Tracks" later in this chapter. Otherwise, all of the techniques described earlier for getting videos into the Movie window, moving them around, trimming them on the Timeline, and splitting and deleting them apply to audio files.

This section takes a quick look at the Audio Clip Properties tool, demonstrates how to load only the Audio track from a captured video file into a project, and describes where to drag your audio files (see the sidebar "Tracking the Audio Tracks" later in this chapter).

To change the duration of an audio file on the Timeline:

1. Do *one of the following*:

   ▲ Trim the audio file on the Timeline using the same techniques as for trimming video files, described in "Trimming a Clip on the Timeline" earlier in this chapter.

   ▲ Launch the Clip Properties tool by selecting the audio file and clicking the Speaker icon at the top left of the Movie window (**Figure 7.81**).

   Studio opens the Audio toolbox.

   If you don't see the Audio Clip Properties tool, click the Scissors icon at the upper left of the screen to open it.

2. To adjust the start and end points of the audio file, use the controls described in "Trimming with the Clip Properties Tool" earlier in this chapter (Figure 7.46).

   Note in particular that most CDs have several seconds of blank space at the end of each clip. To avoid this gap in your production, trim this space as shown in **Figure 7.82**.

Figure 7.81 Click here to open the Audio Clip Properties tool.

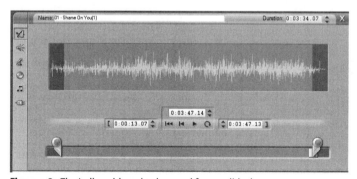

Figure 7.82 The Indigo girls as background for my slideshow.

To add only the audio from a video file:

- From the Video Scenes tab in the Album window, drag a video file to either the Sound Effect track or the Music track.

  Studio inserts only the audio from the video file. See Chapter 11 for more on audio.

✔ Tip

- Studio lets you drag an audio file into a clip in the Storyboard and Text views. However, since there is no indicator of duration, results are unpredictable, so you should work with audio in Timeline view.

Tracking the Audio Tracks

Here are some rules of the road for Studio's audio tracks. (See Chapter 11 for much more on audio.)

- To add an audio file to your production, drag it to either the Sound Effect track or the Music track.

  Be careful, however, if you intend to use Studio's narration recording, CD-ripping, or SmartSound Music track features, because they require that a specific track be open for the files they produce. For narration recording, the Sound Effect track must be open; for CD-ripping and SmartSound, the Music track must be open. So if you drag an audio file onto the Sound Effect track, for example, you won't be able to record a narration track for that segment.

- To add the audio track from a captured video file to your production—without the video—drag it to either the Sound Effect track or the Music track.

- Studio prevents you from adding an audio file to the Audio track if the audio is present. However, if you delete the audio clip by locking the video track and deleting the audio, Studio lets you add audio to that track as well.

- Studio lets you place audio files anywhere in a production, even if it creates a gap in the playback audio. Be careful to avoid these unintended gaps when you place audio files.

- If you drag one audio file into another, Studio always trims the clip you're dragging. This makes it easy to accidentally truncate a clip by dragging it into another clip. (With video files, dragging doesn't trim a clip at all; you have to activate the trim handles.)

8

USING TRANSITIONS

Transitions are effects placed between video clips to help smooth the movement from one scene to another. We've all seen transitions, even if we don't recognize them by that name. In movies, for example, when the screen fades to black at the end of a dramatic scene and then fades back in from black to the next scene, the filmmaker is using a *fade* transition. When two scenes blend together for a moment before the second scene appears clearly, the filmmaker is using a *dissolve* transition.

On *Monday Night Football,* when the halftime stats swing back, down, and under, revealing Al and John, that's a transition, too. However, in most film and television productions, the most frequent transition is a *cut,* which is actually the absence of a transition, or the instantaneous jump from the last frame of the first clip to the first frame of the second clip.

Studio 9 provides three transition collections: Standard Transitions, Alpha Magic, and Hollywood FX for Studio. This chapter describes each group, discusses when to use them, and then explains how to apply and customize them. We'll conclude with a detailed look at some of the advanced transitions available if you upgrade to higher-level versions of Hollywood FX.

Looking in the Box

You access the three transition groups from the Transitions tab of the Album, opened by clicking the Lightning Bolt icon on the left panel of the Album (**Figure 8.1**). In defining how these transitions work, I'll call the first video Video A, and the second, Video B.

Standard Transitions: As you would expect, the Standard Transitions group includes the common transitions used in most video editing. In addition to the dissolves and fades already mentioned, the Standard group includes the following types of transitions:

- *Wipes:* Both Videos A and B remain fixed while an effect hides Video A and reveals Video B. Imagine you're pulling down a shade between two videos. With a wipe, both videos would remain static, and the shade simply hides Video A and reveals Video B. On Studio's Transitions tab, any transition with an arrow that appears to be pulling Video B over Video A, with the arrow visible in both videos, is a wipe.

- *Slides:* Video B slides in over Video A. With the shade example, Video B would be playing on the shade and slowly appear, bottom first, as you pulled the shade down. As with a wipe, Video A remains static and is simply covered up by Video B. On Studio's Transitions tab, any transition with an arrow that appears to be pushing Video B over Video A, with the arrow contained completely in Video A, is a slide.

- *Pushes:* Video B pushes Video A off the screen. If you were pulling down a shade between two videos, Video B would push Video A down, very much like a slide, except that Video A doesn't get covered up; it gets pushed off the screen. On Studio's Transitions tab, any transition with two arrows moving in the same direction is a push.

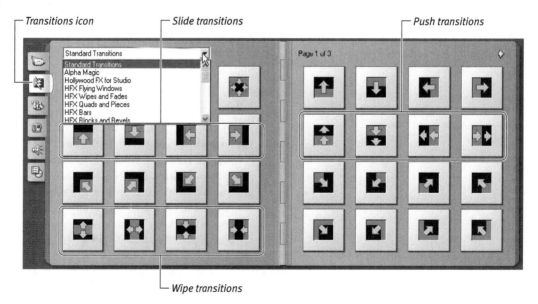

Figure 8.1 You access the Transitions tab by clicking the Lightning Bolt icon. Note how Studio differentiates Push, Slide, and Wipe transitions in the Standard Transitions group.

Using Transitions

Figure 8.2 The word PRO is a watermark and will show up in your transition unless you upgrade to Hollywood FX Mega.

Figure 8.3 Hover your mouse over the Hollywood FX transitions and you can see which version of Hollywood FX you need to use the transition sans watermark.

The Standard Transitions collection includes many other transitions not characterized in these three major groups, so you should definitely explore what else is there. Just click the white arrows at the top of each page to navigate to the next page.

Alpha Magic: Technically, Alpha Magic transitions are wipes that use organic forms as masks to create the effect. In plain English, they're generally more artistic than the standard transitions and often more whimsical.

Hollywood FX: All transitions in the Hollywood FX for Studio collection are yours to use as you wish. However, most transitions in the Hollywood FX collections below this are watermarked, so you can use them, but the annoying watermark will appear in your video unless you purchase upgrades to either Hollywood FX Plus or Mega at www.pinnaclesys.com. For example, the PRO shown in **Figure 8.2** is a watermark.

Pinnacle includes the required version of Hollywood FX in the name, so if you hover your mouse over a transition, you can see if it's a BAS transition (included with Studio), a PLS transition (in the FX Plus collection), or a PRO or MEGA transition (in the FX Mega collection; **Figure 8.3**). Note that Pinnacle changed the name of Hollywood FX Pro to Hollywood FX Mega, and that many Mega transitions are still designated PRO.

✔ Tip

- To see how a transition looks, click it and it will play in the Player window.

Understanding Transitions

As you'll see, using and customizing transitions is easy. Using them effectively is also easy, if you keep three simple concepts in mind.

A little goes a long way

Recognize that you don't have to insert a transition between every two scenes on the timeline. Rather, use a transition only when it highlights a change in place or time that you want the viewer to perceive.

For example, if you're shooting your child's birthday party, you may have a bunch of shots in the dining room: kids eating, shouting, and blowing their horns; parents watching and smiling; and Uncle Ernie discreetly grabbing his third piece of chocolate cake. When you edit these clips, you should simply cut from clip to clip—sans transitions—because they all occur at the same place in time. However, the next major scene is opening presents in the living room. When you move from the dining room to the living room, there is a change in place and time, so a transition is appropriate.

Like meets like

All your transitions should match the extent of change in place and time. For example, when you move from the dining room to the living room, the change is pretty minor. Here you might use a dissolve, or a simple motivated transition, discussed later in this chapter. But you shouldn't fade to black and then fade back in to the dining room scene because a fade to black suggests a very significant change in place and time. However, if the entire birthday party sequence, from start to finish, was part of a longer video, you might fade to black at the end of the party and then fade in from black at the next major scene: Thanksgiving or that trip to Disneyland.

KISS or motivate

Transitions should either be motivated or kept very simple. When I say motivated, I mean a transition that relates to the content of the video or one that moves the viewer from one scene to the next with particular aplomb. This final concept is probably the most difficult to accept, especially if you've been eagerly eyeing Studio's capacious quantity of transitions.

Motivated transitions go a long way toward engaging the audience, and they add a lovely professional touch. For example, in "Hollywood FX Exposed" later in this chapter, I used a snowflake transition between songs at a Holiday concert. I used a transition to help the viewer understand that a different performer was coming on stage, and the snowy transition was motivated by the season and event.

Similarly, I used a golf-tee transition at a golf outing to separate clips from the end of one hole to the start of another. I used a bottle-of-bubbly transition between the wedding ceremony and wedding reception.

Had I not had these motivated Hollywood FX transitions, I would have used a simple fade or dissolve instead. That's because random, complicated transitions that don't relate to the content of the videos confuse and possibly irritate the viewer.

This is the primary reason that I'm such a fan of Hollywood FX: because it allows me to add a fun and professional touch to my videos. Pinnacle offers some alluring transitions in the Basic pack, which is freely accessible to Studio 9 users, and in the free Extra pack you get for registering your copy of Studio with Pinnacle. However, as you'd expect, Pinnacle saves the best Hollywood FX transitions for the optional Plus and Mega upgrades. In addition to the extra transitions, the Plus upgrade offers extensive customization options, and the Mega upgrade lets you customize transitions and even build your transitions from scratch.

If you find yourself using lots of transitions, explore the Hollywood FX samples and consider upgrading to either the Plus or Mega versions.

Using Transitions

The next few pages cover the basics of transitions. Once you've mastered these, you'll be ready to move on to the subsequent sections that illuminate advanced topics: customizing transitions, working with Hollywood FX transitions, and using ripple transitions for slide shows.

To set the default transition duration:

1. Choose Setup > Edit to open the Studio Setup Options screen to the Edit tab (**Figure 8.4**).

2. Change the Transitions default duration value to the desired setting by doing *one of the following*:
   ▲ Use the jog controls (up and down triangles) to the right of the duration.
   ▲ Click the duration to make it editable and directly enter the desired setting.

3. Click OK to close the dialog box.

To identify and preview a transition effect in the Album:

1. If you're at a different panel, click the Lightning Bolt icon in Edit mode to open the Transitions tab in the Album (Figure 8.1).

2. Hover the pointer over the transition to preview it.

   Studio displays the transition name in a tooltip (**Figure 8.5**).

3. Click the transition to preview it in the Player.

   In the preview, A represents the first clip, and B represents the second clip. In Figure 8.5 you can see the heart-shaped transition, with Video B opening up into Video A. For use only for weddings and on Valentine's Day, please.

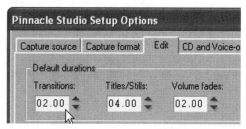

Figure 8.4 Here's where you change the default transition duration.

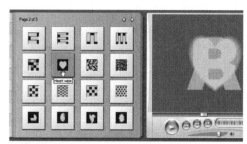

Figure 8.5 Hover your mouse over a transition, and Studio tells you its name; click it, and Studio plays it in the Player. Note the Video A/Video B nomenclature in the Player.

Using Transitions

Figure 8.6 To use a transition in a production, just drag it and drop it at the desired spot, aided by Studio's visual cues.

Figure 8.7 There you go, fading into a clip.

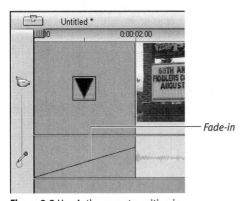

Figure 8.8 Here's the same transition in Timeline view. Note that Studio fades in the audio, too, saving you some work.

To fade into or out of a clip:

1. With at least one clip in the Movie window, drag a fade transition into the Timeline or Storyboard in front of the first clip (to fade in) or behind the last clip (to fade out).

   Studio displays a green box on the Storyboard (**Figure 8.6**) or two vertical green lines on the Timeline whenever you roll over a location where you can apply the effect. You'll also see a small transparent box and plus sign under the pointer.

2. Release the mouse button.

   Studio inserts the fade effect (**Figure 8.7**).

✔ Tips

- You can apply transitions in any Movie window, though the Storyboard and Timeline views are probably most appropriate. **Figure 8.8** shows the fade transition shown in Figure 8.7 in the Timeline view.

- Studio also fades in the audio component when it applies a fade effect. This can be a great convenience, but if you want to do something different with your audio, you can find more detailed information in Chapter 11.

203

To insert a transition between two clips:

1. With at least two clips in the Movie window, drag any transition between any two clips.

   Studio displays a green box on the Storyboard or two vertical green lines on the Timeline whenever you roll over a location where you can apply the effect. Studio also adds a small transparent box and plus sign to the pointer (**Figure 8.9**).

2. Release the mouse button.
   Studio inserts the transition (**Figure 8.10**).

Figure 8.9 When you drag a transition between two clips, a box and a plus sign let you know where you can safely drop the transition.

✔ Tips

- Whenever Studio inserts a transition between two clips, it also inserts a cross-fade between the two audio clips, simultaneously reducing the volume on the first clip from 100 percent to 0 percent and boosting the volume on the second clip from 0 percent to 100 percent. These changes are reflected on the Audio track (**Figure 8.11**). This behavior is appropriate, since most transitions help you move smoothly from one scene to another, and the audio treatment should follow that of the video. However, if you want to reverse this effect and customize your audio treatment, see Chapter 11 for instructions.

- The only exception to Studio's audio cross-fade approach occurs during the fade transition, where Studio fades the scene completely to black (or white) before starting to show the second scene. Here, Studio also fades out the old audio completely to zero before boosting audio on the second track (see Figure 8.20). This behavior is appropriate given that fades are generally used to emphasize the ending of one scene and the beginning of another.

Figure 8.10 The completed dissolve transition.

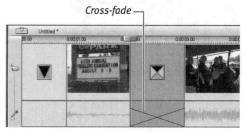

Figure 8.11 The same transition in Timeline view. Note the automatic audio cross-fade.

Using Transitions

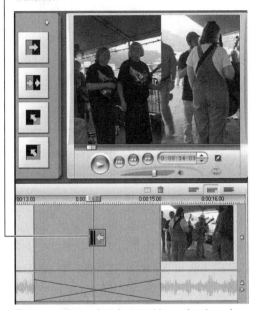

Figure 8.12 To preview the transition, select it on the Timeline and click Play.

Figure 8.13 Inserting a fade into a title uses the same basic technique as for video clips: drag the transition, drop it, move on to the next edit.

Figure 8.14 The completed fade.

To preview a Standard or Alpha Magic transition:

1. Click the transition to make it active (**Figure 8.12**).

2. To start the preview, click the Play button in the Player (or press the spacebar or L).

✔ Tip

- Virtually all Standard and Alpha Magic transitions preview in real time, playing both audio and video, so you can immediately determine whether you like the effect. The Hollywood FX transitions are more complicated; many require rendering (see "Working with Hollywood FX Transitions" later in this chapter).

To fade into or out of a title or other element on the Title track:

1. With at least one title or other element on the Title track, drag a fade transition in front of the target (to fade in) or behind the target (to fade out).

   Studio displays a green box on the Storyboard or two vertical green lines on the Timeline whenever you roll over a location where you can apply the effect. Studio also adds a small transparent box and a plus sign to the pointer (**Figure 8.13**).

2. Release the mouse button.

   Studio inserts the fade effect (**Figure 8.14**).

   continues on next page

✔ Tips

- You preview a fade-in on the Title track in the same way you preview effects dragged to the Video track.

- You can also apply a transition between titles or other elements on the Title track, as shown in **Figure 8.15**. The process is identical to that for inserting a transition between two clips on the Video track.

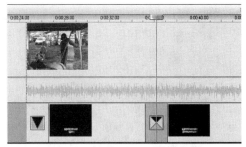

Figure 8.15 You can also insert transitions between titles and other images on the overlay track following the same basic instructions as for video clips.

To change transitions on the Video or Title track:

1. Drag another transition on top of the existing transition.

   Studio shows the same green box or lines and the cursor with the box and plus sign (**Figure 8.16**).

2. Release the mouse button.

   Studio replaces the previous effect, and you're ready to preview (**Figure 8.17**).

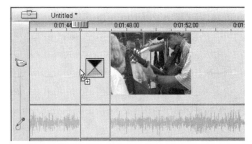

Figure 8.16 To use a different transition, simply drag it and drop it over the old transition.

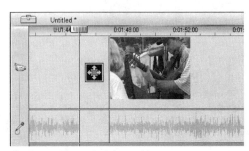

Figure 8.17 The replaced transition.

Transition Timing

Quick question: If you set your default transition time to 2 seconds, how many seconds of video does your transition take? Well, if you guessed 2 or 4, you're right (I'm trying to make this book a positive experience)—but only part of the time (sorry).

The obvious answer is 2, since the transition should take 2 linear, real-time seconds to play. That's true for every transition except fade transitions, where Studio fades out for 2 seconds and then in for 2 seconds. In that case, the total transition time is 4 seconds.

For example, **Figure 8.18** shows two clips, each 6 seconds long, totaling 12 seconds. Then a 2-second dissolve is added between the two clips (**Figure 8.19**). However, if a fade is added, the entire transition takes 4 seconds: 2 seconds to fade out, and 2 to fade in (**Figure 8.20**).

What's also intriguing about Figure 8.19 is that the transition starts at the 4-second point in the first clip, and also that somehow the overall clip is shortened from 12 to 10 seconds (this didn't occur with the fade transition).

continues on next page

Figure 8.18 Two clips, 6 seconds each, 12 seconds total.

Figure 8.19 Insert a 2-second dissolve, and we're down to 10 seconds. Hey, what happened? See Figure 8.21.

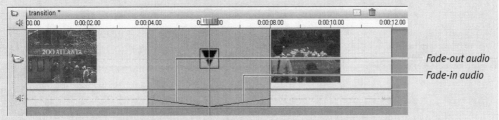

Fade-out audio
Fade-in audio

Figure 8.20 Insert the cross-fade, and the transition takes 4 seconds, though the default duration is 2. Hey, at least the movie is still 12 seconds. Note the complete audio fade-out before the audio fades back in.

Transition Timing *continued*

What happened? To show you, I loaded the same clips into Adobe Premiere, which offers what's called an A/B editing view that shows both the clips on the Timeline and the transition (**Figure 8.21**). (This transition works the same in Premiere as in Studio; it's just presented differently in the Timeline.)

This screen shot reveals that during the 2-second dissolve transition, Studio uses the last 2 seconds of the first clip and the first 2 seconds of the second clip. Since segments from both clips are being used simultaneously, this shortens the video from 12 to 10 seconds.

In contrast, the fade transition—since it doesn't use simultaneous portions of the two clips—allows the clip to stay at 12 seconds (**Figure 8.22**). Obviously, if you used a cut, or no transition between the clips, there would be no overlap at all, and the video would still be 12 seconds long.

Beyond the riddles, what are some practical ways to apply this information?

First, if you plan on using transitions other than cuts, be sure to trim your clips accordingly, leaving the planned durations of your transitions and fades at the beginning and end of each affected clip.

Second, if you're planning on a tight narration or Music track, remember that two 6-second clips don't add up to 12 seconds of video if you have a 2-second dissolve between them. Though it's possible to do the math and compute the duration and precise starting points of each clip, it's generally easier to get the video lined up exactly the way you want it and then produce your audio.

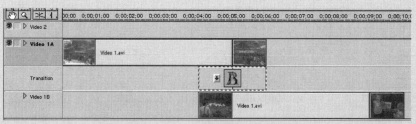

Figure 8.21 A screen shot from Adobe Premiere tells the story. The 2-second dissolve transition overlaps 2 seconds in each video, which is why the video is shorter overall.

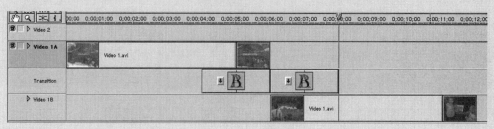

Figure 8.22 The clip isn't shortened with the fade-out and then fade-in, since there is no overlap.

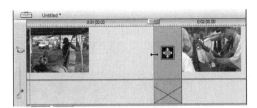

Figure 8.23 The easiest and most visual way to modify transition duration is to use the Timeline, where you can see the key frames in the two affected videos.

Customizing Transitions

Unless you upgrade to Hollywood FX Plus or Mega, Studio allows you to customize only two aspects of a transition: duration and direction.

This section explains how you can change the duration of a transition by dragging the transition to the desired length on the Timeline or by using the Clip Properties tool. It also explains how to reverse the direction of the effect, which can only be done using the Clip Properties tool.

To edit transition duration on the Timeline:

1. Select the target transition and place the pointer over either edge.

   The pointer becomes a bidirectional arrow (**Figure 8.23**).

2. Holding down the mouse button and watching the video frames displayed in the Player, drag the transition to the desired duration.

3. Release the mouse button to set the new duration.

✔ Tip

- If you drag the transition to the right, the Player shows the *first* frame of the second clip that will appear after the transition finishes. If you drag it to the left, the Player shows the *last* frame in the first clip that will appear before the transition starts. This is a great way to fine-tune the starting and ending points of your transition.

Chapter 8

To edit transition duration in the Clip Properties tool:

1. Open the Transitions Clip Properties tool by doing *one of the following*:

   ▲ Double-click the target transition (or right-click it and select Clip Properties from the menu that appears).

   ▲ Select the target transition and then click the Video Toolbox icon at the top left of the Movie window (**Figure 8.24**).

   The Video toolbox opens to the Clip Properties tool for transitions (**Figure 8.25**).

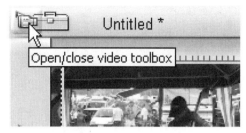

Figure 8.24 You can also open the Video toolbox and use the Clip Properties tool to modify duration.

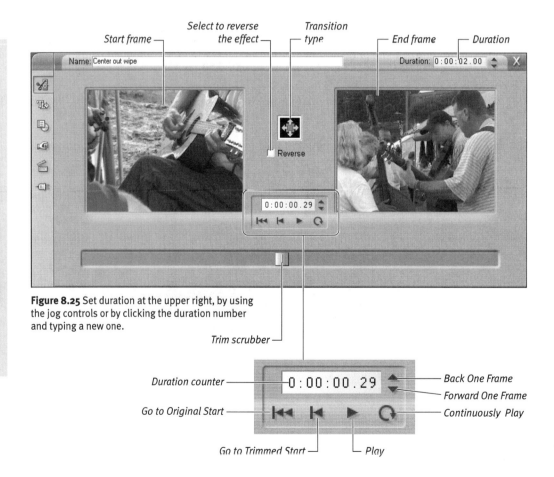

Figure 8.25 Set duration at the upper right, by using the jog controls or by clicking the duration number and typing a new one.

Using Transitions

Figure 8.26 Checking the Reverse box reverses the effect you applied. In this case, Studio converts the selected effect, the center-out wipe, to an outside-to-center wipe.

2. At the upper right, change the duration value to the desired setting by doing *one of the following*:
   ▲ Use the jog controls to the right of the duration.
   ▲ Click the duration to make it editable and directly enter the desired setting.

3. Use the transport controls in the middle of the window to preview the transition.

4. Close the Video toolbox by clicking the X in the upper-right corner or by reclicking the Video Toolbox icon you used to open the window (Figure 8.24).

✔ Tip

- The Video toolbox is great when you want precise transition times, but the Timeline is more helpful when you're making artistic decisions, because it gives you a much better visual representation.

To reverse a transition effect:

◆ In the Transitions Clip Properties tool, click the Reverse check box (**Figure 8.26**). Studio reverses the transition effect.

✔ Tips

- A good example of a transition that's significantly affected by reversal is the "Open curtain" transition, located at the top and on the left of page 2 of the Alpha Magic Transitions album. I often open a movie with that transition in the normal direction (opening the curtain), and at the end of the movie I reverse it to close the curtains.

- If you encounter a Reverse check box that's dimmed for a particular transition, look for a transition in the library that performs the reverse of the selected transition.

Chapter 8

Working with Hollywood FX Transitions

Most Standard and Alpha Magic transitions are fairly simple. That's why you can get real-time previews on fairly old computers.

However, Hollywood FX transitions, even some of the free ones, are much more complex, so Studio can't process them in real time. This makes it hard for you to see how the transition will really look in your final production.

Fortunately, Studio offers several options to provide real-time previews. First, depending on the graphics card in your computer, you can enable what Studio calls hardware acceleration to view the effect—in essence, Studio sends the transition to the graphics card and says, "Here, you render this thing and display it."

If you have a reasonably current graphics card in your computer and the latest drivers, this hardware acceleration should boost performance to real time. For example, on the desktop computer I'm using right now, I have a hot card from NVIDIA that accelerates everything Studio can throw at it in real time. On my laptop, however, which has no three-dimensional capabilities, enabling hardware acceleration has no positive impact, and in fact makes the system a bit less stable.

In that case, I use the other option, rendering the transition as a background task (see the sidebar "About Background Rendering" later in this chapter for a discussion of your choices). With background rendering, Studio renders the actual frames that make up the transition and stores them in a separate file. Although the process takes a few moments, while Studio is rendering I can still be editing elsewhere in the production, and when it's done I can view my transition in real time.

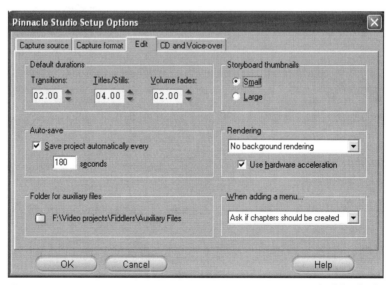

Figure 8.27 Select hardware acceleration and background rendering on the Edit tab of the Studio Setup Options screen

Using Transitions

Figure 8.28 Heed this warning. If your system starts crashing after you enable hardware acceleration, go back and disable it. It should work with most current graphics cards, especially if the drivers are current.

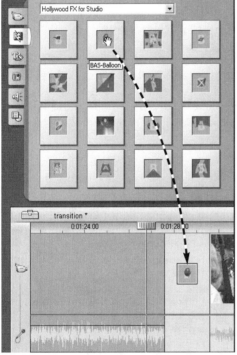

Figure 8.29 Hardware acceleration works only with Hollywood FX transitions like the Balloon transition selected here.

Here's how to set the two options, plus some caveats. Start by saving your project file (see "Saving Your Projects" in Chapter 2).

To enable hardware acceleration:

1. From the Studio menu, choose Setup > Edit.

   The Studio Setup Options screen appears, open to the Edit tab (**Figure 8.27**).

2. In the Rendering box on the right, select Use Hardware Acceleration (or press Alt+H).

   Studio displays a warning (**Figure 8.28**).

   Operation can get unstable if your graphics card doesn't support this operation, so again, before you experiment, be sure to save your project file.

3. Close the warning window by clicking OK.

4. Close the Studio Setup Options dialog box by clicking OK.

5. From the drop-down menu on the Transitions tab of the Album, select the Hollywood FX for Studio transition group (**Figure 8.29**).

6. Drag a transition down to the location where you want it within the clips.

   I'm using the Balloon transition, but background rendering works similarly with all Hollywood FX transitions.

7. Preview the transition by clicking Play in the Player (or pressing the spacebar or L).

   If the transition plays in real time, it's likely that your graphics hardware is compatible with Studio, and you should stay in this mode.

   If the transition stops and starts like your car on a cold morning, your graphics card is not compatible with Studio, and you should return to the Studio Setup Options screen as described in Step 1 and disable Use Hardware Acceleration.

About Background Rendering

Studio is a nondestructive editor, which means that it leaves all captured or imported files untouched and implements your edits by producing a completely new file. This process is called rendering, and depending upon project duration, complexity, and the speed of your computer, rendering can take quite a long time.

When you render at the end of a project, it's a *foreground* task, which means that the program is totally dedicated to rendering, and you can no longer edit. Virtually all programs work this way, not just Studio.

However, Studio also provides an option to render certain effects in the *background*, which means that you can continue to edit while Studio is rendering. Studio 8 rendered only Hollywood FX transitions in the background, but Studio 9 also renders special effects in the background, a major improvement, with a couple of caveats. Let me explain by providing this example:

Chapter 9 discusses special effects. One very useful new special effect is Auto Color Correct, which corrects video shot with incorrect white balancing.

To use Auto Color Correct, you apply the filter and then move on to other editing. If you enable background rendering, Studio 9 will render the effect in the background and allow you to continue editing. When your editing is complete and you're ready to render, Studio will have less rendering to do, and you'll have less time to wait, because Studio already rendered the effects.

Sounds great so far, right? Well, here are the caveats. First, background rendering speeds up only the final rendering if you're outputting your project back to DV tape. If you're producing a DVD or outputting files in RealVideo or Windows Media format, background rendering won't save you any time at all. Here's why:

As shown in **Figure 8.30**, Studio offers two alternatives for background rendering on the Edit tab of the Studio Setup Options dialog: Optimize for Preview and Optimize for Make Tape. If you select the latter option, Studio will render all Hollywood FX transitions and special effects into DV format, performing work it would otherwise have to do before actually outputting to DV tape.

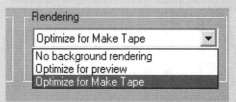

Figure 8.30 Here's where you select your background rendering options.

If you select Optimize for Preview, Studio renders into a lower resolution format that looks fine in the preview window and takes less time to produce than DV files. However, since this format is used only for previewing and not for final output, you won't save any time at final rendering.

So unless you're actually creating a project for output back to DV tape and select Optimize for Make Tape, background rendering won't save time during final rendering. However, you still may want to render in the background, using Optimize for Preview, because this provides the most accurate preview of your effects.

continues on next page

> **About Background Rendering** *continued*
>
> However, here's the second caveat. Rendering in the background may make your system feel sluggish during editing. For example, you may notice that you have to select a video file two or three times before the system responds, that dragging files on the Timeline takes longer than usual, or that scenes in the Album take longer to appear when you select a new video file.
>
> This is because rendering is very computationally intensive, which means that it consumes lots of your computer's processing power. On my 2.4-GHz Pentium 4 HP workstation, I notice very little difference when background rendering is turned on. On my Dell laptop with a 1.6-GHz Mobile Pentium chip, background rendering creates some sluggishness, but it's still worthwhile.
>
> So what's the net/net? If your goal is to output to DV tape, give background rendering a try, selecting Optimize for Make Tape. If your goal is a DVD or output in some other format, give background rendering a try, selecting Optimize for Preview. In both instances, be aware that background rendering may slow performance, and if this becomes unacceptable, turn off background rendering.
>
> In addition, recognize that rendering in the background stresses the system, which may lead to instability and system crashes. If this occurs, turn off background rendering and see if the situation improves.

To render as a background task:

1. From the Studio menu, choose Setup > Edit.

    The Studio Setup Options screen appears, open to the Edit tab

2. In the Rendering list box at the right (Figure 8.30), select one *of the following options:*

    ▲ No Background Rendering, to disable background rendering.

    ▲ Optimize for Preview, to create a low-resolution file for preview.

    ▲ Optimize for Make Tape, to create a file in DV format.

    See the sidebar "About Background Rendering" earlier in this chapter for assistance with this decision.

3. Click OK to close the Studio Setup Options dialog box.

    Studio will now render all transitions as background tasks.

4. From the drop-down menu on the Transitions tab, select the Hollywood FX for Studio transition group (Figure 8.29).

5. Drag the transition to the target location.

6. Preview the transition by clicking Play in the Player (or pressing the spacebar or L).

    You see a small bar above the transition in the Timescale (**Figure 8.31**), at first completely light blue and then a more transparent shade as Studio renders the video. When the entire bar is transparent, Studio has finished rendering, and you can preview your transition in real time.

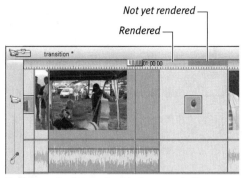

Figure 8.31 Background rendering at work. The transparent bar indicates how much has been rendered, and the blue bar shows how much still needs to be rendered.

Using Transitions

Ripple Transitions for Slide Shows

As discussed in "To create a slide show" in Chapter 7, you can create a slide show from still images by dragging multiple images to the Timeline. As a lovely touch for slide shows, you can add transitions between images, a process that Studio simplifies with a feature called ripple transitions.

Here's how it works.

To insert a ripple transition between slide show images:

1. With your slide show on the Timeline, drag the desired transition between the first and second images (**Figure 8.32**). Studio inserts the transition.

2. Select all slides in the slide show by doing *one of the following*:
   ▲ If your entire presentation is a slide show, choose Edit > Select All from the Studio menu (or press Ctrl+A).
   ▲ If the Timelines contains other assets that you don't want included in the ripple transition, hold down the Shift key and select the first image and then the last image in the slide show.

   Studio highlights all the images in the slide show.

   continues on next page

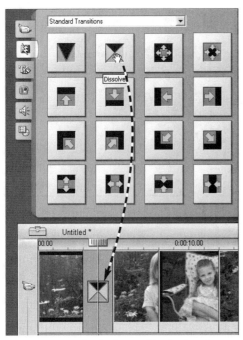

Figure 8.32 Start the ripple transition by dragging the desired transition between the first and second images.

3. Right-click the selected images to reveal the menu and then select Ripple Transition (**Figure 8.33**).

Studio inserts the transition between all still images (**Figure 8.34**).

✔ Tips

- For most video clips, 2-second transitions, which is the default setting for video, are fine. But for still images, a 2-second transition can be a bit long, especially at the default 4-second duration for stills. You may want to change the default transition time when you are applying transitions to slide shows; then change it back to the usual 2 seconds for your video work.

- After you apply a ripple transition, you can customize the duration for any transition as described in "Customizing Transitions" earlier in this chapter.

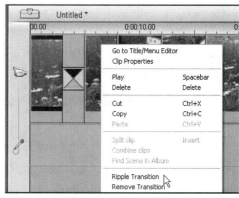

Figure 8.33 Then highlight all images in the slide show, right-click, and select Ripple Transition.

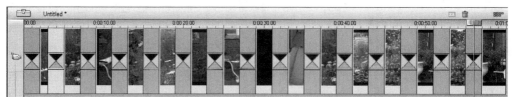

Figure 8.34 Voilà! Multiple transitions, neatly inserted. When I'm feeling really frisky, I use page curls instead of dissolves, creating the appearance of physically scrolling through the images.

Hollywood FX Exposed

Here is my ode to Hollywood FX, or how I used Hollywood FX in various projects in 2003. Though this section may feel a bit over the top, Hollywood FX is one of Studio's most outstanding features, and since textual hyperbole doesn't convey how cool it really is, I felt compelled to show you.

You can download and view short videos showing most of these transitions at my Web site, www.doceo.com/studio9. You'll also find a description of how to create one of my favorite effects, the Picture-in-Picture (P-i-P) effect, with Hollywood FX Plus or Mega. It's a pretty advanced function, which is why it's not in the book, but if you're the adventuresome type, take a look. A screenshot from the video produced using this technique appears at the end of this chapter.

Note that you don't need Hollywood FX to produce P-i-P effects; you can use the procedure illustrated in "Creating P-i-P Effects with Video Thumbnails" in Chapter 12. Hollywood FX provides more options, but you'll need to upgrade first.

Hollywood FX 2003

One of my first video opportunities in 2003 was my daughter's birthday, in January. **Figure 8.35** shows the balloons transition, used to separate play time and cake time at her party. This transition is available with the Family Fun Pack, a $20 pack available after you upgrade to Hollywood FX Plus.

As with all transitions, you can use Hollywood FX transitions at the start of a clip. **Figure 8.36** shows the highly caloric box-of-candy transition into my daughter's Valentine's Day preschool party, February's big event. This transition comes with the Mega upgrade.

Figure 8.35 The bubbles transition, always a favorite at birthday parties.

Figure 8.36 Transitioning into the Valentine's Day video with a box of chocolates.

Here we are in March at Zoo Atlanta. Since the video consists primarily of candid shots of different animals, I wanted a transition that highlighted the change from animal to animal. As shown in **Figure 8.37**, I used the wide-world-of-sports transition, a Mega transition in the sports category. This transition pulls the first video into the big screen on the right, while the scenes on the left scroll downward. Then the tiger zooms out to fill the screen.

Hollywood FX offers many cool wedding effects and is essential even if you're a casual videographer at a wedding, as I was last April when my daughter was a flower girl at a wedding on Saint Simons Island. **Figure 8.38** shows the video transitioning from ceremony to reception with a bottle of bubbly.

May was the month of a gymnastics exhibition. Most of the video consists of my daughter performing various exercises. I chose the Studio AB Plus effect (**Figure 8.39**), which pulled the first video into the monitor on the left and then zoomed the video from the monitor on the right to full screen.

Figure 8.37 The wide-world-of-sports transition highlights the fact that we're showing different animals in these videos.

Figure 8.38 Transitioning from the ceremony to the wedding reception.

Figure 8.39 A cool transition that tells the viewer that we're showing highlights from the gymnastics exhibition.

May also brought Mother's Day, for which mother received a water garden fully dug in and delivered by this writer (who still claims residual soreness). On the left in **Figure 8.40** is the barren starting point, then the blooming flower pot transition—part of the $20 Family Fun pack—and then splendor in the grass. My wife has quite the green thumb, eh?

June was Junior Rodeo month (**Figure 8.41**). Okay, maybe the Wanted poster is a stretch, but it's free with the Extra FX pack you get for registering Studio. Plus I'll bet the cowboys themselves would love it.

August is the Fiddler's Convention. Here I walked around, shooting different bands as they warmed up or performed offstage; I used the triangle block, a Mega effect (**Figure 8.42**), to let the viewers know the band was changing.

Figure 8.40 A flower-pot transition from bare ground to exotic garden.

Figure 8.41 What better transition for a rodeo than a Wanted poster?

Figure 8.42 A nice triangle transition lets the viewer know that we're changing bands.

September was my high school reunion, highlighted by golf with the gang. It's a bit tough to see in **Figure 8.43**, but Paul and Jim, in the first shot, get wrapped up into a golf ball, placed on a tee and then driven off the screen to reveal me teeing off. Most golfers are suckers for this kind of stuff, and I'm no exception. This and many other sports-related transitions are available with the Plus upgrade.

In October, we went to Dollywood in Pigeon Forge, Tennessee. One of the highlights was the trip to the Gatlinburg Aquarium, where you can walk underneath sharks and other toothy carnivores. The video-bites transition shown in **Figure 8.44** was the obvious choice, available as part of the Plus upgrade. I'm not usually big on sound effects, but these were pictures from my digital camera, so they had no accompanying sound. The kids loved the chewing sound effect and went wild when they heard the shark burp. Ah, producing for a five-year-old's sense of humor definitely has its high points. Both sound effects come with Studio; we'll discuss how to access them in "Studio's Sound Effects" in Chapter 11.

Figure 8.43 Wrapping my high school buddies into a tee and then driving them off the screen. Pretty sweet, eh?

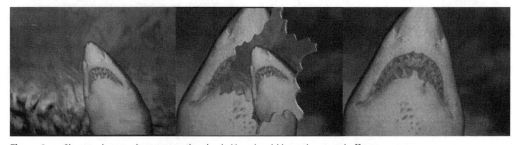

Figure 8.44 Chomp, chomp, chomp goes the shark. You should hear the sound effects.

Halloween is always big fun with the kiddies, and Pinnacle offers several motivated Halloween transitions in the Holiday FX Pack ($20). **Figure 8.45** shows a ghost chasing my little wizard off the screen and introducing a cute shot of my little angel walking with a clown.

I shot the December holiday concert at the fabulous Rex Theater (pronounced Thee-a-tor) with a Sony VX2100 review unit that delivered awesome sound and video quality. The Holiday FX pack included several excellent holiday-related transitions, but I finally chose the snow transition that comes with the free Extra FX pack you get for registering Studio. This is shown in **Figure 8.46**.

Figure 8.45 A ghost transition—perfect for Halloween.

Figure 8.46 Snow falling between acts at the fabulous Rex Theater.

Back at the Fiddler's Convention, I used Hollywood FX Mega to produce the Picture-in-Picture effect in **Figure 8.47**. This shows the country music singers in the background with folks dancing in the foreground. It's a very cool effect, and I describe how to produce it at my Web site, www.doceo.com/studio9.

Picture-in-Picture

Figure 8.47 The Picture-in-Picture effect, Hollywood FX version: band in the background; dancers in the foreground window.

Applying Special Effects

Special effects are filters that change the appearance of video either to fix underlying problems (curative special effects) or enhance the video artistically (artistic special effects). Studio has six classes of special effects: one class curative and five artistic.

As with Hollywood FX and transitions, Studio has standard effects that ship with the program and Plus and Pro Packs of effects that you can buy to add more capabilities. Pinnacle has also opened up Studio's architecture so that third parties can build filters for it, a glorious change that has already produced some great special effects for Studio.

I should say that I'm not a big fan of artistic special effects, mostly because with a few exceptions, it's tough to use them in a way that actually improves the perceived quality of your movies. On the other hand, the curative filters now in Studio rank among the best I've seen, even in professional programs. Also very useful is Studio's automatic music video creation routine, a great program supplement in version 9, and the ability to add motion to still images.

Chapter 9

What's in the Box?

Table 9.1 shows the six classes of special effects in Studio. Those in the first column (Studio 9) are "in the box," or standard with the retail version of Studio 9. Those in the Plus and Pro columns, of course, come with their respective upgrades. At the time of this writing, the third-party plug-ins were not finalized, so I am not able to list them for you.

Although the classes of special effects are essentially self-explanatory, let's run through them quickly:

- **Cleaning Effects:** These are curative filters that fix problems with the underlying video. Auto Color Correct fixes white balance and other color- and brightness-related issues, while Noise Reduction removes noise, usually caused by shooting with poor lighting or capturing from analog sources (more on this in "Video Rescue 101," later in this chapter). Stabilize minimizes unwanted motion in a video, usually produced by shooting with a hand-held camera.

- **Time Effects:** These artistic effects change the speed of the video, either slowing it down or making it faster.

- **Color Effects:** These artistic effects adjust the color of the video, for example, to black and white or sepia.

- **Fun Effects:** These artistic effects change the video in some fundamental way; for instance, the Water Drop effect makes your video look like a pond with water dropping into it. Also included is the Plus: 2D Editor, which allows you to add motion to still images; this editor is demonstrated in "Adding Motion to Still Images," later in this chapter.

- **Style Effects:** These artistic effects change the style of the video; for instance, Old Film makes your video look like it was shot in the 1940s.

- **Pan and Zoom:** These are third-party tools that allow you to add motion to still images; these tools are demonstrated in "Adding Motion to Still Images," later in this chapter.

Table 9.1

Studio's Special Effects

Plug In	Studio 9	Plus Pack	Pro Pack	Plug In	Studio 9	Plus Pack	Pro Pack
Cleaning Effects				**Fun Effects**			
Auto Color Correct		Basic	Advanced	Magnify	Yes		Advanced
Noise Reduction	Yes			Water Wave	Yes		Advanced
Stabilize	Yes			Fractal Clouds	Yes		
Sharpen	Yes			Fractal Tunnel	Yes		
Time Effects				Motion Blur	Yes		
Speed	Yes			Turbulence	Yes		
Strobe	Yes			**Style Effects**			
Color Effects				Blur	Yes		
B/W	Yes			Emboss	Yes		
Color Correction	Yes			Mosaic	Yes		
Posterize	Yes			Old Film		Basic	Advanced
Sepia	Yes			Stained Glas		Basic	Advanced
Invert	Yes			Mirage	Yes		
Shift Channels	Yes			Replication	Yes		
Threshold	Yes			Watercolor	Yes		
Tint	Yes			Bevel Crystal	Yes		
Fun Effects				Minmax	Yes		
2D Editor	Yes			Radial Blur	Yes		
Lens Flare		Basic	Advanced	Stained Glass	Yes		
Noise	Yes			Video Feedback	Yes		
Water Drop		Basic	Advanced	Themes	Third Party		
Fractal Fire	Yes			Lighting Control	Third Party		
Framer	Yes			**Pan and Zoom**			
Hall of Mirrors	Yes			Moving Pictures	Third Party		

Before Getting Started

Let's discuss a few points before jumping in. We'll start with setup options, specifically as they relate to hardware acceleration of effects and background rendering, both discussed Chapter 8.

Briefly, Studio can accelerate the preview of most special effects if you enable hardware acceleration in the Pinnacle Studio Setup Options dialog box (**Figure 9.1**), accessed by choosing Setup > Edit in the main Studio menu. You should give hardware acceleration a try, because it should work for most current graphics cards. As detailed in "Working with Hollywood FX Transitions" in Chapter 8, if you experience any instability, disable hardware acceleration.

The issue of background rendering is more complicated. If you haven't chosen a Rendering setting, read the sidebar "About Background Rendering," in Chapter 8 and choose either Optimize for Preview or Optimize for Make Tape. If you disable background rendering, Studio will preview the effect, but what you see is only an estimate, not the real effect applied to your actual source footage. In my view, rendering in the background using either setting provides a more accurate preview, which is critical when making sensitive adjustments like color correction and noise removal.

Also, be aware that while effects have some similarities in interface and operation (this is discussed in "Learning the Special Effects Interface," later in this chapter), each effect, by necessity, looks and works differently. This is especially true of third-party effects created by companies other than Pinnacle.

Space doesn't allow a comprehensive review of all special effects, so this chapter demonstrates only the most widely used. If you follow along, you'll probably find most other Pinnacle-created effects self-explanatory, but be advised that some third-party effects use different interfaces. If you're not comfortable teaching yourself how to use these effects, before buying a third-party effect, you may want to check whether the vendor provides user documentation.

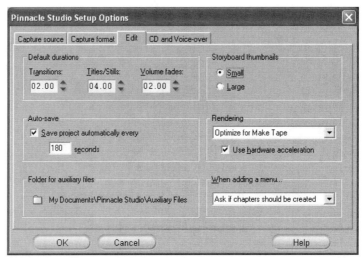

Figure 9.1 The Pinnacle Studio Setup Options screen, where you can select hardware acceleration and background rendering.

Applying Special Effects

Figure 9.2 Click here to open the Video toolbox.

Learning the Special Effects Interface

This section covers the basics of accessing, applying, and configuring special effects. Then we'll move on and explore some key special effects.

Note that some effects, like the Mosaic effect discussed later in this chapter, often look better when gradually inserted into the clip. To accomplish this, Studio offers transition-in and transition-out controls, covered in this section. As you'll see, these are very powerful capabilities that add a lot of useful subtleties to Studio's special effects capabilities.

To access special effects:

1. Place the target clip on the Timeline and select the clip with your pointer.
2. At the upper left of the Movie window, click the Open/Close Video Toolbox icon (**Figure 9.2**).

   The Video toolbox opens (**Figure 9.3**).

   continues on next page

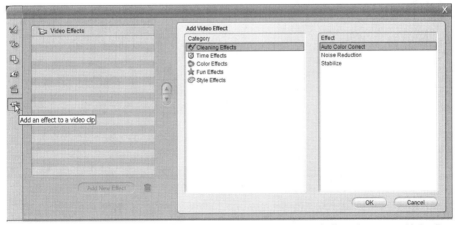

Figure 9.3 Click here to get to the special effects. These are the basic special effects that come with Studio.

229

Chapter 9

3. On the left side of the toolbox, click the Add an Effect to a Video Clip icon.

   Figure 9.3 lists all the special effects categories that come standard with Studio. Compare this to **Figure 9.4**, which lists the Plus and Pro packs and a range of third-party special effects. Note the consistent icon use: the Broom and Dustpan for cleaning effects, the Clock for timing effects, the Color Wheel for color effects, the Star for fun effects, and the Palette for style effects. After applying a special effect to a video clip, Studio places the appropriate icon on the clip in the Timeline to indicate that it has applied the effect.

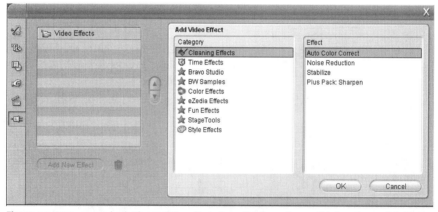

Figure 9.4 Here you see both Plus and Pro effects from Studio and some third-party special effects.

Applying Special Effects

To add and configure a special effect:

1. Click the target effect category.
2. Click the target effect.
3. Click OK (**Figure 9.5**).

   Studio applies the special effect. If it's a Studio effect, Studio then opens the effect settings window (**Figure 9.6**).

   continues on next page

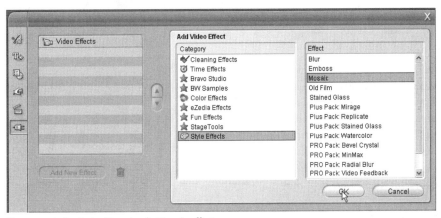

Figure 9.5 Let's start with a simple Mosaic effect.

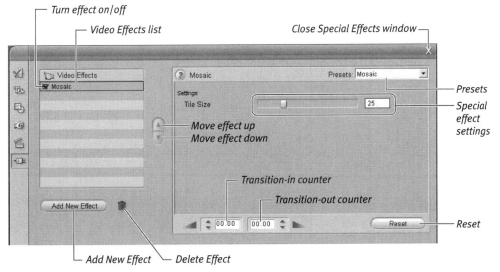

Figure 9.6 The Special Effects settings window.

Chapter 9

If it's a third-party effect, the effects settings window either contains the configurable settings or an Edit button that opens the third-party configuration screen (**Figure 9.7**).

4. To choose special effect settings, while previewing in the Player, do *one of the following*:

   ▲ Choose a value from the Presets list (Figure 9.6).

   ▲ Manually adjust the effect settings.

   Note that you can preview the effect in the Player by clicking Play or by dragging the Player slider around the video.

5. To transition an effect in or out, click the appropriate control and adjust the counter, either by typing thc desired interval or using the arrow keys beside each counter to increase or decrease the interval (**Figure 9.8**).

   Studio prevents you from entering a number larger than the duration of the video clip in either the Transition-in or Transition-out counter.

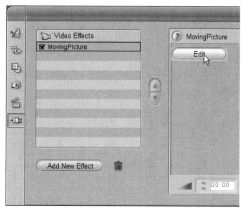

Figure 9.7 You click Edit to edit some third-party effects.

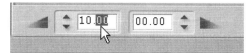

Figure 9.8 Setting the transition-in duration.

Applying Special Effects

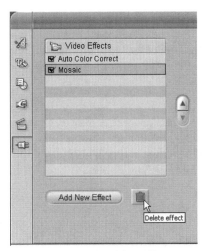

Figure 9.9 Click here to delete effects.

6. When you are finished configuring the special effect, do *one of the following*:

   ▲ Click the X in the upper-right corner to close the Special Effects window.

   ▲ Click the Add New Effect button to select and configure another special effect.

   Studio saves the first effect and returns you to either the Movie window for additional editing or the Special Effects window so you can choose and configure another special effect.

✔ Tip

- Note the Reset button in Figure 9.6. This resets all controls and zeros out the transition-in and transition-out values.

To delete a special effect:

1. Select the target effect in the Video Effects list.

2. Click the Delete Effect button (**Figure 9.9**).

   Studio deletes the effect.

To turn effects on or off:

◆ Click the check box to the left of the effect (**Figure 9.10**) to turn the effect on or off for preview and rendering.

✔ Tips

■ It's often useful to turn an effect on or off when attempting to configure another special effect. For example, in Figure 9.10, I'm trying to configure the Color Correction effect, but the blocks from the Mosaic filter make this hard to do. By turning the Mosaic effect off (**Figure 9.11**), I get a clear view of the video and can effectively set my configuration options.

■ You can adjust the order of special effects by selecting an effect and then clicking the arrows to move the effect up or down (Figure 9.6). You'll see how and why you might want to do this in "Video Rescue 101," later in this chapter.

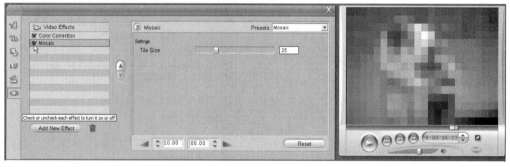

Figure 9.10 Here's how you turn off an effect so you can preview your other effects.

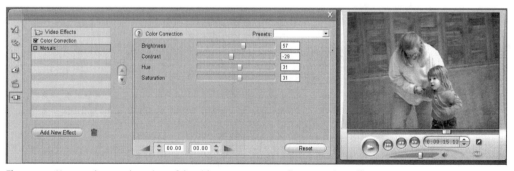

Figure 9.11 Now you have a clear view of the video so you can configure another effect.

Studio's Cleaning Effects

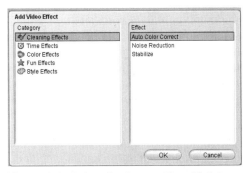

Figure 9.12 Let's start cleaning our video with Auto Color Correct.

One of the benefits of having older siblings is that you get lots of their cool stuff, albeit often after they tire of it and it's a bit worn. Similarly, Studio, with a more full-featured sibling like Pinnacle Liquid Edition, gets lots of cool stuff passed down to it—but without the negatives of hand-me-down clothes.

One of these hand-me-downs is Studio's Auto Color Correct effect, which corrects for improper white balancing and other color deficiencies. Simply stated, this tool is extraordinary. I know this because I tested and found Edition's color correction superior to that of any other prosumer editor, including Adobe Premiere and Apple's Final Cut Pro, in a review I wrote for *EMedia, the Digital Studio Magazine*. Now in Studio, it's a wonderful feature that can dramatically improve video quality. Also passed down from Edition are Stabilization and Noise Reduction effects, both covered in this section.

To apply automatic color correction:

1. Place the target clip on the Timeline and select the clip.

2. At the upper left of the Movie window, click the Open/Close Video Toolbox icon (Figure 9.2).

3. On the left side of the Video toolbox, click the Add an Effect to a Video Clip icon (Figure 9.3).

4. Select the Cleaning Effects category (**Figure 9.12**).

continues on next page

Chapter 9

5. Select Auto Color Correct.

6. Click OK.

   Studio opens the Auto Color Correct window (**Figure 9.13**) showing the standard controls included with all Studio versions. **Figure 9.14** shows the advanced controls available in the Plus version.

7. Adjust the settings as desired; then do *one of the following*:

   ▲ Click the X in the upper-right corner to close the Special Effects window.

   ▲ Click the Add New Effect button to select and configure another special effect.

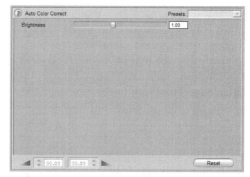

Figure 9.13 Here are the standard controls included with all versions of Studio.

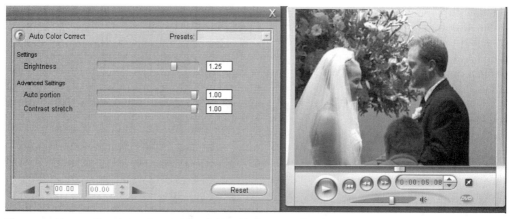

Figure 9.14 Here are the advanced controls available with the Pro pack.

Figure 9.15 Background rendering provides the most accurate preview, but can take a few moments.

✔ Tips

- Usually, when videos need color correction, they often need to be brightened as well, which is why Pinnacle includes the Brightness setting in Studio. I almost always bump up the brightness a bit once I apply color correction.

- Color correction requires precise adjustments, so I always wait for background rendering to complete before finalizing my decision (**Figure 9.15**). If you're applying color correction to a large clip, split out a small segment and apply Auto Color Correct to the segment to identify the proper values. Then apply the effect to the larger clip using the same values. See "Common Tasks" in Chapter 7 for information on splitting clips.

- Pinnacle advises that the Auto Color Correct filter "may introduce video noise into the clip as a side-effect of processing" and recommends that you apply the Noise Reduction effect shown in Figure 9.12 to counteract this problem.

- If you split a clip with special effects, Studio applies all effects to both clips. Studio prevents you from combining two clips if one of them has special effects.

Chapter 9

To apply the Stabilize effect:

1. Place the target clip on the Timeline and select the clip.

2. At the upper left of the Movie window, click the Open/Close Video Toolbox icon (Figure 9.2).

3. On the left side of the Video toolbox, click the Add an Effect to a Video Clip icon (Figure 9.3).

4. Select the Cleaning Effects category (Figure 9.12).

5. Select the Stabilize effect (Figure 9.12).

6. Click OK.

   Studio adds Stabilize to the Video Effects list, but presents no user-configurable settings (**Figure 9.16**). To understand how Studio stabilizes the image, see the sidebar, "About Stabilization."

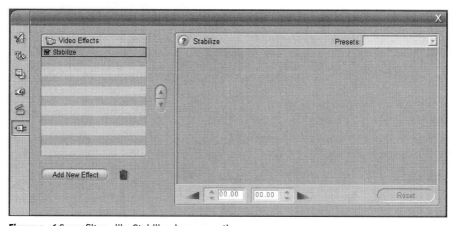

Figure 9.16 Some filters, like Stabilize, have no options.

About Stabilization

Whereas Auto Color Correct corrects for incorrect white balancing, Stabilize bails you out for not using a tripod or for failing to hold the camera steady.

Interestingly, Stabilize works exactly like electric image stabilization (EIS) in a DV camera. That is, most EIS systems capture a larger frame than is necessary for the ultimate video frame. For example, in a DV camera, the CCD may capture an 800 x 600 frame that will ultimately be reduced to 720 x 480 resolution.

Then, when the motion sensor chips in the camera sense motion, the camera compensates by shifting the image within that larger frame. For example, if the camera detects an inadvertent five-pixel jerk to the right, it compensates by shifting the image five pixels to the left.

Similarly, if the algorithms used by Studio detect a five-pixel jerk to the right, Studio moves the image five pixels to the left. However, since Studio doesn't start with a larger-than-necessary frame, it must zoom into the image to free up pixels on the borders to enable the necessary shifting.

This is evident in **Figure 9.17**. On the left is the original frame, and on the right is the frame after stabilization. As you can see, my daughter, the cute blonde in the middle, is noticeably larger in the frame on the right, and the little girl on the left in the original frame has been cut out of the picture. You might also notice that my daughter's face is slightly less sharp on the right.

The key benefit is that the video is vastly easier to watch because Studio eliminated most of the motion injected by my walking alongside my daughter. Though the visible area in the frame and the detail are both slightly reduced, overall the video is much more watchable.

Once you know the trade-offs to look for, you can easily try stabilizing footage with noticeable jerkiness, making sure that the cure isn't worse than the disease. Most of the time, your video will end up looking much, much better.

Figure 9.17 Stabilize works by zooming into the image to create space on the top, bottom, and sides to remove minor camera motion. That's why the original clip shows more area than it does after stabilization.

Chapter 9

To apply the Noise Reduction effect:

1. Place the target clip on the Timeline and select the clip.

2. At the upper left of the Movie window, click the Open/Close Video Toolbox icon (Figure 9.2).

3. On the left side of the Video toolbox, click the Add an Effect to a Video Clip icon (Figure 9.3).

4. Select the Cleaning Effects category (Figure 9.12).

5. Select the Noise Reduction effect (Figure 9.13).

6. Click OK.
   Studio opens the Noise Reduction settings window (**Figure 9.18**).

7. Adjust the setting as desired.
   See the sidebar "About Noise Reduction Filters" for assistance.

8. When you're finished, do *one of the following*:
   ▲ Click the X in the upper-right corner to close the Special Effects window.
   ▲ Click the Add New Effect button to select and configure another special effect.

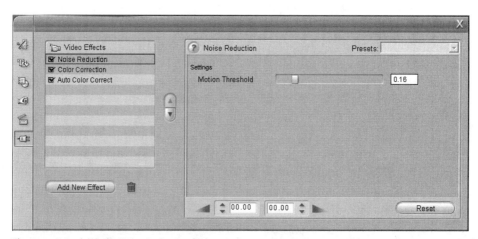

Figure 9.18 Applying the Noise Reduction filter.

Video Rescue 101

There's no one-size-fits-all panacea for poorly shot video, but here's one procedure I used to help correct some footage shot in a dark restaurant without a light and with a single-chip, consumer-quality DV camcorder. Hey, it was reunion weekend, and I was definitely not breaking out the good equipment.

Figure 9.19 shows the four stages of the video, with the overly dark original video at the upper left. I first applied Auto Color Correct, with brightness boosted to the max, shown at the upper right. This brightened the image considerably, but it wasn't enough, so I applied manual Color Correction as well.

This brightened the video even more, but also produced significant noise that resembled an indoor snowstorm, which I mostly removed with the Noise Reduction effect. This isn't easy to see in the figure, but it's readily apparent when playing the clip in real time.

continues on next page

Figure 9.19 Video Rescue 101, from unusable to reasonably good quality.

Video Rescue 101 *continued*

One interesting part of the exercise was a realization that the order of special effects affects the way in which Studio applies them and the visual result. For example, **Figure 9.20** shows the three filters applied with Noise Reduction applied last; now the video is very dark. **Figure 9.21** shows the same three filters applied to the same source video in a different sequence, with a completely different result. I rendered both files to make sure the previews were accurate, and the rendered files looked just like previews. When applying special effects, order definitely matters.

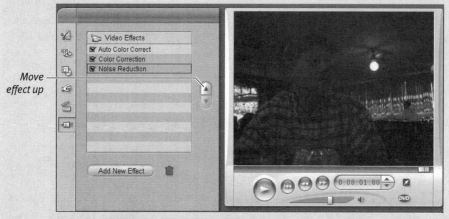

Figure 9.20 Shifting the effect order. Here you can barely see the video.

Figure 9.21 Same effects, different order, completely different result.

Varying Playback Speed

Changing the playback speed of your clips is useful in a variety of circumstances, whether it's to showcase a child's look of delight or slow your golf swing to better reveal its flaws. Studio offers two modes for resetting playback speed. By using a slider control, you can specify any speed from one-tenth the original to five times faster. Or you can drag the clip to the desired duration, a useful method during insert edits or any time you need a clip to fill a defined space.

Studio also offers a *strobe* mode, which essentially displays the same frame multiple times, producing a stuttering strobe-light effect without those distracting flashes. You can use this mode in conjunction with changes in playback speed or as a stand-alone effect.

Note that whenever Studio changes playback speed, it automatically mutes the audio from the Video track, since playback speed changes produce disturbing audio distortion. (You can prevent the audio muting by locking the audio track before implementing playback speed variations, though you'll have an overlap if you make the clip faster, or a gap if you make it slower.)

About Noise Reduction Filters

Noise reduction filters work by attempting to distinguish between real motion that occurs from frame to frame, like a hand waving or lips speaking, and noise, which is random graininess and other artifacts (video defects) caused by a number of factors, including shooting under poor lighting conditions or using poor equipment.

The slider bar shown in Figure 9.18 sets the threshold between noise and real motion. The farther you move the slider to the right (higher value) the more motion Studio assumes is noise. This increases the filtering, enhancing noise removal, but also potentially producing artifacts caused by the elimination of real motion. Move the slider to the left (lower value), and Studio uses a lower threshold, assumes that more motion is real motion, and removes less noise, reducing the cleansing effect.

Noise reduction can work wonders when you're working with very poor quality video (see the sidebar "Video Rescue 101"), but it must be used judiciously because higher thresholds can and do produce artifacts. This means that you should render in the background to get the best possible preview before selecting your final settings.

To change playback speed via the slider:

1. Place the target clip on the Timeline and select the clip.

2. At the upper left of the Movie window, click the Open/Close Video Toolbox icon (Figure 9.2).

3. On the left side of the Video toolbox, click the Add an Effect to a Video Clip icon (Figure 9.3).

4. Select the Time Effects category.

5. Select the Speed effect.

6. Click OK (**Figure 9.22**).

   Studio opens the Speed settings window (**Figure 9.23**). In our example, the original duration of the clip is three seconds.

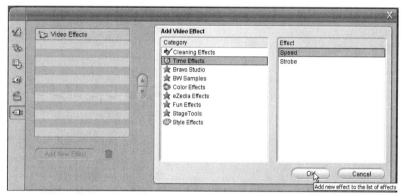

Figure 9.22 Slowing down my chip shot so that I can visualize my errors.

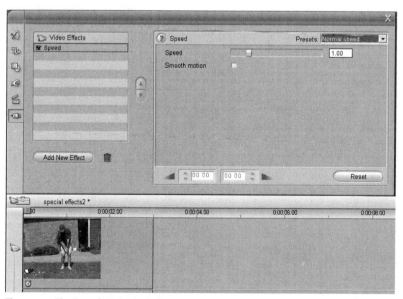

Figure 9.23 The Speed settings window.

Applying Special Effects

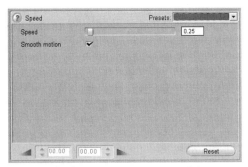

Figure 9.24 Cut the speed to 25 percent of the original, and the video extends from 3 to 12 seconds.

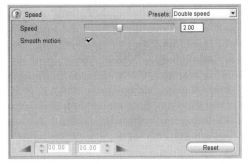

Figure 9.25 Double the speed, and you cut the video in half, down to 1.5 seconds.

7. To adjust video speed, do *one of the following:*

   ▲ To decrease playback speed and produce a slow-motion effect, drag the playback speed slider to the left, reducing speed to a fraction of the original (**Figure 9.24**).

   By reducing speed to 25 percent of the original, you quadruple playback duration, to 12 seconds.

   ▲ To increase playback speed and produce a fast-motion effect, drag the playback slider to the right, accelerating speed to a multiple of the original (**Figure 9.25**).

   By doubling the playback speed, you cut playback duration to 1.5 seconds.

8. When you're finished, do *one of the following:*

   ▲ Click the X in the upper-right corner to close the Special Effects window.

   ▲ Click the Add New Effect button to select and configure another special effect.

✔ Tip

- Whenever you slow clip speed below 1X, be sure to select the Smooth Motion check box, which produces interpolated frames between the original frames, smoothing overall motion. This control has no effect when you increase playback speed, so you might as well leave it checked all the time.

245

To change playback speed on the Timeline:

1. Place the target clip on the Timeline and select the clip.
2. At the upper left of the Movie window, click the Open/Close Video Toolbox icon (Figure 9.2).
3. On the left side of the Video toolbox, click the Add an Effect to a Video Clip icon (Figure 9.3).
4. Select the Time Effects category.
5. Select the Speed effect.
6. Click OK (Figure 9.22).
   Studio opens the Speed Settings window (Figure 9.23). In our example, the original duration of the clip is three seconds.
7. Move the pointer to the right edge of the clip on the Timeline.
   The pointer changes to the Speed Change cursor (**Figure 9.26**).
8. Drag the clip left to increase the playback speed, or right to decrease it (**Figure 9.27**).
9. When you're finished, do *one of the following*:
   ▲ Click the X in the upper-right corner to close the Special Effects window.
   ▲ Click the Add New Effect button to select and configure another special effect.

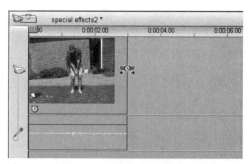

Figure 9.26 Or you can change speed manually by dragging the slider to the desired value.

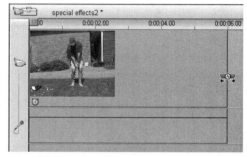

Figure 9.27 Here's the extended clip.

✔ Tip

■ Adjust speed on the Timeline when you're attempting to match clip duration with audio or other Timeline content. Otherwise, using the slider control is generally easier.

To produce a strobe effect:

1. Place the target clip on the Timeline and select the clip.

2. At the upper left of the Movie window, click the Open/Close Video Toolbox icon (Figure 9.2).

3. On the left side of the Video toolbox, click the Add an Effect to a Video Clip icon (Figure 9.3).

4. Select the Time Effects category.

5. Select the Strobe effect.

6. Click OK (**Figure 9.28**).

   Studio opens the Strobe settings window (**Figure 9.29**).

7. Drag the Strobe Repetition slider to the desired value.

   The slider setting indicates the number of times that Studio repeats each frame before playing an additional frame. Note that Studio drops frames to make room for the repeated ones.

8. When you're finished, do *one of the following*:

   ▲ Click the X in the upper-right corner to close the Special Effects window.

   ▲ Click the Add New Effect button to select and configure another special effect.

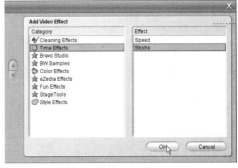

Figure 9.28 Let's apply the Strobe effect to our two young dancers.

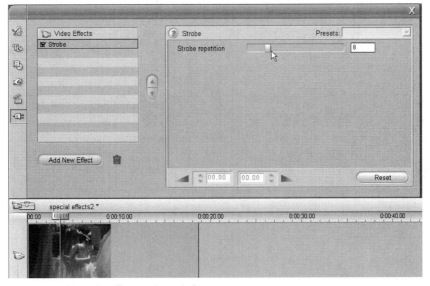

Figure 9.29 The Strobe Effect settings window.

Adding Motion to Still Images

The ability to add motion to still images is often called the Ken Burns effect, after the director who created movies about the Civil War and baseball exclusively by panning (moving around an image) and zooming into and away from images. I've been creating video slide shows since about 1998, but I had to use Adobe Premiere to get it done. Now Studio offers at least two options.

We'll look first at the 2D Editor, available as part of the Plus pack, which is good for simple projects like one-direction zooms and pans. Then we'll take a quick fly-by of a more sophisticated tool called MovingPicture, from a company called Stage Tools, that's now available as a Studio plug-in.

Adding motion with the Plus: 2D Editor:

1. Place the still image to be edited on the Timeline and select the image.
2. At the upper left of the Movie window, click the Open/Close Video Toolbox icon (Figure 9.2).
3. On the left side of the Video toolbox, click the Add an Effect to a Video Clip icon (Figure 9.3).
4. Select the Fun Effects category.
5. Select the Plus: 2D Editor effect (**Figure 9.30**).
6. Click OK.

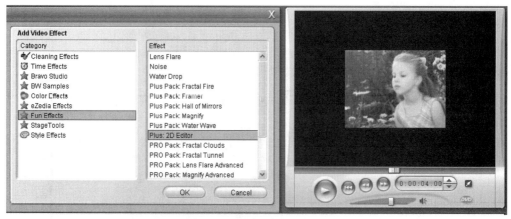

Figure 9.30 Let's zoom in on this beauty with the Plus: 2D Editor, adding motion to a still image.

Applying Special Effects

7. Studio opens the Plus: 2D Editor settings window (**Figure 9.31**).

   In the beta version of the software I used, Studio opened the 2D Editor with the Half Size Centered preset selected, which is why my daughter is showing up that way in the Player window in Figure 9.30. Let's reverse that first.

8. Click Reset.

   Studio resets the controls to zero, and Whatley fills the screen (**Figure 9.32**). Note that this won't happen immediately unless you've disabled background rendering.

   continues on next page

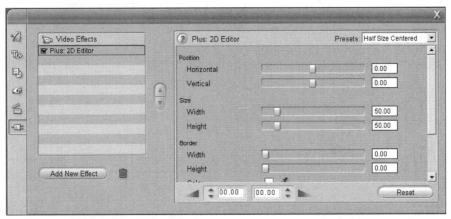

Figure 9.31 The Plus: 2D Editor settings window. Note the default of Half Size Centered. Click Reset to start over.

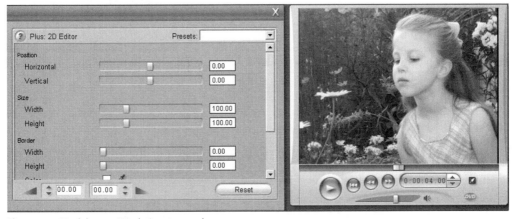

Figure 9.32 Much better. Now let's get even closer.

9. To zoom into the image, do *one of the following*:

   ▲ Drag the Width and Height sliders to 150 (to increase image size by 50 percent.

   ▲ Click the Size counters to the right of the slider bar and enter 150 directly (**Figure 9.33**).

   Note that Studio won't maintain the aspect ratio if you don't set the width and height to the same values.

   The size is now right, but the picture is off center. Let's correct this (the pan portion of the adjustment).

10. To center the image, adjust the Horizontal and Vertical Position sliders as desired (**Figure 9.34**).

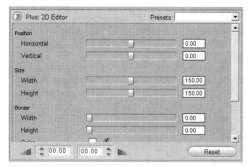

Figure 9.33 Looks good, but a bit off center.

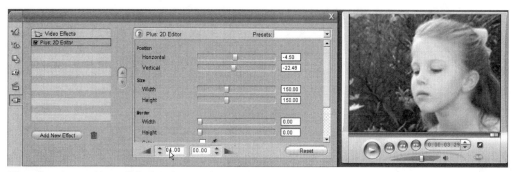

Figure 9.34 Centered beautifully; now let's set the transition to create the Pan and Zoom effect.

11. At the bottom left of the settings window, set the Transition in counter to the same duration as the image on the Timeline.

    This is the special sauce that forces Studio to create the pan and zoom effect. Essentially, we used the controls to set the desired *end* point of the video. By transitioning into that end point, we're telling Studio to create all intermediate frames between how the image looked in Figure 9.32 and how it looked in Figure 9.33. The video produced will both zoom into the image and pan across it.

✔ Tips

- To pan out of the image, use the sliders to set the size at a fraction of the original image size. Then you can create borders and shadows as shown in **Figure 9.35**.

- Unless your computer is a lot faster than my computer, you'll probably want to disable background rendering while setting up an image pan, which will improve responsiveness dramatically.

- The Plus: 2D Editor has two very significant limitations. First, it can handle only one zoom or pan sequence per image. Second, either the starting point or the ending point must be the image at the original resolution. This makes it impossible to create multi-step pans and zooms on the same image by using multiple copies of the same image (the trick I had to use in Premiere). If you're looking to produce complicated effects, you'll have to try MovingPicture, from Stage Tools.

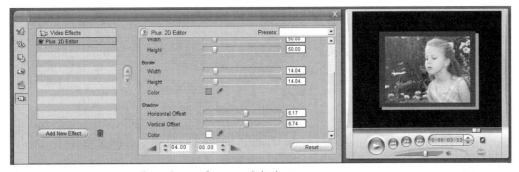

Figure 9.35 Or you can go smaller and create frames and shadows.

About MovingPicture

MovingPicture, from Stage Tools, is a third-party tool used to create multipart pan and zoom effects. For example, in **Figure 9.36**, I'm creating a video of my wife's water garden consisting of six camera views, all from different locations in the garden at different zoom ratios. The squiggles that look like a sideways figure 8 in the middle are the path the camera takes around the garden.

Creating the movie is simple. You start by manipulating the camera box, which represents the part of the image that's actually displayed in the video, to the starting size and position using the Viewer as a guide. All controls are WYSIWIG—what you see is what you get—so you grab, move, and resize the camera box directly.

Once you have the camera set, you touch a later point on the Key Frame Timeline to create a key frame, which is a fixed point where you can reset the camera box to a different position and size.

Do this multiple times, and you've created several key frames with different camera views. While rendering, the program simply creates the various key frames and all necessary points in between to create a video file of the garden tour.

The tool, priced at $199, is very similar to products like Canopus Imaginate, which has a few more functions and also costs $199. The ability to access capabilities like these within Studio offers compelling potential and shows why opening up the architecture for third-party developers was a great move for Pinnacle.

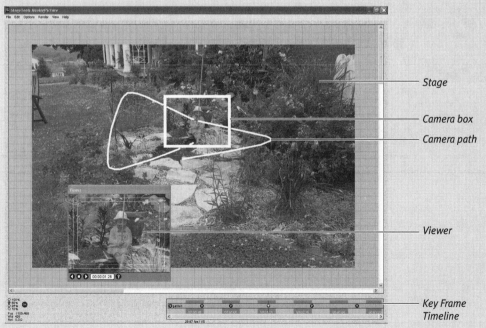

Figure 9.36 For serious work, however, you'll need a full-featured tool like MovingPicture from Stage Tools.

Creating Music Videos Automatically

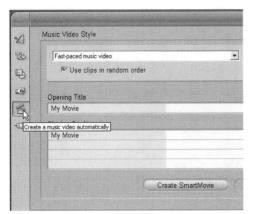

Figure 9.37 Let's create a SmartMovie. Click here to start.

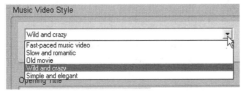

Figure 9.38 Pick your music video style here.

One of the more exciting features of Studio 9 is the ability to automatically create a music video. This capability is ideal for footage like the 10 minutes of video I took of my daughters roller skating the other day: footage with no plot, no highs, no lows, nothing to turn into an interesting story. Even condensed, it would be painful for the grandparents to watch.

However, cut it up into short, tasty segments, add a zesty background music clip, and you've got a four-minute music video that will have viewers tapping their toes and clapping their hands. While this could take hours to make manually, Studio does it all automatically.

To automatically create a music video:

1. Drag the target video footage to the Video track.

    Note that the video footage should be at least twice as long as the background music you'll be using. You can (and should) edit out scenes as desired before producing the music video.

2. Drag the target background audio clip (a WAV file from a CD, a WAV or MP3 from your hard drive, or a song created by SmartSound) to the Music track.

3. At the upper left of the Movie window, click the Open/Close Video Toolbox icon (Figure 9.2).

4. On the left side of the Video toolbox, click the Create a Music Video Automatically icon (**Figure 9.37**).

5. From the Music Video Style list, choose the target style (**Figure 9.38**).

continues on next page

6. Do *one of the following*:
   ▲ Select the Use Clips in Random Order check box (**Figure 9.39**).
   Studio will use the clips in random order, promoting smoothness but losing continuity.
   ▲ Don't select the Use Clips in Random Order check box.
   Studio will maintain narrative continuity, but will limit Studio's choice of clips, which could degrade the smoothness of the music video.

7. Enter the opening title and closing credits.

8. Set the Relative Volume slider completely to the right to prioritize background music over the original audio from the video.
   There may be situations where you want to maintain the original audio, but I can't think of any, since it will be completely chopped up and placed in random order by Studio while creating the music video.

9. Click Create SmartMovie.
   Studio loads the background audio file and then starts creating the SmartMovie (**Figure 9.40**). The techniques used are proprietary, but Pinnacle seems to be pulling out all the facial close-ups, using these as the primary video content and then matching the beat of the song to transition and effect timing.
   Studio produces the SmartMovie (**Figure 9.41**).

Figure 9.39 Now enter the rest of your settings.

Figure 9.40 Working! Working!

✔ Tips

- If you don't like the resulting video, you can select another music video style, click Create SmartMovie and try again. Or, you can click Reset and restore the timeline and all assets to their pre-SmartMovie condition.

- You can edit any component of the completed SmartMovie as desired, though significant edits, like shifting clips on the Timeline, could result in a loss of synchronization.

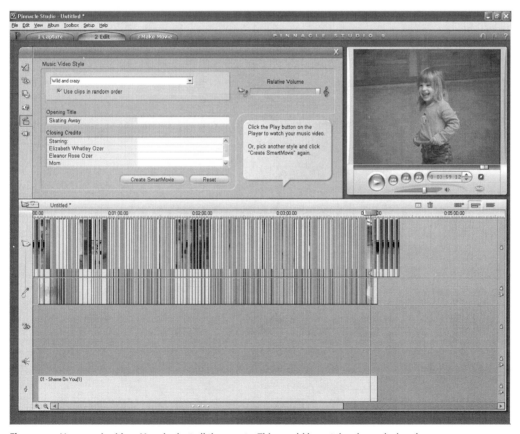

Figure 9.41 Your music video. Man, look at all those cuts. This would have taken hours by hand.

Designing Titles and Menus

10

Studio's Title editor is one of Studio's most important tools, performing double duty to create both titles and DVD menus. Fortunately, the Title editor, formerly known as Title Deko, has always been both elegant and easy to learn.

To start, here's a quick function flyover. First, for all video productions, DVD or otherwise, the Title editor creates full-screen titles, positioned on the Video track, that introduce the movie or new sections, or show final credits.

Second, again for all video productions, the Title editor produces *overlay* titles, positioned on the Title track, which are displayed over your videos. These are useful for adding logos or text descriptions that enhance the video. For example, you could have the title "Billy's First Birthday" running along the bottom of a clip showing the happy child with chocolate cake all over his face.

Finally, the Title editor also produces the menus needed to navigate through and around your DVD titles.

Note that the Title editor works identically for both 4:3 and 16:9 projects. Just be sure to be in the proper mode before starting your title or menu because the dimensions are completely different. See "Working with the Album's Views and Tools" in Chapter 6 for details on switching between the two aspect ratios.

Chapter 10

Opening the Title Editor

At last count, there were approximately 6,583 ways to open the Title editor, but I'm sure I missed a few. Just joking, of course, but here are the easy ways to get the job done.

To open the Title editor:

1. Position the Timeline scrubber at the desired title insertion point (**Figure 10.1**).

2. From the Studio menu, choose Toolbox > Create Title (**Figure 10.2**).

   The title creation screen opens (**Figure 10.3**).

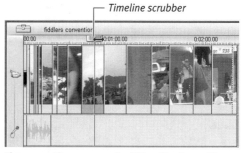

Figure 10.1 You can open the Title editor from either the Video track or the Title track. First position the Timeline scrubber where you want the title inserted.

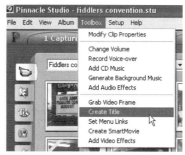

Figure 10.2 One of the many ways to open the Title editor.

Figure 10.3 Here's where you choose between a title overlay and a full-screen title.

Designing Titles and Menus

3. Do *one of the following*:

   ▲ Click the Title Overlay button to create a title that appears *over* your video on the Title track.

   The Title editor opens, displaying the video that will appear behind the title to help you design and place your title (**Figure 10.4**).

   ▲ Click the Full Screen Title button to create a title that appears *instead* of video.

   The Title editor opens, with no video displayed since the full-screen title displaces the video on the Video track.

Figure 10.4 The Title editor for a title overlay, with the underlying video displayed. Get comfortable; you're going to be here for a while.

OPENING THE TITLE EDITOR

259

To open the Title editor (easier):

Do *one of the following:*

1. From the Edit screen, click the Show Titles icon at the left of the Album (**Figure 10.5**).

    The Titles tab opens (**Figure 10.6**).

2. Select the desired title and do *one of the following:*
    - ▲ Drag the title to the Video track to create a full-screen title (**Figure 10.7**).
    - ▲ Drag the title to the Title track to create an overlay title (**Figure 10.8**).

3. Once the selected title is on the track, double-click the title (**Figure 10.9**).

    The Title editor opens with the selected title (**Figure 10.10**).

Or

- ◆ Double-click the Title track at the desired location for the title overlay. The Title editor opens, displaying the underlying video (Figure 10.4).

    Note that this way (the easiest method) works only for overlay titles.

✔ Tips

- The Title track is beneath the Video track. To make Studio display a title over the video, you actually place it under the Video track.

- If you work with titles a lot (and who doesn't?), the F11 (don't save) and F12 (save title) keys become pretty handy. Often it's easier to deep-six a title by pressing F11 and starting over than it is to attempt the multiple undos necessary to get back to square one.

Figure 10.5 Studio includes an album of very useful titles. Here's where you find them.

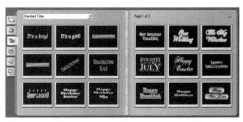

Figure 10.6 Three pages of time-savers and idea generators.

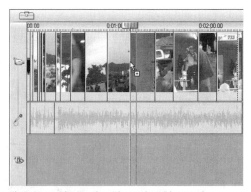

Figure 10.7 Placing the title on the Video track.

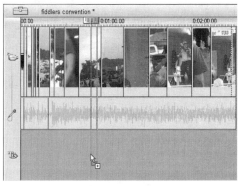

Figure 10.8 Placing the title on the Title track.

Designing Titles and Menus

Figure 10.9 Double-click an existing title to open the Title editor.

Figure 10.10 Here you go, ready to edit.

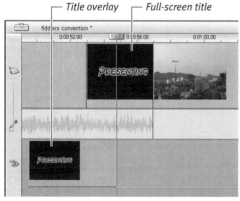

Figure 10.11 Where full-screen and title overlays end up on the Timeline.

- **Figure 10.11** illustrates the positioning of full-screen and overlay titles. As mentioned earlier, Studio places full-screen titles on the Video track, where they *displace* the video for their duration. In contrast, Studio places overlay titles on the Title track, where they appear *over* other videos. If you change your mind about whether you want your title to appear in overlay or full-screen mode, but don't want to redo your design, simply drag the title into the other track at the same position in the Timeline.

- You can only place full-screen titles between scenes, before the first scene, or following the last scene. Drag a title to a position on the Video track and Studio will place it at the nearest scene change. In contrast, you can place overlay titles at any point in the Title track.

To close the Title editor and save your work:

- Do *one of the following*:
    ▲ Click OK in the bottom right corner.
    ▲ Choose File > Close Title Tool (or press F12).
    ▲ Click the X at the upper right of the Title editor.

To close the Title editor without saving:

- Do *one of the following*:
    ▲ Click the Cancel button at the bottom right.
    ▲ Choose File > Cancel Title Tool (or press F11).

Looking at the Title Editor

Once you've opened the Title editor, take a look at its interface and tool sets (**Figure 10.12**). You can access many of these functions by using the Studio menu as well as by clicking the onscreen icons.

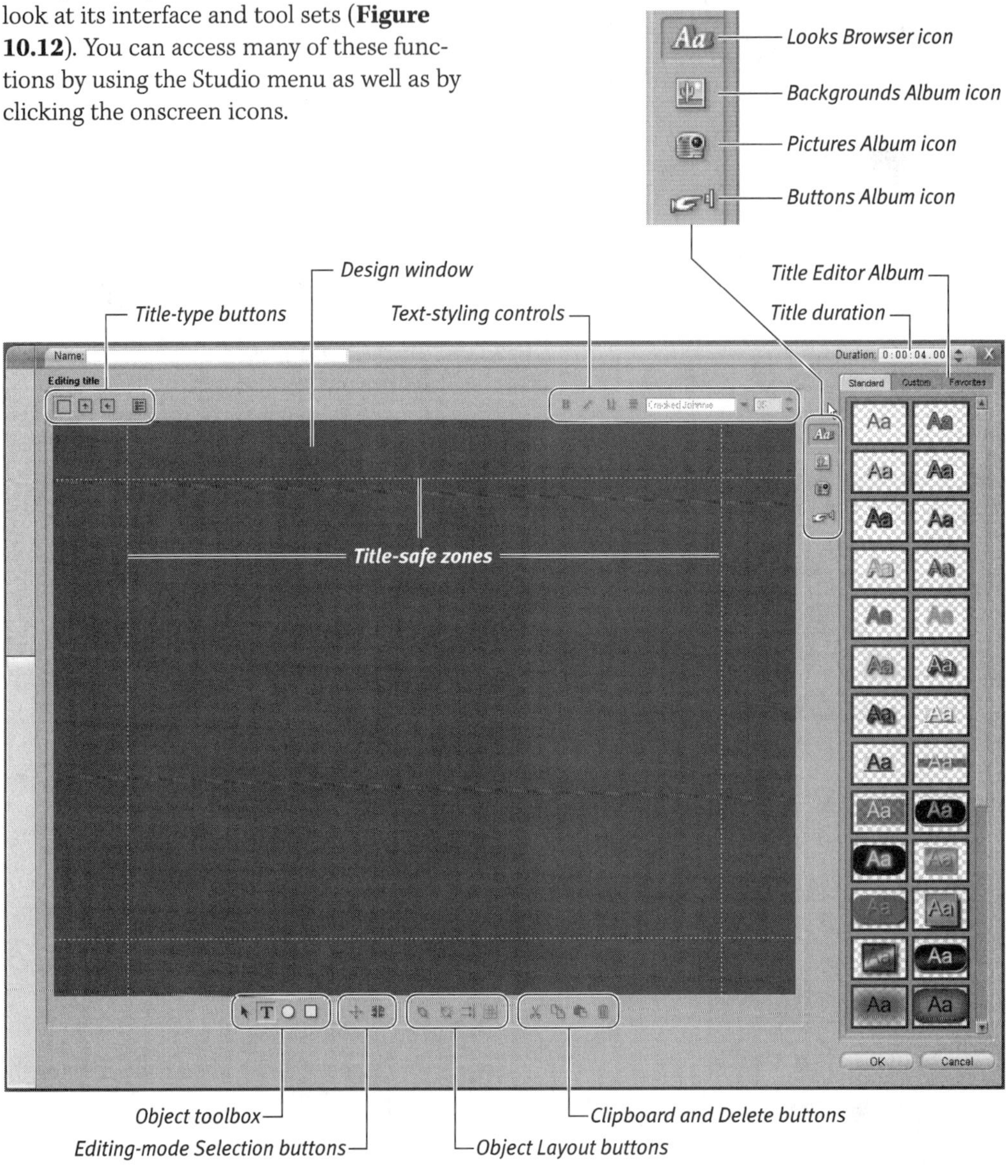
Looks Browser icon
Backgrounds Album icon
Pictures Album icon
Buttons Album icon
Design window
Title Editor Album
Title-type buttons
Text-styling controls
Title duration
Name:
Editing title
Duration: 0:00:04.00
Standard
Custom
Favorites
Title-safe zones
OK
Cancel
Object toolbox
Clipboard and Delete buttons
Editing-mode Selection buttons
Object Layout buttons

Figure 10.12 The Title editor for a full-screen title, which takes over the entire screen.

Designing Titles and Menus

Design window: Studio's Design window is a WYSIWYG (what you see is what you get) design area. When you're designing title overlays, you'll see the underlying video in the Design window (Figure 10.4). But when you're working with full-screen titles, the Design window starts out empty.

Title-safe zones: When creating titles for DVD and other productions viewed primarily on a TV, keep all title elements inside these zones. Otherwise, they may be truncated.

Title-type buttons: These buttons control the type of title: whether static, rolling up and down, crawling sideways, or DVD menu.

Text-styling controls: These controls are similar to those in most word processing programs, with the addition of some excellent alignment and word-wrapping tools.

Object toolbox: These controls allow you to create and position text-, circle-, and square-based objects that serve as either design elements or menu buttons.

Editing-mode selection buttons: Use these buttons to switch into and out of advanced editing modes for kerning text and deforming objects.

Object layout buttons: My favorite. Nothing is more irritating than menu components that are out of alignment or not quite the right size. These tools let you group, align, and resize objects for a more uniform appearance.

Clipboard and deletion buttons: When you're designing titles and menus, often the simplest approach is to copy and paste text attributes and other labels. These tools simplify these common tasks.

Title Editor Album: Studio includes libraries of looks, backgrounds, pictures, and menu elements to use in your productions. Generally, you can customize these, add your own, and save them in a Favorites Album.

Title duration: Here's where you can customize the duration of your title (as with still images, you can also accomplish the same goal by dragging the title to the desired length on the Timeline).

Chapter 10

Adding and Editing Text

Studio's titles can be composed of text and imported images, as well as circles, squares, and derivatives thereof drawn with the Title editor's own drawing tools.

We'll start with text and then examine other components and how they all work together.

To add menu text:

1. Open the Title editor using any of the techniques described earlier in this chapter.

   An *I* should be adjacent to the pointer, indicating that the Text tool is active. If you don't see the *I*, click the *T* in the Object toolbox at the bottom of the screen (**Figure 10.13**).

2. In the Design window, click where you want the text to appear.

   Studio displays a bounding box for your text (**Figure 10.14**).

3. Type the desired text.

4. Click anywhere outside the box to set the text (**Figure 10.15**).

Figure 10.13 Click the Text tool to insert text. Studio rewards you with a special text-insert pointer.

Figure 10.14 The bounding box is ready to receive your text.

Figure 10.15 Pretty bland, eh? We'll spice it up in a minute.

264

Designing Titles and Menus

Figure 10.16 Select the box to edit the text. See the thin text-insert pointer after the word *to*?

Figure 10.17 Studio highlights the text you're about to replace.

Figure 10.18 The new text.

To change menu text:

1. Select the menu text.

   A bounding box appears around the text (**Figure 10.16**). The thin insert bar after the colon is the text-entry pointer.

2. Move the text-entry pointer to the desired location by using the arrow keys or by clicking the pointer in the desired spot.

3. Type the desired text.

   Studio adds the text.

4. To set your changes, click anywhere outside the box.

To replace menu text:

1. Select the menu text.

2. Drag over the text that you want to replace or hold down the Shift key and use the arrow keys to select the text you want to replace.

   Studio highlights the selected text (**Figure 10.17**).

3. Type the desired text.

   Studio replaces the text (**Figure 10.18**).

4. To set your changes, click anywhere outside the box.

265

To move text:

1. Select the text.

   A gray bounding box appears around the text object (Figure 10.18).

2. Click the bounding box.

   Yellow control points appear around the box, a green dot appears above the box, and the pointer turns into the move-object pointer (**Figure 10.19**).

   The move-object pointer will disappear if it's moved outside the bounding box.

3. Drag the text to the desired location.

✔ **Tip**

- You can use the arrow keys to move text (and all objects) one pixel in any direction—a great way to fine-tune your positioning.

Figure 10.19 Select the text twice to move or resize it. First you get the gray bounding box and then these control points.

Designing Titles and Menus

Figure 10.20 Studio's alignment controls work like those in most programs.

Figure 10.21 To change text attributes, simply highlight the text and change the attributes.

Figure 10.22 Just love that Cracked Johnnie font for blue grass music.

To change font, text attributes, and alignment:

1. Select the text.

   A gray bounding box appears around the text object (Figure 10.18).

2. Click the bounding box.

   Yellow control points appear around the box, a green dot appears above the box, and the pointer turns into the move-object pointer.

   All text-styling controls are now active. You know the drill for bold, italics, underlining, font, and font size.

3. To change the alignment, do *one of the following*:

   ▲ Click the Text Justification icon at the top and select Left, Center, or Right alignment (**Figure 10.20**).

   ▲ From the Studio menu, choose Title > Justify Text. Then choose the desired alignment.

4. To change font or text attributes such as size, boldfacing, italics, and underlining, drag over the text that you want to modify and then choose the desired attributes (**Figure 10.21**).

   Studio changes the attributes (**Figure 10.22**).

✔ Tip

- The shrinking, scaling, and word-wrap options in Figure 10.20 are discussed later in this chapter, since most users pick their styles before fine-tuning their text.

Using Studio's Styles

There are more extensive text-editing capabilities to explore, but if you're like me, you'll produce the most professional-looking titles by using styles contained in Studio's Looks browser.

When you create your first text title, Studio applies the default style at the top left of the Looks browser (**Figure 10.23**), which is open by default when you open the Title editor. Otherwise, to open the Looks browser, click the Looks icon at the left of the browser window or go to the Studio menu and choose Title > Album > Looks.

As you scroll down the Looks browser, you'll see increasingly creative title presets. The upcoming tasks show you how to apply and customize Studio's looks. Note that changing styles doesn't affect font, font size, alignment, or any other text attribute.

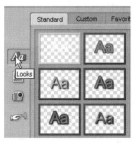

Figure 10.23 Studio's styles are a real blessing for creatively challenged individuals (like me); you can apply them to text and other objects.

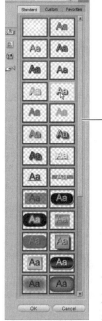

Scroll bar

Figure 10.24 Select the text to change; then select a new style, and you're done. Use the scroll bar on the right to scroll down the browser.

To apply a new look to text:

1. Select the text to adjust and click the gray bounding box to display the control points (Figure 10.19).

2. Using the scroll bar on the right of the Looks browser, scroll down to the desired style (**Figure 10.24**).

3. Select the style with the pointer.
   As soon as you select the style, Studio applies it to the selected text.

✔ Tips

- If you hover your pointer over any style, Studio displays a submenu containing eight styles with different combinations of color, edge, and shadow (**Figure 10.25**). Move your mouse, and the submenu disappears, or you can click the X in the upper-right corner.

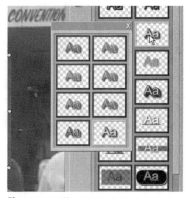

Figure 10.25 Hover your mouse over a style to see a submenu containing eight similar styles.

Designing Titles and Menus

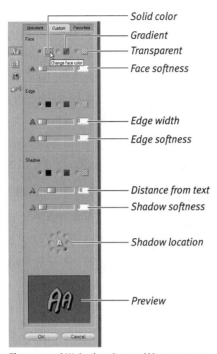

Figure 10.26 Wait, there's more! You can even customize the styles. Note the Solid color, Gradient, and Transparent color swatches for the text face, edge, and shadow.

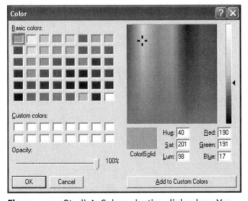

Figure 10.27 Studio's Color selection dialog box. You can store your custom colors, a useful feature when you need to repeat them.

Figure 10.28 Here's where you edit the gradients. Each color box opens the Color Selection screen.

To customize a solid text color:

1. Select the style to customize (Figure 10.24).

2. In the Looks browser, select the Custom tab (**Figure 10.26**).

3. In the Face section, select the radio button next to the solid-colored box with the tooltip Change Face Color.

4. Click the solid-colored box.
   Studio's Color selection dialog box opens (**Figure 10.27**).

5. Choose the desired color by selecting it from the Basic Colors or Custom Colors palette or by clicking a color on the spectrum.

6. If you want, save your custom color by clicking the Add to Custom Colors button (Ctrl+A).
   Saving your custom color helps you maintain uniformity as you work.

7. Click OK to close the dialog box.

To customize a gradient text color:

1. Select the style that you want to customize.

2. In the Looks browser, select the Custom tab.

3. In the Face section, select the radio button next to the gradient-colored box.

4. Click the Gradient box.
   Studio's Gradient Selection screen opens (**Figure 10.28**). The boxes at each corner of the Gradient preview box control the gradient blend.

5. Click any box to open its Color Selection dialog box. You can configure each of the four colors independently.

6. Click the X in the upper-right corner to close the Gradient Selection dialog box.

USING STUDIO'S STYLES

269

To adjust text softness:

1. Select the style that you want to customize.

2. In the Looks browser, select the Custom tab.

3. In the Face section, select the solid or gradient radio button and adjust the face softness with the Face slider, viewing the results in the Preview window (**Figure 10.29**).

   Softness controls the definition of the text face. At zero the face is completely sharp, while at 30 it's very indistinct, causing the text to blend into the background.

   If you have text selected in the Title editor, Studio applies these modifications to the title in near real time.

To adjust text edges:

1. In the Edge section, select the solid or gradient radio button and then change the text color as described in "To customize a solid text color" or "To customize a gradient text color" earlier in this chapter.

2. Use the Edge sliders to modify the edge width and softness.

   Width refers to the width of the edge, while edge softness, like face softness, relates to how sharply Studio defines the edge. The easiest way to get a feel for this is through experimentation.

Shadow location

Figure 10.29 Our day is fading into memory. Use the softness sliders to control text strength; click the desired radio button to set shadow location.

Designing Titles and Menus

Figure 10.30 The Favorites Album can come in very handy, especially when you decide to change a style.

Figure 10.31 Click the Suitcase icon to you're your style.

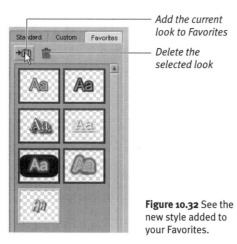

Figure 10.32 See the new style added to your Favorites.

To adjust text shadows:

1. In the Shadow section, select the solid or gradient radio button and then change the text color as described in "To customize a solid text color" or "To customize a gradient text color" earlier in this chapter.

2. To modify the distances of the shadow from the original text and shadow softness, use the Shadow sliders.

3. To change the position of the shadow, click the button for the desired Shadow location.

✔ Tip

- There are no customization options for the transparent text style.

To add a style to the Favorites Album:

1. Select the Favorites tab to open the Favorites Album (**Figure 10.30**).

2. Click the Suitcase icon to add the currently selected style (**Figure 10.31**).

   Studio adds the style to the Favorites Album (**Figure 10.32**).

To delete a style from the Favorites Album:

1. From within the Favorites Album, select the offending style.

2. Click the Trash Can icon to delete the style.

✔ Tips

- Saving styles in your Favorites Album is very convenient when you're changing the styles of multiple objects. Otherwise, you have to hunt through the Looks browser each time you apply the style.

- You can save any style in the Favorites Album; it doesn't have to be one that you've edited.

- Think twice before deleting a style, because you cannot bring the style back with Undo.

About Text Scaling and Word Wrapping

Studio's word-wrapping and text resizing controls (**Figure 10.33**) can be confusing at first, so I thought I would explain a couple of concepts that made them easier for me to understand.

First, the top two controls, Shrink to Fit and Scale to Fit, are basically inactive until you resize the text in a title by grabbing one of the edges as described in the next section, "Resizing and Justifying Text."

Second, consider the difference between *shrink* and *scale* as the terms relate to these controls. Briefly, when you select Shrink to Fit and then resize the text box, Studio makes the text larger and smaller along with the box, but it doesn't change the aspect ratio, or—to be technical—squish the text to make it fit. In contrast, when you select Scale to Fit, Studio scales, or squishes, if you prefer, the text to make it fit into the newly defined confines.

Figure 10.33 Your shrinking, scaling, and word wrap controls.

Figure 10.34 illustrates the difference between *shrink* and *scale*. The starting point is the top title. The middle title is the result after resizing with Shrink to Fit selected; the text is smaller, but each letter has the same basic form. Contrast this with the bottom title, resized using Scale to Fit. Here Studio stretched the text to fit the entire text box.

So if you just want to customize text size, but don't want to change the proportions, use Shrink to Fit. If you want to actually change the proportions of the letters, use Scale to Fit. You can switch between these two alternatives any time the text box is activated; you don't have to resize the text box with these controls enabled to achieve the desired effect.

continues on next page

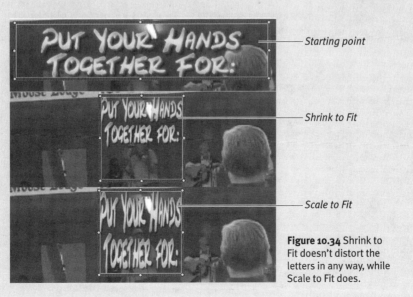

Figure 10.34 Shrink to Fit doesn't distort the letters in any way, while Scale to Fit does.

Designing Titles and Menus

About Text Scaling and Word Wrapping *continued*

The word-wrapping controls work like this. When you select Word Wrap On and then resize the text box, Studio resizes the box and rewraps the words to make them fit, but does not change the size. **Figure 10.35** illustrates this point, working from the same starting point as Figure 10.34. Here, I selected Word Wrap On and made the box smaller. As you can see at the top of the figure, the text size is the same, but Studio adjusted the word wrap to make the text fit.

Then I selected Word Wrap Off, and Studio essentially returned the title to its original position.

Between you, me, and the fencepost, I find Studio's word-wrapping controls unintuitive and not particularly useful, and so I insert carriage returns in my titles to control word wrapping directly.

Figure 10.35 Select Word Wrap On, and Studio wraps your text for you, but doesn't change font size. Word Wrap Off returns you to the status quo.

Resizing and Justifying Text

Even after applying Pinnacle's wonderful styles, you still may have to resize and/or justify your text. When resizing, note that Studio will adjust your text differently depending on which scaling, shrinking, or word-wrapping option you've selected. See the preceding sidebar, "About Text Scaling and Word Wrapping," for details.

To justify text, you use a control to place the text in one of nine divided areas, a simple way to ensure consistency among menus.

To resize text:

1. Select the text that you want to adjust and click the gray bounding box to display the control points.

2. If the Move, Scale, and Rotate tool isn't selected at the bottom of the Title Editor window, click the icon to enable the tool (**Figure 10.36**).

3. To shrink or expand the text, do *any of the following*:

   ▲ Hold the pointer over a corner control point of the bounding box to convert it into a two-sided arrow (**Figure 10.37**). Press the mouse button and drag the control point in or out to shrink or expand the text as desired. If you've selected Shrink to Fit or Word Wrap On, you can freely resize the height and width of the text, but if you've selected Scale to Fit, Studio restricts your scaling so that the aspect ratio of the text doesn't change.

Figure 10.36 Click the Move, Scale, and Rotate tool to resize your title text.

Figure 10.37 With this double arrow, you can adjust both the text height and width.

Figure 10.38 Note the small double-arrow pointer on the right control point. Drag this to adjust width but not height.

Figure 10.39 You knew this was coming. The small double-arrow pointer on the bottom is used to adjust height but not width.

Designing Titles and Menus

Figure 10.40 Use the Justify tool to place your text in one of nine positions.

Figure 10.41 Note that Studio respects the title-safe zone when it justifies the text.

▲ Hold the pointer over the left- or right-side control point to convert it into a two-sided arrow (**Figure 10.38**). Press the left mouse button and drag the control point in or out to shrink or expand the text.

▲ Hold the pointer over either the top or bottom control point to convert it into a two-sided arrow (**Figure 10.39**). Press the left mouse button and drag the control point in or out to shrink or expand the text.

To justify text:

1. Select the text that you want to adjust and click the gray bounding box to display the control points.

2. Do *one of the following*:

   ▲ On the Title Editor toolbar at the bottom of the screen, click the Justify tool, which looks like a tic-tac-toe board (**Figure 10.40**).

   ▲ From the Studio menu, choose Title > Justify.

3. Select the desired area in the Justify tool. Studio aligns the text accordingly (**Figure 10.41**).

   After positioning your text, the Justify tool displays a black dot in the selected spot, reflecting the current positioning.

✔ Tip

- The Justify tool is easily confused with the Text Justify (text alignment) tool discussed in "To change font, text attributes, and alignment" earlier in this chapter. The Text Justify tool justifies or aligns the text within the text object itself, like the alignment tools in a word processor. In contrast, the Justify tool aligns the text object to a location in the menu or title.

275

Kerning and Leading Text

Occasionally you may want to adjust the space between letters or characters, a process called *kerning*, or change the vertical space between lines of text, called *leading*. Here's how.

To kern text:

1. Select the text that you want to adjust and click the gray bounding box to display the control points.

2. On the Title Editor toolbar at the bottom, click the Set Kerning, Leading, and Skew tool (**Figure 10.42**).

3. Position the pointer over one of the side control points.

    The pointer changes to the kern pointer (**Figure 10.43**).

4. Drag the pointer in or out to achieve the desired spacing.

    Studio changes the distance between the letters (**Figure 10.44**).

To change the leading between text lines:

1. Select the text that you want to adjust and click the gray bounding box to display the control points.

2. On the Title Editor toolbar at the bottom, click the Set Kerning, Leading, and Skew tool (Figure 10.42).

3. Position the pointer over either the top or bottom control point (not the corner).

    The pointer changes to the kern pointer.

4. Drag the pointer up or down to achieve the desired spacing.

    Studio changes the distance between the words (**Figure 10.45**).

Figure 10.42 This font is too compressed for my taste. Fix it by clicking the Set Kerning, Leading, and Skew tool.

Figure 10.43 Place the kern pointer over a control point on the right or left and stretch out the text.

Figure 10.44 Note how much more space there is between the letters.

Figure 10.45 Place the kern pointer over the top or bottom control point to change the leading.

Designing Titles and Menus

Figure 10.46 Use the top control point to rotate the text.

Figure 10.47 Rotate your text to the desired position.

Figure 10.48 You can also skew your text. Just grab and stretch.

Figure 10.49 Here's what happens.

Rotating and Skewing Text

Here are two additional design options: rotate and skew.

To rotate text:

1. Select the text that you want to adjust and click the gray bounding box to display the control points.

2. If the Move, Scale, and Rotate tool isn't selected, click the icon to enable the tool (Figure 10.36).

3. Move the pointer over the green control point atop the text object.

   The pointer changes to the rotate pointer (**Figure 10.46**).

4. Drag the pointer to rotate the text to the desired position.

   A dotted-line bounding box follows your progress.

5. Release the pointer when your text is in the desired position (**Figure 10.47**).

To skew text:

1. Select the text that you want to adjust and click the gray bounding box to display the control points.

2. On the Title Editor toolbar at the bottom, click the Set Kerning, Leading, and Skew tool (Figure 10.42).

3. Position the pointer over one of the control point corners.

   The pointer changes to the skew pointer (**Figure 10.48**).

4. Drag the text to the desired location.

   A dotted-line bounding box follows your progress.

5. Release the pointer when your text is in the desired position (**Figure 10.49**).

Using Full-Screen Titles

As you may recall, a full-screen title is any title that lives on the Video track, since it replaces the video completely, taking up the full screen. All full-screen titles initially have black backgrounds (**Figure 10.50**). You can go with that minimalist approach, or you can add a background, which can be a solid color, gradient, or full-screen image.

You can choose from Studio's range of useful background images or use your own. Just remember: all images used as a background run full screen and can't be resized and used as foreground design elements such as logos. For information on using images as logos, see "Adding Logos to Video" later in this chapter.

Figure 10.50 Here's what a full-screen title looks like when you first create it. It has no background—but we'll fix that in a hurry.

To create a single-color background:

1. In the Title editor, do *one of the following*:
   ▲ Click the Backgrounds icon at the left of the Title Editor Album (**Figure 10.51**).
   ▲ From the Studio menu, choose Title > Album > Backgrounds.
   The Backgrounds Album opens (**Figure 10.52**).

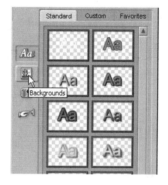

Figure 10.51 Getting to the Backgrounds Album.

Designing Titles and Menus

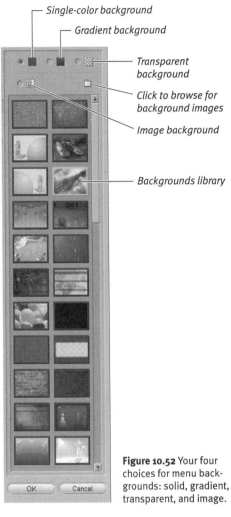

- Single-color background
- Gradient background
- Transparent background
- Click to browse for background images
- Image background
- Backgrounds library

Figure 10.52 Your four choices for menu backgrounds: solid, gradient, transparent, and image.

2. Select the single-color background radio button (Figure 10.52).

3. To change colors, click the colored box next to the radio button.
   Studio's Color Selection dialog box opens (**Figure 10.53**).

4. Choose the desired color by selecting it from the Basic Colors or Custom Colors palette or by clicking a color on the spectrum.

5. If you want, save your custom color by clicking the Add to Custom Colors button (Ctrl+A).
   Saving your the custom color helps you maintain uniformity as you work.

6. Click OK to close the dialog box.
   Studio replaces the background with the selected color.

Figure 10.53 The familiar Color Selection dialog box.

To create a gradient background:

1. In the Title editor, click the Backgrounds icon at the left of the Title Editor Album (Figure 10.51).

   The Backgrounds Album opens (Figure 10.52).

2. Select the gradient background radio button.

3. To change colors, click the colored box next to the gradient radio button.

   Studio's Gradient Selection dialog box opens (**Figure 10.54**). The boxes at each corner of the Gradient preview box control the gradient blend.

4. Click any box to open its Color Selection dialog box (Figure 10.53). You can configure each of the four colors independently.

5. Click the X in the upper-right corner to close the Gradient Selection dialog box.

   Studio replaces the background with the selected gradient.

Figure 10.54 This is where you choose your gradient colors.

To create a transparent background:

1. In the Title editor, click the Backgrounds icon at the left of the Title Editor Album (Figure 10.51).

   The Backgrounds Album opens (Figure 10.52).

2. Select the transparent background radio button.

   This is the default setting for the background, for which there are no options. The background simply appears as black behind the menu or title components.

Designing Titles and Menus

Figure 10.55 To change the background, just select the image you want.

Figure 10.56 Or use your own images as backgrounds.

To select an image background:

1. In the Title editor, click the Backgrounds icon at the left of the Title Editor Album (Figure 10.51).

    The Backgrounds Album opens (Figure 10.52).

2. Select the image background radio button.

3. Do *one of the following:*

    ▲ To use an image from the Album, select the desired image.

    Studio replaces the background with the selected image (**Figure 10.55**).

    ▲ To use an image from another location, click the Folder icon to browse for images elsewhere (Figure 10.52). In the standard Open dialog box that appears, navigate to and select the desired image file.

    Studio replaces the background with the selected image and populates the Image browser on the right with the new files (**Figure 10.56**).

✔ Tips

- The original location of Studio's excellent background images is Program Files > Pinnacle > Studio 9 > Backgrounds, should you need to find these images again.

- If a selected image doesn't fill the screen in either height or width, Studio stretches the image proportionately (without distorting it) to fill either height or width, whichever is closer. For the most predictable results, prepare your background image files at your target output resolution, using 640 x 480 pixels for DVD, the resolution used for Pinnacle's background files.

- For a complete discussion of image preparation, see "Editing Still Images" in Chapter 5.

USING FULL-SCREEN TITLES

281

Adding Logos to Video

Placing logos over videos is a nice professional touch, though in this situation Studio presents a minor catch-22. Simply stated, from the Title editor, you can place, move, and resize a logo over your video, but you can't make it transparent.

Alternatively, you can drag an image to the Title track from the Still Images tab in the Album and make it transparent (assuming that you follow the rules discussed here), but you can't move or resize the image or it becomes a full-screen logo.

These are the general rules; this section describes how to work within them. An exception to the rules is discussed in the sidebar "The Art of Being Transparent," later in this chapter.

Figure 10.57 Click the Pictures icon to open the Pictures Album.

Click to browse for pictures

Figure 10.58 The Pictures Album.

To overlay a logo on video:

1. Double-click the Title track at the desired location for the logo overlay.
   The Title editor opens.

2. In the Title editor, do *one of the following*:
   ▲ Click the Pictures icon at the left of the Title Editor Album (**Figure 10.57**).
   ▲ From the Studio menu, choose Title > Album > Pictures.
   The Pictures Album opens (**Figure 10.58**).

3. If necessary, click the Folder icon to navigate to the directory containing your logos.

Designing Titles and Menus

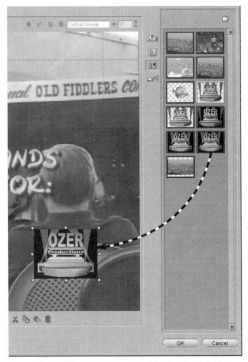

Figure 10.59 Drag the image into the Design window. Unlike a background image, an image dragged from the Pictures Album can be scaled or moved.

4. Drag the image into the Design window (**Figure 10.59**).

5. Move and resize the image as described in "To resize text" earlier in this chapter.

   Note that you can't skew or rotate the image, only resize and move it.

✔ Tips

- Although you can't argue with the sheer elegance of the logo shown in Figure 10.59 (pretty cheesy, eh?), you probably wish the black background would go away. The sidebar "The Art of Being Transparent," later in this chapter, describes how to accomplish this.

- The program of choice for creating titles and logos is Ulead Systems' Cool 3D Studio, available at www.ulead.com. Using a supplied template, I created the logo shown in Figure 10.59 in about two minutes.

To make a logo transparent:

1. From the Still Images tab, drag the logo to the Title track (**Figure 10.60**).

    In the Player, Studio zooms the image to full screen and makes it transparent, so you can see segments of the video behind it.

2. Double-click the logo to open the Title editor (**Figure 10.61**).

    The logo is full screen and shows no transparency in the Title editor. In addition, selecting the logo raises no control points. The image looks fuzzy (though perhaps not in your small version of it) because the 160 x 120–resolution image was zoomed to full screen.

Figure 10.60 To make an image transparent, you must load it from the Album. See how this logo is transparent now?

Figure 10.61 Notice how the same logo shows no transparency in the Title editor.

Designing Titles and Menus

Figure 10.62 Since you can't resize images placed on the Title track from the Album, you have to premake your logo files like this.

Figure 10.63 Here's how the logo looks in use.

✔ Tips

- Studio assumes that the top-left pixel is the transparent color and eliminates this color when displaying the logo. In the Ozer Productions logo, the top-left pixel is black, the same color as the background to be eliminated. When you want to make an image transparent, computer-generated images work best, or real-world images carefully edited to produce a single, consistent background image.

- Since you can't resize the logo when pulling it down from the Album, the best solution is to create a full-screen (640 x 480) image with the logo as a small component in the desired location (**Figure 10.62**). Remember to observe the title-safe zones when creating images in this fashion. **Figure 10.63** shows the image overlaying the video.

The Art of Being Transparent

This section's introduction describes Studio's catch-22 when it comes to transparent logo overlay: if you drag in an image from the Title editor, you can move and resize it, but you cannot make it transparent; if you drag in an image from the Still Images tab of the Album, you can make it transparent, but you cannot move or resize it.

There is one undocumented exception to this catch (Quick! Call Geraldo). If you create a 32-bit image with an alpha channel for the desired transparency region, Studio recognizes and eliminates this region from the Title editor, allowing full moving and resizing control.

For example, of the three logos in **Figure 10.64**, two are transparent—including the Ozer Productions spinning globe, which has active edit points, proving that the logo is both resizable and movable. These were produced as 32-bit video overlays in Targa (TGA) format in Ulead's Cool 3D Studio. The third logo was output as a simple 24-bit bitmap file, and as you can see, it's not transparent. Note that Studio displays the two images as transparent in the Looks browser (it also displays another transparent logo not used in this example), showing a checkered gray pattern behind them instead of the pure black backgrounds of the other images.

In retrospect, it's not surprising that Studio recognizes a transparent alpha channel in images, since the program uses this technique to recognize transparent areas in DVD buttons (see "Working with Buttons" later in this chapter).

The bottom line is that if you understand how to produce 32-bit images with an alpha channel in programs like Adobe Photoshop, Cool 3D Studio, or Jasc's Paint Shop Pro, you can make your images transparent in Studio so that you can move and resize them at will in the Title editor. Check www.doceo.com/Studio9 for details on creating a transparent logo in Cool 3D Studio and Photoshop.

Figure 10.64 Contrary to what the Studio manual says, the Title editor can recognize transparency masks on 32-bit images with an alpha channel, providing the best of both worlds.

Designing Titles and Menus

Figure 10.65 Studio lets you draw ellipses and rectangles in your titles.

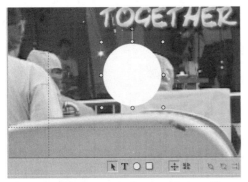

Figure 10.66 You can manipulate an object at will once it's inserted.

Figure 10.67 You can even apply styles to the object.

Creating and Editing Title Objects

Now that you're comfortable with text, it's time to touch briefly on adding and editing title objects: ellipses and rectangles that you can use in your titles. Title objects serve quite nicely as text backgrounds or as stand-alone design components.

Studio's title objects are very flexible and can be assigned looks, customized, skewed, resized, and repositioned at will. You accomplish these tasks the same way as for text.

To create an ellipse or rectangle:

1. From the Title editor, click the Add Ellipse or Add Rectangle icon in the Object toolbox (**Figure 10.65**).

2. In the Design window, drag the pointer to draw the text object (**Figure 10.66**). Studio creates the object (**Figure 10.67**).

To edit or customize a title object:

- Do *any of the following*:
  ▲ To move the title object, see "To move text" earlier in this chapter.
  ▲ To apply or customize a new style, see "Using Studio's Styles" earlier in this chapter.
  ▲ To resize or justify the object, see "Resizing and Justifying Text" earlier in this chapter.
  ▲ To rotate or skew your object, see "Rotating and Skewing Text" earlier in this chapter.

Working with Buttons

Buttons are interactive links on a menu that let viewers play content like video or a slide show, or jump to other menus. Studio supplies an album of buttons, and you can convert any ungrouped object to a button. Once you add a button to a title, it magically becomes a menu. Like titles, menus can be either full screen or overlays displayed over an underlying video track.

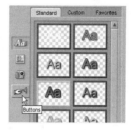

Figure 10.68 Time to start authoring! Step 1: open the Buttons Album.

Studio's Title editor is a great place to produce attractive, custom menus, but you can also choose from an extensive range of customizable menus on the Disc Menus tab of the Album, accessible from the Edit menu. The easiest way to get started is to use the supplied templates, described in "Using Menu Templates" in Chapter 12, which also describes how to link content to buttons. The current chapter focuses exclusively on the mechanics of menu creation.

To add a button to a title:

1. In the Title editor, do *one of the following*:
   - ▲ Click the Buttons icon at the left of the Title Editor Album (**Figure 10.68**).
   - ▲ From the Studio menu, choose Title > Album > Buttons.

   Studio opens the Buttons Album.

2. Drag the desired button into the Design window (**Figure 10.69**).

   Studio inserts the button into the title.

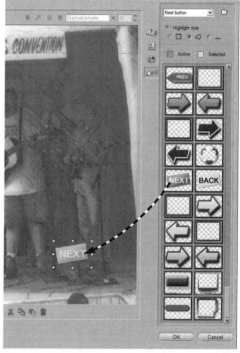

Figure 10.69 Drag the button from the Buttons Album to the Design window.

✔ Tip

- If you've created your own album of buttons, use the folder to the right of the drop-down menu at the top of the Buttons Album (Figure 10.71) to navigate to the appropriate folder.

Designing Titles and Menus

Figure 10.70 Or convert any menu object—text, ellipse, rectangle, image—to a button with this control.

To convert an object to a button:

1. Select the object that you want to convert and click the gray bounding box to display the control points (**Figure 10.70**).

2. At the top of the Buttons Album, open the drop-down menu (**Figure 10.71**).

3. Choose Normal Button.

   Studio converts the text to a button and highlights it with the default-selected color (**Figure 10.72**). When you return to the Menu view, you'll see that the Menu track is now active, and that the label M1, for *Menu 1,* appears at the top of the menu (**Figure 10.73**). Congratulations; you're now authoring a DVD!

Figure 10.71 The four button types: Normal, Thumbnail, Previous, and Next.

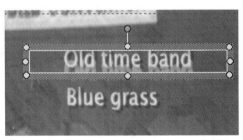

Figure 10.72 After converting text to a button, Studio highlights it with the default-selected color. This is the faint shadow you see beneath the highlighted text.

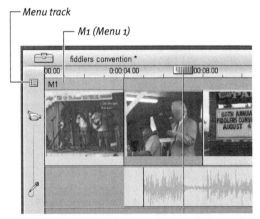

Figure 10.73 Adding a button converts a title to a menu. Now the Menu track is activated, and Menu 1 in place.

289

WORKING WITH BUTTONS

To set a highlight style for a button:

1. Select the button that you want to modify and click the gray bounding box to display the control points (Figure 10.72).

2. At the top of the Buttons Album, choose one of the following highlight styles (**Figure 10.74**):
   - ▲ **Follow Shape:** Makes the highlighting follow the object's shape.
   - ▲ **Box:** Displays a box around the button.
   - ▲ **Underline:** Underlines the button.

   Figure 10.75 shows the styles.

✔ Tip

- Studio provides no feedback in the Title editor after you select the button style, so you have to preview the buttons in the Clip Properties tool.

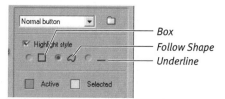

Figure 10.74 Buttons can have three highlight styles, shown here.

Figure 10.75 Here's what the three highlight styles look like when applied to a title.

A Taxonomy of Buttons

As you can see in the drop-down menu in Figure 10.71, Studio has the following four button types:

Normal Button: Links to a video, slide show, or another menu.

Thumbnail Button: Links to a video or slide show and displays a thumbnail inside the button (usually shaped like a frame).

Next Button: Links to the next page. Appears on all but the final page of multimenu productions automatically created by Studio from menu templates.

Previous Button: Links to the previous page. Appears on the second and subsequent pages of multimenu productions automatically created by Studio from menu templates.

If you're building your own menus one by one, always select either the Normal or Thumbnail Button option, even when creating links to previous or next pages.

Use the Previous and Next Button options *only* when you're creating menu templates for Studio autocompletion (see "Creating DVD Menu Templates" later in this chapter). Studio uses these buttons to enable navigation between menus that it automatically creates from these templates.

Designing Titles and Menus

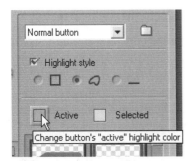

Figure 10.76 You can customize the highlight color for the active or selected state.

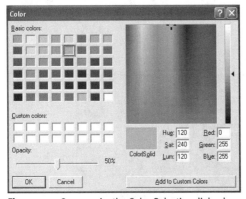

Figure 10.77 Once again, the Color Selection dialog box.

To set active and selected colors:

1. Select the button that you want to modify and click the gray bounding box to display the control points (Figure 10.72).

2. At the top of the Buttons Album, choose the color box next to the state (Active or Selected) that you want to change (**Figure 10.76**).
   Studio's Color Selection dialog box opens (**Figure 10.77**).

3. Choose the desired color by selecting it from the Basic Colors or Custom Colors palette or by clicking a different color on the spectrum.

4. If you want, save custom color by clicking the Add to Custom Colors button (Ctrl+A).
   Saving your custom color helps you maintain uniformity as you work.

5. Click OK to close the dialog box.

Working with Multiple Objects

Studio includes a wealth of grouping, alignment, sizing, and sequencing tools that can be used with all text, graphic, and other objects. You will find them especially helpful for DVD menu design, where they can shave countless minutes off work time you would otherwise spend ensuring that objects are properly sized, spaced, and aligned.

This section explores these features while creating a DVD menu that you will save as a Studio template.

To make objects the same size:

1. Select the objects that you want to resize by doing *one of the following:*
   - ▲ Hold down the Ctrl key and click each object; the last object you select should be the object whose size you want the others to replicate.
   - ▲ Drag an area that includes only the objects to be resized; the last object you select should be the object whose size you want the others to replicate.

   Studio places white highlights around each object except the last one selected; it places yellow highlights around the final object (**Figure 10.78**).

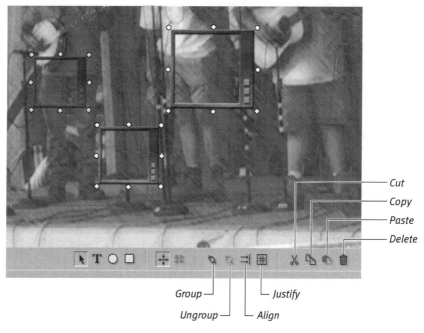

Figure 10.78 To make all objects the same size, select them, choosing last the one you want all the others to conform to (it should have a yellow bounding box around it).

Designing Titles and Menus

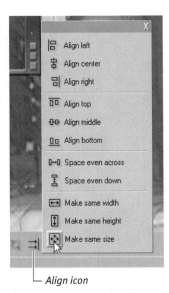

Align icon

Figure 10.79 Click the Align icon; then select Make Same Size at the bottom of the menu.

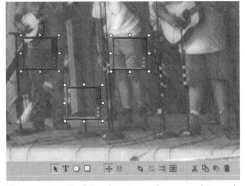

Figure 10.80 All of the objects are the same size now!

2. Click the Align icon at the bottom of the Design window.

   Studio displays the Align menu (**Figure 10.79**).

3. Select Make Same Size at the bottom of the Align menu.

   Studio resizes all objects to the size of the last object selected (**Figure 10.80**).

✔ Tips

- This method works best if you've already made your objects and need to resize them en masse. But often it's easier to copy and paste buttons and other objects to ensure that they're identical (see "To copy and paste objects" later in this chapter).

- The Align menu also includes options for making objects the same height and width. Use the same procedures described in the preceding task to operate these functions.

- You can also access sizing functions from the Studio menu by choosing Title > Align.

- In truth, these controls have worked sporadically for me in the past. If you find that they're not working for you, use the copy and paste method discussed in the first tip if you can; otherwise, mutter (quietly) under your breath and resize your objects manually.

WORKING WITH MULTIPLE OBJECTS

293

To evenly space objects vertically or horizontally:

1. Move the two outside objects to the external boundaries for all the objects that will be spaced.

2. Select the objects that you want to space by doing *one of the following:*
   - ▲ Hold down the Ctrl key and click each object.
   - ▲ Drag an area that includes only the objects to be spaced (**Figure 10.81**).

3. At the bottom of the Design window, click the Align icon.
   Studio displays the Align menu (Figure 10.79).

4. Select Space Even Across.
   Studio spaces all objects evenly between the two objects at either extreme (**Figure 10.82**).

✔ Tips

- Studio does *not* space the objects evenly on the page, only between the objects at either extreme. To obtain the desired spacing, place the two outside objects at the desired location, and Studio spaces all other selected objects evenly between these two.

- Operation is identical when spacing objects vertically.

- You can also access spacing functions from the Studio menu by choosing Title > Align.

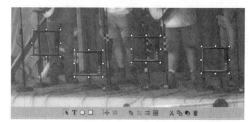

Figure 10.81 Now to get the objects evenly spaced, first move the two outside boxes to the desired locations. Studio spaces the images inside these extremes.

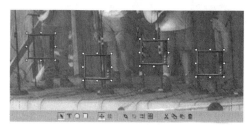

Figure 10.82 Now that the objects are spaced evenly, time to get them aligned. When selecting the images, choose the one in the desired position last (it should have a yellow bounding box).

Designing Titles and Menus

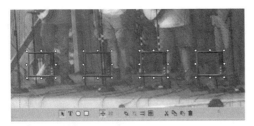

Figure 10.83 Alignment achieved.

To align objects vertically or horizontally:

1. Select the objects that you want to align by doing *one of the following*:
   ▲ Hold down the Ctrl key and click each object; the last object you select should be the object with which you want the other objects aligned (Figure 10.82).
   ▲ Drag an area that includes only the objects to be aligned; the last object you select should be the object with which you want the other objects aligned.

   The object with the yellow control points will be the reference object. All other objects will shift to align with this object.

2. Click the Align icon at the bottom of the Design window.

   Studio displays the Align menu (Figure 10.79).

3. Click the desired alignment—in this case, Align Bottom.

   Studio aligns all objects on the bottom of the reference object (**Figure 10.83**).

✔ Tips

- Operation is identical when using the other alignment functions.
- You can also access the alignment functions from the Studio menu by choosing Title > Align.

To group and ungroup objects:

1. Select the objects that you want to group by doing *one of the following:*
   - ▲ Hold down the Ctrl key and click each object.
   - ▲ Drag an area that includes only the objects that you want to group.
2. Click the Group icon at the bottom of the Design window (**Figure 10.84**).
   Studio groups the objects together. To ungroup the objects, click the Ungroup icon next to the Group icon.

✔ Tip

- Once you've grouped the objects, you can perform extensive edits that affect all of the objects. For example, with the thumbnail buttons shown in Figure 10.84, you can modify the size, active color, and highlight style for all grouped objects at once—a very efficient editing procedure.

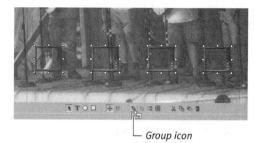

Figure 10.84 Group the objects so you can position them en masse. Use the Group icon.

Designing Titles and Menus

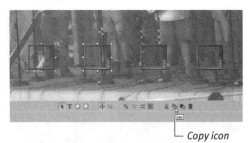

Copy icon

Figure 10.85 To copy two of the objects to move them above the others, select them and click the Copy icon.

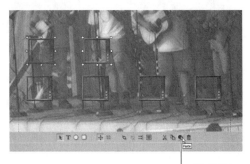

Paste icon

Figure 10.86 Next, paste them atop the originals using the Paste icon. Then drag them to the desired location.

To copy and paste objects:

1. Select the objects that you want to copy by doing *one of the following*:
   ▲ Hold down the Ctrl key and click each object.
   ▲ Drag an area that includes only the objects to be copied (**Figure 10.85**).

2. Click the Copy icon at the bottom of the Design window.

3. Click the Paste icon to paste the objects. Studio pastes the objects directly on top of the original objects.

4. Drag the pasted objects to the desired location (**Figure 10.86**).

WORKING WITH MULTIPLE OBJECTS

Chapter 10

In the next task, a frame (a rectangle object) was created after the thumbnail button was created and thus obscures the thumbnail when dragged to the same location. Here's how to place the frame behind the thumbnail.

To change object layers:

1. Select the object or objects that you want to move forward or backward (**Figure 10.87**).

2. From the Studio menu, choose Title > Layer; then choose the desired action— in this case, Send Back One Layer (**Figure 10.88**).

   Studio moves the object back one layer, displaying the thumbnail button over the frame (**Figure 10.89**).

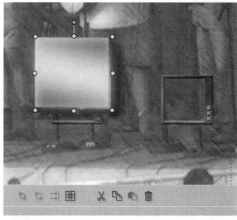

Figure 10.87 Suppose you want to use a rectangle as a frame for this thumbnail button. The problem is that when you create the rectangle, Studio places it over the thumbnail.

Figure 10.88 Use these controls to move objects to different layers.

Figure 10.89 Now the frame is behind the button, where you can move it to serve as a frame for the thumbnail button.

Creating DVD Menu Templates

One of Studio's coolest features is its menu template function. You can create menu templates that Studio automatically populates when you add videos to the Timeline. Through your work in the previous section, "Working with Multiple Objects," the template is almost complete.

A complete template has three components: buttons for linking content, Next buttons, and Previous buttons. These allow Studio to automatically create menus and controls for navigating. Text and cute backgrounds are nice but not required. Our template-in-progress already contains the buttons for linking content; you will now see how to add the Next and Previous buttons.

See Chapter 12 for more on DVD menus.

Figure 10.90
To complete the template menu, you need Next and Previous buttons.

To use existing Next and Previous buttons in your template:

1. Browse the Buttons Album until you find suitable buttons with the words *next* or *previous* in the name (**Figure 10.90**).

2. Drag the buttons to the desired locations (**Figure 10.91**).

Figure 10.91 Drag the Next and Previous buttons to the desired locations.

To create your own Next and Previous buttons:

1. Create the desired text or object (**Figure 10.92**).

2. Open the drop-down menu at the top of the Buttons Album and choose Next Button.

3. Repeat Steps 1 and 2 to create the Previous button.

To save a menu as a template:

1. From the File menu, choose File > Save Menu As.

   Studio opens the Save Menu As dialog box.

2. Name the file and save it in the Program files > Pinnacle > Studio 9 > Menus > My Menus folder (**Figure 10.93**).

   Studio should default to this menu location; you should need to hunt for it only if you've saved menus before in another location.

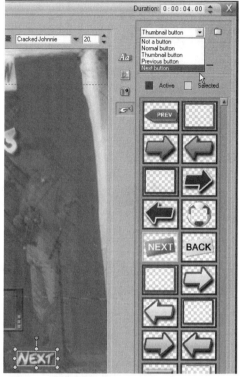

Figure 10.92 You also could use any object as a Next or Previous button and simply assign it the appropriate value.

Figure 10.93 Save the template.

Creating Rolls and Crawls

After all this work, there's only one way to close this chapter: with "The End" rolling onto the screen, or crawling across the screen—you pick. The grandparents are screaming for this DVD.

With rolls, you place the title object where you want it to end up, and Studio moves it from off-screen at the bottom of the window to the specified location.

With crawls, Studio moves the title object from off-screen on the right to off-screen on the left. You set the object at the desired height, and Studio does the rest.

To create a rolling title:

1. In the Title editor, position the title object at the desired stopping point (**Figure 10.94**).

2. Among the title-type buttons at the upper left, click the Roll icon.

    Studio produces the effect, which you can preview only in the Movie window.

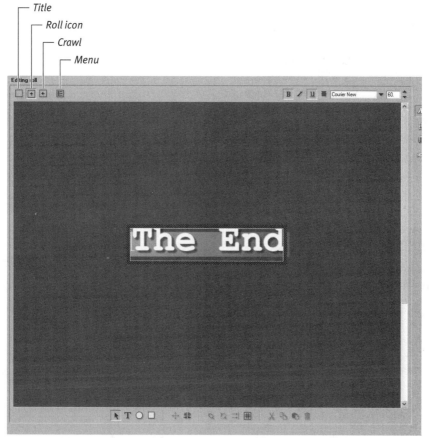

Figure 10.94 The perfect way to end this chapter: a rolling "The End" title, pulled from Studio's Album, of course.

To create a crawling title:

1. In the Title editor, position the title object at the desired height.

2. Among the title-type buttons at the upper left, click the Crawl icon (Figure 10.94). Studio produces the effect, which you can preview only in the Movie window.

✔ Tips

- To make the title roll or crawl more slowly, simply make the title longer by dragging it on the Timeline or entering a longer duration in the Title editor as shown in Figure 10.12.

- You can easily mix effects—for instance, a scrolling title that fades to black—by placing two titles sequentially on the timeline. Be sure that the text in the second title aligns precisely with the stopping point of the text in the first title. Make this happen by copying the first title, pasting it into the Timeline next to the first title, and then reversing the motion on the second clip as described in the following tip.

- To reverse a crawl or a roll and convert back to a static menu, click the Title icon among the title-type buttons (Figure 10.94).

- Menus (that is, titles with buttons) can't roll or crawl.

- Studio includes a "The End" title in the Titles Album, which provides the easiest way to create this effect.

Working with Audio

11

The last ten chapters have focused largely on video, perhaps leading the casual observer to believe that audio is less important. However, as serious producers will tell you, this just isn't so. The Internet experience is probably the best barometer: Many viewers will tolerate grainy, postage-stamp-size video, but let the audio break once or twice, and satisfaction quickly wanes. That's why streaming technologies from Apple, Microsoft, and RealNetworks all prioritize the delivery of audio over video.

Like most programs, Studio offers three audio tracks, for original audio, narration, and background music. It also provides tools for taking music from CD tracks and converting them to sound files, known as *ripping* CD tracks, and recording narration.

But what sets Studio's audio feature apart is three things. First is SmartSound, which produces thematic background music of any customizable length. Also exceptional is Studio's Volume tool, a real-time mixer that lets you customize audio volume on all tracks simultaneously. Finally, Studio now offers audio effects for critical functions like noise removal and equalization, allowing producers to improve sound quality dramatically. Together, these tools let you easily create and integrate professional-quality audio into your productions.

About Audio Tracks and Workflow

Studio has three audio tracks (**Figure 11.1**), which operate as follows:

- **Audio track.** This track always starts with audio from the video file above it. If you lock the Video track, you can delete the original audio file and insert an audio file from the Album or drag one from any other track. The Audio track is referred to as the Original Audio track in Studio Help files.

- **Sound Effect track.** Studio places narrations created with the Voice-Over tool in this track. By designation, Pinnacle also suggests that sound effects should be placed in this track, but you can place the sound effects in any open track. The Sound Effect track is referred to as the Sound Effect and Voice-Over track in some Studio Help files.

- **Music track.** Studio places files from both the CD Audio tool and SmartSound tool in this track, which can otherwise contain any audio file. It's referred to as the Background Music track in some Studio Help files.

You can place any audio file from the Album in any track, but you should reserve the designated tracks for their namesake items if you plan to create narration or background audio files. Once Studio creates these files, it lets you move them to any track, thus providing additional design flexibility.

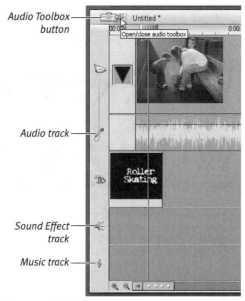

Figure 11.1 Studio has three audio tracks: one for the audio included in the captured file, one for sound effects and voice-overs and one for music. At the top is the Audio Toolbox button.

Getting audio to the Timeline

As we've seen, Studio populates the Audio track with audio associated with the video file.

You can add only the audio from any video file by dragging the file from the Album to either the Sound Effect track or the Music track. (For details, see "Working with Audio Files" in Chapter 7.)

Studio can also import WAV and MP3 files for dragging to the audio tracks. (For details, see the section "Working in the Sound Effects Tab" in Chapter 6.)

The Audio toolbox

Studio's Audio toolbox, accessed by clicking its namesake button at the top of the Movie window (Figure 11.1), contains the various tools used to create, edit, and mix audio on the respective tracks (**Figure 11.2**). Here are those tools (top to bottom):

Figure 11.2 The Audio toolbox contains six tools.

Labels (top to bottom): Audio Clip Properties tool, Volume tool (mixer), Voice-Over tool, CD Audio tool, SmartSound tool, Audio Effects tool

- **Audio Clip Properties tool:** For trimming audio files.

- **Volume tool (mixer):** For adjusting the volume of the various audio tracks.

- **Voice-Over tool:** For recording narration segments placed on the Sound Effects track.

- **CD Audio tool:** For ripping CD audio tracks that are placed on the Music track.

- **SmartSound tool:** For creating background music placed on the Music track.

- **Audio Effects tool:** For adding audio effects to any audio track.

✔ Tip

- Create your audio tracks last, after all your video edits are finalized. That way, adjustments to the video tracks won't throw off the synchronization of the Music and Sound Effect tracks with the video.

Setting Recording Options

There are two ways to capture audio from an audio CD. The better one is to capture the tracks digitally, a process known as ripping—basically just a file transfer from the CD to your hard drive. Very much like DV capture, it's fast, high-quality, and simple, requiring no real options to set.

If that's not available, you can capture CD audio through your sound card, essentially performing an analog-to-digital conversion. You have to set some parameters for the conversion, but they're simple and described in the next task.

To set CD-ripping options:

1. From the Studio menu, choose Setup > CD and Voice-over.

    The Pinnacle Studio Setup Options screen opens to the CD and Voice-Over tab (**Figure 11.3**).

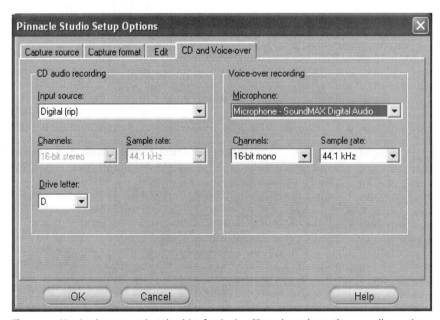

Figure 11.3 Here's where you select the drive for ripping CD tracks and set other recording options.

Working with Audio

Figure 11.4 Most people rip audio digitally. If this option isn't available, select the appropriate input source and digitize at 16-bit stereo, 44.1 kHz.

2. In the lower-left corner of the screen, select the drive containing the CD audio disc.

3. Do *one of the following*:
    ▲ If your CD drive is set to Digital (rip) in the Input source drop-down box (Figure 11.3), you're set.
    ▲ If your CD drive is not set to Digital (rip), click the Input source drop-down menu and choose the appropriate recording option for your sound card (**Figure 11.4**). Then click the Channels drop-down menu (still in the CD audio recording area on the left) and choose 16-bit stereo. Finally, click the Sample rate drop-down menu and choose 44.1 kHz.

✔ Tips

- If you have multiple CD/DVD drives, try to find a drive that you can set to Digital (rip), and use that drive.

- Unfortunately, all sound cards are different, so it's impossible to tell which options are available on each individual card.

To set voice-over recording options:

1. Follow Step 1 of the previous task.

2. In the Voice-over Recording section on the right, make sure the Microphone drop-down menu is set to the correct microphone input source (**Figure 11.5**).

3. In the CD Audio Recording section of the screen, click the Channels drop-down menu and choose 16-bit mono (Figure 11.4).

4. Click the Sample rate drop-down menu and choose 22.05 kHz.

5. Click OK to close the dialog.

✔ Tips

- Pinnacle recommends using 16-bit mono at 22.05 kHz for narration because speech is less complex than music, and this format saves space without any perceptible change in quality. If the quality isn't good enough for your ear, or if you record your audio with music in the background, bump it up to the 16-bit stereo, 44.1 kHz, used for ripping CD tracks. It'll cost you an extra 128 KB per second, or about 3.5 percent of what DV video costs you.

- If you're creating auxiliary audio files, it helps to know where the system is storing them so that you can reuse or delete them. See "Setting Auxiliary File Location" in Chapter 2 for details.

Figure 11.5 Studio does a pretty good job finding the microphone input, but if it doesn't on your computer, here's how you select it.

Working with Audio

Figure 11.6 Position the Timeline scrubber where you want Studio to place the ripped CD audio.

Ripping CD Audio

If you're used to fully functional jukebox products like those from MusicMatch, Microsoft, and RealNetworks, Studio's CD Audio tool will seem mundane. But while it doesn't compare to these products in flash and features, at least you'll know the files you create using the CD Audio tool will be compatible with Studio.

To rip a CD audio track:

1. In the Movie window, place the Timeline scrubber where the audio should be inserted (**Figure 11.6**).

2. To open the CD Audio tool, do *one of the following*:

   ▲ Click the Audio Toolbox icon (Figure 11.1), then click the CD to switch to the CD Audio tool.

   ▲ In the Studio menu, choose Toolbox > Add CD Music.

   The Audio toolbox opens to the CD Audio tool (**Figure 11.7**).

   continues on next page

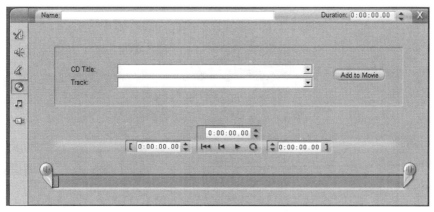

Figure 11.7 The CD Audio tool.

Chapter 11

3. Place a CD in the CD audio drive.

    Studio performs *one of the following* actions:

    ▲ If the CD is new, Studio prompts you to enter the name of the CD (**Figure 11.8**). Enter the appropriate name.

    ▲ If you've ripped tracks from this CD previously, Studio automatically recognizes the CD and inserts the name (**Figure 11.9**).

4. Select the desired track.

5. If desired, select the Start and End locations by doing *one of the following*:

    ▲ Slide the Trim calipers to the desired location.

    ▲ Type the desired setting in the transport controls or use the Trim scrubber to move to the desired location, and then click the controls that set your Start and End locations.

    ▲ Use the Jog buttons next to the Start and End Location counters.

Figure 11.8 Studio tracks your CDs by the title you enter here. Let's give peace a chance.

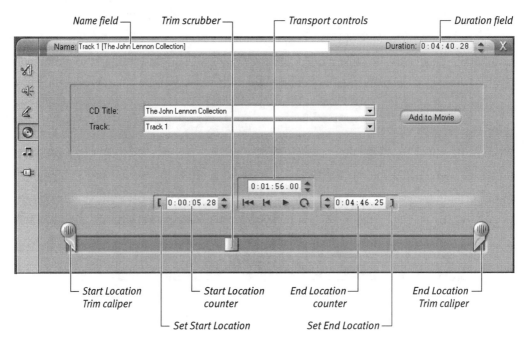

Figure 11.9 Use the Trim calipers to delete the silence at the start and end of the track.

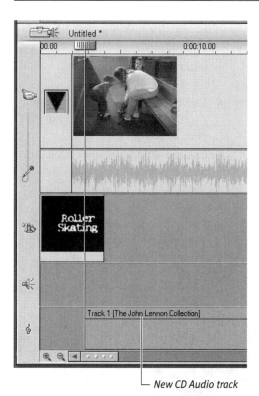

New CD Audio track

Figure 11.10 Studio adds the track. Note that Studio doesn't actually rip the track until you preview, so preview as soon as you place the track, or you'll have to find the CD again during final rendering.

Figure 11.11 Here's Studio asking for the CD.

6. Click the Add to Movie button.

   Studio adds the track to the selected location (**Figure 11.10**).

✔ Tips

- There's usually some silence at both the start and end of a CD audio clip. It's a good idea to eliminate this before you rip a track; otherwise it's another step with the Audio toolbox (Figure 11.9).

- Studio doesn't actually rip the track until you preview the video at that location. At that time, if the CD is not in the drive, Studio prompts you to insert the audio CD (**Figure 11.11**). To keep things simple, you should preview right after inserting the track; that way Studio rips and inserts the audio right away, and you won't have to track down the CD later.

- If you're a digital audio aficionado, you'll probably be much happier using any of the players from the companies I mentioned in the introduction to this section (MusicMatch's Jukebox, Microsoft's Media Player, or RealNetworks' RealOne) to rip tracks from your audio CD. All these programs can search the Internet and name your CDs and tracks, and rip the files for instant use and later reuse. But many people will probably find that the CD Audio tool works just fine.

- If you use a third-party player, note that Studio can be finicky during import, and might fail to load MP3 files that are not 128 Kbps, or WAV files that are not 16-bit stereo at 44.1 kHz (the standard for CD audio). If you use another tool, rip a track or two and see if Studio can load it before ripping your entire collection. And remember, Studio can't load Windows Media files or QuickTime, so don't even think about it.

Creating Background Tracks Using SmartSound

With the buildup I gave it in the intro, SmartSound can't possibly live up to its billing. So, I'll try the low-key approach, walk you through the tool quickly, and let you decide for yourself.

Note that you can't have CD audio and SmartSound files in the same location on the Music track (though you can certainly have both at different locations). I'll delete John Lennon and start with a clean background audio track.

To add SmartSound background music:

1. To select the scenes to which SmartSound can synchronize the audio, do *one of the following*:

   ▲ Holding down the Shift key, select contiguous scenes with the pointer (**Figure 11.12**).

   ▲ Starting with any unpopulated area on the Timeline, drag a box around the scenes.

   ▲ From the Studio menu, choose Edit > Select All (Ctrl+A) to select the entire Timeline.

   Studio turns the selected tracks blue.

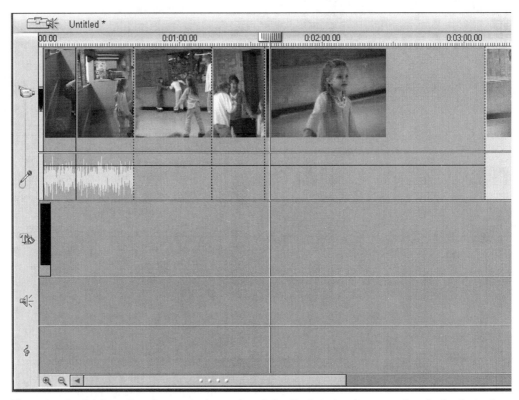

Figure 11.12 Studio's SmartSound creates background music for all selected tracks, so start by selecting the tracks.

Working with Audio

Figure 11.13 The SmartSound tool. Studio ships with a lot of choices, and you can buy additional tracks at www.smartsound.com.

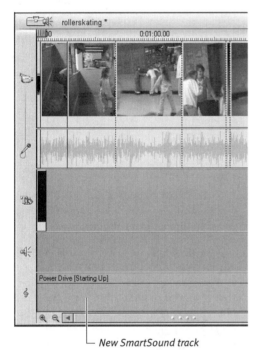

— *New SmartSound track*

Figure 11.14 Studio adds the track to the selected videos.

2. To open the SmartSound tool, do *one of the following*:
   ▲ Click the Audio Toolbox icon (Figure 11.1), and then click the SmartSound Tool icon, which is the second from the bottom on the left of the Audio Toolbox panel (Figure 11.2).
   ▲ From the Studio menu, choose Toolbox > Generate Background Music.
   The SmartSound tool opens (**Figure 11.13**).
   If you didn't install SmartSound during installation, Studio prompts you to insert the setup disc.

3. Choose a style from the Style list.
4. Choose a song from the Song list.
5. Choose a version from the Version list.
6. Click the Preview button anytime to listen to your selection.
   You can change your selection and preview again anytime.
7. When complete, click the Add to Movie button.
   Studio adds the background audio track to the selected clips (**Figure 11.14**).

✔ Tips

- As with CD audio, Studio doesn't create the track until you preview.

- Each time you change the duration of the videos on the Timeline, Studio adjusts the duration of the SmartSound track, creating noticeable delays on longer projects as Studio creates the new audio track. This is another reason to add audio as the last editing step.

- Click the SmartSound button (Figure 11.13) to see more about SmartSound, including the URL for the SmartSound Software (formerly Sonic Desktop) Web site (www.smartsound.com), which offers an excellent selection of additional audio tracks.

CREATING BACKGROUND TRACKS

313

Chapter 11

Recording Narrations

Narrating your videos and slide shows is a great way to add context to the visual presentation, and Studio makes narrations simple to create and use. Even with an inexpensive microphone, you can create high-quality audio, but with the wrong gear or wrong setup, you'll be disappointed with the quality. For more details, see the sidebar "Getting the Most from Your Narrations."

To connect for narration:

1. Connect your microphone to the microphone port on your sound card or computer.

    Note that the internal settings for *line-in* are different from those of the microphone, so you're not likely to get good results using this connector.

2. Connect your headphones (if available) to the speaker port on your sound card or computer.

✔ Tip

- Many computers (like my Sony VAIO) designate the microphone connector with a red plug, which sometimes matches the plug on the microphone itself.

Getting the Most from Your Narrations

There are two aspects to a good-quality narration: technical and artistic.

From a technical perspective, you can achieve great results with an inexpensive microphone, but I recommend that you use a microphone that's part of a headset. Microphones and headsets are often sold together for use in Internet videoconferencing.

If you're using a stand-alone microphone, ditch your external speakers and use a set of headphones during recording. Otherwise, you'll produce *feedback*—an annoying screeching sound caused by the microphone picking up output from the speakers.

From an artistic standpoint, you'll get the best results by scripting your narration and taking the time to try multiple takes until you get it right. Keep your comments short and to the point, or you'll complicate both the scripting and the performance.

If you're going to wing it without a script, adjust your expectations downward. While you may strive to emulate the baritone splendor of James Earl Jones, the fluidity of Bryant Gumble, or the mellifluous tones of yoga maven Tracey Rich, you'll never get finished if you insist on that level of perfection.

Finally, there are tools out there that can stretch or compress your narration to the duration of the corresponding video with minimal distortion, which can save oodles of time compared to re-recording a four-minute track to shave 15 seconds either way. Sony Pictures' CD Architect is a good place to start (www.mediasoftware.sonypictures.com).

Working with Audio

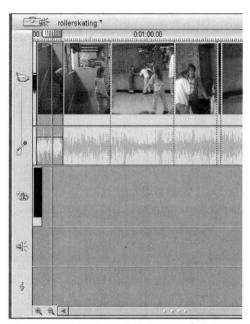

Figure 11.15 As with CD audio, start your narration by placing the Timeline scrubber at the desired location.

To record your narration:

1. In the Movie window, position the Timeline scrubber to the desired insert point (**Figure 11.15**).

    There must be at least one video or still image on the Timeline to record a narration, and there can't be audio in the Sound Effect track at the desired insert point.

2. To open the Voice-Over Narration tool, do *one of the following*:

    ▲ Click the Audio Toolbox icon (Figure 11.1), and then in the Audio toolbox, click the icon for recording a voice-over narration—the third icon from the top.

    ▲ From the Studio menu, choose Toolbox > Record Voice-over.

    The Voice-Over Narration tool opens (**Figure 11.16**).

    The volume meter on the right is completely unlit, meaning the microphone is hearing no audio—a good thing. When you have a noisy room or a poor microphone, the meter jumps, signifying noisy audio.

continues on next page

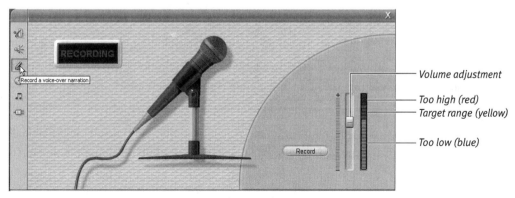

Figure 11.16 The Voice-Over Narration tool. Use the Volume Adjustment tool to customize recording volume.

315

3. Speak into the microphone, and use the Volume Adjustment tool on the right to position the audio level so that it is at the top of the blue level or into the yellow level, but never touches the red.

   Touching the red may clause *clipping*, which often sounds like a mechanical click on the audio, or it can distort your voice.

4. After setting the appropriate level, click the Record button to start the recording.

   Studio first lights a "Standby" sign in the Recording box, then numbers count down from three, to two, to one. Then the Recording light turns on, and blinks slowly during the recording (**Figure 11.17**).

   While recording, watch the audio levels to maintain the appropriate volume.

   If the Recording button doesn't light up, it's most likely because the Timeline scrubber is positioned above a point in the Sound Effect track that already contains audio. So move, edit, or delete the old audio, or change locations to a blank place in the track.

5. Press Stop to stop recording (Figure 11.17).

   When Studio stops recording, it creates and stores the audio file (you'll see the word *Standby* light for a moment), then posts the file in the Sound Effect track (**Figure 11.18**).

6. In the Player, press Play to hear your recorded audio.

   Since the proper levels haven't yet been set for the narration and other tracks, it may be difficult to hear the narration over the other tracks. To learn how to set the respective volumes, see "Using the Volume Tool" later in this chapter.

   After you've finished recording, the narration track is just like any file that you can trim, split, move, or delete. For example, if you don't like the recorded track, simply select it, press Delete, and it's gone.

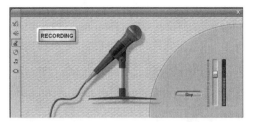

Figure 11.17 Once you're recording, try to keep the level predominantly in the yellow, avoiding the red at all costs.

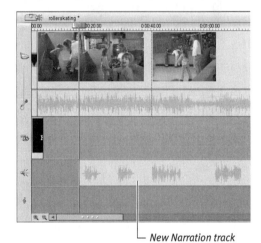

— New Narration track

Figure 11.18 The completed narration track.

Working with Audio

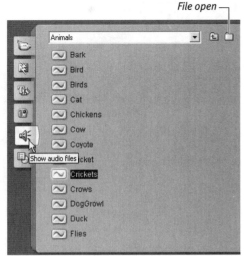

Figure 11.19 Studio's sound effects.

Using Studio's Sound Effects

Pinnacle includes a range of sound effects with Studio, which you access by clicking the Audio Files tab on the left of the Edit Album. I'm not a big sound effects guy, but every once in a while they come in handy, like the chewing effect I used to spice up a slide show on sharks, or adding applause to my daughter's gymnastics exercises.

When you first run Studio, the list of sound effects are displayed when you open the Audio Album (**Figure 11.19**). However, once you change folders to import other files, Studio doesn't automatically return to this default view. Assuming you installed Studio using all default file locations, you should be able to reload the sound effects into the Album by clicking the yellow Folder icon (Figure 11.19), which produces the Open dialog, and then navigating to C:\Program Files\Pinnacle\Studio 9\SoundEffects.

317

Editing Audio Clips

Chapter 7 described how to edit audio files on the Timeline. All of those principles apply equally to audio files created by the three tools discussed earlier.

In addition, you can edit audio files with Studio's Clip Properties tool, also discussed in Chapter 7. Since the Audio Clip Properties tool presents a slightly different face when editing a CD-Audio clip and a SmartSound clip, I'll address each separately below.

To edit Audio from a CD:

1. Double-click the Audio track in the Movie window to edit (**Figure 11.20**).

    Studio opens the CD Audio Clip Properties tool (**Figure 11.21**).

    Studio stores the track-related information, so you don't need the audio CD right away. However, Studio will need it if you make any changes and preview, so don't let the disc get too far away.

2. Make the desired edits (**Figure 11.22**).

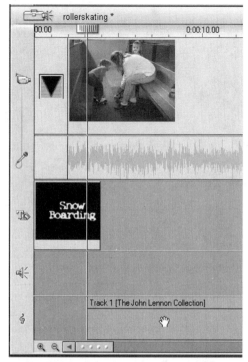

Figure 11.20 To edit the track, double-click it. What opens?

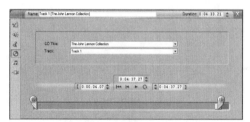

Figure 11.21 The Clip Properties tool for CD audio.

Figure 11.22 Make the desired edits.

Working with Audio

Figure 11.23 Then preview, and Studio rips the track.

Figure 11.24 Once again, if the audio CD isn't present, Studio prompts you.

3. To save edits, click the X in the upper right to close the Clip Properties tool or touch another tool.

4. Click Preview in the Player to rip the CD track immediately.

   Studio rips the track (**Figure 11.23**) and then plays the clip. If the CD isn't in the drive, Studio prompts you to insert the disc (**Figure 11.24**).

To edit a SmartSound clip:

1. Double-click the track to edit it (**Figure 11.25**).

   Studio opens the SmartSound tool (**Figure 11.26**).

2. Make the desired changes and click the Accept Changes button (**Figure 11.27**). Studio makes the changes.

Figure 11.25 Editing SmartSound is pretty similar. Start by double-clicking on the track.

Figure 11.26 The SmartSound tool opens.

Figure 11.27 Make the desired changes and click Accept Changes.

Using the Volume Tool

Now that you've created these multiple audio tracks, it's time to blend them into a synergistic audio experience by adjusting their relative volume.

Studio offers two tools, the Volume tool discussed here, and the adjustment handles on the Timeline discussed in the next section. Both these tools are designed to complement each other, so you can use the adjustment handles on the Timeline to modify any adjustments you made using the Volume tool, and vice versa.

There are three sets of volume controls, one each for the Audio track, the Sound Effects track, and the Music track. Here's how they operate:

- **Mute:** Mutes the *entire* track.

- **Global Volume:** Adjusts the volume of the *entire* track.

- **Volume Adjust:** Adjusts the volume *at the current edit location*. This tool is best used in real time with the audio playing, so you can listen to the volume and adjust as necessary.

- **Volume Meter:** Reflects track volume at that location.

- **Fade-in** and **Fade-out:** Perform their namesake tasks at the current edit location.

- **Balance:** Adjusts the audio balance between the left and right speaker, and the position of each track front to back as perceived by the listener (this is also called a *fade*).

Working with Audio

To open the Volume tool:

◆ Do *one of the following*:
  ▲ Click the Audio Toolbox icon in the Movie window (Figure 11.1), and then click the Speaker icon on the left of the Audio Toolbox panel.
  ▲ In the Studio menu, choose Toolbox > Change Volume.

The Volume tool opens above the Movie window (**Figure 11.28**).

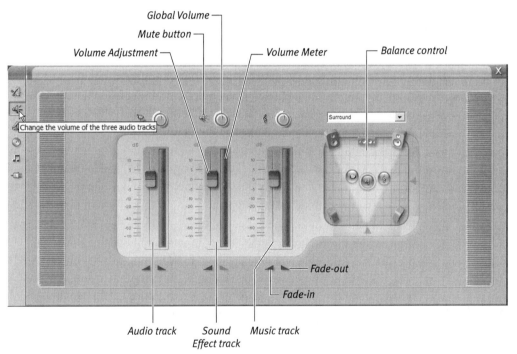

Figure 11.28 Studio's cool Volume mixer. Each of the three tracks has a complete set of controls.

Chapter 11

To mute a track:

1. Follow Step 1 of the previous task.

2. Click the Mute button for the respective track.

   Studio places a red line over the Mute button and adjusts track volume to zero, placing a red line at the bottom of the track (**Figure 11.29**).

To adjust track global volume:

1. Follow Step 1 in "To open the Volume tool."

2. Adjust the Global Volume tool to the desired level by turning it clockwise (to increase volume) or counterclockwise (to decrease volume) (**Figure 11.30**).

   Studio adjusts the volume of the entire track and places a blue line at the adjusted level (**Figure 11.31**).

Figure 11.29 A muted track. Note the line at the bottom of the Audio track—it will be more easily visible when you try this on your projects.

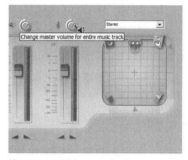

Figure 11.30 This control adjusts volume for the entire audio clip.

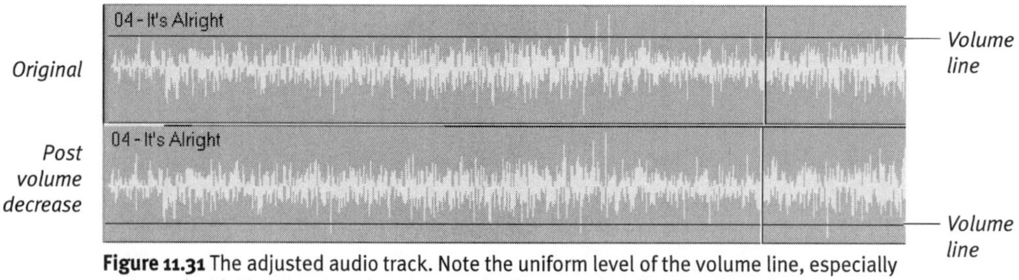

Figure 11.31 The adjusted audio track. Note the uniform level of the volume line, especially compared with Figure 11.33, where I created adjustment handles to edit track regions, rather than the entire track.

Working with Audio

Figure 11.32
This control adjusts volume *at that location*, as opposed to uniformly over the entire clip.

To adjust track volume:

1. Follow Step 1 in "To open the Volume tool."

2. Position the Timeline scrubber at the target location.

3. Move the volume adjustment downward or upward (**Figure 11.32**).

   Studio creates an adjustment handle and adjusts the clip volume on the track at the target location (**Figure 11.33**).

   Once Studio creates the adjustment handle, you can move it around manually. As you'll see in the next section, you can also create adjustment handles directly on the Timeline.

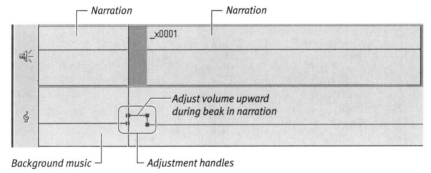

Figure 11.33 Here I'm adjusting the Music track upwards during a break in narration.

Chapter 11

To fade in audio:

1. Follow Step 1 in "To open the Volume tool."

2. Position the Timeline scrubber where the fade-in should start—that is, the point where volume should be zero before it starts to increase (**Figure 11.34**).

   Normally, this is the absolute start of a scene or audio clip.

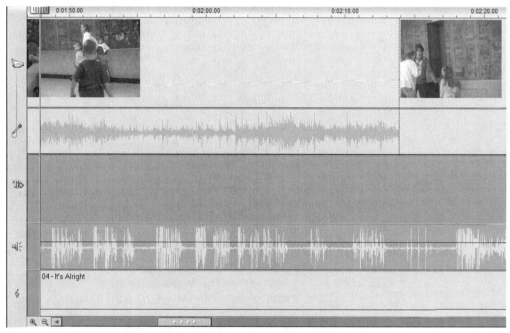

Figure 11.34 To fade in audio, first place the Timeline scrubber where you want the fade-in to start—that is, where audio volume is set to zero. Normally, this is the start of the audio file.

Working with Audio

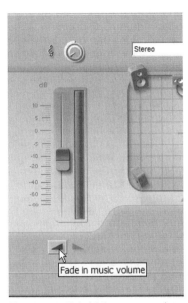

Figure 11.35 Click this button to produce the fade-in.

3. Click the Fade-in icon for the target audio track (**Figure 11.35**).

   Studio fades in the audio using the default fade-in/fade-out duration (**Figure 11.36**). To adjust this default setting, see "Setting Default Durations" in Chapter 2.

✔ Tips

- If your track has multiple files and you want each to fade in, you have to apply the effect separately to each audio file. For example, if you have multiple CD or narration tracks and want each to fade in, you must apply the fade-in to each file manually.

- When you apply transitions between clips, Studio automatically creates a cross-fade between the two original audio tracks, unless you apply the fade transition (in which case Studio fades the first track out and fades the second one in). Note that you can customize this cross-fade manually—see "Adjusting Volume, Balance and Fade on the Timeline," later in this chapter.

- If the track's Fade-in control is not active, click the target track with your pointer to make it the active track. Studio will turn the Fade-in and Fade-out controls black and make them active.

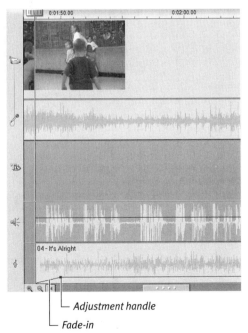

Figure 11.36 Fade-in accomplished. Again, note the small blue dot, which is the adjustment handle you can manually move.

325

To fade out audio:

1. Follow Step 1 in "To open the Volume tool."

2. Position the Timeline scrubber where the fade-out should end—that is, the point where volume should be set to zero (**Figure 11.37**).

   Normally, this is the absolute end of a scene or audio clip.

3. Click the Fade-out icon for the target audio track (**Figure 11.38**).

   Studio fades out the audio (**Figure 11.39**) using the default fade-in/fade-out duration. To adjust this default setting, see "Setting Default Durations," in Chapter 2.

✔ Tip

- If your track has multiple files and you want each to fade out, you have to apply the effect separately to each audio file. For example, if you have multiple CD or narration tracks and want each to fade out, you must apply the fade-out to each file manually.

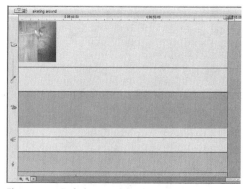

Figure 11.37 To fade out, place the Timeline scrubber at the point you want volume to be set to zero—normally, the end of the clip.

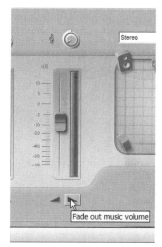

Figure 11.38 Click this button to fade out.

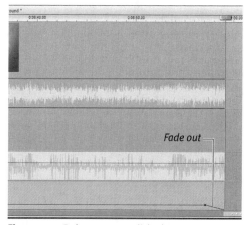

Figure 11.39 Fade-out accomplished.

About the Balance Control

The Balance control adjusts two characteristics of an audio clip: the clip's position with reference to the left and right speakers (called the balance, or *pan*) and its position front to back (or the *fade*) as perceived by the listener.

These controls are useful under several circumstances, including the following:

- If you recorded the left and right audio tracks of an event separately (balance).
- To change the perceived location of a sound, such as a train or car, from one direction to another to create the impression that the train or car was moving from left to right (balance).
- To make a clip sound more faint toward the end (fade).
- To place background music clearly behind the Audio or Sound Effect track (fade).
- To place a voice narration track more clearly in front of the audio from the video clip.

It's important to note, however, that Studio doesn't provide track-wide balance or fade control in the same way it does with the other volume adjustments.

For example, if you're not at the first frame of an audio file when you adjust the balance or fade using the Balance control, Studio creates an adjustment handle and adjusts the balance or fade value *from that position forward*, which is often not the desired effect. But if you position the Timeline scrubber at the absolute start of an audio clip and then adjust the Balance control, Studio adjusts the balance or fade values for the entire clip.

So if you use balance and fade controls extensively, you may find it easier to make these adjustments on the Timeline rather than using the Balance control (see "Adjusting Volume, Balance and Fade on the Timeline" later in this chapter for more information). The easiest way to set the Timeline scrubber to the absolute start of an audio clip is to position it a few frames before the start of an audio clip, and then press the right arrow key, which is the shortcut that directs Studio to select the next clip.

Note that all three tracks start at the same exact position in the Balance control, front and center. Each track is represented by the same icon that represents the track in the Timeline (**Figure 11.40**). To select the track to adjust, either click the desired icon in the Balance control or click the target track in the Timeline.

Also note that when balance and fade are adjusted jointly, Studio refers to these adjustments as *surround* controls. This is different from true *surround sound*, which is used primarily for the creation of Dolby Digital DVD audio, allowing you to customize the placement of up to five audio tracks in relation to five speakers.

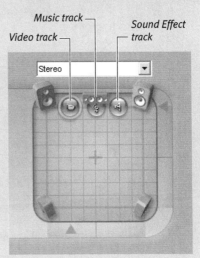

Figure 11.40 A close up of the Balance control. Note the icons for the three tracks.

To adjust balance using the Balance control:

1. Follow Step 1 in "To open the Volume tool."

2. Position the Timeline scrubber where the balance adjustment should begin: at the start of the audio clip for clip-wide adjustments, or at any other position to adjust the value from that position forward (**Figure 11.41**). (See the sidebar "About the Balance Control" for more information.)

3. Do *one of the following* to select the track to adjust:
   - ▲ Click the target track on the Timeline.
   - ▲ Click the Target icon in the Balance control (Figure 11.40).

   To access the icon in the Balance control directly, you may have to move one of the other icons out of the way, which obviously changes its balance value. So, remember to move it back to the desired value after you've adjusted your target track (just another reason why it's easier to adjust these values on the Timeline).

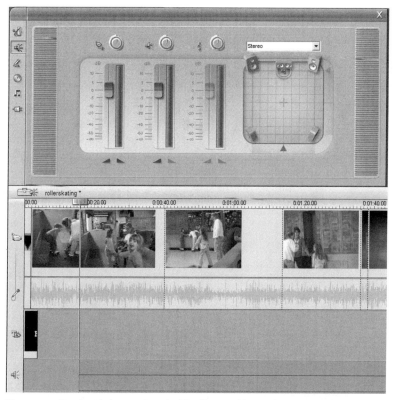

Figure 11.41 To adjust balance, place the Timeline scrubber at the point to adjust.

Working with Audio

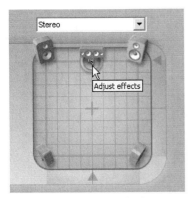

Figure 11.42 Click the icon for the target track and move it to the left or right.

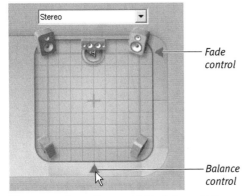

Figure 11.43 Or use the green triangle beneath the Balance control. Note the brown fade control to the right, which you can use to adjust fade position.

Figure 11.44 Choose Surround to adjust both balance and fade position.

4. Do *one of the following* to adjust track balance:
   ▲ Click the icon and move it to the left or right (**Figure 11.42**).
   ▲ Click the green triangle beneath the Balance control and move it to the left or right (**Figure 11.43**).
   Studio adjusts the track's balance.

To adjust fade using the Balance control:

1. Follow Step 1 in "To open the Volume tool."

2. Position the Timeline scrubber where the fade adjustment should begin: at the start of the audio clip for clip-wide adjustments or at any other position to adjust the value from that position forward (Figure 11.41). (See the sidebar "About the Balance Control" for more information.)

3. Click the drop-down box at the top of the Balance control and choose Surround (**Figure 11.44**).

4. Do *one of the following* to select the track to adjust:
   ▲ Click the target track on the Timeline.
   ▲ Click the Target icon in the Balance control (Figure 11.40).

   Note that to access the icon in the Balance control directly, you may have to move one of the other icons out of the way, which obviously changes its balance value. So, remember to move it back to the desired value after you've adjusted your target track (just another reason why it's easier to adjust these values on the Timeline).

   continues on next page

329

5. Do *one of the following* to adjust track fade position:
   ▲ Click the icon and move it in front of the other icons or behind them (**Figure 11.45**).
   ▲ Click the brown triangle to the right of the Balance control and move it to the front or back (Figure 11.43).
   Studio adjusts the track's fade position.

To perform real-time, multi-track audio mixing and balance adjustments:

One of Studio's best features is the ability to adjust volume, balance and fade for all three tracks in real time, which is the fastest and easiest way to produce the desired values.

1. Follow Step 1 in "To open the Volume tool."
2. Position the Timeline scrubber where you'd like to start adjusting the volume, fade and balance (**Figure 11.46**).

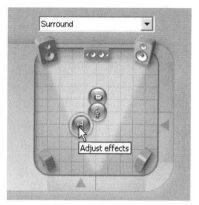

Figure 11.45 Then click the icon for the target track and move it to the front or back.

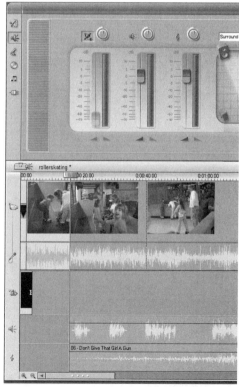

Figure 11.46 Now for some fun: real-time, multitrack mixing. Position the Timeline scrubber at the starting point.

Working with Audio

3. In the Preview window, press Play.

4. As you listen to the audio, adjust the volume, balance and fade position for each track using the appropriate controls in the Volume tool.

Studio creates adjustment handles and adjusts the three parameters in real time (**Figure 11.47**). Don't feel like you need to make this perfect; you'll learn how to manually fine-tune these settings in the next section.

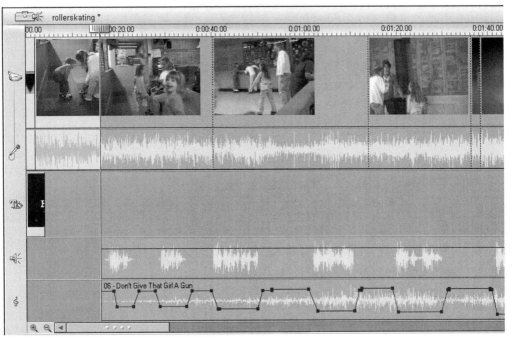

Figure 11.47 The adjusted volumes.

Adjusting Volume, Balance and Fade on the Timeline

You can use the Timeline to modify the adjustments you made using the Volume or Balance controls or create your own adjustment handles and edit them manually. This section shows you how to do both (and how to delete unwanted adjustment handles).

To adjust audio volume:

1. Touch the target track.

    Studio turns the track blue. Note that the cursor has two states for audio editing. The cursor resembles a hand when hovering over any part of the audio track except the blue audio level line (**Figure 11.48**). In this state it's called the Location Adjustment cursor, and it lets you move the track to a different location on the same track or to a different track.

    When you hover the pointer over the blue audio level line, it converts to a speaker and becomes the Volume Adjustment cursor, which you can use to create or adjust the levels of adjustment handles (**Figure 11.49**).

2. With the Volume Adjustment cursor, do *one of the following*:

    ▲ To create an adjustment handle and adjust the volume, touch the audio line and move it to the desired volume level.

    Studio creates an adjustment handle and adjusts the level (**Figure 11.50**).

    ▲ To adjust a previously created adjustment handle, touch and drag it to the new volume level (**Figure 11.51**).

    You can drag the adjustment handle in all four directions: up, down, left, and right.

Figure 11.48 When the pointer looks like this hand, you can move the file to a different location on the track or a different track.

Figure 11.49 When the pointer looks like a speaker, you can create and move the adjustment handles.

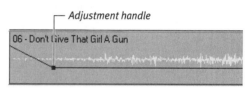

Figure 11.50 You can create an adjustment handle by touching the volume line, and dragging the volume down.

Figure 11.51 Here I've increased the volume.

Working with Audio

Figure 11.52 To delete an adjustment handle, just grab it and pull it down quickly.

To delete an adjustment handle:

◆ With the cursor in Volume Adjustment mode, touch an adjustment handle, drag it straight down quickly, and release (**Figure 11.52**).

Studio removes the adjustment handle.

To remove all volume changes:

1. Select the track or multiple tracks on the same Timeline to adjust the volume back to its pre-edited state (**Figure 11.53**).

2. Right-click and choose Remove Volume Changes (**Figure 11.54**).

Studio removes all volume changes on the selected track (**Figure 11.55**).

✔ Tip

■ Removing volume changes only works on a single track. Studio lets you select clips on different tracks and activate the tool via the right-click menu, but only removes volume changes from the top track.

Figure 11.53 Say you don't like these adjustments and simply want to start over. First select all the affected clips.

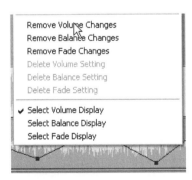

Figure 11.54 Then choose Remove Volume Changes from the right-click menu.

Figure 11.55 You're back at square one with a pristine volume line.

To switch track displays:

1. Select the target track.
2. Right-click and choose the target display (**Figure 11.56**).
   Studio switches to the selected display.

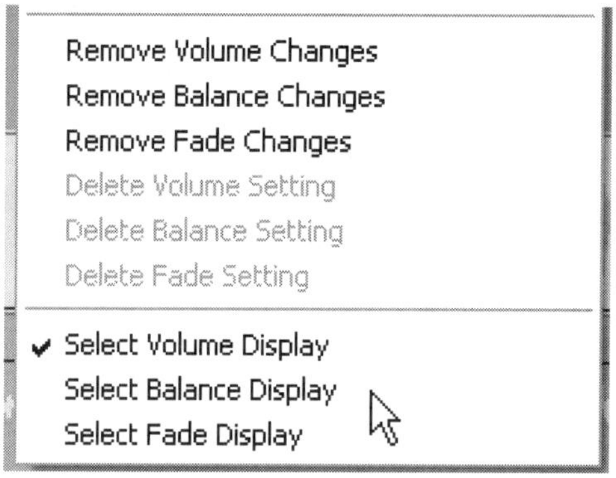

✔ Tips

- Studio color codes the displays: The Volume display is blue, the Balance display green and the Fade display a ghastly orange (where's the Queer Eye for the Straight Guy when you need them?).

- As you would expect, moving the volume line up increases volume while moving it down decreases volume. Similarly, moving the fade line down pushes the audio toward the back, while moving it upward brings the audio closer to the front. Moving the balance line toward to the top moves the audio to the left, while moving it downward shifts the audio to the right.

- You can delete all balance and fade changes to a track by right clicking on the track and choosing Remove Balance Changes or Remove Fade Changes. The technique is identical to the steps outlined in the previous track, "To remove all volume changes."

Figure 11.56 Here's how you switch between the different Track displays.

Using Adjustment Handles: A Primer

Let's make it sound like a train is moving from left to right as an exercise on how to use adjustment handles. If you're interested in following along, you'll find the train sound in the Vehicles folder of Studio's sound effects, though you can practice these techniques on any Audio track. Once the target Audio track is on the Timeline, switch to Balance display as described in "To switch track displays." Your track should look like **Figure 11.57**.

Figure 11.57 Starting point for panning a train.

Let's start by moving the audio track all the way to the left. Click the balance line near the start on the left to create an adjustment handle (**Figure 11.58**). Then drag the adjustment handle as far as possible to the left and to the top of the track (**Figure 11.59**). While you're not at the precise start of the track, you're close enough that your viewers won't hear the difference.

Figure 11.58 Click the balance line to create an adjustment handle.

Figure 11.59 Then drag it to the upper left, which represents the right speaker.

Go to the end of the audio clip, create an adjustment handle (**Figure 11.60**) and drag it to the bottom right corner (**Figure 11.61**). Play the clip by pressing Play in the Preview window, and if you have stereo speakers set up, you should hear the train moving from your left speaker to the right. You can use the same procedure (in Fade display) to move a sound from front to back.

Figure 11.60 Create your adjustment handle on the right.

I use the Volume and Balance controls primarily for real time mixing, but find working on the Timeline more effective for track-wide effects.

Figure 11.61 And drag it down to the bottom, representing the left speaker.

Chapter 11

Using Studio's Audio Effects

In addition to the video effects discussed in Chapter 9, Studio includes several audio effects that perform both curative and artistic functions. It also supports third-party audio effects that conform to the VST plug-in specification, so you can supplement the audio effects that ship with the program using additional effects from Pinnacle and third-party vendors.

This last section of the chapter begins with an overview of the audio effects included with Studio, and then provides a general description of how you select, configure and operate them. As you would expect, these effects operate very much like Studio's video effects, so if you're familiar with those, you'll have no problem working with these. The section concludes by showing you how to use Studio's new Noise Reduction filter.

What's in the box?

Studio's audio offering includes three curative effects that make your audio sound better:

- **Noise Reduction:** Removes unwanted background noise from your audio.

- **Equalizer:** Similar to controls on receivers and amplifiers that allow you to fine-tune your audio across ten supported bands (**Figure 11.62**).

- **Leveler:** For standardizing the volume of all audio clips included in a production.

Studio's artistic effects are more varied; here are some highlights.

- **Grungelizer:** Adds noises like the crackle from a record player, electric static, or the hum of AC current to your audio to provide a dated feel.

- **Reverb:** Simulates the audio from a range of environments, such as a concert hall, car, church, corridor, or cavern.

- **Alien:** Converts the audio to one or more alien voices.

- **Karaoke:** Removes the vocals from a song so that you can sing along with the background music.

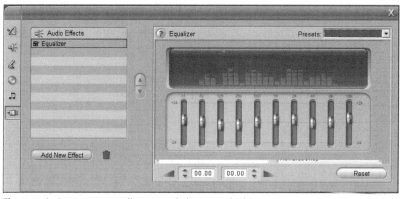

Figure 11.62 Pretty sexy equalizer control, don't you think?

Other effects that don't ship with the program but should be available from Pinnacle include the NewBlueWind effect, which makes voices sound like the wizard from the Wizard of Oz, and the NewBlueChorus effect, which makes single voices sound like a chorus. You can apply and test any audio effect in real time, which makes them very simple to sample and configure.

The special effects interface

Let's take a look at how to access, apply, and configure audio effects. As you'll see, operation is very similar to Studio's video effects (see Chapter 9), so if you're familiar with their operation, you can skip this part.

Figure 11.63 You know the drill—click here to open the Audio toolbox.

To access audio effects:

1. Place the target audio clip on the Timeline and select the audio clip with your pointer.

2. In the upper left corner of the Movie window, click the Open/close Audio Toolbox icon.

3. On the left side of the Audio toolbox that appears, click the Add an Effect to an Audio Clip icon (**Figure 11.63**).

   In the Add Audio Effect section on the right side of the screen (**Figure 11.64**), note the two types of effects, indicated by the little icons to the left of each category name in the Category window: The Broom and Dustpan icon represents cleaning effects, while the Electric Plug icon with the VST label represents plug-in effects.

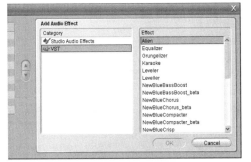

Figure 11.64 Click here to add an effect.

To add and configure a special effect:

1. Follow Steps 1 through 3 of the preceding task.

2. In the Category window, click the target category of the type of effect you want to use (**Figure 11.64**).

3. In the Effects list on the right, click the target effect (**Figure 11.64**).

4. Click OK.

   Studio applies the special effect and, depending on the effect you chose, will either open a Settings window with configuration options (**Figure 11.65**), or a screen with a button for opening a different configuration screen (**Figure 11.66**).

5. To adjust the audio effect settings, do *one of the following*:
   ▲ Choose a value from the Presets list box (Figure 11.65).
   ▲ Manually adjust the effect settings.
   Note that you can preview at any time by pressing Play in the Player window.

6. To transition an effect in or out, click the appropriate control and adjust the counter, either by typing the desired interval or using the arrow keys beside each counter to increase or decrease the interval (**Figure 11.67**).

   Studio prevents you from entering a number longer than the duration of the audio clip in either the Transition-in or Transition-out counters.

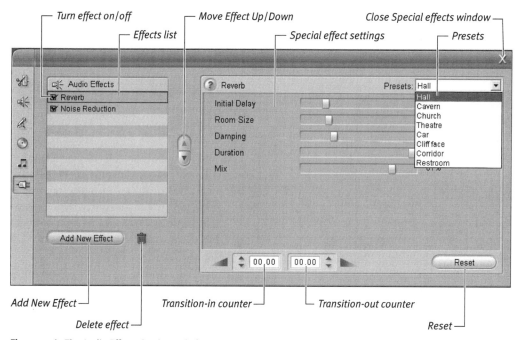

Figure 11.65 The Audio Effects Settings window.

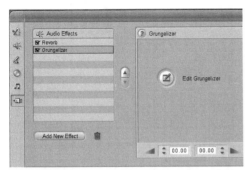

Figure 11.66 If the adjustments aren't in the Settings window, you'll typically see an Edit button like you do here.

Figure 11.67 Here's where you set the transition in and out durations.

7. When you're finished configuring the audio effect, do *one of the following*:
   ▲ Click the X in the upper right corner to close the Special Effects window (Figure 11.65).
   ▲ Click the Add New Effect button to select and configure another special effect.

   Studio saves the first effect and either returns to the Movie window for additional editing or to the Audio Effects window to chose and configure another special effect.

✔ Tip

- The Reset button (Figure 11.65) resets all controls, converting the transition-in and transition-out values to zero.

To delete a special effect:

1. Follow Steps 1 and 2 of "To access Audio Effects."
2. In the Category window, click the target category of the type of effect you want to delete (Figure 11.63).
3. Select the target effect in the Audio Effects list with your pointer (Figure 11.64).
4. Click the Trash Can icon (Figure 11.65). Studio deletes the effect.

To turn an effect on or off:

◆ Deselect the Effect On/Off checkbox to turn the effect off for preview and rendering, or select the checkbox to turn it on (**Figure 11.68**).

✔ Tips

- It's often useful to turn an effect on or off when attempting to configure another audio effect.

- You can also adjust the order of special effects by selecting them and then clicking the Move Effect Up or Move Effect Down arrows (Figure 11.65). The order does impact how the resultant audio sounds, so you should experiment with the order to achieve the desired effect.

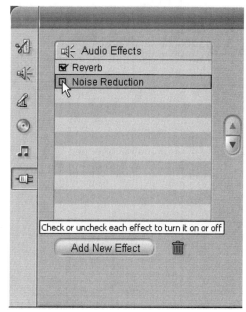

Figure 11.68 This control turns the effect on and off so that you can fine-tune other controls.

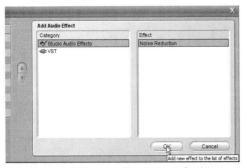

Figure 11.69 Getting to Studio's Noise Reduction effect.

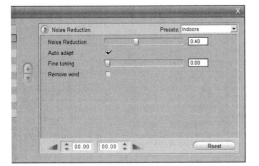

Figure 11.70 The controls for Studio's Noise Reduction effect.

Cleaning Your Audio

Studio's Noise Reduction audio effect attempts to remove unwanted background noise from your audio files. The key word here is *attempts*. It generally works best on consistent noises like the hum of air conditioning or the recording noise from your camcorder, and works poorly, if at all, with random noises like a dog barking or a car horn.

You should never count on any Noise Reduction effect—Studio's or any other—as a panacea that can fix any problem. The best course is to eliminate the background noise before shooting, because Noise Reduction is never a sure thing.

In the next task, I'm removing the crackle of a poor microphone from a narration I'm going to add to the Roller Skating video.

To apply the Noise Reduction effect:

1. Place the target audio clip on the Timeline and select the audio clip with your pointer.

2. In the upper left corner of the Movie window, click the Open/close Audio Toolbox icon (Figure 11.63).

3. On the left side of the Audio toolbox, click the Add an Effect to an Audio Clip icon (Figure 11.64).

4. Click the Studio Audio Effects Category (Figure 11.64).

5. Click the Noise Reduction effect (**Figure 11.69**).

6. Click OK.

   Studio opens the Noise Reduction settings window (**Figure 11.70**).

continues on next page

7. Do *one of the following*:
   ▲ Choose one of the three presets (Indoors, Outdoors or Music Restoration) and proceed to Step 9.
   ▲ Manually adjust the controls as described in the next step.
8. If you're manually adjusting the controls:
   ▲ Adjust the Noise Reduction setting to match the noise in the video, setting it higher for loud background noises and lower for slight hums.
   ▲ Select the Auto Adapt option to have the effect automatically modify itself for changing conditions.
   ▲ Adjust the Fine-tuning control to specify the level of cleaning.
   ▲ Select the Remove Wind option when background wind is the problem.
   Preview the effect frequently while modifying these settings. The most commonly experienced problem is distortion, which can make the audio sound heavily metallic or hollow. Also preview at different points in the audio clip to test for distortion, especially if conditions change.

9. Do *one of the following*:
   ▲ Click the X in the upper right corner to close the Special Effects window.
   ▲ Click the Add New Effect button to select and configure another special effect.
   Studio saves the first effect and either returns to the Movie window for additional editing or to the Audio Effects window to chose and configure another special effect.

✔ **Tip**

■ If Noise Reduction produces unacceptable distortion, try using the Equalizer control and reducing levels in one or more bands (Figure 11.62). If the offending background noise is mostly contained in one or two bands, often you can remove the background noise without distorting the original audio.

12

DVD Authoring

The problem with linear video is that it's so, well, linear. While it can seemingly take forever to create a 30-minute video from your four hours of vacation tapes, you still might have trouble quickly locating that cute spot where little Sally and cousin Johnny were holding hands, watching the July 4 parade.

That's the beauty of DVD. It's pretty much infinitely linkable, allowing you to find the most important scenes quickly. And, though you can dress up your videos as much as you like, you can also choose to break them into scenes (or let scene detection do the work for you) and create menus with links to the good parts.

It's a parent's dream: simple, fast, and better than VHS quality, with tape-like playback simplicity. Just open the player and pop in the disc. With recordable drive and media prices dropping every time you turn around, it's also alluringly inexpensive.

Whereas Springsteen was "born to run," Studio was born to author DVDs, the first program ever with an integrated editing and authoring environment. It's enough to get my creative juices flowing—how 'bout yours?

About DVD Authoring

With a buildup like that, it's a letdown to start in tutorial mode, but you gotta walk before you can run. So spend some time learning about DVD authoring before diving in.

When planning your DVD, you have two basic issues to consider: video flow and menu structure.

Video flow

Video flow relates to the way the video plays over the course of the DVD. There are two extremes, with many points in between.

◆ **Linear production:** At one extreme is a linear movie that simply happens to be on DVD. You've designed it to flow from beginning to end, like a Hollywood movie, and you're using DVD simply as a convenient distribution medium, perhaps in addition to dubbing to VHS tape.

Maybe you want viewers to be able to jump in at certain points, but once the video starts, it will play from start to finish unless interrupted by the viewer.

When planning a linear production, you have to build the entire movie on the Timeline first and then start adding the interactivity. The key link between DVD menus and the video content on the Timeline are chapter points that connect menu buttons with the video scenes you select during authoring. Studio makes these chapter points easy to spot by creating flags on the menu track, which are labeled sequentially, starting with C1 (**Figure 12.1**). At the end of each chapter, you can also choose whether viewers automatically continue on to the next video scene or return to the menu so that they can choose another option. If you choose the latter approach, Studio places Return to Menu flags on the Menu track.

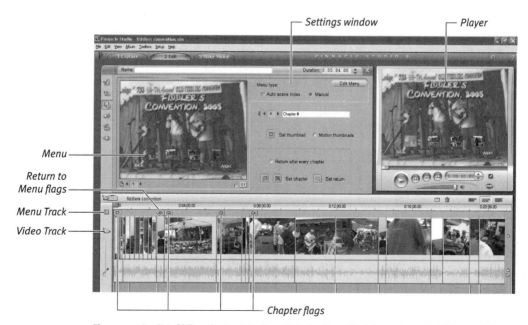

Figure 12.1 Studio's DVD authoring interface. Note the Menu Track icon above the Video Track icon, and the Menu Clip Properties tool, where you'll do most of your linking and customization.

◆ **Disparate videos or slide shows:** The opposite of linear productions are collections of related but essentially disparate videos or slide shows that don't flow from start to finish. Perhaps you're converting your three-month tape from last summer, which covered little Johnny's trip to the Little League World Series, Sally's diving championship, and that ridiculously expensive trip to Disney World. In addition to the videotapes, you also shot pictures with a digital still-image camera, and you'd like to build them into a slide show viewable from the DVD.

You'll spend some time consolidating scenes from each event into a discrete movie, but you don't expect viewers to watch the video from start to finish. After each movie or slide show, you want viewers to return to the original menu so that they can choose another sequence.

When planning this second type of production, you start by building all individual movies and slide shows on the Timeline. You again use chapter flags to link to the various movies and scenes within the movies. Then, using techniques discussed in this chapter, you insert Return to Menu flags (Figure 12.1), which return viewers to a menu after the video or slide show finishes.

The net-net is that two tools control video flow. Chapter flags allow viewers to jump to any spot in the video, and Return to Menu flags let you direct where viewers go after watching any particular video.

Some Words of Advice

The best advice I can give to those new to DVD authoring is to be unambitious. In general, most DVD authoring tools, like Studio, offer a cornucopia of development options. Once you start to experiment, development time can go through the roof, and advanced options like video thumbnails and menus lengthen rendering time drastically. With your first DVD projects, it's better to be unambitious and finished than frustrated with no end result.

And while Studio is a mature, ninth-generation video editor, it's only a second-generation DVD authoring program. If you scan the Pinnacle message boards, you'll notice a disproportionate share of messages that relate to exotic DVD authoring attempts. In my experience, with all authoring programs, not just Studio, the more you push the design envelope, the more likely you are to find yourself immersed in untested waters. So get a few simple and successful projects under your belt before going crazy on the authoring front.

Irrespective of the production type you choose, it's best to get the video and slide show production done first and then start your DVD authoring.

Menu structure

Menu structure determines the way menus link to each other. Studio uses three basic types:

- **Linear menus:** Linear menus flow sequentially backward and forward, as shown in **Figure 12.2**. You create these by using any Studio template or by building your own template, as described in Chapter 10.

When you use a linear menu, Studio automatically builds enough menus so that each chapter in your video has a link. Viewers move through the menus sequentially, using links between the menus that Studio automatically inserts. Because Studio does all the work for you, using linear menus is fast and easy.

However, though linear menus are acceptable for linear movies, they're poor choices for disparate collections of content. For example, if the trip to Disney World was the last event of the summer, you may have to toggle through 10 menus to see that killer sunset from the hotel room balcony—definitely not optimal.

Figure 12.2 Linear menus flow sequentially. Studio builds them automatically, making them easy to create, but they're not the best tools for navigation to content.

The Two Faces of DVD

Recordable DVDs have two basic roles in life. The first is to serve as a place to store data, similar to a CD-recordable disc but with a 4.7 GB capacity rather than 653 MB or 700 MB.

More to our interests, however, is the recordable DVD's second role, as a medium for playing back interactive productions on DVD players connected to TV sets and computers with DVD drives and the necessary player software.

Whereas any program capable of writing data to a disc can use DVD-R and DVD+R discs in their first capacity, only an authoring program like Studio can produce titles that play on DVD players.

- **Custom menus:** When working with disparate collections, you may want to consider building your own *custom menus*, which have direct links from one to many menus, as shown in **Figure 12.3**. In my production, I created separate pages for different topics at the Fiddler's Convention: one for interesting bands, one for instruments, and one for the sites. If viewers want to see that killer band from Virginia Tech, they need click only twice rather than multiple times.

Studio provides tremendous flexibility in this regard, allowing you to customize menus and link menu to menu at will. Though you'll get vastly improved navigation, the obvious downside is you have to build multiple menus and perform most of your linking manually. You'll also have to build links from these pages back to the home page and insert Return to Menu flags at the end of each main sequence.

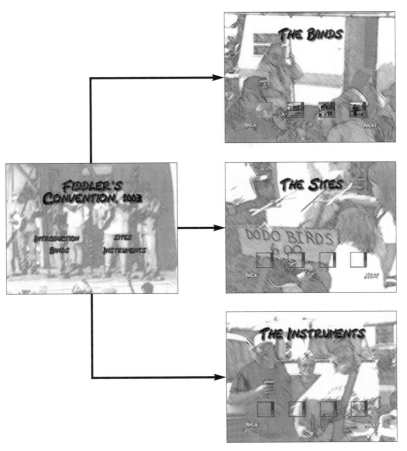

Figure 12.3 You build 'em, you link 'em—custom menus are more work, but are customized for your content.

- **Hybrid menus:** The third menu structure, shown in **Figure 12.4**, is a hybrid structure that includes both linear and custom menus. This is the structure used in my Fiddler's Convention project, because several of the menus had more sequences than I could fit on one page.

    For example, the Instruments section contained eight videos, requiring two menu pages. Since I used a linear rather than a custom menu, Studio built the second Instruments menu for me, along with links back and forth between the first and second Instruments menus.

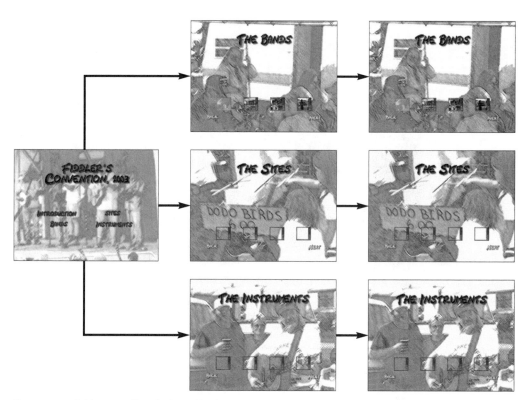

Figure 12.4 Hybrid menus offers the best of both worlds: they provide great navigation, and Studio handles some of the linking for you.

If you study the custom menus in Figure 12.4, you'll notice they all look somewhat similar. That's because to speed production, I created the first menu by hand, saved it, and then swapped the background image and title by section, saving each menu as I went along. (Total production time for the five custom menus was about 10 minutes.)

For a $100 program, Studio is surprisingly adept at authoring, with elegant touches such as displaying only linked buttons on a menu and hiding those that are inactive, as shown in the Player window on the right in **Figure 12.5**.

In the figure, the Menu Clip Properties window on the left shows the linear menu template, and the Preview window on the right shows how the menu will look during playback. The single unpopulated video icon (with *??* at the upper left) is not displayed during playback, and neither are the Previous (left arrow) and Next (right arrow) buttons, which are unnecessary because this section has only one menu.

On the other hand, Studio also lacks link-checking capabilities and didn't notice the *??* in the middle bottom of the page, which is supposed to be a link back to the home page. Had I produced this disc without the link, navigation would have been awkward. To avoid producing a disc with incomplete links, you need to thoroughly preview and check links before burning the disc. You'll learn how later in this chapter.

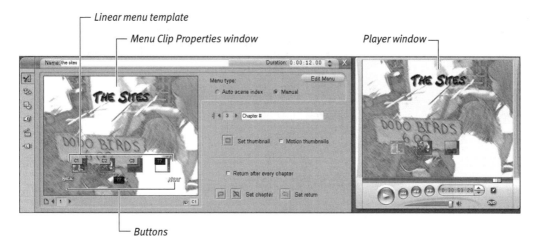

Figure 12.5 The linear menu template and the Preview window, showing only the populated buttons.

Using Menu Templates

If you're a new Studio user, I recommend that you produce your first few DVD projects using templates. Keep in mind that the key to success isn't what you'll learn on these pages, as production is largely automated, but how you've prepared your videos beforehand.

Specifically, Studio automatically inserts chapter flags at the start of each scene. If you have too many scenes, you'll have multiple menu pages, which are cumbersome to navigate. To avoid this problem, combine scenes in the Album (see Chapter 6) or the Movie window (see Chapter 7) before starting your DVD. Also see Chapter 10 for more on menus.

The one downside of this approach is that you can't trim or place transitions between scenes and then combine them. If this limitation prevents you from combining your scenes into usable chunks, you should tell Studio not to automatically create chapter links when you drag in your first menu, and simply create the links manually (see "To Create a Chapter Link" later in this chapter).

As it turns out, the template approach worked well for a holiday concert DVD I produced while writing this book. I'll use this project to demonstrate the use of templates and then get back to the Fiddler's Convention for the rest of the chapter.

Figure 12.6 All assets for my holiday-concert project have been placed on the Timeline.

To use a menu template:

1. In Edit mode, place all project assets on the Timeline (**Figure 12.6**).

2. Click the Show Menus icon to open the Disc Menus tab of the Album (**Figure 12.7**).

   Studio identifies motion menus, or menus with video as a background, with an icon at the bottom right. Also, if you've created your own menus, you access them by choosing My Menus from the list of menus.

3. Drag the desired menu to the front of the project, placing it on the Video track.

   Studio opens the Adding Menu to Movie dialog box (**Figure 12.8**).

4. Click Yes to create links automatically to each scene after the menu.

   Studio automatically creates as many menus as necessary for all video scenes, inserts the Next and Previous buttons where necessary, and populates the thumbnail buttons with videos from the Timeline.

   continues on next page

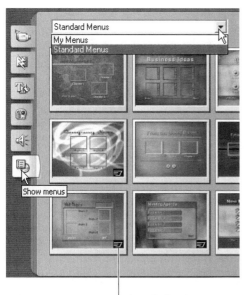

Icon designates menu has video as background

Figure 12.7 Welcome to the Menu Album. Note that the menus you create are stored in a separate folder.

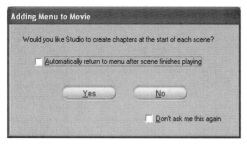

Figure 12.8 Click Yes, and Studio practically builds the DVD for you.

✔ Tips

- Studio automatically uses the first video frame as the menu thumbnail, not the thumbnail you've selected for either the Album or the Timeline (see Chapter 10).

- When you use a menu template, Studio shows only one copy of the menu on the Timeline, even though the program may ultimately produce multiple menus. See "To select the next menu page" later in this chapter for information on navigating through these pages in the Menu Clip Properties window.

- Studio enables four options when you select a menu, as shown in **Figure 12.9**. I stick with the default option, Ask If Chapters Should Be Created, so that I can easily opt out of Studio's automatic menu creation, which I usually do. To access this dialog box, choose Setup > Edit from Studio's main menu.

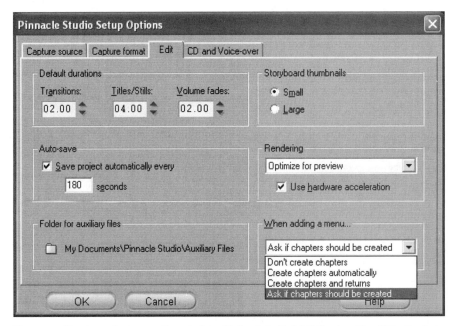

Figure 12.9 Chapter and returns options. I stick with the default, Ask If Chapters Should Be Created.

To edit the menu:

1. Double-click the menu.
   Studio opens the Menu Clip Properties tool (**Figure 12.10**).

2. At the upper right, click Edit Menu.
   The Title editor opens (**Figure 12.11**). See Chapter 10 for editing details.

3. Make your edits; then do *one of the following*:

   ▲ At the lower right, click OK (or press F12) to save the menu and return to the Edit window.
   Studio overwrites the original menu on the Timeline, but doesn't change the menu in the Menu Album.

   ▲ Choose File > Save Menu As to save the file using a unique name, preserving the original Studio menu for reuse. Then click OK to return to the Edit window.

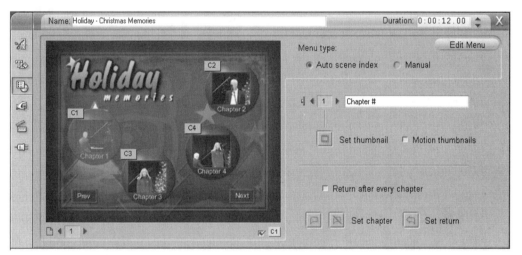

Figure 12.10 The initial menu showing the first four chapter links.

Figure 12.11 The Title editor, where you can customize this template (I added 2003 to the description).

To create a chapter link:

1. Using the Timeline scrubber or the Player controls, navigate to the target starting point of the new chapter (**Figure 12.12**).

2. Do *one of the following:*
   - ▲ Right-click the Menu track and choose Set Disc Chapter (**Figure 12.13**).
   - ▲ Right-click the Video track and choose Set Disc Chapter.

   Studio creates the new chapter link, in this case C5 (**Figure 12.14**).

✔ Tip

- You can move a chapter flag by dragging it to any location on the Menu track. See "Previewing Your DVD" later in this chapter for details.

Figure 12.12 To create a chapter flag to link to from the menu, first choose the frame.

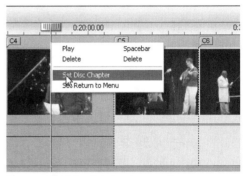

Figure 12.13 Right-click the Menu track to see your options.

Figure 12.14 The new chapter link is created.

Maintaining Order—Or Not

If you elect to have Studio automatically create chapter points at all scenes (Figure 12.8) and then later add chapter points at other locations on the Timeline, Studio automatically places each new scene in its chronological sequence. For example, in Figures 12.12 through 12.14, I added a chapter point between C4 and C5, which Studio automatically named C5; Studio then incremented all subsequent chapter points on the Timeline by one number. In Studio parlance, this means that the menu type is Auto Scene Index, which you can see at the upper right of Figure 12.10.

In contrast, if you elect to assign chapter points manually and then insert a chapter point between two current chapter points, Studio inserts the next available chapter point at the selected location and doesn't automatically reorder the chapters. This is shown in **Figure 12.15**, where I added all chapter points manually. Here, the inserted chapter point is C12, rather than C5. This means that this chapter point will appear on the third menu, rather than the second, and will be out of sequence when played from the menu. This menu type is Manual, shown at the upper right of Figure 12.10.

Note that you can convert from Manual to Auto Scene Index at any time by clicking the Auto Scene Index check box in the Menu Clip Properties window, and Studio will reorder the chapter points into sequential order. This process is described in "To change menu type" later in this chapter.

Here's the lesson: So long as your videos are laid out sequentially on the Timeline in the order you want your viewers to access them, and you have a reasonable number of scenes, you can have Studio automatically assign chapter points. This approach is also easier if you delete chapter points, since Studio will automatically reorder all subsequent videos and close any gaps in the menu.

On the other hand, if you want to customize the menu order of the chapter points, you have to use the second approach and manually assign all chapter points. Note that if you delete any chapter points under this approach, Studio doesn't automatically fill the gaps, and you'll have unassigned buttons in your menus. You can easily address this issue by switching to Auto Scene Index mode, but then all chapter points will be assigned sequentially, and you'll lose the custom order you've already created.

Figure 12.15 Here's the way the link would look if I selected Manual rather than Auto Scene Index.

To manually assign chapter points:

1. In Edit mode, place all project assets on the Timeline (Figure 12.6).

2. Click the Show Menus icon to open the Disc Menus tab of the Album (Figure 12.7).

   Note that Studio identifies motion menus, or menus with video as a background, with an icon at the bottom right. Also, if you've created your own menus, you can access them by choosing My Menus from the list box shown at the top of Figure 12.7.

3. Drag the desired menu to the front of the project, placing it on the Video track.

   Studio opens the Adding Menu to Movie dialog box (Figure 12.8).

4. Click No to create links manually to each scene after the menu.

5. At the bottom of the Menu Clip Properties tool, click the Show Link Numbers check box (**Figure 12.16**).

Show Link Numbers check box

Figure 12.16 Click here to see the links (or the absence of links).

DVD Authoring

Figure 12.17 Drag the scene into the target frame to create the link.

6. Link scenes to the menu buttons by doing *one of the following:*

   ▲ In the Timeline, drag the target scene into the target button frame (**Figure 12.17**).

   ▲ Click the target button frame in the Menu Clip Properties tool (Studio highlights the frame). Click the target scene on the Timeline (Studio highlights the scene). Then click the Create Chapter Link button in the Menu Clip Properties tool (**Figure 12.18**).

   Studio lists C1 in the button frame and C1 on the Timeline and places the first frame of the video as a thumbnail (**Figure 12.19**).

   continues on next page

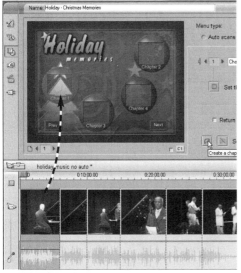

Figure 12.18 Or click the frame and then the scene and then click here.

Figure 12.19 The C1 on the button indicates which chapter point the button is linked to on the Timeline.

Chapter 12

7. Repeat Step 6 until you populate all button frames on the first menu (**Figure 12.20**)

8. At the bottom of the Menu Clip Properties tool, click the Show Next Page icon.

   Studio advances to the next menu page, identified as Menu Page 2 in the page selector (**Figure 12.21**).

9. Repeat Steps 6 through 8 until all desired scenes are added to the menu.

✔ Tip

- The order of Studio's menus can be different than expected. For example, in the Holiday template I used, the first button frame, designated in Figure 12.16 as Chapter 1, is on the far left, and the second button frame, designated as Chapter 2, is at the upper right. Use the chapter numbers on the buttons as a guide when linking your videos.

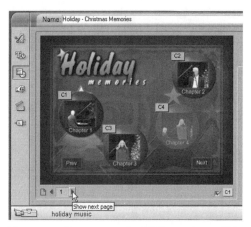

Figure 12.20 Once you create all links on a page, click here to see the next page.

— Page selector
Figure 12.21 Here we are at Page 2.

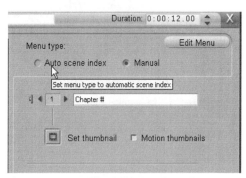

Figure 12.22 To reorder the chapter flags after inserting a new chapter point, select Auto Scene Index.

DVD Authoring

Figure 12.23 Order restored. Compare this figure to Figure 12.15.

To change menu type:

◆ In the Menu Clip Properties tool, select Auto Scene Index (**Figure 12.22**).

Studio sorts the chapter flags sequentially and updates all affected menus (**Figure 12.23**).

To delete chapter links:

◆ To delete chapter links, do *one of the following*:

▲ In the Menu Clip Properties tool, select the button linked to the target chapter link. Click the Delete the Current Chapter icon or press *V* (**Figure 12.24**).

▲ On the Menu track, select the chapter flag, right-click, and choose Delete.

▲ On the Menu track, select the chapter flag and press the Delete key.

Studio deletes the chapter flag and clears the menu link (**Figure 12.25**).

Figure 12.24 To clear chapter links (and delete chapters), select the chapter and then click the Delete Current Chapter icon.

Figure 12.25 The chapter flag and link created in Figure 12.14 are both gone.

359

To change a button caption:

1. Select the button in the Menu Clip Properties tool; then select the button caption description to make the field active.

2. Insert the new text.

3. Press Enter to save the text (**Figure 12.26**). Studio saves the new description and changes the menu.

To change a button thumbnail:

1. Select the button in the Menu Clip Properties tool; then use the Timeline scrubber or Player controls to navigate to a new thumbnail frame.

2. Do *one of the following:*
   ▲ Right-click the Video track and choose Set Thumbnail.
   ▲ In the Menu Clip Properties tool, click the Set Thumbnail icon (**Figure 12.27**).

   Studio changes to the new thumbnail.

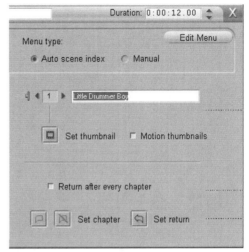

Figure 12.26 Enter the button description here.

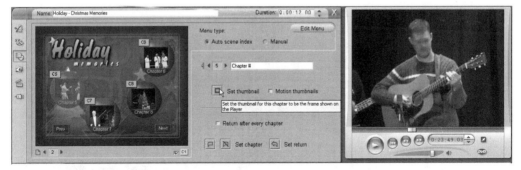

Figure 12.27 To change the thumbnail, navigate to the target frame and click Set Thumbnail.

DVD Authoring

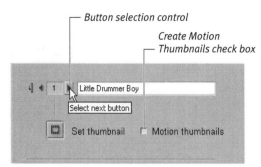

Figure 12.28 Use the button selection control to move from button to button.

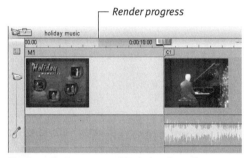

Figure 12.29 Expect some rendering time when you select Motion Thumbnails, especially with multimenu productions.

Figure 12.30 Click here to display the next menu page.

✔ Tips

- Use this procedure to move through the sequential menus automatically created by Studio, to access all linked chapters.

- To select a completely different menu, double-click that menu on the Timeline.

To select another button to edit:

◆ In the Menu Clip Properties tool, do *one of the following*:

  ▲ Click the button to edit.

  ▲ Use the button selection control to move to the button you want to edit (**Figure 12.28**).

To create video buttons:

◆ In the Menu Clip Properties tool, select Motion Thumbnails (Figure 12.28).

  Studio replaces the still-image thumbnail with a tiny version of the video, creating a video button.

✔ Tips

- The video button will play for the duration of the menu and then restart. Video buttons are most aesthetically pleasing when menus have a duration of at least one minute. See "To change menu duration" later in this chapter.

- Because video buttons must be separately rendered before they appear, these won't immediately show up when you preview your video. If you selected background rendering (see Chapter 8), you'll see the rendering progress reported above the menu (**Figure 12.29**).

- Maybe it's just me, but video buttons are irritating, take a long time to render, and slow the computer when rendering in the background. These head my list of "don't try this at home" features.

To select the next menu page:

◆ In the Menu Clip Properties tool, click the Show Next Page icon (**Figure 12.30**).

USING MENU TEMPLATES

To set Return to Menu links:

1. On the Menu track, double-click the target menu.

   Studio displays the menu in the Menu Clip Properties tool.

2. Click the video that, after playback, should return the viewer to the target menu (rather than automatically moving to the next scene on the Timeline).

3. Do *one of the following*:
   - ▲ In the Menu Clip Properties tool, click the Return to This Menu icon (**Figure 12.31**).
   - ▲ Right-click the Menu track and choose Set Return to Menu.
   - ▲ Right-click the Video track and choose Set Return to Menu.

   Studio sets the Return to Menu flag (**Figure 12.32**).

✔ Tip

- Studio always sets the Return to Menu flag at the end of the video, figuring you'd probably never want to interrupt playback of a clip in the middle. If your intent is to interrupt the clip in the middle, simply drag the flag to the desired location.

To change menu duration:

- ◆ To change the menu duration, do *one of the following*:
   - ▲ Select the menu and drag it to the desired length (see Chapter 7 for details).
   - ▲ At the upper right of the Menu Clip Properties tool, change the Duration field by typing the desired duration or using the controls to the right of the field (**Figure 12.33**).

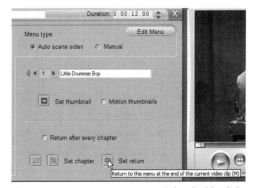

Figure 12.31 To set Return to Menu links, double-click the menu to open it in the Menu Clip Properties tool and then click this icon or press M.

Figure 12.32 Whatever method you use, look for the flag. It should be the same number as the menu you want to return to (in this case, M1 = Menu 1) and blue.

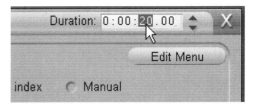

Figure 12.33 You can set the menu duration here, or simply drag the menu to the desired length, just like a still image.

DVD Authoring

Figure 12.34 Here's the main menu for my DVD.

Using Custom Menus

Before starting work here, you should have at least two menus: a main menu (**Figure 12.34**) with buttons to link to your section menus, and the section menus themselves (**Figure 12.35**).

The section menus should have three navigational button links: Previous and Next buttons that link to the namesake pages, and a Home button to link to the main menu.

Start by getting your main menu and section menus on the Timeline. Then link the menus to scenes on the Timeline and then to each other.

Previous button
Links to scenes
Next button
Home button (link to main menu)

Figure 12.35 Here's one of five section menus. Note the Next and Previous buttons, which handle navigation if Studio creates multiple menus, and the link to the main menu.

Chapter 12

To insert the main menu:

1. In Edit mode, place all project assets on the Timeline (Figure 12.6).

2. Click the Show Menus icon to open the Disc Menus tab in the Album (Figure 12.7).

3. At the upper left of the Menus Album, choose My Menus from the list box.

   Studio opens the Album that contains your custom menus.

4. Drag the main menu to the front of the project, placing it on the Video track (**Figure 12.36**).

   Studio opens the Adding Menu to Movie dialog box (Figure 12.8).

5. Click No to manually create all links.

   Studio inserts the menu and opens the Menu Clip Properties tool to the Set Menu Links window (**Figure 12.37**).

✔ Tip

- If your custom menu has numbers in front of the menu items (**Figure 12.38**), it's probably because Studio is configured to produce a VideoCD or SuperVideoCD. See "Burning a DVD Title" later in this chapter to learn how to configure Studio to produce a DVD, which will eliminate the numbers from the menu.

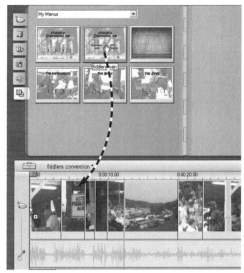

Figure 12.36 Clicking the Show Menus icon opens the Disc Menus tab.

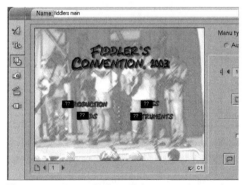

Figure 12.37 Oops—look at all those question marks, representing open links. You'll fill them in a moment.

Figure 12.38 The roman numerals in front of the text buttons indicate that Studio is set up to produce a VideoCD or SuperVideoCD.

DVD Authoring

To insert and link a section menu:

1. From the Disc Menus tab, drag the section menu to the Timeline in front of the first video clip you will link to this menu (**Figure 12.39**).

   Studio opens the Adding Menu to Movie dialog box. Note that the Introduction button in the main menu will link directly to the first song on the Timeline, which I linked using techniques described in "To create a chapter link" earlier in this chapter.

   continues on next page

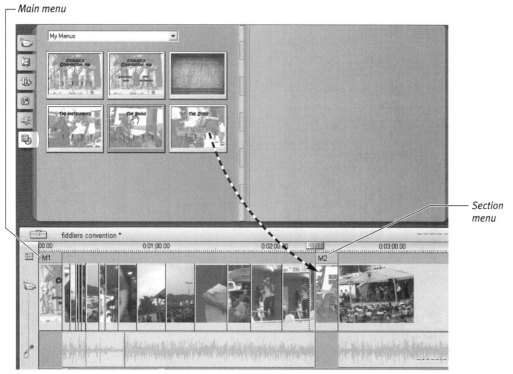

Figure 12.39 Drag the section menu to the Timeline.

Chapter 12

2. Click No to manually create all links. Studio inserts the menu (**Figure 12.40**).

3. If Studio doesn't automatically open the Menu Clip Properties tool, double-click the menu to open it.

4. Drag the main menu to the Home button in the section menu (**Figure 12.41**).

   Studio links the main menu to the section menu, allowing the viewer to navigate back to the main menu from the section menu (**Figure 12.42**), and places an M1 on top of the link because the Show Link check box, at the bottom right in the figure, is checked.

   I find that links can get disorganized if I don't complete the menu links first, which is why I do this first.

Figure 12.40 Here's the section menu, begging to be linked.

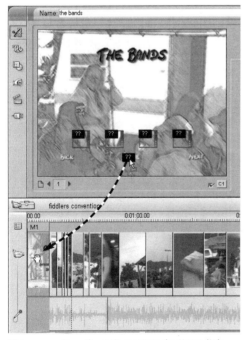

Figure 12.41 Drag the main menu to the Home link.

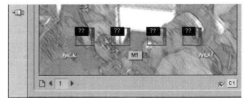

Figure 12.42 The M1 tells you that the link is accomplished.

DVD Authoring

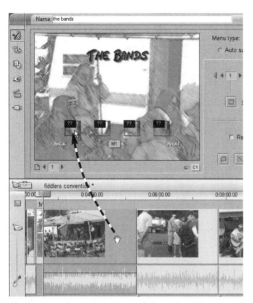

Figure 12.43 Start dragging and dropping videos on the buttons.

Figure 12.44 Or select a menu button, select a video, and click this button. This is the best method when Studio gets a bit balky and refuses to set the link.

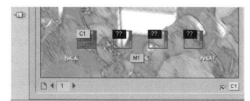

Figure 12.45 Link accomplished. While you can't see it in this black-and-white image, the C1 link in the Menu Clip Properties tool is coded the same color as the menu.

5. To link project assets on the Timeline to the menu buttons, do *one of the following*:

▲ Drag a video to a button in the Menu Clip Properties tool (**Figure 12.43**).

▲ Select a button in the Menu Clip Properties tool; then right-click the Menu track at the desired location and choose Set Disc Chapter.

▲ Select a button in the Menu Clip Properties tool; then right-click the Video track at the desired location and choose Set Disc Chapter.

▲ Select a button in the Menu Clip Properties tool; then select the target video and click the Create a Chapter Link for the Selected Button icon (**Figure 12.44**).

Studio creates the new chapter flag, in this case C1 (**Figure 12.45**), and links the chapter flag to the selected button.

continues on next page

USING CUSTOM MENUS

367

6. Populate the rest of the buttons on the section menu using these same procedures (**Figure 12.46**). If you need more than one menu, click the Show Next Page icon, shown in Figure 12.46, or the Select Next Button icon, shown in Figure 12.28.

7. Add and populate any other section menus.

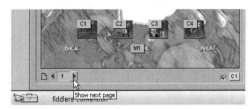

Figure 12.46 First menu done.

✔ Tips

- At times, Studio gets a bit finicky about accepting a link via drag and drop. When this happens, select the target button and then the target scene and click the Create a Chapter Link for the Selected Button icon.

- If Studio won't let you turn the menu page, it's because you haven't linked all buttons on that menu yet. When this happens, it's usually the Return to Home button that's still unlinked.

- Studio resets the chapter flag number for each menu and color codes menus, chapter links, and Return to Menu links.

DVD Authoring

Figure 12.47 Time to link the section menu to the main menu. Double-click the main menu to open it in the Menu Clip Properties tool.

To link section menus to the main menu:

1. Double-click the main menu.

    Studio opens the main menu in the Menu Clip Properties tool (**Figure 12.47**).

2. Drag the section menu to the appropriate link on the main menu (**Figure 12.48**).

    Studio creates the link.

    continues on next page

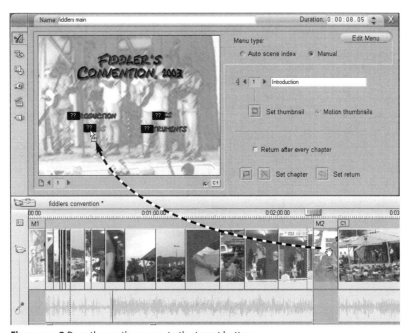

Figure 12.48 Drag the section menu to the target button.

3. Repeat Step 2 for all section menus or videos directly linked directly to the main menu (**Figure 12.49**). Menus are shown as M2, M3, and M4, and the direct link to a chapter point is shown as C1.

✔ Tips

- If you're using a hybrid menu structure and your section menu has multiple pages, you'll have to link the first and all subsequent menus to the main menu to enable viewers to return to the main menu from each menu. For example, Figure 12.46 shows the menu link to the main menu as complete (as indicated by the M1 designation), but once you turn to the next menu page, the link (like all the others) is empty (**Figure 12.50**).

- Again, sometimes Studio gets a bit finicky about accepting a link via drag and drop. In these instances, make sure the target link is selected in the Menu Clip Properties tool, select the target asset, and then click the Create a Chapter Link for the Selected Button icon (Figure 12.44).

Figure 12.49 Menu 2 linked and ready for duty.

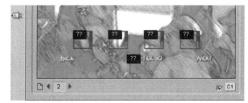

Figure 12.50 If you're using a hybrid menu structure, you have to link *each menu* to the Home page. Here we turn to page 2 of this menu, and the link to Home is empty.

DVD Authoring

Figure 12.51 To set a Return to Menu flag, choose the last video in the section.

To set Return to Menu flags:

1. Double-click the target menu.
   Studio displays the menu in the Clip Properties tool.

2. On the Timeline, select the final video linked to that menu (**Figure 12.51**).

3. Set the Return to Menu link using one of the techniques described earlier in "Using Menu Templates."
   Studio sets the Return to Menu link for that menu (**Figure 12.52**).

4. Set Return to Menu links for all section menus.

✔ Tip

- If the Return to Menu flag has a different number than the menu number, you may be returning to the wrong menu—obviously okay if you wanted to return to a different menu than where you started from, but also a fairly common mistake.

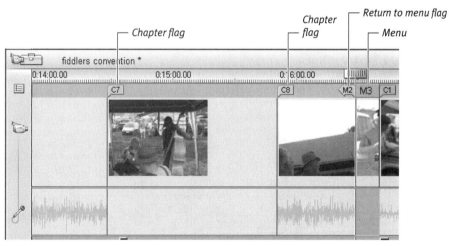

Figure 12.52 Return to Menu link set.

Chapter 12

Previewing Your DVD

Given Studio's DVD design flexibility, it's difficult to set rules for previewing your titles. Generally, I like to check the major intermenu links first, because if these are wrong, viewers won't be able to access certain menu pages. Then I check the Return to Menu links and finally the video links themselves.

Note that even if you let Studio build the production for you from a template, you should check the intermenu links, especially if you created your own template. That way, if you made a mistake creating the menu, you'll catch it before you burn your DVD.

Basically, the best practice is to go through each link on each menu. It's not so much the media cost that will kill you if you have to reburn your DVD; it's the rendering and production time, which can easily take hours, even for short productions.

Figure 12.53 Click here to start the DVD preview.

To preview your DVD:

1. In the Player window, click the Start DVD Preview icon (**Figure 12.53**).

   The Player switches to DVD Preview mode with DVD-specific playback controls (**Figure 12.54**).

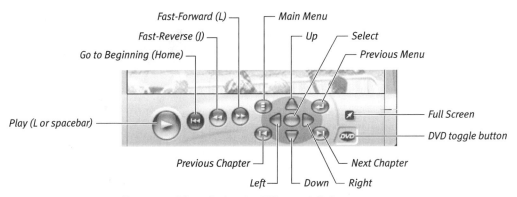

Figure 12.54 Whoee, look at that DVD control. Makes me want to grab a beer and put my feet up!

Figure 12.55 Start by checking all links to section menus.

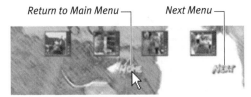

Figure 12.56 And then back to the main menu.

Figure 12.57 After clicking to the next menu, click here to return to the previous menu.

2. Check all links from the main menu to the section menus (**Figure 12.55**).

3. Check all links back to the main menu from the section menus (**Figure 12.56**).

4. From each section menu with multiple pages, check the links between each menu (Figure 12.56 and **Figure 12.57**).

5. If you inserted Return to Menu flags, play the last video in each section to test whether you return to the proper menu. You can use the Timeline scrubber to move to near the Return to Menu flag and then click Play, which may be faster than waiting for the video to play (**Figure 12.58**).

6. Check each movie link in each menu.

continues on next page

Figure 12.58 Drag the Timeline scrubber to the end of the video to speed things up.

✔ Tips

- If your chapter flags aren't in the desired locations, you can drag them to any frame desired (**Figure 12.59**).

- If you toggle to full-screen mode during preview, you no longer have access to any of the preview controls. Press Esc on your keyboard to return to the main Studio menu.

- Studio may stall and simply stop playing during preview at times. If this occurs, simply toggle out of Preview mode by clicking the Start DVD Preview icon (Figure 12.53) and then toggle back in and try again. If that doesn't work, try rebooting (saving your work first, of course).

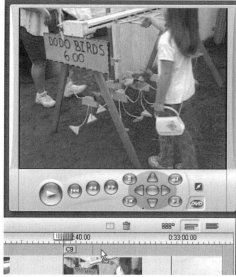

Figure 12.59 You can drag chapter flags to new locations, using the Player as a guide.

DVD Authoring

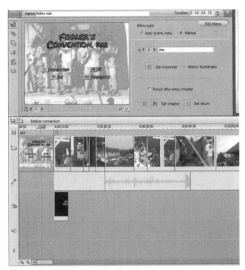

Figure 12.60 To add audio to your menu, start by double-clicking the menu to load it in the Menu Clip Properties tool.

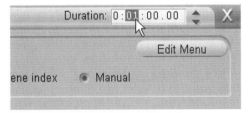

Figure 12.61 Extend the duration to at least one minute (for aesthetics, not due to a Studio limitation).

Figure 12.62 Close the Video toolbox.

Creating Audio Menus

Many Hollywood DVDs play audio while displaying the menu, an effect that Studio can duplicate with ease. You can use any audio track you create or import into Studio (see Chapter 11) as background for your menu tracks.

For simplicity, the tasks here will use a CD audio track previously ripped to disk, but you can rip tracks at will or use SmartSound to create audio for your menus.

Few things are as irritating as music repeated over and over every 12 seconds. So if you're going to use audio menus, remember to extend the duration of your menus to at least one minute, preferably longer.

To create an audio menu:

1. Double-click the target menu.
   Studio opens the menu in the Menu Clip Properties tool (**Figure 12.60**).

2. Extend the duration of the menu to at least one minute (**Figure 12.61**).
   (See "To change menu duration" earlier in this chapter for instructions.) The one-minute rule is for aesthetics, not any limitation in the Studio program.

3. At the upper left of the Movie window, click the Camcorder icon to close the Video toolbox (**Figure 12.62**), or click the X in the upper-right corner of the Menu Clip Properties tool.

continues on next page

375

4. Do *one of the following*:
   ▲ To find an audio file to use as background music, click the Show Sound Effects icon to open the Sound Effects tab in the Album.
   ▲ To use the audio from a video file as background music for the menu, click the Show Videos icon (**Figure 12.63**).

   I'm using the music from a killer band from Virginia Tech as background music.

Figure 12.63 I'm using background audio from one of the video scenes, a great little band from Virginia Tech.

5. Drag the desired audio track to either the Sound Effect track or Music track and trim to the same duration as the DVD menu using techniques discussed in "To change the duration of an audio file on the Timeline" in Chapter 7.

6. If you like, fade the background audio in and out. See "Using The Volume Tool" in Chapter 11 for details (**Figure 12.64**).

   If you use an MP3 file as background, when you first preview your DVD with background music enabled, Studio will load the audio file into memory before playing it (**Figure 12.65**). Thereafter, preview should proceed just as it does with titles that don't have audio menus.

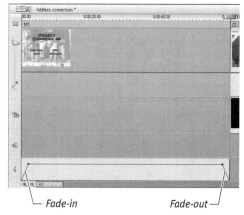

Figure 12.64 Fade the audio in and out for a bit of extra polish.

✔ Tips

- Audio backgrounds work automatically with templates; Studio inserts the audio into all sequential menus. However, the track starts over each time you move between menus, which may prove irritating.

- Creating an audio menu doesn't modify any menu settings, making it simple to insert audio backgrounds as the final development step. In contrast, video menus integrate most smoothly when planned from the start.

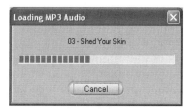

Figure 12.65 Before you can preview an MP3 file, Studio has to load the audio track.

DVD Authoring

Figure 12.66 Insert the background video on the Video track.

Figure 12.67 Trim the video to the desired length; once again, a minute or more works best.

Creating Video Menus

Motion menus have video playing underneath the buttons to amuse viewers while they're making their menu selection. Note that video menus are easiest to use if you include them in your design from the start, since plugging them in at the end may break the links in the affected menus, forcing you to relink.

Video menus are subject to the same caveat as audio menus: when they're short and repetitive, they get irritating. Plan on using video clips of at least one minute for your video menus.

Finally, like video buttons, video menus take time, add design complexity, and push the developmental envelope. Get a few successful DVDs under your belt before implementing these.

To create a video menu:

1. Drag the background video onto the Video track where the menu will be located (**Figure 12.66**).

2. If necessary, trim the video to the desired length, which should be at least one minute (**Figure 12.67**); use the techniques described in "Trimming a Clip on the Timeline" in Chapter 7.

   The one-minute rule is for aesthetics, not any limitation in the Studio program.

   continues on next page

377

Chapter 12

3. Click the Show Menus icon to open the Disc Menus tab in the Album.

 If you're dragging down a custom menu, you'll have to choose My Menus from the top of the Menu Album.

4. Drag the desired menu to the Title track so it corresponds with the video background (**Figure 12.68**).

 Studio opens the Adding Menu to Movie dialog box (Figure 12.8).

5. Do *one of the following:*
   - ▲ Click Yes to automatically create links to each scene after the menu.
   - ▲ Click No to link all videos and menus manually.

 Studio inserts the menu without the background image, making it transparent.

6. Drag the menu to the same duration as the background video.

7. If necessary, link the main menu to the section menus and link the videos.

8. In the Player, click the DVD icon to preview your work (**Figure 12.69**).

 Looks pretty cool, if I do say so myself.

✔ **Tip**

■ Video backgrounds work automatically with templates; Studio inserts the video behind all sequential menus.

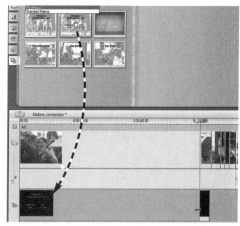

Figure 12.68 Locate the menu in the Album and drag it to the Title track and to the same duration as the video file.

DVD icon

Figure 12.69 Here's the completed video menu in the preview window.

378

Choosing Your DVD Recorder

In the beginning, there was DVD, and it was good. Then DVD-RAM. Then DVD+RW. Then (in non-sequential order) DVD-R, DVD-RW, and DVD+R/RW. Then DVD+R/RW/-R and DVD-R/RW +R/RW and DVD+RAM/-R. Or is it DVD-RAM/+R? I'm not sure.

This is not a misprint—in fact, I'm sure I've forgotten a few formats. Overall, if the DVD industry set out to confuse potential buyers of DVD recorders, it couldn't have done a better job.

But here are the details you need to know:

First, make sure that whatever recorder you buy supports either -R or +R, the two formats most widely compatible with set-top DVD players. DVD-RAM or DVD+RW without an R option should be avoided at all costs. All DVD-RW drives support -R as well, and say so. To be completely sure, look for a statement like "compatible with DVD players" on the box or marketing literature, although this is not 100 percent true for any of the formats.

Second, make sure that whatever device you choose, you purchase the correct media. That is, a DVD+R drive can't write to DVD-R media, and vice versa. The only exceptions are drives from Sony, Pioneer, and several other vendors that support DVD-R/RW and DVD+R/+RW, but most drives support only one or the other.

I started out in the DVD-R camp with Pioneer burners, but have worked a lot lately with an HP xw4100 workstation with a DVD Writer 300n +R/RW drive. The only problem, and it's a big one, is that discs produced by the 300n won't play on my Pioneer DVD player.

This isn't a slur against the HP burner, which has batted 1,000 in creating discs I've sent to friends, family, and business associates. It also doesn't mean that every disc created by the 300n will be incompatible with all Pioneer players. Several of my colleagues have had great success playing DVD+R disks in Pioneer players.

Unfortunately, no DVD burner or format can claim 100 percent compatibility, an issue explored in the sidebar "The Dark Side of Recordable DVD."

Burning a DVD Title

The big moment has arrived; you've created, previewed, tinkered, and then tinkered some more. The babies are crying, the spouse complaining, and the grandparents doubting they'll ever see this DVD. It's time to shoot the videographer and ship the movie.

Let's burn, baby, burn.

To burn a DVD title:

1. Put blank media in your DVD burner.
2. Do *one of the following*:
   ▲ At the upper left of the program window, click Make Movie (**Figure 12.70**), then click Disc (**Figure 12.71**), and then click Settings.
   ▲ From the Studio menu, choose Setup > Make Disc (**Figure 12.72**).

   Studio enters Make Movie mode, and the Pinnacle Studio Setup Options dialog box opens to the Make Disc tab (**Figure 12.73**).
3. In the Output Format section, choose DVD.
4. In the Burn Options section, choose *one of the following:*
   ▲ **Burn Directly to Disc:** Choose this to render and burn the current project directly to DVD.
   ▲ **Create Disc Content but Don't Burn:** Choose this to render the current project and save it to your hard disk.
   ▲ **Burn from Previously Created Disc Content:** Choose this to burn from previously created content. Studio burns the content from the currently open project; this option is available only if the project was already burned to disc or saved as a disc image.

Figure 12.70 Click Make Movie to start the DVD production process.

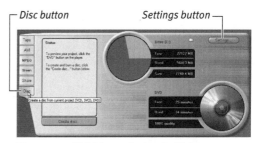

Figure 12.71 Click Disc to display the Diskometer.

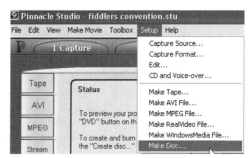

Figure 12.72 Or choose Setup > Make Disc.

5. At the left side of the Video Quality/Disc Usage section, click Automatic.

   This tells Studio to automatically determine the optimal data rate for the amount of content on your disc, which is the simplest of the four options. If you select Best video quality, Studio encodes at 8 mbps but limits your disc to about 59 minutes of video. If you select Most video on disc, Studio encodes at 3 mbps, which allows up to approximately 124 minutes of video, but will encode at 3 mbps even if you have less video, which is suboptimal. Or you can choose custom and set your own target data rate.

6. At the right side of the Video Quality/Disc Usage section, do *one or more of the following:*

   ▲ Select Filter Video if your input video is of poor quality.

   Studio uses a smoothing filter, which can improve quality but usually blurs the video.

   ▲ Select Draft Mode to encode more quickly but with some sacrifice in quality.

   ▲ Select MPEG Audio to encode audio in MPEG format.

   Select this option if you're getting short on disc space. If you don't select MPEG Audio, Studio will burn pulse-code modulated (PCM) audio to the disc, which provides slightly better quality and may be more compatible.

   continues on next page

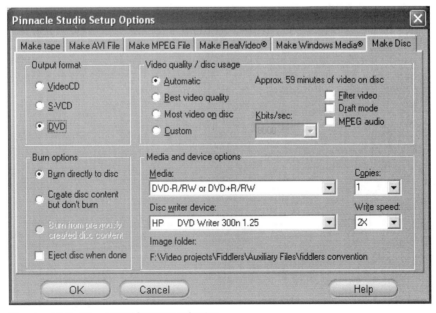

Figure 12.73 Decision central for DVD production.

Note that all DVD Players sold in the U.S. are *required* to be compatible with AC-3 and PCM audio. In contrast, though compatibility with MPEG Audio is almost ubiquitous, it isn't *required*, which is why PCM is a safer choice if you have the disc space.

Figure 12.74 Setting the number of DVD copies.

7. In the Media and Device Options section, do *one of the following*:

   ▲ From the Media list, choose DVD-R/RW or DVD+R/RW.

   ▲ From the Disc Writer Device list, choose your DVD-recordable drive.

   ▲ From the Copies list, choose the number of copies you want to produce (**Figure 12.74**).

   Studio will create the set number of copies sequentially, prompting you for additional discs when required.

   ▲ From the Write Speed list, choose 1X. See the sidebar "The Dark Side of Recordable DVD" later in this chapter for details.

8. Click OK to close the Pinnacle Studio Setup Options dialog box.

   Studio returns to the Make Movie window, and a Status box appears. You'll see an error message if the project is too large to fit on the recordable disc (**Figure 12.75**) or if the hard disk doesn't have sufficient space to stage the disc image.

9. Click Create Disc to start encoding.

Figure 12.75 Studio isn't shy about letting you know when there's a problem.

DVD Authoring

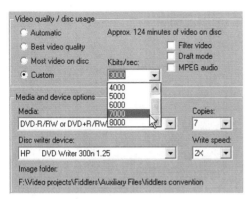

Figure 12.76 Encoding at a lower rate may resolve playback problems.

✔ Tips

- Though technically Studio can burn projects of any length, once you go over 80 minutes or so, Studio must increase compression to fit the video on the disc, degrading quality. All DVD authoring programs have this issue, not just Studio.

- If you're having problems playing your DVDs, particularly if they stutter and stop during playback, you may want to encode at a lower rate (see the sidebar "The Dark Side of DVD-R" later in this chapter). Try encoding between 6000 and 7000 Kbits/second, using the controls shown in **Figure 12.76**.

- Note the Image folder listed at the bottom of Figure 12.76. I typically use the same directory as my capture directory for these files, so they're easy to find and delete when I'm finished with a project. "Setting the Auxiliary File Location" in Chapter 2 describes how to select your Image folder. Note that it's not advisable to change the Image folder location in the middle of a project, since some users have reported problems when switching in midstream. It's especially inadvisable to change location just before burning—it would be a shame to throw a wrench in the works this late in the process.

383

What's happening?

After you start the DVD burn process, Studio has three tasks to perform:

- **Encoding:** Studio has to convert the video and other assets to the proper formats. Depending upon the length of content and speed of your computer, this can take anywhere from several minutes to several days. While encoding, Studio moves the Timeline scrubber through the Timeline and updates the Player to show the video being encoded.

    A progress bar sits under the Player showing overall progress in encoding, compiling and burning to DVD (**Figure 12.77**).

- **Compiling:** Studio converts the encoded files to DVD-formatted files and stores the files to disk. This is called the Compiling Disc phase, as shown in the Status window (**Figure 12.78**).

- **Burning the DVD:** Studio updates the Status screen and reports "Writing disc content" (**Figure 12.79**).

Make Movie progress

Figure 12.77 This bar shows progress through the encoding, compilation, and disc burning processes.

Figure 12.78 The next step is compiling.

Figure 12.79 Then writing disc content (burning). Getting close now.

DVD Authoring

Figure 12.80
Thank you, sir—
may I have another!

When the process is completed, Studio ejects your freshly minted DVD. Time to address the envelope, lick the stamps, and get this disc off to the grandparents. If you elected to create more than one DVD, Studio asks you to insert another blank disc (**Figure 12.80**).

✔ Tip

- Occasionally, especially with more complex projects, Studio may crash while encoding and writing to disc. When this occurs, I typically reboot and give Studio another try. If it crashes again, I remove the menus from the project and render the entire video as an AVI file using the DV format for video and 48 KHz for audio (see "To encode a project in DV format" in Chapter 14 for details). Then I insert the completed AVI file into the project, split the video where I need to insert menus, and insert and relink all menus. Then I try to burn the project again; invariably, the problem is resolved, and Studio produces the DVD.

Creating P-i-P Effects with Video Thumbnails

A Picture-in-Picture, or P-i-P, effect merges two video files with one in the background and another in a frame in the foreground. It's a fun effect in a number of situations; in the task here, I use it to show my wife watching our daughter's gymnastics routine.

I first create a video menu using the background video, and then insert the foreground video as a video thumbnail into the menu. Then I output the video menu as an AVI file that contains both the video menu and the second file as a tail, which I then trim when I reinsert the file into Studio.

It all sounds more difficult that it is, so I'll shut up and get started.

To create a P-i-P effect with video thumbnails:

1. Insert the background video on the Timeline (**Figure 12.81**).

2. Insert the foreground video behind the background video on the Timeline.

3. Double-click the Title track beneath the background clip.

   Studio opens the Title editor (**Figure 12.82**). Note that if the menu isn't beneath a background video, it will appear blank.

4. At the upper right of the Title editor, click the Buttons icon to open the Buttons library.

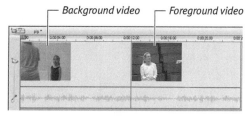

Figure 12.81 Starting point for the P-i-P: background video in front of the foreground video.

Figure 12.82 Here we are in the Title editor, getting ready to insert the button frame.

DVD Authoring

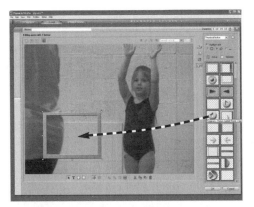

Figure 12.83 Drag in the frame and size it to please—not too big, or you'll surely block some critical video.

Figure 12.84 Have to clear the button selection color. Start here.

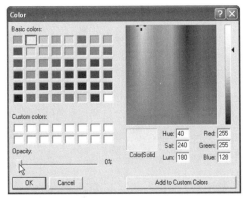

Figure 12.85 Set Opacity to 0 percent so that you can no longer see the button selection color.

5. Drag a frame button into the menu and resize it as desired (**Figure 12.83**). See "Working with Buttons" in Chapter 10 for details.

   Obviously, the location and size of the button frame shouldn't conflict with the background video.

   Note that all frame buttons have the word *frame* in the name, which you can see by hovering the pointer over the frame.

6. At the upper right of the Menu Editor, click Change Selected Highlight Color (**Figure 12.84**).

   Studio opens the Color dialog box.

7. At the bottom left of the Color dialog box, drag the Opacity slider all the way to the left to produce a 0 percent value (**Figure 12.85**).

   Since this menu has only one button, it's always selected. Setting Opacity to zero removes the tint that Studio would otherwise place over the button to let the viewer know that it is the selected button.

   continues on next page

8. Click OK to close the dialog box.

9. At the bottom right of the Title editor, click OK to close the Title editor.

10. If necessary, drag the new menu so that it has the same duration as the background video (**Figure 12.86**).

11. Double-click the menu.

    Studio opens the Menu Clip Properties tool showing the frame as the only button (**Figure 12.87**).

12. Drag the foreground clip into the menu frame (**Figure 12.88**).

13. In the Menu Clip Properties tool, select Motion Thumbnails.

    You won't see the foreground movie play in the preview window unless you have background rendering enabled. See "About Background Rendering," in Chapter 8, for details.

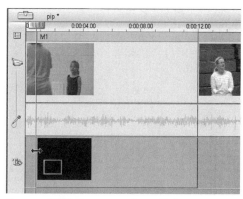

Figure 12.86 Fit the menu underneath the background video.

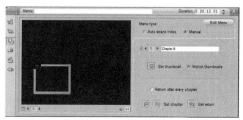

Figure 12.87 Back in the Menu Clip Properties toolbox.

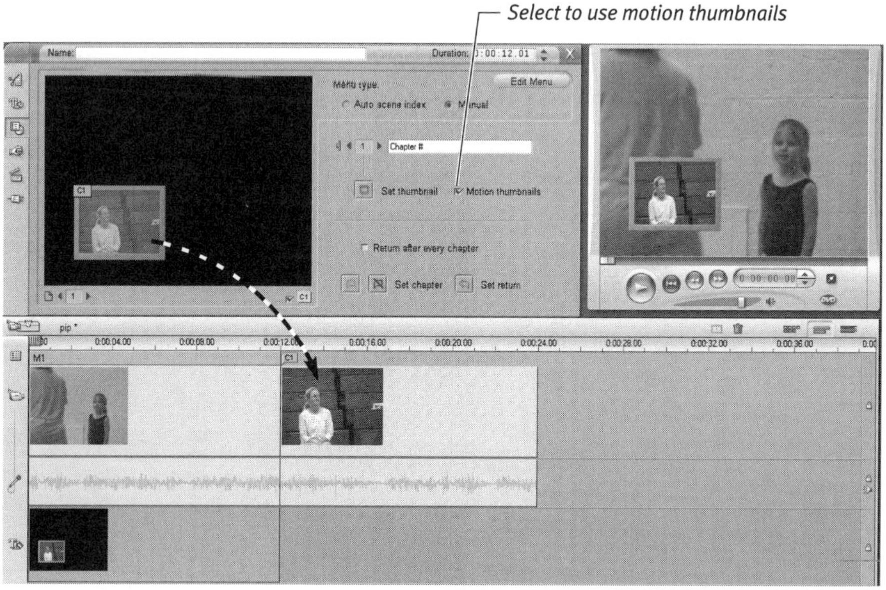

Figure 12.88 Drag the foreground clip to the button frame.

Figure 12.89 Now we have to cut off the back end. Move to the first frame without the P-i-P and press S.

14. Render the clip as an AVI file using the DV format

    See "To encode a project in DV format" in Chapter 14 for details.

15. Reload the clip in the Album and drag it to the Timeline.

16. Drag the Timeline scrubber to the frame after the last frame with a P-i-P (**Figure 12.89**).

17. Press *S* on the keyboard to trim away all video not containing the P-i-P effect (**Figure 12.90**).

18. Render the trimmed file as in Step 14 and then integrate it into your project.

✔ Tip

- Before getting started, you should consider the audio side of the equation. As the procedure is described here, Studio will mix both audio tracks at equal sound levels. You can also mute one of the tracks before rendering, or adjust the audio balance differently. See "Using the Volume Tool" in Chapter 11 for details.

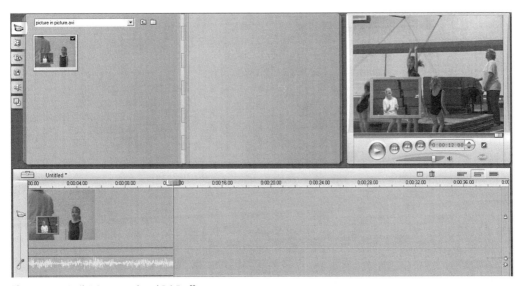

Figure 12.90 Voila! Our completed P-i-P effect.

About VideoCD and Super VideoCD (S-VCD)

In theory, VideoCD and Super VideoCD (S-VCD) are CD-R-based formats that play on computers and DVD players. Sounds great, and sounded even better back in the day when DVD recorders cost $5000 or more.

In practice, however, using a variety of programs, I've had poor luck creating VideoCDs or S-VCDs that play reliably on either computers or DVD players. And since DVD recorders now cost under $200, I have pretty much given up on the format.

If you're going to burn these types discs, stick strictly to the default settings that Studio selects for you, to optimize your chances for compatibility.

The Dark Side of DVD Recordable

Okay—so you work for 10 hours getting your masterpiece on disc and then ship it off to the grandparents. What are the odds that it will play?

Well, anywhere from 63 to 90 percent, depending upon format and who's doing the figuring. These figures come from Mark Hachman, in an article titled "DVD Compatibility: It's as Ugly as Ever" (*ExtremeTech*, October 29, 2002). The article describes the results of studies by Pioneer and Intellikey. The researchers in the Intellikey study tested 100 players manufactured between 1999 and 2002 and found compatibility issues at least 10 percent of the time across all media, though problems were less frequent on newer players. Both studies found -R and +R media more compatible than -RW and +RW. Some newer studies show -R and +R compatibility as high as 95 to 96 percent, but no format ever achieves 100 percent compatibility.

What's a budding videographer to do? In addition to distributing your work on -R or +R media, you can follow the advice of Ralph LaBarge in an article titled "DVD Compatibility Test" (*DV Magazine*, July 2002).

LaBarge's first recommendation is to buy name-brand media, which he found to produce lower error rates than off-brand media. He also recommends burning videos at 7 megabits per second or less; at these rates, if reading errors occurred, the drive could reread the segment and potentially play it back normally without a visible pause. (Normally, I let Studio pick the burn data rate, but I would try using a lower rate if I experienced compatibility problems with a particular player or were distributing discs widely.)

Interestingly, LaBarge also found that off-brand media performed better when burning at slower speeds; since reading this, I've restricted all my burning to 1X speed.

To this list I would add that once you find a solution that works, stick with it. Once you find a burner/media combination that works on most of your target players, don't change just to save a penny or two.

Finally, I never send out a disc without a caveat, usually something like "these recordable DVDs don't work on 100 percent of the drives out there; let me know if you have a problem, and I'll come up with a plan B." That way, if the disc doesn't play, the recipient knows it's a fact of life, not my foul-up. If a problem does occur, you can try loading at lower bit rates or lower speeds or using a different burner.

Part IV: Other Output

Chapter 13 Writing to Tape 393

Chapter 14 Creating Digital Output 403

Chapter 15 Using StudioOnline 425

13

WRITING TO TAPE

Most video producers render to tape to distribute or archive their productions.

When you work in DV, you typically will write to DV tape and then dub to VHS or some other widely supported analog format for distribution to the grandparents.

When you work in analog video, you'll want to write each distribution tape directly from Studio, rather than dubbing one tape to VHS and then dubbing additional tapes from there. This approach avoids the quality loss associated with analog-to-analog copies, which is like photocopying a photocopy.

Writing to tape is a three-step process. First you set up your hardware, which is nearly identical to connecting for capture. Then Studio renders the project, essentially implementing all of your editing work, inserting transitions, mixing audio, and overlaying titles. Sounds like hard work, doesn't it? But it's all transparent; no user intervention required. When rendering is complete, you begin the final stage: actually writing the video to tape.

I took a break from the Fiddler's Convention DVD to bang out a quick edit of the Holiday Concert at our local Rex Theater. The back you'll see is the fabulous Eddie Davis (note to self: when shooting a pianist, always sit on the side the pianist is facing).

Setting Up Your Hardware

Hardware setup involves three discrete actions: getting connected to your camera or deck, getting the camera or deck ready, and getting your computer ready.

To set up your hardware:

1. Connect your camera or deck to the computer.

    For more information on DV capture, see Chapter 3; for more information on analog capture, see Chapter 4.

2. Make sure the camera or deck is in VTR, VCR, or Play mode.

3. If the camcorder has an LCD display, open the LCD and use the camcorder controls to display all tape location and recording/playback information (if available).

    Sony camcorders usually have a Display button that reveals this information.

4. If the camera or deck has an Input/Output selector, select Input.

    I haven't seen this in a while, but my venerable Sony Hi-8 CCD-TR81 had an Input/Output switch that needed to be set before writing to tape.

5. If there is no LCD, or you're writing to a stand-alone deck, connect a television or other analog monitor to the camera or deck.

    The only way to be sure you're actually writing to tape is to see the video in the camera or deck. If you don't have an LCD or TV you can connect, you should be able to track progress in the viewfinder.

6. Check the time codes of the tape in the deck to make sure you have sufficient space for your production

7. Check that any copy-protection features on the tape are disabled.

    Most DV tapes have a copy-protection tab on the back panel, a great way to make sure you don't overwrite your valuable video.

    In my tests, Studio didn't detect that copy protection was enabled and played the video out to the DV camera anyway. No harm was done, as the camera didn't overwrite the video, but nothing got recorded either.

8. Close all extraneous programs on your computer and don't perform any other tasks on the computer while writing to tape.

✔ Tip

- Like capture, writing to tape is an extremely demanding process, and one slip can ruin the tape. Try not to touch the computer or camera over the course of this procedure.

Writing to Tape

Figure 13.1 Click the Make Movie tab to get started.

You may want to consider some minor adjustments when converting a DVD production to tape-based output (see the sidebar "Outputting DVD Projects to Tape" later in this chapter), but otherwise your project should be on the Timeline, complete and itchin' to be written.

To write your project to tape:

1. Do *one of the following*:
   - ▲ At the top of the Studio interface, click Make Movie (**Figure 13.1**). Then, at the upper left of the Make Movie panel, click Tape (**Figure 13.2**).

continues on next page

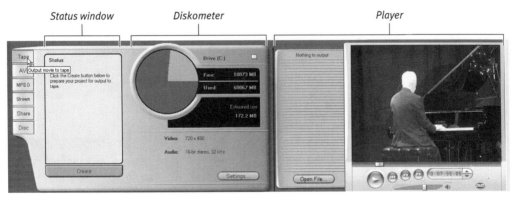

Figure 13.2 The Make Tape controls. Note the Status window, which delivers instructions and warnings; the Diskometer, which details disk requirements and capacity; and the Player, which controls writing to tape.

Chapter 13

▲ From the Studio menu, choose Setup > Make Tape (**Figure 13.3**).

Studio displays the Make Tape controls in the Make Movie window.

Note that Studio will immediately compute the project's disk requirements and warn you in the Status box if you don't have the necessary disk space.

2. Below the Diskometer in the middle of the Make Movie window, click Settings.

The Pinnacle Studio Setup Options dialog opens to the Make Tape tab (**Figure 13.4**).

3. Choose the appropriate audio and video output devices:

   ▲ If outputting DV, as in Figure 13.4, choose DV camcorder.

   ▲ If outputting analog video, choose both the device and the audio output (**Figure 13.5**) and the format (S-Video is preferred when available).

4. For a DV camcorder, select the Automatically Start and Stop Recording check box to allow Studio to control the DV camera, and adjust the Record Delay Time value, if necessary.

All DV camcorders have a short delay between the time they receive the Record command and the time they start recording. Stick with the default (1 second, 27 frames), unless you notice that your camcorder is not capturing the first few moments of the video; then you should extend the duration.

For an analog camcorder or deck, the automatic recording option won't be available (Figure 13.5); you'll manually start the recording.

Figure 13.3 Another route to the Make Tape controls is the Setup pull-down.

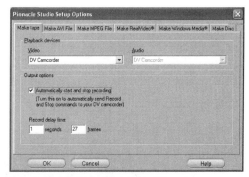

Figure 13.4 The Make Tape tab in DV mode.

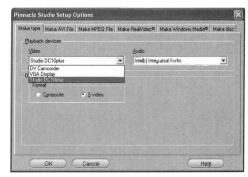

Figure 13.5 The Make Tape tab in analog mode.

Writing to Tape

Figure 13.6 Studio tells you when it's rendering.

Figure 13.7 You can track your progress by watching the Timeline Scrubber, or the progress bar under the Player.

Figure 13.8 Itchin' to be written!

5. At the bottom of the Status box in the Make Movie window, click Create (Figure 13.2).

   Studio starts to render the project. The Status box presents the message "Rendering. Please wait" (**Figure 13.6**), the Timeline scrubber moves through the production as it's rendered, and the status bar under the Player reflects progress through the project (**Figure 13.7**).

   When rendering is complete, Studio displays the message shown in **Figure 13.8**.

6. If you have an analog camcorder or deck (or are manually cueing your DV deck), start your device recording now.

   If you selected Automatically Start and Stop recording, Studio will start and stop the DV tape automatically.

   continues on next page

397

7. Click Play in the Player to start playback (**Figure 13.9**).

    Studio starts playing the video out the device selected in Step 3. The only progress you'll see on your computer is the Player counter advancing through the video.

    You should see video in the camcorder LCD panel (**Figure 13.10**) and/or on the television or other monitor attached to your analog device. You should generally also see a red light or other indicator on your camcorder to show that the video is being recorded.

    If you don't see video, it's likely that you're not sending the video out to the device, so you should recheck your setup.

Figure 13.9 Studio preserves CPU resources and provides very little feedback during the actual writing, only updating the Player counter.

Figure 13.10 Your camcorder or deck should display the incoming video, with a red ball on the upper right of the window indicating the recording.

✔ Tips

- To stop Studio during rendering, click Cancel in the status window (Figure 13.6). To stop Studio while rendering to tape, click the Pause button in the Player (Figure 13.9) or press the spacebar.

- Don't go away during rendering. If Studio needs a CD to rip a track, or if you used SmartCapture and Studio needs to recapture video, you'll need to be there to respond.

- Studio saves all temporary files created during rendering, so if you want to write another tape, simply load the project, enter Make Movie mode, and everything should be rendered and ready to go.

- Some older DV cameras use nonstandard commands to start and stop recording and may not recognize Studio's commands. If Studio doesn't automatically start your DV recorder, uncheck the Automatically Start and Stop Recording check box and manually set the record function.

- Before recording a long segment to tape, try a one- or two-minute sequence, just to make sure everything is working. Writing back to tape is one of those "tough to get it right the first time" activities, at least for me, so test your setup with a shorter project to catch any errors.

Intelligent Rendering

When working with DV source footage, Studio uses a process called Intelligent Rendering to produce the stream it sends out to tape. Rather than rendering the entire project into one huge file, Studio renders the edited portions of the project, like transitions, titles, and special effects, into discrete separate files, leaving unchanged segments alone. Then, when writing back to tape, Studio switches between the rendered files and the original captured files to dynamically create the stream.

This process is much faster than rendering the entire project, and it's more disk-efficient, since fewer new files are created. It can be demanding on lower-powered computers, however.

If you experience problems writing back to tape, compile the project into one DV file (see "To encode a project in DV format" in Chapter 14) and then write this file back to tape, which should be a bit less strenuous on the computer.

The only caveat is that the size of the project file can't exceed the maximum file size for the operating system you're running and the way you've formatted your drives. (See "Windows File Size Limitations" in Chapter 3.)

Writing Disk Files to Tape

Use this technique when writing disk-based AVI files to tape.

To write disk-based files back to tape:

1. Do *one of the following*:
   ▲ In the upper-left corner of the Studio interface, click Make Movie (Figure 13.1). Then, in the upper-left of the Make Movie interface, click Tape.
   ▲ From the Studio menu, choose Setup > Make Tape (Figure 13.2).
   Studio displays the Make Tape controls (Figure 13.3).

2. To the left of the Player, click the Open File button (**Figure 13.11**).

3. Select and load the target file (**Figure 13.12**).
   Studio's status screen should tell you that the file is loaded and ready to play (**Figure 13.13**).

4. If you have an analog camcorder or deck (or are manually cueing your DV record), start your device recording now.
   If you selected Automatically Start and Stop Recording, Studio will start and stop the DV tape automatically.

5. Click Play in the Player to start playback.
   The operation should proceed as described in "Writing to Tape" earlier in this chapter.

Figure 13.11 Start here to write a disk-based AVI file.

Figure 13.12 Then load the file.

Figure 13.13 Studio's Status box tells you you're ready to go.

✔ Tips

- You can write multiple copies to tape without re-rendering the project simply by duplicating this procedure. Some Studio 9 users have reported the loss of sound synchronization when making multiple copies, which you can avoid by rebooting between copies.

- Never copy an analog tape from one deck to another, since the quality drops very, very dramatically when you do. Writing to tape multiple times from Studio is shorter (no rewind time) and will produce much better quality.

Outputting DVD Projects to Tape

You've created this awesome DVD project and then realize Aunt Janie hasn't made the leap to DVD. VHS will just have to do.

What's the absolute bare minimum you have to do to convert your DVD project to tape output? Well, actually, nothing. You're in great shape. Studio simply treats the menus as still images and compiles them into the program normally.

Of course, the menus may look a bit bizarre, with all those windows and links and arrows and such (not that Aunt Janie would notice). So you may want to simply delete them and then write to tape. Remember to save your DVD project first so you don't lose any work.

CREATING DIGITAL OUTPUT

Chapter 12 addressed DVD creation, and Chapter 13 covered writing back to tape. This chapter covers options for creating digital files for playback on your hard disk, copying to a CD or DVD, sending your productions via email, and posting your work to a Web site. It focuses on three options on the Studio output pane: AVI, MPEG, and Stream.

Choosing among these formats is simple. If you're outputting for disk-based playback or CD distribution, choose MPEG, which has largely supplanted AVI files as a distribution format. If you're posting your files to a Web site or sending them via email, use a streaming format.

Note that this chapter discusses CD and DVD as data-storage devices, not specialized formats that play in a player attached to your television. That is, if you want to produce an MPEG file to copy to a CD or DVD to send to a friend to play on a computer, you're in the right place. If you want to author a production that can be viewed on a DVD player and TV set, go to Chapter 12.

A Brief Overview of Compression

Though compression sounds complicated, in use the concept is simple: video files are extremely large, and compression technologies, or *codecs*, make the files smaller. DV video is clean and pristine, but at 3.6 megabytes per second (MB/sec), you can fit only about three minutes worth on a 700-MB CD. The higher compression rates offered by technologies like MPEG, RealVideo, and Microsoft's Windows Media make digital video distributable, and that's why compression is so important.

When folks started distributing digital video in 1994, the main distribution medium was the CD, for playback on computers. The computers of the day, 80386 and Pentium computers with 1X CD drives, could retrieve only 150 to 300 kilobytes per second (KB/sec) of data, and the only codecs that could play on these computers were Cinepak and Indeo, which sacrificed visual quality to achieve the 15 frames-per-second (or more) playback speed necessary for a production to actually look like video.

MPEG-1 technology was around back then and offered vastly superior visual quality, but the underpowered computers of the day couldn't play the files without hardware assistance, so the technology never really caught on. On today's much faster computers, MPEG-1 playback is a walk in the park, especially since both Microsoft and Apple ship MPEG-1 playback software with their operating systems. Since MPEG-1 offers better quality than all AVI codecs and can play on virtually all computers, AVI files now are seldom used as a format for distributing video; for distributing your video, MPEG formats are typically better choices.

AVI is still tremendously vital as a capture and editing format, however, and is used by Studio and most other Windows-based programs to capture DV video.

MPEG-1 versus MPEG-2

So which do you use, MPEG-1 or MPEG-2? Well, MPEG-2 offers better resolution—720 x 480 pixels versus 320 x 240 for MPEG-1—and better quality, though it generally requires about four times the disk space of MPEG-1. More important, however, is that MPEG-1 players have been included free with every Windows and Macintosh computer shipped since the late 1990s, whereas MPEG-2 playback requires software that typically costs $10 to $20.

The cost may not be great; however, you can assume that everyone can play any MPEG-1 files you send them, but you can't make the same assumption for MPEG-2 files. If you're sending your CD to an audience that you know can play MPEG-2, and if you have sufficient space on your CD or DVD, use MPEG-2. If you're distributing your videos to a broader audience with unknown MPEG-2 capabilities, MPEG-1 is a safer choice.

Streaming media technologies

Streaming media technologies are advanced codecs that deliver much higher quality than their predecessors at fantastically reduced bit rates. That's what makes them ideal for email and essential for streaming video from a Web site. For casual users, both RealVideo and Windows Media technologies are free, and qualitative differences between the two are minor. Both are great choices for email or posting to a Web site.

Decoding Your Compression Parameters

Before you start encoding, take a quick look at the parameters you'll be selecting.

Video resolution: Video resolution refers to the number of horizontal and vertical pixels in a video file. By way of reference, DV video starts life at 720 pixels wide and 480 pixels high, or 720 x 480. You capture and edit in this format to maintain the best possible quality, and then you generally *scale* to a lower resolution to distribute your videos. The only exception is MPEG-2, which, as you can see in **Table 14.1**, is encoded at 720 x 480 as well.

Why scale the other formats to lower resolutions? Generally, when video is compressed to lower and lower data rates (defined later in this chapter), the individual frames look better when you start with lower resolution frames. That's why most Web-based videos have a resolution of 320 x 240 or less, especially those distributed at modem speeds.

Table 14.1

Common Compression Parameters			
TECHNOLOGY	RESOLUTION	DATA RATE (IN KILOBITS PER SECOND)	FRAME RATE (FPS)
MPEG-2	720 x 480	4000–8000 Kbps	29.97
MPEG-1	320 x 240	1150–2400 Kbps	29.97
AVI codecs	320 x 240	200–300 KB/sec	15
Windows Media	160 x 120 and 320 x 240	22–500 Kbps	8–30
RealVideo	160 x 120 and 320 x 240	22–500 Kbps	8–30

You'll learn which resolutions to use in various circumstances later in this chapter, in the sections that discuss the individual compression formats. However, the general rule for video resolution is that if the video is bound for playback on computers, use a 4:3 aspect ratio, the same as that used for still-image capture. If the video will be viewed on a TV, use 720 x 480, or an aspect ratio of 4:2.66.

Data rate: Data rate is the amount of data associated with a specified duration of video, usually one second. For example, as seen in Table 14.1, MPEG-2 usually has a data rate of between 4000 and 8000 kilobits per second (Kbps), while streaming formats like RealVideo and Windows Media can be as low as 22 Kbps.

The most important factor in determining data rate is the capacity of the medium on which the video is played. If you exceed this capacity, the data can't keep up, and playback is interrupted, something we've all experienced with Internet-based video.

DVDs are capable of retrieving more than 10 megabits per second (Mbps) leaving a comfortable margin over the 4 to 8 Mbps used for most DVDs. On the other hand, if a computer is connected to a Web site via a 28.8 modem, retrieval capacity is down to around 22 Kbps, requiring the much lower rate. RealVideo and Windows Media technologies make selecting the right data rate simple by using presets for common devices such as dial-up modems, local area networks, and DSL modems.

Frame rate: The frame rate is the number of frames per second (fps) included in an encoded file. For both MPEG-1 and MPEG-2, this rate is always 29.97 fps, a parameter that Studio doesn't allow you to change. Both RealVideo and Windows Media technologies dynamically assign a frame rate to a file based on the target distribution medium (modem or broadband) and video content, so you won't see a frame rate option in either encoding interface.

This leaves the AVI format as the only option for which you need to choose a frame rate. For the most part, if you've chosen AVI, you want to play video on older computers, which is why Table 14.1 shows 15 fps for this format. If your target computer is more recent (for example, Pentium II or above), MPEG-1 is probably a better choice.

With this prologue complete, let's compress some video.

Compressing to AVI Format

If your computer is having difficulty using Studio's Intelligent Rendering technique (see the sidebar "Intelligent Rendering" in Chapter 13), you may want to produce a DV-based AVI file as a workaround. You'll learn this procedure first and then we'll describe how to produce an AVI file for distributing your videos (but remember: MPEG-1 or MPEG-2 are almost always superior choices).

To encode a project in DV format:

1. After completing your project, do *one of the following*:
   ▲ At the top of the Studio interface, click Make Movie (**Figure 14.1**). Then, at the left of the Make Movie panel, click AVI (**Figure 14.2**).
   ▲ From the Studio menu, choose Setup > Make AVI File (**Figure 14.3**).

   continues on next page

Figure 14.1 The encoding process begins in the Make Movie window.

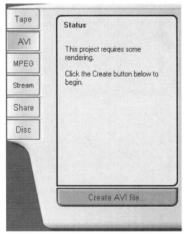

Figure 14.2 Start outputting digital files in AVI, MPEG, and streaming formats by clicking the appropriate button in the Make Movie window.

Figure 14.3 Another route to the Make AVI File tab.

Chapter 14

Studio enters Make Movie mode, providing AVI controls (**Figure 14.4**).

Note that Studio immediately computes the project's disk requirements and warns you in the Status box if you don't have the necessary disk space.

Studio also displays the currently selected encoding parameters for both audio and video.

2. Below the Diskometer, click the Settings button.

   The Pinnacle Studio Setup Options dialog box opens to the Make AVI File tab (**Figure 14.5**).

3. In the Video Settings section, select Include Video in AVI File.

4. In the Compression list, choose DV Video Encoder.

   Because DV is a highly standardized format, when you make this selection, all other video compression options become dimmed, helping to ensure compatibility between computer and camera.

5. In the Audio Settings section, in the Sample Rate list, choose the sample rate used in the original DV source video (**Figure 14.6**).

   If you don't know the sample rate and the project contains DV videos originally captured from your camera, click the Same as Project button. Studio will scan the DV files on the disk and determine the sample rate.

   If you're using disk-based assets, use 48 kHz.

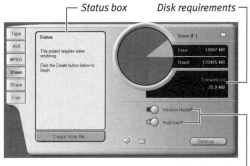

Figure 14.4 The AVI file screen. Note that Studio shows the estimated disk requirements and will alert you if you're short. The current encoding parameters are also displayed here.

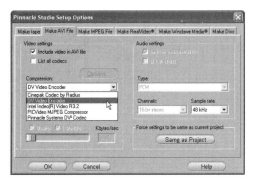

Figure 14.5 DV Video Encoder should be the default encoder, but select it here if it isn't.

Figure 14.6 Choose your audio sample rate here.

Creating Digital Output

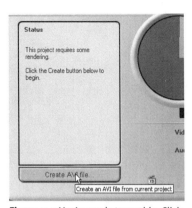

Figure 14.7 You're ready to rumble. Click Create AVI File to get started.

6. Click OK to return to the Make Movie dialog box.

7. At the bottom of the Status box, click Create AVI File (**Figure 14.7**).

    Studio opens the Create AVI File dialog box (**Figure 14.8**).

8. Type the file name and change the location if desired.

9. Click OK to close the dialog box.

    Studio starts encoding. You should see the Timeline scrubber moving through the video, the video updating in the Player, and progress in the bars beneath the Player window (**Figure 14.9**).

    continues on next page

Figure 14.8 Choose a file name and target location.

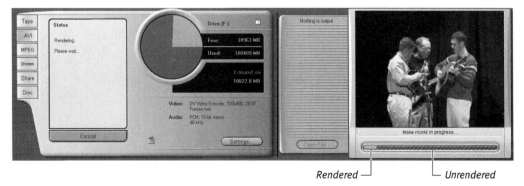

Rendered — — Unrendered

Figure 14.9 Encoding in progress. You'll see the Timeline scrubber moving over the video being encoded, and you can track Studio's progress under the Player window.

Chapter 14

10. To play the video after encoding, click the Open File button on the Diskometer (**Figure 14.10**). To open the file for output to tape, click the Open File button on the Player and follow the instructions in Chapter 13.

✔ **Tip**

- If you're working with an analog capture card and want to create an AVI file for output to tape, substitute the codec used by your capture card for DV Video Encoder in Step 4 of the preceding task.

Figure 14.10 File encoded, ready to play or write back to tape.

Creating Digital Output

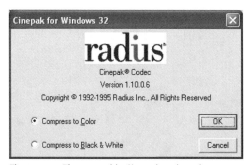

Figure 14.11 The venerable Cinepak codec; choose between color and black and white.

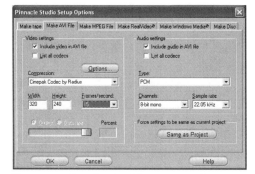

Figure 14.12 Choosing the right parameters for your AVI file. Note that the data rate option is dimmed, a significant issue for those placing AVI video on CD.

To encode a project in AVI format for distribution:

1. Follow Steps 1 through 3 in the preceding task.

2. In the Compression list, choose either Cinepak Codec by Radius or Intel Indeo(R) Video R3.2 (Figure 14.5).

   These two codecs provide the best playback on lower-power computers.

3. If you choose Cinepak, the Options button above the Compression list will become active. Click Options to open the Cinepak for Windows 32 options box and select Compress to Color (**Figure 14.11**). Then click OK.

4. Change the resolution to 320 x 240 (**Figure 14.12**).

5. Change the frame rate in the Frames/second box to 15.

6. In the Audio Settings section, select Include Audio in AVI File if desired.

7. In the Type list, choose PCM.

8. In the Channels list, choose 8-bit mono.

9. In the Sample Rate list, choose 22.05 kHz.

10. Click OK to return to the Make Movie window.

11. At the bottom of the Status box, click Create AVI file.

    Studio opens the Create AVI File dialog box.

12. Type the file name and change the location if desired.

13. Click OK to close the dialog box.

    Studio starts encoding. You should see the Timeline scrubber moving through the video, the video updating in the Player, and progress in the bars beneath the Player window (Figure 14.9).

continues on next page

14. To play the video after encoding, click the Open File button on the Diskometer (Figure 14.10).

    The Open File button on the Player should be dimmed because you can't upload a Cinepak or Indeo file back to a camera.

✔ **Tips**

- Studio provides poor data-rate controls for encoding AVI files, forcing you to choose a quality percentage rather than a data rate when encoding with Indeo and most other formats (**Figure 14.13**). You'll have to experiment with different quality percentages to hit your data rate target.

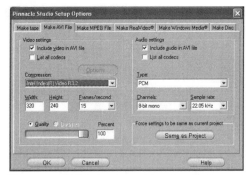

Figure 14.13 With Indeo 3.2, you have to adjust quality to arrive at your target data rate, which usually involves trial and error.

- Even though most current CD drives can retrieve data at a rate of 24X or higher, don't encode at data rates higher than 300 kilobytes per second (KB/sec) for two reasons: First, though you'll see dramatic quality improvements between 150 KB/sec and 250 KB/sec, improvements slow thereafter. Second, even a 24X drive may start to choke at data rates of 500 KB/sec and higher, especially on lower-powered computers, resulting in choppy playback.

Figure 14.14 Studio recommends working only with tried-and-true codecs (I second that emotion).

- The audio parameters listed here are conservative numbers for primarily speech-based audio. At full CD quality, the audio rate is 176 KB/sec, and this is in addition to the video data rate. At the listed parameters, the audio data rate is approximately 44 KB/sec, which is much more reasonable.

- If you select List All Codecs in the Video Settings section, Studio will open the warning dialog box shown in **Figure 14.14**. Basically, Studio displays only known and proven compatible codecs in both the Audio and Video Settings sections. Unless you want to experiment, you should probably stick to these codecs.

Creating Digital Output

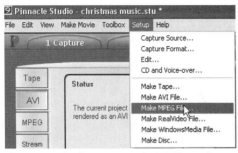

Figure 14.15 The direct route to the MPEG encoding tools.

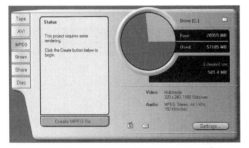

Figure 14.16 The MPEG encoding screen. Note the estimated file requirements and current encoding settings.

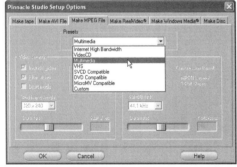

Figure 14.17 Stick with the Studio presets for MPEG encoding. This Multimedia preset is appropriate for creating MPEG-1 files for playing from a hard disk or CD.

Producing MPEG Files

Studio simplifies the production of MPEG files with excellent presets for most common MPEG distribution situations. You can also customize your options completely, but most users are better off sticking with the presets.

To produce an MPEG file:

1. After completing your video project, do *one of the following*:

    ▲ At the top of the Studio interface, click Make Movie (Figure 14.1). Then, at the left of the Make Movie window, click MPEG.

    ▲ From the Studio menu, choose Setup > Make MPEG File (**Figure 14.15**).

    Studio enters Make Movie mode, providing MPEG controls (**Figure 14.16**).

    Note that Studio immediately computes the project's disk requirements and warns you in the Status box if you don't have the necessary disk space.

    Studio also displays the currently selected encoding parameters for both audio and video.

2. Below the Diskometer, click the Settings button.

    The Pinnacle Studio Setup Options dialog box opens to the Make MPEG File tab (**Figure 14.17**).

    continues on next page

413

Chapter 14

3. In the Presets list, do *one of the following*:
   ▲ To create files intended for a disc, choose VideoCD, SVCD Compatible, or DVD Compatible, depending on the type of disc you want to create.
   ▲ To create files for writing to MicroMV-compatible devices, choose MicroMV Compatible.
   ▲ To create files for playback on computers, choose Multimedia.
   ▲ To create your own parameters, choose Custom (**Figure 14.18**).

4. Click OK to close the dialog box and return to the Make Movie window.

5. At the bottom of the Status box, click Create MPEG File.
   Studio opens the Create MPEG File dialog box (**Figure 14.19**).

6. Type the file name and change the location if desired.

7. Click OK to close the dialog box.
   Studio starts encoding. You should see the Timeline scrubber moving through the video, the video updating in the Player, and progress in the bars beneath the Player window (Figure 14.9).

8. To play the video after encoding, click the Open File button on the Diskometer.

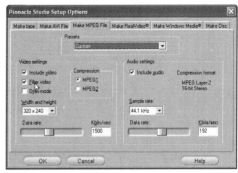

Figure 14.18 You may need to select Custom to disable filtering or boost the data rate.

Figure 14.19 Choose a file name and target location.

✔ Tips

- Note that all presets use filtering, which can cause blurriness in certain videos. If quality is unacceptable, note the default settings, select Custom encoding, and re-enter all preset values, making sure not to select the Filter Video check box.

- The Multimedia preset uses a data rate of approximately 1500 Kbps, which may be inadequate for very-high-motion videos. If so, note the other preset settings, select Custom encoding, and re-enter all preset values, boosting the data rate to no more than 2400 Kbps.

- Do not use custom settings when creating files for DVD, VideoCD, or Super VideoCD (S-VCD) format. These formats are specifically defined, and straying from the general guidelines could produce files incompatible with the specification.

- Select Draft Mode to improve the encoding speed of your video, at some cost in quality.

Creating RealVideo Files

The RealVideo format was created by RealNetworks. To view files encoded in this format, viewers need the RealOne Player, which is available for free downloading at www.realnetworks.com. Available in Macintosh and a number of Unix flavors, RealVideo supports a broader audience than Windows Media format, and quality at low bit rates is considered slightly better.

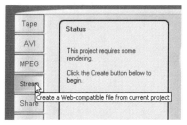

Figure 14.20 Ready to go streaming? Start here.

Like Windows Media, RealVideo can produce files that support multiple bit-rate connections, but only when streaming from a RealNetworks server. Note that if you're creating a file with multiple bit rates, all the bit rates must share the same resolution (which is why so many sites displaying RealVideo content have links for modem and broadband connections).

Figure 14.21 Or start streaming here.

Though functional, Studio's tools for RealVideo encoding lack filtering, variable-bit-rate encoding, and other advanced options available in RealVideo's free encoding tools. Studio is great for encoding videos for email and for other casual projects, but for high-volume production and real-time encoding (which Studio doesn't perform), you're better off using other tools.

To create RealVideo files:

1. After completing your video project, do *one of the following*:
   ▲ At the top the Studio interface, click Make Movie. Then, at the left of the Make Movie window, click Stream (**Figure 14.20**). Below the Diskometer in the Make Movie window, click the RealVideo button.
   ▲ From the Studio menu, choose Setup > Make RealVideo File (**Figure 14.21**).
   Studio enters Make Movie mode, providing Stream controls.

Creating Digital Output

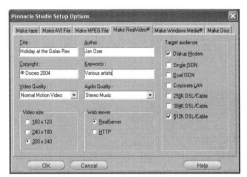

Figure 14.22 RealVideo encoding parameters.

Figure 14.23 Your title and author information appear in RealOne Player.

Figure 14.24 Customize video encoding for your footage.

Note that Studio immediately computes the project's disk requirements and warns you in the Status box if you don't have the necessary disk space.

2. Below the Diskometer, click the Settings button.

   The Pinnacle Studio Setup Options dialog box opens to the Make RealVideo tab (**Figure 14.22**).

3. Type title, author, and copyright information.

   This information will appear when the file is played (**Figure 14.23**).

4. Type the desired keywords in the Keywords box.

   If the video is posted to a Web site, this information will be used to categorize the video by Internet search engines.

5. In the Video Quality list (**Figure 14.24**), do *one of the following:*

   ▲ For clips with normal motion (no extremely high motion or low motion), choose Normal Motion Video. During encoding, RealVideo will balance frame rate and image clarity.

   ▲ For talking-head and similar clips with very limited motion, choose Smoothest Motion Video. During encoding, RealVideo will produce a higher frame rate and smoother motion.

   ▲ For high-action clips, choose Sharpest Image Video. During encoding, RealVideo will reduce the frame rate and produce fewer frames of higher quality.

   ▲ For slide shows, choose Slide Show. During encoding, RealVideo will reduce the video to a series of high-quality still photos.

continues on next page

6. In the Audio Quality list (**Figure 14.25**), select the description that best matches your audio content.

   During encoding, Studio will use the appropriate audio codec and data rate for your audio content.

7. In the Video Size section, select *one of the following resolutions:*

   ▲ For video to be streamed via dial-up modems, choose 160 x 120.

   ▲ For video to be streamed via single a ISDN line, choose 240 x 180.

   ▲ For all other available categories of video, choose 320 x 240.

8. In the Web Server section, do *one of the following:*

   ▲ If the ISP hosting the video has a RealServer installed, choose RealServer. Streaming files with RealServer is the preferred method, since it provides several valuable options, including the ability to create files that serve multiple target audiences and the ability to adjust playback performance to changing line conditions. If you don't know whether RealServer is installed, ask your ISP.

   ▲ To stream videos from an HTTP server without RealServer installed, choose HTTP; however, this produces a file that serves only one connection speed. Also use this option for email.

Figure 14.25 Customize audio encoding for your soundtrack.

Creating Digital Output

Figure 14.26 Choose a file name and target location.

9. In the Target Audience section, choose the connections that your viewers will use to view the video.

   If you selected RealServer in Step 8, you can choose multiple options and produce a file that can serve a diverse range of connection speeds.

   If you selected the HTTP option in Step 8, you can select only one profile.

10. Click OK to return to the Make Movie window.

11. At the bottom of the Status box, click Create Web File.

    Studio opens the Create Web File dialog box (**Figure 14.26**).

12. Type the file name and change the location if desired.

13. Click OK to close the dialog box.

    Studio starts encoding. You should see the Timeline scrubber moving through the video, the video updating in the Player, and progress in the bars beneath the Player window (Figure 14.9).

Chapter 14

To play RealVideo files:

1. At the bottom of the Diskometer, click the RealPlayer icon. (After encoding is completed, the RealPlayer icon at the bottom of the Make Movie window becomes active, as shown in **Figure 14.27**.)

   Studio opens the Open Media Player dialog box with the most recently encoded file selected (**Figure 14.28**).

2. Click Open.

   Studio opens RealOne (or whatever RealPlayer you have installed) and plays the file.

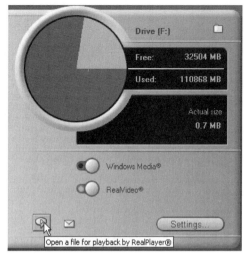

Figure 14.27 Click here to play the file in the RealOne Player.

Figure 14.28 Select the file and click Open.

Creating Digital Output

Figure 14.29 Click here to send the file via email.

Figure 14.30 Choose the file and click open.

Figure 14.31 Choose the profile in Outlook or other MAPI-enabled email client.

Figure 14.32 Oops. You'll have to send the file to another computer and mail it from there, or load a MAPI-compatible program.

To send RealVideo files via email:

1. At the bottom of the Diskometer, click the Envelope icon. (After encoding is completed, the Send File by Email icon becomes active, as shown in **Figure 14.29**.)

   Studio opens the Select File to Email dialog box with the most recently encoded file selected (**Figure 14.30**).

2. Click Open.

   If you have an email client installed on your computer that is Messaging Application Programming Interface–compatible (MAPI-compatible), such as Microsoft Outlook or Outlook Express, Studio opens an email message with the compressed file attached. Just insert the target email address and send the message. If your email client has multiple profiles, Studio opens the Choose Profile dialog box (**Figure 14.31**). Choose a profile and click OK, and Studio will open the email message with the file attached. If Studio can't find a MAPI-compatible email program, Studio displays an error message (**Figure 14.32**).

✔ Tips

- If you're sending a file via email, the recipient's bandwidth shouldn't control how you encode the file. Even if the recipient has a slow connection, the recipient may be willing to wait to download the file. The only practical issue is the attached file limitation imposed by many ISPs. For example, Earthlink allows attachments of no more than 5 MB, and Hotmail and Yahoo impose even more stringent limitations. Be sure to consider this when producing your file.

- Remember that your recipient will need RealPlayer installed to view the video, or Windows Media Player to view Windows Media videos.

CREATING REALVIDEO FILES

421

Creating Windows Media Files

Microsoft's streaming technology is called Windows Media. To view files encoded in this format, viewers need Microsoft's Windows Media Player, which ships with all Windows computers and is freely downloadable at www.microsoft.com/windowsmedia. Microsoft offers players for all relevant Windows flavors, Macintosh (8.01 to OS X), and Sun Solaris, but no Linux version (quel surprise!).

Like the RealNetworks technology, the Microsoft technology can produce files that support multiple-bit-rate connections, but only when streaming from a Windows Media server, which is available only for Windows XP, or from a RealNetworks Helix server. Microsoft's most recent release of Windows Media 9 supports multiple-resolution files within the multiple bit rates, but if you're working at this level, you should use Windows Media Encoder, not Studio. Studio is a great tool for casual Windows Media encoding, but doesn't expose all relevant encoding controls and doesn't support real-time encoding.

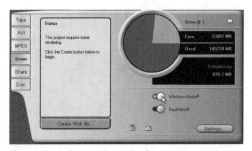

Figure 14.33 The starting point for creating Windows Media files.

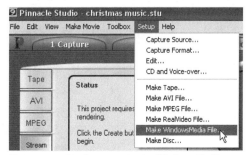

Figure 14.34 Another route to the Windows Media encoding screen.

To create Windows Media files:

1. After completing your video project, do *one of the following*:

   ▲ At the top of the Studio interface, click Make Movie. At the left of the Make Movie window, click Stream (**Figure 14.33**). Below the Diskometer, click the Windows Media button.

   ▲ From the Studio menu, choose Setup > Make WindowsMedia File (**Figure 14.34**).

   Studio enters Make Movie mode, providing streaming controls.

Creating Digital Output

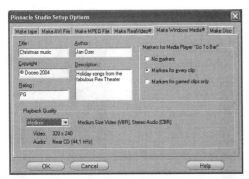

Figure 14.35 Windows Media encoding parameters.

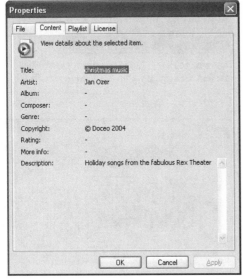

Figure 14.36 Here's where the viewer sees the title, author, and description.

Figure 14.37 Choose your playback quality.

Figure 14.38 Custom encoding parameters.

Note that Studio immediately computes the project's disk requirements and warns you in the Status box if you don't have the necessary disk space.

2. Below the Diskometer, click the Settings button.

   The Pinnacle Studio Setup Options dialog box opens to the Make Windows Media tab (**Figure 14.35**).

3. Type information in the Title, Author, Copyright, Rating, and Description boxes.

   This information will appear when the file is played (**Figure 14.36**). If the video is posted to a Web site, the description will be used to categorize the video by Internet search engines.

4. In the Playback Quality list (**Figure 14.37**), select *one of the following*:

   ▲ **Low:** Studio encodes files at a resolution of 160 x 120 and a data rate of 48 Kbps, which is appropriate for 56-Kbps modems and single-channel ISDN.

   ▲ **Medium:** Studio encodes files at a resolution of 320 x 240 and a data rate of approximately 412 Kbps (or about 80 kilobytes per second), appropriate for downloadable and CD-based video.

   ▲ **High:** Studio encodes files at a resolution of 720 x 480 and a data rate of approximately 1922 Kbps, appropriate for transfer via CD or DVD or for high-quality hard disk drive–based playback.

   ▲ **Custom:** This option offers a range of other encoding parameters (**Figure 14.38**).

continues on next page

423

Chapter 14

5. In the Markers for Media Player "Go To Bar" section, select the desired option.

   If you insert markers in the clip, viewers can jump to these markers using a menu in Microsoft's Windows Media Player B (**Figure 14.39**).

   If you enable markers and don't name your clips, Studio will enter a default name based on the project name and clip start point.

   To name your clip, open it in the Clip Properties tool and enter the desired name in the Name field (**Figure 14.40**). See "Trimming with the Clip Properties Tool" in Chapter 7 for more information on the Clip Properties Tool.

6. Click OK to return to the Make Movie window.

7. At the bottom of the Status box, click Create Web File.

   Studio opens the Create Web File dialog box (**Figure 14.41**).

8. Type the file name and change the location if desired.

9. Click OK to close the dialog box.

   Studio starts encoding. You should see the Timeline scrubber moving through the video, the video updating in the Player, and progress in the bars beneath the Player window (Figure 14.9).

✔ Tip

- To play or send your Windows Media files via email, see "To play RealVideo files" and "To send RealVideo files via email," earlier in this chapter.

Figure 14.39 Here is how the viewer uses the file markers to navigate within the Windows Media file.

Figure 14.40 Windows Media markers are the only reason I know for naming your clips in the Clip Properties tool. Here's where you enter the name.

Figure 14.41 Choose a file name and target location.

USING STUDIOONLINE

15

The Internet is the ultimate mechanism for sharing videos, and Pinnacle makes the process simple with StudioOnline, its Internet-based video distribution site. After you're done editing, Studio can automatically publish your videos to StudioOnline, or you can manually upload files yourself. StudioOnline can then send custom email messages to your intended audience, build an address book for frequently used contacts, and even schedule messages for later transmittal.

There are two major caveats: First, you get only 10 MB of storage space on the site, which you can't upgrade. When you're working with video, that ain't much. More important, if you upload the video directly from Studio, StudioOnline converts it to relatively low-bit-rate files in Real and Microsoft formats and then distributes these files—often visually degraded—to your target viewers.

Pinnacle may change this procedure in the future. However, unless and until it does, you'll get better results encoding the file yourself and then manually uploading it to StudioOnline. The only downside to this approach is that you can't pick the thumbnail image used by StudioOnline to represent your video.

Uploading Videos to StudioOnline

You can get your files up to StudioOnline in two ways: directly from Studio or manually through a browser.

Figure 15.1 Once you're ready to transmit, click Make Movie.

To upload to StudioOnline from Studio:

1. After completing your project, click Make Movie (**Figure 15.1**).
   Studio opens the Make Movie window.

2. At the left of the Make Movie panel, click Share (**Figure 15.2**).

3. To change the thumbnail image used to represent your video once it's uploaded to StudioOnline, navigate to the target frame using the Timeline scrubber or the Player controls and click the Set Thumbnail button (**Figure 15.3**).

Figure 15.2 Then click Share to upload your video to StudioOnline.

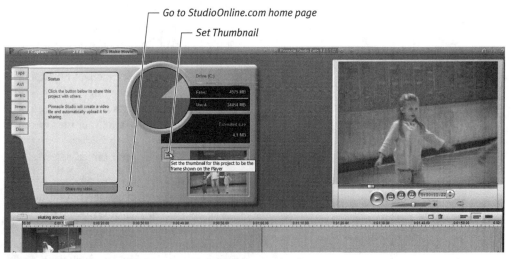

Figure 15.3 When you upload from Studio, you can pick the thumbnail image.

Using StudioOnline

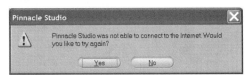

Figure 15.4 Oops. You can't upload a file if you're not online. If your video-editing station isn't connected to the Internet, you can encode and upload manually from another computer.

Figure 15.5 The Status box reports that my video file arrived safely.

4. At the bottom of the Status box, click Share My Video.

   Studio starts encoding the file. You should see the Timeline scrubber moving through the video, the video updating in the Player, and progress in the bars beneath the Player window.

   If your computer is not connected to the Internet, Studio will prompt you to connect to the Internet with the message shown in **Figure 15.4**. You must be online to continue.

   If you are online, Studio will encode and automatically upload your file, letting you know when it's finished with the message shown in **Figure 15.5**.

   Studio will also open your default browser to the StudioOnline login screen (**Figure 15.6**).

   If Studio doesn't open your browser automatically, click the Go to StudioOnline.com Home Page button (Figure 15.3).

   continues on next page

Figure 15.6 The StudioOnline login screen.

UPLOADING VIDEOS TO STUDIOONLINE

427

5. Do *one of the following*:
   ▲ If you've already registered, enter your user name and password and click Login.
   ▲ If you haven't registered, click Create New User Account and register for your account. StudioOnline will send you an email message and a link that you can click to sign in and upload your video.

   You should see a screen that looks like **Figure 15.7**. From here, you can start sending videos as described in "Sending Videos from StudioOnline" later in this chapter.

✔ Tips

- If you attempt to produce a file longer than 4 minutes, expect an error message like that shown in **Figure 15.8**.

- For information on how to actually get your videos to your audience, see "Sending Videos from StudioOnline" later in this chapter.

Figure 15.7 Here's where you end up after automatically uploading a file to StudioOnline.

Figure 15.8 What you'll see if you try to send a video longer than about 4 minutes.

Using StudioOnline

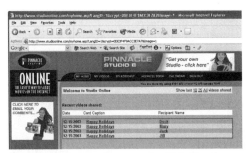

Figure 15.9 When you first enter StudioOnline, the first screen you'll see is a list of the most recent cards that you sent.

Figure 15.10 Click here to start manually uploading a video.

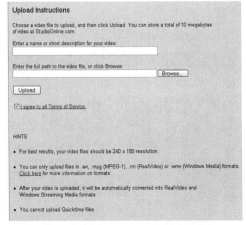

Figure 15.11 Upload instructions. Note the rules (particularly that QuickTime files need not apply).

To manually upload to StudioOnline:

1. From your browser, surf to StudioOnline at www.studioonline.com and log in to your account.

   StudioOnline opens a screen similar to **Figure 15.9**.

2. At the top of the StudioOnline page, click My Videos.

   StudioOnline opens the My Videos page (**Figure 15.10**).

3. Click Upload a Video.

   StudioOnline opens the Upload Instructions page (**Figure 15.11**). Note that StudioOnline recommends uploading files encoded at 240 x 180 resolution, in AVI, MPEG-1, RealVideo, or Windows Media format.

   Contrary to the third bullet point on the screen, in my test StudioOnline did not convert the uploaded files to RealVideo or Windows Media format.

   continues on next page

Chapter 15

4. Click Browse.

   StudioOnline opens the Choose File dialog box (**Figure 15.12**).

5. Choose the file to upload and click Open.

   Studio returns to the Upload Instructions page.

6. Type the desired description for your video and select the box to indicate that you agree with the terms of service (**Figure 15.13**).

   StudioOnline displays an error message if you don't enter a description or accept the agreement terms.

7. Click Upload.

   StudioOnline uploads the file and adds it to the My Videos page (**Figure 15.14**). Note that videos uploaded by Studio have a thumbnail image, while those uploaded manually show a Pinnacle template of sorts.

✔ Tip

- Though StudioOnline can accept AVI and MPEG-1 files, you'll get the best bang for your bandwidth buck (in English, the best quality for a particular file size) using RealVideo or Windows Media. See Chapter 14 to learn how to output digital files in all these formats.

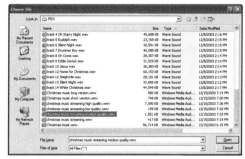

Figure 15.12 You know this drill. Select the file you want to upload and click Open.

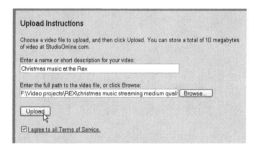

Figure 15.13 Enter a name or description and click to accept the service terms or StudioOnline won't upload your file.

Uploaded from Studio

Uploaded manually

Figure 15.14 File successfully uploaded. Note that only the files uploaded via Studio have actual thumbnails, not the files you uploaded manually.

Using StudioOnline

Figure 15.15 Click the envelope to send an email announcement to the target recipient.

Figure 15.16 Choose the video postcard to display your video.

Sending Videos from StudioOnline

Once your file is available online, you can email people to let them know it's ready for viewing. Email recipients simply click a link to go online and watch the video.

To send a video from StudioOnline:

1. From your browser, surf to StudioOnline at www.studioonline.com.

   StudioOnline opens a screen similar to Figure 15.9.

2. On the top of the StudioOnline page, click My Videos.

   StudioOnline opens the My Videos page.

3. Choose a video to send and click the Envelope icon underneath the video (**Figure 15.15**) to open the screen shown in Figure 15.7.

4. Click the desired video postcard (**Figure 15.16**).

5. Complete the information shown in **Figure 15.17**.

continues on next page

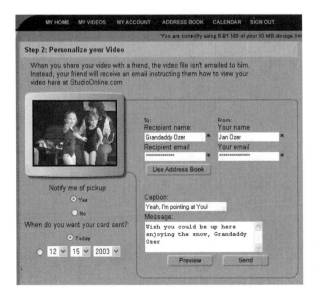

Figure 15.17 Note that you can ask to be notified when your video is viewed, and you can schedule email for later transmission.

431

Chapter 15

6. Do *one of the following:*

   ▲ Click Send to send the email. Studio sends it.

   ▲ Click Preview to preview the appearance of your video on the screen when an email recipient accesses it (**Figure 15.18**). Click Back to perform more edits, or Send to send the email.

   StudioOnline sends the email to the recipient (**Figure 15.19**), who will be instructed to click a link to view the video, and lets you know that the email has been sent (**Figure 15.20**).

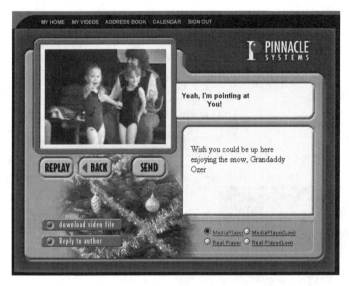

Figure 15.18 Here's a preview of what the email recipient will see.

```
Jan Ozer has sent you a video. You can view it by clicking on:

http://www.studioonline.com/playvideos.asp?crypt=F29BF81C15E38183

Learn how to share your own videos on the Internet! Click here:

http://www.pinnaclesys.com/HomeMovieMaking.asp
```

Figure 15.19 Here's the actual email your recipient will receive.

Using StudioOnline

Once the remote viewer clicks the page, the video starts playing automatically, and remote viewers can select the video stream best suited to their available bandwidth and configuration, download the file, and/or send an email back to you (**Figure 15.21**).

continues on next page

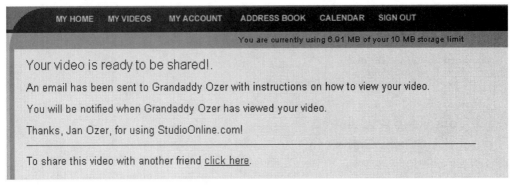

Figure 15.20 Here's your notice that your email was sent.

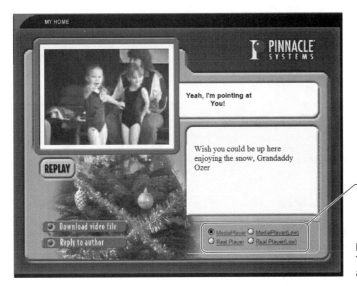

— *Four available video files*

Figure 15.21 Live playback of the file. The recipient can download the file and send an email back at you.

433

✓ Tips

- Note in Figure 15.17 that you can request notification that the email recipient actually watched the video (**Figure 15.22**), or you can schedule the card to be sent in the future.

- In the My Home section that appears when you log in to your account (Figure 15.9), StudioOnline keeps a log of all videos you've sent. This is a convenient way to keep track of your email, and you can view a presentation by clicking it in the Card Caption column.

Your video was viewed
Admin@StudioOnline.com

To: jozer@mindspring.com

```
Hello Jan Ozer, good news!

The video you sent on 12/15/2003 5:53:00 PM was viewed by
Grandaddy Ozer on 12/15/2003.

Thank you for using Studio Online. Please visit us again
to see what's new!
The Studio Online team
http://www.studioonline.com
```

Figure 15.22 Here's notice that the video was actually viewed.

Managing Videos in StudioOnline

Figure 15.23 When you have only 10 MB of space, spring cleaning is a year-round occupation. Click here to delete the file.

StudioOnline will refuse to accept additional videos once you reach your 10-MB limit, making frequent maintenance critical.

To delete videos from StudioOnline:

1. From your browser, surf to www.studioonline.com and log in to your account.

   StudioOnline opens a screen similar to Figure 15.9.

2. At the top of the StudioOnline page, click My Videos.

   StudioOnline opens the My Videos page.

3. Click the Trash Can icon on the video to be deleted (**Figure 15.23**).

4. Studio opens the Delete Video dialog box (**Figure 15.24**).

5. Click Delete.

   Studio deletes the file and restores drive space.

Figure 15.24 Yes, you really mean it. Click here to let StudioOnline know.

✔ Tips

- You access StudioOnline's Address Book by clicking Address Book in the top menu bar (Figure 15.9). The procedure for adding and deleting contacts is self-explanatory.

- You access StudioOnline's Calendar function by clicking Calendar in the top menu bar. Though you can enter events in the Calendar manually, you can schedule the future transmission of an email only by working through the process described earlier in "To send a video from Studio-Online," using the controls shown in Figure 15.17. In my tests, when I scheduled an email message for later transmission, StudioOnline didn't show it on the Calendar, but did send it as scheduled.

435

Part V: Reference

Appendix A Keyboard Shortcuts 439

Appendix B Troubleshooting 441

Index 455

Keyboard Shortcuts

The terms *Left*, *Right*, *Up* and *Down* in this table refer to the arrow (cursor) keys. *Plus* and *Minus* refer to the + and − keys. Note that Studio's manual and tool tips designate *K* as the key to press to start video playback. In my tests (as of Studio version 8.5), this didn't work, but pressing *L* did. So, if you have a version after 8.5, and *L* doesn't work, try *K*.

Table A.1

Main Studio Interface	
Spacebar	Play and stop
J	Fast-reverse (hit multiple times for faster playback)
K	Stop
L	Play or fast-forward (hit multiple times for faster playback)
X or Ctrl+Up	Step forward 1 frame
Y or Ctrl+Down	Step back 1 frame
A or I	Mark in
S or O	Mark out
Ctrl+Left	Trim in point by -1 frame
Ctrl+Right	Trim in point by +1 frame
Alt+Left	Trim out point by -1 frame
Alt+Right	Trim out point by +1 frame
Alt+Ctrl+Left	Rolling trim out point by -1 frame (trims following clip too)
Alt+Ctrl+Right	Rolling trim out point by +1 frame
G	Clear mark in and mark out
D	Go to mark in (in Clip Properties tool)
F	Go to mark out (in Clip Properties tool)
E or Home	Go to start
R or End	Go to end
Left	Select previous clip
Right	Select next clip
Delete	Delete selected clip(s)
Insert	Split clip at Scrubber position
Page Up	Go to next page of Storyboard or Timeline
Page Down	Go to previous page of Storyboard or Timeline

continues on next page

Appendix A

Table A.1

Main Studio Interface *continued*	
+	Zoom in the Timeline
–	Zoom out the Timeline
C	Set menu chapter
V	Clear menu chapter
M	Set Return to Menu flag
Ctrl+Page Up	Go to previous menu chapter
Ctrl+Page Down	Go to next menu chapter

Table A.2

Title Editor	
Alt+Plus	Bring to front
Alt+Minus	Send to back
Ctrl+Plus	Bring forward one layer
Ctrl+Minus	Send back one layer
Ctrl+0	Text justification off
Ctrl+1	Text justification: bottom-left
Ctrl+2	Text justification: bottom-center
Ctrl+3	Text justification: bottom-right
Ctrl+4	Text justification: middle-left
Ctrl+5	Text justification: middle-center
Ctrl+6	Text justification: middle-right
Ctrl+7	Text justification: top-left
Ctrl+8	Text justification: top-center
Ctrl+9	Text justification: top-right
Ctrl+K	Kern, leading, and skew
Ctrl+M	Move, scale, and rotate
Shift+Left	Expand character selection left
Shift+Right	Expand character selection right
Ctrl+Left	Reduce horizontal scale of, or squeeze (kern), text selection depending on current edit mode (move/scale/rotate or kern/skew/leading)
Ctrl+Right	Increase horizontal scale of, or stretch (kern), text selection
Ctrl+Down	Reduce scale or leading of text selection depending on current edit mode
Ctrl+Up	Increase scale or leading of text selection
Shift+Ctrl+Left	Same as Ctrl+Left (larger adjustment)
Shift+Ctrl+Right	Same as Ctrl+Right (larger adjustment)
Shift+Ctrl+Down	Same as Ctrl+Down (larger adjustment)
Shift+Ctrl+Up	Same as Ctrl+Up (larger adjustment)
Alt+Left	*In text selection:* Move characters left *No selection:* Move left all text from cursor to end of line
Alt+Right	*In text selection:* Move characters right *No selection:* Move right all text from cursor to end of line
Shift+Alt+Left	Same as Alt+Left (larger adjustment)
Shift+Alt+Right	Same as Alt+Right (larger adjustment)

TROUBLESHOOTING

Video capture, editing, and output to tape are without question the most demanding activities most computers ever perform. For this reason, it's not surprising that video editing reveals more "imperfections" in computers than surfing the Web or word processing.

Studio works on Windows 98 (Second Edition), but if you're running this operating system, you're likely running at least three-year-old hardware and perhaps drivers. This is the equivalent of running the Paris to Dakar road race in that jalopy you drove back in college—you may get there, but you're likely to experience a breakdown or two.

Keep in mind that not all programs run on all computers (something I've learned testing hundreds of products over the last few years). If you're having problems you can't resolve through techniques in this appendix, through Pinnacle's extensive online help facilities, or directly through technical support, cut your losses. Either try Studio on another computer or return the software. Life is way too short to make a quest of it.

Finally, a complete troubleshooting guide for all computers and operating systems that Studio supports would be a book in its own right, and definitely not a book I care to write. These next sections will hopefully hit the high points.

Optimizing Your Capture Computer

Since you can avoid most installation and operational hassles by using a new computer with current drivers, I'll start there, and then discuss how to give your current computer its best chance to make a good first impression with Studio. Then I'll move on to troubleshooting.

If a rich friend called and asked what kind of computer to buy to run Studio (i.e., price is no concern), this is what I would tell her to get:

- Intel Pentium 4 at 3.2 GHz with HT Technology
- 512 MB RAM
- Windows XP Professional
- Graphics card from ATI, Matrox, or NVIDIA. 32 MB RAM is more than sufficient. 3D gaming power not needed and not recommended, given that this would encourage her to play games on the computer. Dual monitor output is cool but wouldn't help with Studio, which doesn't support multiple monitors.
- Any DirectX-compatible sound card
- Dual hard-disk drives, both Serial ATA-100 drives—one for the system (at least 40 GB), and one for video (at least 120 GB)
- Pinnacle DV card (Studio DV is fine) if one isn't embedded on the motherboard
- Pioneer DVD-R/RW burner (A06 is the most current model)
- 10/100/1000 gigabit (Gb) Ethernet

A bigger monitor is always better. Any mouse with two buttons and a wheel should work just fine. The computer absolutely must be online, with broadband preferred, to manage the file downloading and uploading inherent to video production.

In terms of care and feeding of her powerful beast, I would recommend that my rich friend load as few extraneous programs as possible. Games and other multimedia programs in particular often ruin a perfectly functioning computer.

I know it's tough for many parents to dedicate a computer to editing, but the more programs you load on your computer, the greater chance you have of overwriting some critical driver or causing a conflict that hinders or interrupts Studio's performance. This is especially so with other video editors and DVD authoring programs. I've been fortunate, having tested many additional software programs on my primary Studio test bed, including many other video editors, with few problems. Still, computer issues seem to hit those least equipped to resolve them (e.g., my parents and certain friends), and each additional program loaded involves a small but real risk.

If you plan on installing Studio on your current computer, here are some steps you should take to smooth the transition.

To ensure a smooth installation:

1. If you're not running Windows XP Professional, consider upgrading.

   At the very least, check the Microsoft Web site to make sure you've installed the most current Service Pack and all critical updates of your current operating system (http://v4.windowsupdate.microsoft.com/en/default.asp).

2. Check the Web sites of your graphics card, motherboard, and sound card vendors and make sure you have the latest updates.

3. Make sure you have the latest update of Microsoft's Direct X installed (www.microsoft.com/directx).

4. Uninstall any extraneous programs on your computer, including games and other multimedia programs.

   If you're running Windows XP, you might even want to restore your system to its pristine state at a date before you installed those other applications. It won't affect any files or documents you've created in the meantime, and it will clear out unnecessary drivers you might not notice in your own cleaning efforts.

5. Defragment all hard disks (as described in Chapter 2).

   Consider buying a separate capture drive if you don't already have one.

   continues on next page

6. Check that your CD or DVD drive is *not* on the same IDE cable as your video drive, which can slow operation.

   The optimal configuration is the video drive on its own cable.

7. Remove all extraneous programs from background operation (see the sidebar "Optimizing System Disk Performance" in Chapter 2).

8. Make sure there are no viruses on the system.

9. Install Studio.

   Studio should prompt you to see if there is an update available (**Figure B.1**).

10. Click Yes to see if there is an update.

    If so, download it (it's free). If Studio doesn't prompt you for some reason, choose Help > Software Updates (**Figure B.2**) to open the same dialog and check for an update. Note that you may have to register the program to download the upgrade.

11. After installing Studio and any updates, test your capture drive as described in Chapter 2.

    If performance is acceptable, your system should be ready.

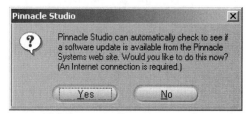

Figure B.1 Always let Studio check for updates after installing.

Figure B.2 If you start experiencing problems, search and load the latest update first.

Troubleshooting Common Problems

Again, the following section is by no means comprehensive. If you run into problems with Studio that aren't addressed here, check Pinnacle's Web site or technical support.

DV card and camera

Note that Studio doesn't interface with your capture card or camera directly; it does so through facilities provided by all Windows operating systems. During DV capture, if you see the error message in **Figure B.3**, and the suggested activities don't resolve the issue, check whether Windows sees the DV card and camera components in the Windows Device Manager.

To troubleshoot your DV card and camera:

1. From the Windows Taskbar, choose Start > Control Panel (**Figure B.4**).

    (In Windows 98 and Windows 2000, choose Start > Settings > Control Panel.)

    Windows opens the Control Panel (**Figure B.5**).

    continues on next page

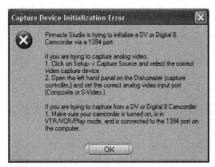

Figure B.3 Studio doesn't see your camera. Try the appropriate suggestions.

Figure B.4 Getting to the Windows Control Panel.

Figure B.5 Click here to open the System Properties window.

445

Appendix B

2. At the bottom of the Control Panel, click System.

   Windows opens the System Properties dialog (**Figure B.6**).

3. At the top of the System Properties dialog, select the Hardware tab.

4. On the Hardware tab, click the Device Manager button.

   Windows opens the Device Manager dialog (**Figure B.7**).

5. Click the plus sign next to IEEE 1394 Bus host controller.

   You should see something close to the description shown in Figure B.7, a device listed with OHCI in the title. If such a device is present, and there is no yellow exclamation or question mark signifying a problem (like there is with the USB Controller), you have the necessary DV hardware and it is properly running.

   If there is no device present, or there is a yellow exclamation mark, check the documentation that came with your computer or DV card to troubleshoot further.

6. If the DV card is present, click the plus sign (+) next to Imaging Devices.

   You should see something close to the description shown in Figure B.7, Sony DV Camcorder. If not, the camera is turned off, it's in the wrong mode (should be in Play mode), or the cable is bad.

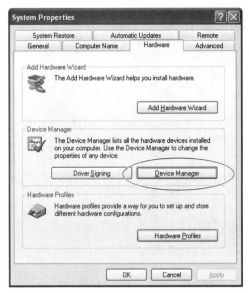

Figure B.6 Click here to open the Device Manager.

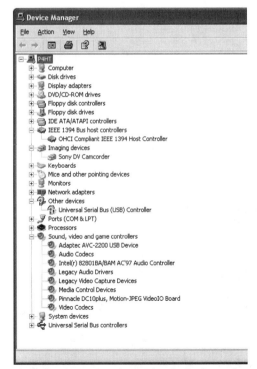

Figure B.7 The Device Manager details the status of all system hardware. Oops, looks like a problem with USB! Better diagnose this one before installing any USB devices.

Troubleshooting

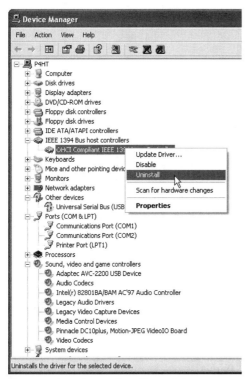

Figure B.8 Sometimes uninstalling and then reinstalling solves the problem.

Figure B.9 If you're having trouble finding the Device Manager, check your Help files.

✔ Tips

- If Windows doesn't see your FireWire card, shut the system down, remove the card, restart Windows, shut down again, reinsert the card, restart, and see if Windows recognizes the newly reinstalled card upon boot up. If Windows doesn't even try to install the card, try the same procedure in a different PCI slot. If this doesn't work, try a different FireWire card.

- If Windows sees the FireWire card, but Studio doesn't, uninstall the card by clicking the card in the Device Manager, then right-click and choose Uninstall (**Figure B.8**). Then reboot, let Windows find the card, and reinstall all necessary driver software. (You may need your Windows disc handy to accomplish this, especially for Windows 98 SE. Don't uninstall unless you can locate the disc.)

- When troubleshooting an analog capture card, click the plus sign in front of Sound, video and game controllers, which is where Windows installs analog cards.

- Note that the route to the Device Manager is slightly different among all Windows flavors. If it doesn't work for you, check the Windows Help files (**Figure B.9**) for instructions on how to open this dialog.

447

No video or distorted video during DV capture

This section assumes Studio found the DV camera and did not produce the error message shown in Figure B.3. If you did receive the error message, see "To troubleshoot your DV card and camera," earlier in this chapter.

If Studio "sees" your DV camera, but doesn't display video in the Player when the camera is running, try the following solutions.

To troubleshoot no video or distorted video in the Player during DV capture:

1. Remove and reinsert the FireWire cable in both the camera and computer to ensure that it is properly seated.

2. Make sure you're running the latest graphics driver for the graphics card installed in your computer.

3. Make sure you're running the latest version of Direct X (www.microsoft.com/directx).

4. Make sure you're running the latest Studio update (Figure B.2).

5. Try different display resolutions and color depths. To do so, right-click on the Windows Desktop and choose Properties (**Figure B.10**).

   Windows opens the Display Properties dialog (**Figure B.11**).

6. Click the Settings tab.

7. Try all available resolutions above 800 x 600 and 16-bit, 24-bit, and/or 32-bit (if available) to find a combination that displays the videos.

8. Try a new FireWire cable.

✔ Tip

- If this doesn't work, check Pinnacle support at www.pinnaclesys.com/support for help with DirectX and advice specific to your graphics card.

Figure B.10 Accessing the Display Properties dialog.

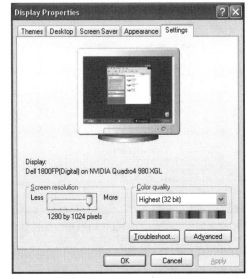

Figure B.11 Here's how you adjust display resolution and color depth.

Troubleshooting

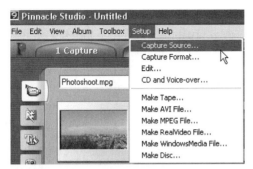

Figure B.12 Getting to the Capture source tab to check Studio setup options.

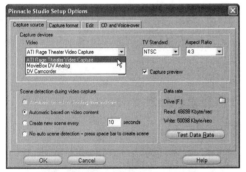

Figure B.13 Make sure you've got the right analog capture device selected.

No video or distorted video during analog capture

If you're having problems with your analog capture card, start by taking the steps described in "To troubleshoot your DV card and camera" to make sure the card is properly installed under Windows. If it is not properly installed, check your capture card documentation.

If the card is properly installed, try these steps to resolve your problem.

To troubleshoot no video or distorted video during analog capture:

1. Remove and reinsert the analog capture cable in both the camera and computer to ensure it is properly seated.

2. From the Studio menu, choose Setup > Capture Source (**Figure B.12**).

    Studio opens the Setup Options dialog open to the Capture source tab (**Figure B.13**).

3. Confirm that the proper video capture device is selected.

4. If the TV Standard box is active (not grayed out), ensure that it's set to the proper standard (NTSC in the United States.).

5. If the Capture Preview check box is enabled, ensure that it's enabled by deselecting it and then reselecting it one more time, and then click OK.

continues on next page

6. In the Capture mode Video input screen, make sure the correct input is selected (**Figure B.14**).

7. Make sure you're running the latest graphics driver for the graphics card installed in your computer.

8. Make sure you're running the latest version of Direct X (www.microsoft.com/directx).

9. Make sure you're running the latest Studio update (Figure B.2).

10. Try different display resolutions and color depths. To do so, right-click on the Windows Desktop and choose Properties. Windows opens the Display Properties dialog.

11. Click the Settings tab.

12. Try all available resolutions above 800 x 600 and 16-bit, 24-bit, and/or 32-bit (if available) to find a combination that displays the videos.

13. Try a different analog capture cable.

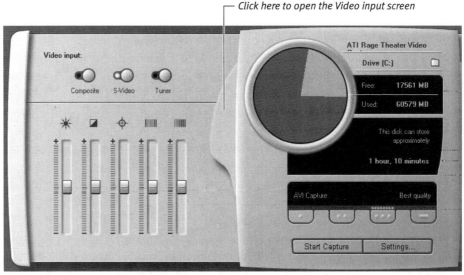

Figure B.14 And the right analog input.

Troubleshooting

Figure B.15 Turn your screen saver off.

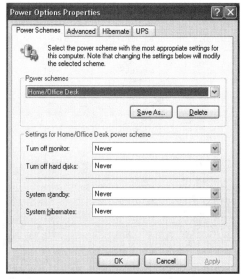

Figure B.16 Disabling your power-saving schemes.

Dropped frames

If you're having trouble with dropped frames, start with the steps described earlier in "To ensure a smooth installation," which should work with most computers. If all else fails, try the following additional steps.

To troubleshoot frames dropped during capture or writing back to tape:

1. Save your project, reboot the system, and reload Studio before writing a project to tape.

2. During capture and writing back to tape, disable the network by pulling the cable from the network interface card.

3. Right-click on the Windows Desktop and choose Properties.

    Windows opens the Display Properties dialog (**Figure B.15**).

4. Click the Screen Saver tab.

5. Choose None from the Screen saver drop-down box.

6. On the bottom-right of the Screen Saver tab, click Power.

    Studio opens the Power Options Properties dialog open to the Power Schemes tab (**Figure B.16**).

continues on next page

Appendix B

7. Choose Never in the Turn Off Monitor, Turn Off Hard Disks, and System Standby drop-down boxes.

8. Close all extraneous programs by doing one of the following:

▲ Close them one- by- one using normal program controls (if available).

▲ Press Ctrl+Alt+Delete to load the Windows Task Manager, select the target program, and click End Task (**Figure B.17**).

✔ Tip

■ If you click the Processes tab in the Windows Task Manager (**Figure B.18**), you'll see a lot more services and programs running. Resist the urge to freelance here and remove random programs, as you might unload a necessary service and crash the system (though Windows typically attempts to prevent this). You're better off working with a good start-up manager program (see Chapter 2).

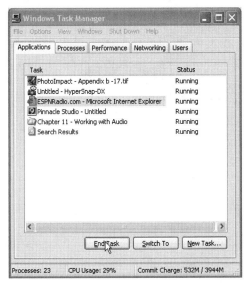

Figure B.17 Closing all extraneous applications.

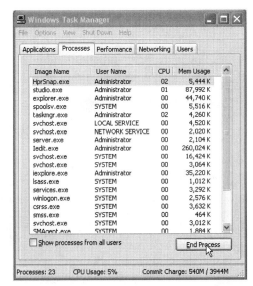

Figure B.18 Beware here, because you may end a crucial process.

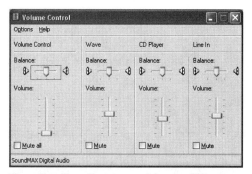

Figure B.19 Many times you can't hear audio because the volume is turned down (imagine that)!

No audio

Note that Studio doesn't play audio when capturing from DV. If you're not hearing audio during analog capture or during normal preview, read this section.

To troubleshoot no audio during capture or playback:

1. Load a file with known good audio in Windows Media Player or another application to see if the audio plays normally. If it doesn't, it's a system problem. Do the following:

   ▲ Check that speakers are turned on.

   ▲ Make sure speaker volume is turned up.

   ▲ See if the speaker cable is connected to both the speaker system and computer.

   ▲ See if the speaker cable is connected to the proper plug (usually the headphones icon).

   ▲ Double-click the speaker in your Taskbar, or choose Start > Programs > Accessories > Entertainment > Volume Control to load Volume Control. Make sure that Wave Balance isn't muted and that both Wave and the Master Volume control are at reasonable levels (**Figure B.19**).

   ▲ If available, plug in a set of headphones or alternate speakers and test whether these work. If they do, it's a speaker problem.

   ▲ Following Steps 1 to 4 under "To troubleshoot your DV card and camera," open the Device Manager dialog, click the plus sign next to Sound, video and game controllers, and make sure your audio device is listed and working properly.

continues on next page

Appendix B

2. If Media Player plays the file normally, check to ensure that audio is captured with the file. In Windows Explorer, navigate to your capture directory and double-click a captured file, which should load into Media Player or other player program.

   If you can't hear audio during playback, somehow audio didn't get captured, normally only an issue with analog capture, since there's almost no way Studio can capture DV video without the audio.

   Verify your audio capture setup:

   ▲ Remove and reinsert the analog audio cables into both the computer and camcorder.

   ▲ Make certain the audio is plugged into the Line-in, not the Microphone port.

3. If audio isn't captured with the file, return to Studio in Capture mode.

4. In the Audio capture screen (**Figure B.20**), make sure Audio capture is turned on and that volume is not completely turned down. Start your camcorder and observe whether the audio meter is responding to the incoming audio. If there is no movement in the audio meter, audio is not getting to the system.

   If you've taken all the actions described in Steps 1 and 2, try swapping audio input cables.

5. If audio is captured with the file, and you still don't hear audio during preview, it's likely you muted the audio tracks or turned the sound down too low. Check "Using the Volume Tool" and "Adjusting Volume on the Timeline" in Chapter 11.

Figure B.20 If your volume button doesn't flicker during capture, your captured files won't have any audio.

Index

* (asterisk), 44
2D Editor effect, 227, 248–249
4-pin cables/connectors, 68, 69
4:3 aspect ratio, 13. *See also* aspect ratios
6-pin cables/connectors, 68, 69
12-bit audio, 13
16-bit audio, 13
16:9 aspect ratio, 13, 114, 119. *See also* aspect ratios
32-bit images, 286

A

A/V ports, 90
acceleration, hardware, 213, 228
Add Ellipse icon, 287
Add Rectangle icon, 287
Address Book, StudioOnline, 435
adjustment handles, 320, 323, 332–333, 335
Adobe Photoshop, 286
Adobe Premiere, 248
AE modes, 10
Album, 119–141
    and 16:9 video, 119
    accessing transition groups in, 198
    adding scene comments in, 82
    and analog capture, 86, 103
    in Capture mode, 37, 64–65, 86
    combining scenes in, 125–126
    displaying files in, 121–122
    and DV capture, 37, 64–65
    in Edit mode, 31
    finding scenes in, 169
    importance of, 119
    loading video files into, 121–122
    opening, 120, 137, 140
    playing videos in, 123–124
    previewing transitions in, 202
    Sound Effects tab, 140–141
    splitting scenes in, 127–128, 130
    Still Images tab, 137–139
    switching views in, 81, 103, 131–132
    viewing captured video in, 83
Alien effect, 336
Align icon, 293, 294
Align menu, 293, 294
alignment
    object, 293–295
    text, 267, 275
alpha channels, 286
Alpha Magic transitions, 197, 199, 205
Analog A/V ports, 69
analog camcorder
    capturing still images with, 108–114
    capturing video with. *See* analog capture
    connecting computer and, 89–91
    and Make Tape controls, 397
analog capture, 85–105
    adding scene comments to, 104
    adjusting incoming audio volume for, 98–99
    adjusting incoming video for, 96–97
    and Album views, 103
    checking audio volume for, 99, 102
    choosing parameters for, 92–95
    complexity of, 85
    connecting camera/computer for, 89–91
    contrasted with DV capture, 85, 96
    and flicker reduction, 114
    and frame rate, 94
    interface, 39, 86–87
    setting options for, 87
    steps in process, 100–102
    troubleshooting, 449–450
    and video resolution, 94
    viewing, 105
analog-to-digital conversion, 96, 306

Index

analog video
    capturing, 100–102. *See also* analog capture
    and scene detection, 88
    writing to tape, 393
Apple Computer, 68
artistic special effects, 225, 226–227, 336
aspect ratios
    16:9 *vs.* 4:3, 13
    and Album views, 81, 103, 132
    and analog capture, 102
    and DV camcorders, 59
    and DV capture, 63
    and image cropping, 118
    mixing, 59–60
    switching between, 81, 103, 132
    and Title editor, 257
    for TV sets, 56, 60
assets
    arranging, in Storyboard view, 153
    assigning default durations to, 55
    gathering, x
    storing, 119
asterisk (*), 44
audio, 303–342. *See also* audio files
    12- *vs.* 16-bit, 13
    background, xii, 312–313
    balance. *See* Balance control
    capturing, 95, 306. *See also* ripping
    cleaning, 340–341
    Continuity system for, 23
    effects, 55, 203, 204, 336–340
    importance of, 303
    improving quality of, 16
    mixing, 330
    removing unwanted noises from, 340–341
    setting recording options for, 306–307
    troubleshooting, 453–454
Audio Album, 317
audio backgrounds, 376
Audio Capture Devices menu, 92
Audio Clip Properties tool, 194, 305, 318
Audio Effects tool, 305
audio fades, 55, 203, 204, 324–326
audio files
    changing duration of, 194
    and Clip Properties tool, 174, 194
    displaying duration of, 140
    dragging to tracks, 195
    editing, 174, 180, 318–319
    how Studio treats, 193, 195
    loading, 141
    playing, 141
Audio Files tab, 32
audio menus, 375–376

Audio toolbox, 36, 305, 337
Audio Toolbox button, 304
Audio track
    adding audio files to, 195
    illustrated, 155
    locking, 180
    purpose of, 156, 304
audio tracks
    adjusting volume of, 322–323
    creating, 305
    descriptions of, 304
    disk requirements for, xii
    muting, 322
    ripping, 303, 306, 309–311
    and Studio workflow, 304–305
    synchronizing with video tracks, 148
Audio Volume control, 99
authoring. *See* DVD authoring
Auto Color Correct effect, 227, 235–237, 241
auto-exposure modes, 10
Autodesk, 122
automatic focus, 12
Autosave feature, 45, 56
auxiliary files, 57–58, 308
AVI codecs, 405
AVI files, 122, 141, 400, 404, 407–412

B

B/W effect, 227
background audio/music, xii, 312–313
Background Music track, 304
background rendering, 214–215, 216, 228
backgrounds
    audio, xii, 312–313, 376
    gradient, 280
    image, 281
    single-color, 278–279
    transparent, 280
    video, 378
Backgrounds Album, 278
Balance control, 320, 327–331, 335
balloons transition, 219
BAS transitions, 199
Beach & Ski mode, 10
Bevel Crystal effect, 227
Blur effect, 227
BMP format, 111, 139
breakout boxes, 91
Brightness setting, 95, 237
Broom and Dustpan icon, 230, 337
burning DVDs, 380–385
Burns, Ken, 190, 248

Index

buttons
    adding to titles, 288
    changing captions for, 360
    changing thumbnails for, 360
    converting objects to, 289
    creating video, 361
    editing, 361
    setting active/selected colors for, 291
    setting highlight styles for, 290
    types of, 290
Buttons Album, 287, 290

C

cables
    FireWire, 69
    four- *vs.* six-pin, 68, 69
    S-Video, 89–90
Calendar function, StudioOnline, 435
camcorder
    analog *vs.* DV, 63, 96
    capturing still images with, 107, 108–114
    choosing settings for, 10–13
    composing shots with, 17–27
    connecting computer and, 68–69, 89–91
    improving sound quality for, 16
    shooting with, 14–15
    stabilizing, 19
    troubleshooting, 445–447
Camcorder Controller, 37, 38, 65
Camcorder icon, 34
camera. *See* camcorder
Canon, 68
captions, button, 360
capture drive, 48–54
    defragmenting, 51–52
    selecting, 48–49
    testing, 53–54
capture footage, disk requirements for, xii
capture format
    for analog capture, 93
    for DV capture, 66, 76
Capture mode, 37–39, 64, 70–71
capture resolution, 94
Capture Source command, 48, 53
Capture Source tab, 66, 67, 75
Capture tab, 37, 64
Capture Video dialog box, 100
capturing
    from analog sources, 39. *See also* analog capture
    audio, 95, 306. *See also* ripping
    from DV sources, 37–38. *See also* DV capture
    optimizing computer for, 442
    quality considerations, 63
    still images, 108–114

CD, editing audio from, 318–319
CD Architect, 314
CD audio ripping, 303, 306–307, 309–311
CD Audio tool, 305, 309
CD-Recordable drives, xi
CD-Rewritable drives, xi
chapter flags, 350, 354, 359, 374
chapter links, 354, 359
chapter points, 355, 356–358
Cinepak codec, 411
Cleaning effects, 226, 227, 235–240
Clip Properties tool, 170–174
    controls provided by, 171
    editing transition duration with, 210–211
    illustrated, 170
    opening, 173
    purpose of, 170
    vs. trimming on Timeline, 175
Clipboard button, 262, 263
clips. *See also* video clips
    changing playback speed of, 243–247
    defined, 6
    detecting scenes in, 129
    fading into/out of, 203
    inserting transitions between, 204
    splitting, 165
Clock icon, 230
close-up shots, 28
codecs, 404, 411. *See also* compression
Color Correction effect, 227, 235–237
Color effects, 226, 227
Color Selection dialog box, 269, 279, 280, 291
color swatches, 269
Color Wheel icon, 230
Combine Clips command, 167
Combine Scenes feature, 125–126
Comment view, 81, 103, 131
Compiling Disk phase, 384
composition
    advanced, 24–27
    basic, 17–23
    defined, 6
compression. *See also* encoding
    MPEG-1 *vs.* MPEG-2, 404
    parameters, 405–406
    purpose of, 404
    and streaming media technologies, 404
computer
    connecting camera and, 68–69, 89–91
    installing Studio on, 443–444
    optimizing performance of, 54, 442
    system requirements, xi–xii
connectors
    4-pin, 68, 69
    6-pin, 68, 69
    FireWire, 68

457

Index

connectors *(continued)*
    RCA, 90, 91
    S-Video, 89–90
    Y-coupling, 91
Continuity system, 20–23
Contrast setting, 95
Cool 3D Studio, 283, 286
Copy icon, 297
Crawl icon, 301, 302
crawling titles, 302
cropping images, 118
cross-fade effect, 204, 325
curative special effects, 225, 226, 336
custom menus, 347, 349, 363–371
cutaways, 26–27

D

Data Rate Test dialog box, 53
data rates, 53–54, 406
date/time settings, 13
date/time stamps, 72
default duration settings, 55–56, 202
defragmenting, 51–52
deleting
    special effects, 233
    styles, 271
    tracks, 158
    video clips (from Timeline), 164
    videos (from StudioOnline), 435
Dell, 68
Design window, 262, 263, 264
Detect Scenes commands, 129
Device Manager, 447
digital effects, 13
digital output, 403–424
    in AVI format, 407–412
    choosing format for, 403
    compression considerations, 404–406
    in MPEG format, 413–415
    in RealVideo format, 416–421
    in Windows Media format, 422–424
digital zoom, 13
DirectX, xi, 442
Disc Menus tab, 32
Disk Defragmenter utility, 51–52
disk optimization, 54
disk requirements, xi, xii
Diskometer
    and analog capture, 86, 87
    and DV capture, 38, 65–66
    illustrated, 37
Display Properties dialog, 448
Display Tool Tips command, 47

dissolves, 4, 197
distortion
    image, 115
    video, 448–450
DMA, 54
drives
    capture, 48–54
    defragmenting, 51–52
    network, 49
dropped frames, 75, 102, 451–452
duration settings, default, 55–56, 202
Dustpan icon, 230, 337
DV camcorder. *See also* camcorder
    aspect ratios supported by, 59
    capturing still images with, 108–114
    choosing settings for, 10–13
    connecting computer and, 68–69
    EIS feature, 239
    and FireWire, 68
    and Make Tape controls, 396
    shooting with, 14–15
DV capture, 63–83
    adding comments to, 82
    choosing capture format for, 76
    connecting camera/computer for, 68–69
    contrasted with analog capture, 85, 96
    in DV format, 73–75
    entering Capture mode for, 70–71
    and flicker reduction, 114
    handling of audio during, 71
    interface, 37–38, 64–66
    in MPEG format, 77–80
    and scene detection, 67
    starting/stopping, 73
    troubleshooting, 70, 448
    viewing, 83
DV cards, 442, 445–446
DV connectors, 68
DV format
    and Diskometer controls, 66, 76
    encoding projects in, 407–410
DV ports, 69
DV tape
    and time codes, 72
    writing to, 393–401
DVD authoring, 343–390
    advice for getting started with, 345
    and audio menus, 375–376
    compatibility considerations, 390
    creating P-i-P effect, 386–389
    interface, 344
    and menu structure, 346–349
    previewing your work, 372–374
    purpose of, xi
    using custom menus, 363–371

Index

using menu templates, 350–362
and video flow, 344–346
and video menus, 377–378
DVD burners, 379, 442
DVD compatibility studies, 390
DVD files, disk requirements for, xii
DVD formats, 379
DVD menus
creating templates for, 299–300
designing, 292–298
editing, 353
DVD players, 60, 346, 379, 382
DVD Preview mode, 372
DVD-R discs, 346
DVD-RAM, 379
DVD-Recordable drives, xi
DVD-Rewritable drives, xi
DVD slide shows, 345
DVD+R discs, 346
DVD+RW drives, xi, 379
DVDs
authoring. *See* DVD authoring
burning, 380–385
playing, 60, 346, 382

E

Edge sliders, 270
Edit line, 155, 156
Edit List view, 34, 146
Edit mode
interface, 31–36
playing captured video in, 105
viewing captured video in, 83
editing. *See also* edits
advanced Timeline, 179–189
audio files, 174, 180, 318–319
buttons, 361
Continuity system for, 20–23
menus, 353
nonlinear, 8–9
steps in process, x–xi
still images, 115–118
undoing/redoing, 41–42
Editing-mode selection buttons, 262, 263
editing tools
Audio toolbox, 36
Video toolbox, 34–35
editors
nondestructive, 214
still-image, 111
title. *See* Title editor
video, 3, 7

edits
insert, 179–186
ripple, 176–177
rolling, 176, 178
split, 187–189
effects. *See* special effects
EIS systems, 239
electric image stabilization, 239
Electric Plug icon, 337
email
and RealVideo files, 404, 416, 421
sending still images via, 111
sending videos from StudioOnline via, 431–434
and streaming formats, 403, 404
and Windows Media files, 404, 424
Emboss effect, 227
Encoder, Windows Media, 422
encoding. *See also* compression
in AVI format, 411–412
in DV format, 407–410
and DVD burn process, 384
in MPEG format, 413–415
in RealVideo format, 416–419
in Windows Media format, 422–424
End Frame Trim caliper, 174
Equalizer effect, 336, 342
establishing shots, 21, 28
Exit command, 45
exposure settings, 10
eyes, 18

F

Fade controls, 320
fade to black, 4
fade transitions, 197, 203, 205
fades, audio, 55, 203, 204, 324–326
Family Fun Pack, 219
Favorites Album, 271
file formats. *See also* specific formats
analog capture, 94
audio, 141
compression, 404, 405
DV capture, 76–80
still-image, 111, 139
video, 122
file size limitations, Windows, 75
files
auxiliary *vs.* captured, 57–58
encoding. *See* encoding
naming, 44, 50
saving, 43–45
filming, 6
filters, 225. *See also* special effects

459

Index

Find Scene in Album command, 169
Find Scene in Project command, 134
FireWire
    cables, 69
    cards, 68, 447
    connectors, 68
    and DV capture, 68–69
    technology, 68
flicker reduction, 114
focus, automatic *vs.* manual, 12
folders
    creating, 43, 50
    naming, 50
    saving projects in, 44
fonts, 267
formats. *See* file formats
four-pin cables/connectors, 68, 69
Fractal Clouds effect, 227
Fractal Fire effect, 227
Fractal Tunnel effect, 227
frame-advance controls, 111
frame capture, 108
Frame Grab tool, 37, 109, 113
frame rate, 94, 406
Framer effect, 227
frames, cutting unwanted, 130
Frames Dropped counter, 75, 102
Full Screen Title button, 259
full-screen titles, 259, 261, 278–281
Fun effects, 226, 227, 248

G

garnishing, xi
GIF format, 139
Global Volume tool, 320, 322
Grab button, 110, 114
gradients, 269, 280
graphics cards, xi, 442
Group icon, 296
Grungelizer effect, 336
guided tour, Studio 9, 29, 30
gun microphones, 16

H

Hachman, Mark, 390
Hall of Mirrors effect, 227
Halloween transitions, 223
hard disks. *See also* drives
    calculating space required on, xii
    cost considerations, 48
    defragmenting, 51–52
    optimizing, 54
    system requirements, xi, xii
hardware acceleration, 213, 228
hardware requirements, xi–xii, 442
hardware setup, tape, 394
HDTV, 59, 60
heads, 170
headsets, 314
Help button, 31
Help screen, 46
highlight styles, 290
Holiday FX Pack, 223
Hollywood FX for Studio, 197, 199
Hollywood FX transitions
    and background rendering, 214
    and program versions, 199, 201
    watermarking of, 199
    working with, 212–213, 219–224
Hue setting, 95
hybrid menus, 348, 370

I

IEEE 1394, 68
iLink, 68
image backgrounds, 281
Image folder, 383
image stabilization, 12
images. *See also* still images
    32-bit, 286
    capturing, 107, 108–114
    cropping, 118
    dropping into Video track, 190
    editing, 115–118
    how Studio works with, 115
    optimizing, 116–117
    resizing, on Storyboard, 149
    resolution considerations, 111, 114, 115–117
    saving, 111
insert edits, 179–186
installing program, 443–444
Intel Pentium, xi, 442
Intelligent Rendering process, 399
Intellikey, 390
interface
    analog capture, 86–87
    DV capture, 37–38, 64–66
    DVD authoring, 344
    Edit mode, 31–36
    special effects, 229–234
    Title editor, 262–263
Invert effect, 227

J

J-cuts, 187, 189
jaggies, 13
Jog controls, 113
JPEG format, 111, 139
JPG format, 139
Jukebox, 311
Justify tool, 275

K

Karaoke effect, 336
Ken Burns effect, 190, 248
kerning, 263, 276
keyboard shortcuts
　for main Studio interface, 439–440
　for playing back video, 124
　for Storyboard, 154
　for Timeline, 161
　for Title editor, 440
　viewing online, 47
keywords, selecting scenes based on, 136
Kissco, 54

L

L-cuts, 187–188
LaBarge, Ralph, 390
Landscape mode, 10
layers, object, 298
lead room, 18
Lens Flare effect, 227
Leveler effect, 336
Lighting Control effect, 227
lights, 15
linear menus, 346
linear video, 343, 344
links
　chapter, 354, 359
　menu, 369–370
logos, 282–286
　adding to video, 282–283
　creating, 283
　making transparent, 284–285, 286
　resizing, 285
long shots, 28
look room, 17
Looks browser, 268–270, 286
low-light, shooting video in, 14–15, 241–242
low-light modes, 11
LP mode, 13

M

Macintosh, 416
Magnify effect, 227
Make AVI File command, 407
Make Disc command, 380
Make Movie mode, 40
Make Movie tab, 395
Make MPEG File command, 413
Make Tape controls, 395–396, 400
manual, Studio 9, x, 46
manual focus, 12
Media Player, Microsoft, 311
medium shots, 21, 24, 28
medium two-shots, 21
MEGA transitions, 199
Menu Album, 351
Menu Clip Properties tool, 353
Menu Clip Properties window, 349
menu structure, DVD, 346–349
Menu track, 156, 289
menus
　adding text to, 264
　audio, 375–376
　changing duration of, 362
　changing/replacing text in, 265
　creating templates for, 299–300
　custom, 347, 349, 363–371
　designing, 292–298
　hybrid, 348
　linear, 346
　linking, 369–370
　moving text in, 266
　video, 377–378
Menus Album, 364
MicroMV devices, 37, 38, 79
microphones, 16, 314, 316
Microsoft Media Player, 311
Minmax effect, 227
Mirage effect, 227
mixing, audio, 330
modes
　camera, 10
　scene-detection, 67
　Studio 9, 31–40
monitors, 442
monopods, 19
Mosaic effect, 227, 229, 231
Motion Blur effect, 227
motion menus, 377
motion techniques, 18–20
Move tool, 274
movie, 6. *See also* video
Movie button, 113
Movie window, 34–36

461

Index

applying transitions in, 203
Audio toolbox, 36
audio/video synchronization in, 148
dragging and dropping items in, 151
illustrated, 31
importance of, 145
setting thumbnails in, 168
switching among views in, 147
Video toolbox, 34–35
views available in, 34, 146–147
Moving Pictures effect, 227
moving subjects, 18
MovingPicture, 252
MP3 files, 141, 305
MPEG
    compression parameters, 405
    and DV capture, 76, 77–80
    encoding tools, 413–415
MPEG-1, 80, 94, 122, 405
MPEG-2
    and analog capture, 94
    compression parameters, 405
    decoders, 80
    encoding engine, ix
    importing, 122
    and MicroMV capture, 79
    vs. MPEG-1, 404
MSDI microphone, 16
Music track, 155, 156, 158, 304
music videos, 253–255
MusicMatch, 309, 311
Mute button, 320, 322

N

narration tracks, xii
narrations, recording, 314–316
NewBlueChorus effect, 337
NewBlueWind effect, 337
Next button, 290, 299–300
night-shot modes, 11
Noise effect, 227
Noise Reduction effect, 237, 240, 241, 336, 340–341
noise reduction filters, 243
nonlinear editing, 8–9
Normal button, 290
nose room, 17

O

Object Layout buttons, 262, 263
Object toolbox, 262, 263

objects. *See also* images
    aligning, 293–295
    copying and pasting, 297
    grouping/ungrouping, 296
    moving to different layers, 298
    resizing, 292–293
    spacing, 294
Old Film effect, 227
online help, 46–47
"Open curtain" transition, 211
optical zoom, 13
Optimize for Make Tape option, 214
Optimize for Preview option, 214, 215
optimizing
    hard disks, 54
    still images, 116–117
Original Audio track, 156, 304
output, creating digital, 403–424
output settings, 40
over-the-shoulder shots, 25, 28
overlay titles, 257

P

P-i-P effect, 219, 224, 386–389
Pan and Zoom effects, 227, 250, 252
panning, 4, 19
Paste icon, 297
PC Magazine, ix, 54
PCI card slot, 68
Pentium, xi, 215, 442
performance
    and background rendering, 215
    optimizing disk, 54
Photos and Frame Grabs tab, 32
Photoshop, 139
Picture-in-Picture effect, 219, 224, 386–389
Pictures Album, 282
Pictures icon, 282
Pinnacle Studio Setup Options dialog box, 48. *See also* setup options
Pinnacle Systems, ix, 425
Pioneer
    DVD compatibility study, 390
    DVD players, 379
    DVD-R/RW burner, 442
pixilation, 13
playback controls, 83, 124, 154, 243–247
Player
    and analog capture, 86
    in Capture mode, 37, 38, 65, 86
    controls, 33, 113
    and DV capture, 65
    scrubber, 124, 154, 155, 156

Index

PLS transitions, 199
point-of-view shots, 24, 25, 28
Portrait mode, 10
ports, 68, 69, 90
Posterize effect, 227
Power Launcher Plus, 54
preview-quality capture, 76
previewing
    DVD authoring, 372–374
    transitions, 199, 202, 205
    video clips, 154, 161
Previous button, 290, 299–300
PRO transitions, 199
processor speed, xi, xii
production footage, disk requirements for, xii
programmed auto-exposure modes, 10
projects
    calculating disk requirements for, xii
    creating folders for, 43
    encoding. *See* encoding
    mixing aspect ratios in, 59–60
    naming, 44
    saving, 43–45
    setting auxiliary file location for, 57–58
    setting options for, 29
    writing to tape, 395–399
PSD format, 139
Push transitions, 198

Q

Question Mark icon, 46
QuickTime files, 122, 141

R

Radial Blur effect, 227
RAM, xi, xii, 442
Razorblade icon, 34
RCA connectors, 90, 91
reaction shots, 24, 28
RealAudio files, 141
RealNetworks, 309, 311, 416
RealOne, 311
RealOne Player, 416
RealVideo files, 122, 405, 416–421
recording
    narrations, 314–316
    setting options for, 306–307
Redo button/command, 31, 42
Reduce Flicker button, 114
rendering
    background, 214–215, 216, 228

    defined, 214
    and editing/production process, xi
    with Intelligent Rendering, 399
    setting options for, 214–216
    stopping Studio during, 399
Rendering box, 213
Replication effect, 227
Reset button, 339
resolution
    analog capture, 94
    MPEG-1 *vs.* MPEG-2, 404
    still-image, 111, 114, 115–117
    video, 404, 405
Return to Menu flag, 362, 371
Reverb effect, 336
Reverse check box, 211
ripping CD audio, 303, 306–307, 309–311
ripple edits, 176–177
ripple transitions, 217–218
Roll icon, 301
rolling edits, 176, 178
rolling titles, 301
Rotate tool, 274, 277
rule of thirds, 17–18

S

S-VCDs, 390
S-Video
    cables/connectors, 89–90
    ports, 69
saddle points, 17
Saturation setting, 95
Save As dialog box, 44
Save Menu As dialog box, 300
Save Project As command, 44
Save Project command, 44
saving
    menu templates, 300
    project files, 43–45
    still images, 111
    titles, 260
Scale to Fit control, 272
Scale tool, 274
scene comments
    adding to captured video, 82, 104
    changing, 135
    customizing, 126, 130
    searching for scenes based on, 136
    and split/combined scenes, 126, 130
scene detection
    and analog footage, 88
    and DV footage, 67
    modes, 67, 75

Index

Scene view, 81, 103, 131
scenes. *See also* video clips
    adding comments to, 82, 104, 135
    combining, 104, 125–126, 166–167
    defined, 6
    detecting, 129
    finding, 134, 136, 169
    grouping, 126
    inserting clips between, 152, 159
    manually creating, 67
    numbering of, 126
    splitting, 127–128, 130
    subdividing, 129
Scissors icon, 194
SCSI, xi, 48
search function, 136
Select Scenes by Name command, 136
Sepia effect, 227
sequences, 6
Set Thumbnail command, 133, 168
setup options
    analog capture, 87, 92–93
    Autosave feature, 56
    auxiliary file location, 57–58
    background rendering, 214–215
    capture format, 76, 78–80
    capture parameters, 66
    Capture Source settings, 48–49, 53
    CD-ripping, 306–307
    default duration settings, 55–56
    DVD productions, 381
    hardware acceleration, 213
    special effects, 228
    Storyboard Thumbnails, 149
    Transitions default duration, 202
Shadow sliders, 271
Sharpen effect, 227
Sharpness setting, 95
Shensoft Power Launcher Plus, 54
Shift Channels effect, 227
shooting video
    choosing camera settings for, 10–13
    guidelines for, 5
    terms associated with, 6
shortcuts. *See* keyboard shortcuts
shot composition
    advanced, 24–27
    basic, 17–23
    defined, 6
shotgun microphones, 16
shots
    defined, 6
    types of, 28
Show Menus icon, 364
Shrink to Fit control, 272

six-pin cables/connectors, 68, 69
Skew tool, 277
Slide transitions, 198
slideshows
    creating, 192
    on DVD, 345
    inserting ripple transitions in, 217–218
    narrating, 314
slow motion, 111
SmartCapture feature, 76
SmartMovie, 253–255
SmartSound
    creating background tracks with, 312–313
    editing tracks with, 319
    purpose of, 303, 305
    Web site, 313
Smooth Motion check box, 245
Softness controls, 270
Sony
    camcorders, 10
    CD Architect, 314
    and FireWire, 68
    iLink, 68
    MicroMV format, 79
    microphones, 16
sound cards, xi, 307
Sound Effect track, 155, 156, 158, 304
sound effects, 317
Sound Effects tab, 140–141
SP mode, 13
Speaker icon, 36, 98, 140
special effects, 225–255
    accessing, 229–230
    adding/configuring, 231–233
    adjusting order of, 234
    classes of, 226–227
    deleting, 233
    interface, 229–234
    setting duration for, 232
    setup options for, 228
    Studio's built-in, 227, 230, 336
    third-party, 226, 227, 230, 231, 252
    turning on/off, 234
Speed effect, 227, 244
split edits, 187–189
Split Scene command, 128
Sports mode, 10
Spotlight mode, 10
stabilization, image, 12
Stabilize effect, 227, 238–239
Stage Tools, 252
Stained Glass effect, 227
Standard Transitions group, 197, 198–199, 205
Star icon, 230
Start Capture button, 66, 73, 100

Index

Start DVD Preview icon, 372
Start Frame counter, 173
Start Frame Trim caliper, 173
Startup Cop, 54
Startup Manager, 54
static screens, 4
still-image editors, 111
still images, 107–118
    adding motion to, 248–251
    capturing, 107, 108–114
    changing duration of, 191
    creating slideshows of, 192
    cropping, 118
    displaying file names for, 138
    editing, 115–118
    and flicker reduction, 114
    how Studio works with, 115, 190
    loading, 138
    optimizing, 116–117
    resolution considerations, 111, 114, 115–117
    saving, 111
    scaling, 111
    setting default duration for, 55
Still Images tab, 137–139
Stop Capture button, 73, 101
Storyboard, 148–154
    arranging assets on, 153
    dragging video clips to, 150–151
    housekeeping tasks, 164–169
    increasing size of images on, 149
    inserting video clips between scenes on, 152
    keyboard shortcuts, 154
    previewing video clips on, 154
    purpose of, 148
    viewing clip-related information on, 153
Storyboard view
    accessing, 34
    applying transitions in, 203
    customizing, 149
    illustrated, 146
    purpose of, 147
storyboards, 148
Stream controls, 416
streaming technologies, 404, 416, 422
Strobe effect, 227, 247
strobe mode, 243
Strobe Repetition slider, 247
.stu files, 44
Studio 9
    awards, ix
    ease of use, ix, 29
    exiting, 45
    guided tour, 29, 30
    installing, 443–444
    manual, x, 46

    modes, 31–40. *See also* specific modes
    movie creation options, ix, x
    as nonlinear editing tool, 8–9, 343
    online help, 46–47
    system requirements, xi–xii
StudioOnline, 425–435
    Address Book, 435
    Calendar function, 435
    caveats regarding, 425
    deleting videos from, 435
    file formats accepted by, 430
    login screen, 427
    purpose of, 425
    sending videos from, 431–434
    storage space provided on, 425, 435
    uploading videos to, 426–430
Style effects, 227
styles, 268–271
    adding to Favorites Album, 271
    customizing, 269–271
    deleting, 271
    selecting, 268
Subdivide Scenes command, 129
Suitcase icon, 271
Sunset Moon mode, 10
Super VideoCDs, xi, 390
synchronization, audio/video, 148
system requirements, xi–xii, 442

T

tails, 170
tape
    converting DVD projects to, 401
    hardware, 394
    recording speed, 13
    writing to, 393–401
taping, 6. *See also* tape
Targa format, 111, 139
television sets, aspect ratio for, 56, 60
templates, DVD menu, 299–300, 350–362
terms, video production, 6
Test Data Rate button, 53
text. *See also* titles
    adding, 264
    aligning, 267
    applying styles to, 268–271
    changing, 265
    changing font for, 267
    changing leading between lines of, 276
    justifying, 275
    kerning, 263, 276
    moving, 266
    replacing, 265

Index

text *(continued)*
    resizing, 274–275
    rotating, 277
    scaling, 272–273
    skewing, 277
    wrapping, 272–273
Text Justify tool, 275
Text-styling controls, 262, 263
Text tool, 264
Text view, 34, 146, 147
TGA format, 139
Themes effect, 227
Threshold effect, 227
Thumbnail button, 290
thumbnails
    button, 360
    setting/resetting, 133, 168
    Storyboard, 149
    video, 386–389
TIFF format, 111, 139
tilting shots, 19, 20
time code
    automatically detecting scenes based on, 75
    contrasted with time/date stamp, 72
    interpreting, 72
time/date settings, 13
time/date stamps, 72
Time effects, 226, 227, 244
Timeline, 155–163. *See also* Timeline view
    adjusting audio volume on, 332–334
    adjusting Timescale of, 163
    arranging video clips on, 160
    changing duration of audio files on, 194
    changing duration of still images on, 191
    changing playback speed on, 246
    changing transition duration on, 209
    combining scenes on, 166–167
    components of, 155–156
    deleting video clips from, 164
    dragging video clips to, 157–158
    editing techniques, 176–189
        insert edits, 179–186
        ripple edits, 177
        rolling edits, 178
        split edits, 187–189
    getting audio to, 305
    inserting video clips between scenes on, 159
    keyboard shortcuts, 161
    moving around on, 162
    previewing video clips on, 161
    splitting video clips on, 165
    trimming video clips on, 175–178
Timeline scrubber, 113, 155, 156, 161
Timeline slider, 155, 156, 162

Timeline view. *See also* Timeline
    accessing, 34, 147
    applying transitions in, 203
    customizing, 162–163
    illustrated, 146
    purpose of, 147, 155
Timescale, 155, 163
Tint effect, 227
Title Deko, 139, 257
Title editor, 257–267
    adding buttons to titles with, 288
    adding/editing text in, 264–267
    adding logos to video with, 282–285
    closing, 261
    creating/editing Title objects in, 287
    creating full-screen titles with, 278–281
    creating rolls/crawls with, 301–302
    illustrated, 262
    interface/tools, 262–263
    keyboard shortcuts, 440
    opening, 258–261
    purpose of, 257
Title Editor Album, 262, 263
title objects, 287
Title Overlay button, 259
Title-safe zones, 263
Title track
    changing transitions on, 206
    fading into/out of elements on, 205–206
    illustrated, 155
    placing title on, 260
    purpose of, 156
Title-type buttons, 262, 263
titles. *See also* text; Title editor
    adding, 264
    adding buttons to, 288
    adding Title objects to, 287
    aligning, 267
    applying styles to, 268–271
    changing, 265
    changing font for, 267
    crawling, 302
    full-screen *vs.* overlay, 259, 261, 278–281
    justifying, 275
    moving, 266
    replacing, 265
    resizing, 274–275
    rolling, 301
    saving, 260
    scaling, 272–273
    setting default duration for, 55
    setting duration of, 263
    wrapping, 272–273
Titles tab, 32
Toolbox icon, 34

Index

tooltips, 47
tour, Studio 9, 29, 30
tracks. *See also* Audio track; Video track
    deleting, 158
    editing, 319
    locking, 158, 180
    synchronizing audio/video, 148
transition collections, 197, 198–199
transitions, 197–224
    accessing groups of, 198
    customizing, 209–211
    defined, 4, 197
    editing duration of, 209–211
    examples of, 197
    Hollywood FX. *See* Hollywood FX transitions
    key concepts regarding, 200–201
    previewing, 199, 202, 205
    reversing, 211
    ripple, 217–218
    setting default duration for, 55, 202
    timing of, 207–208
Transitions icon, 198
Transitions tab, 32, 198
transparent backgrounds, 280
Trash Can icon, 34, 339
Trim calipers, 310
Trim scrubber, 173, 174
trimming, 170–178
    with Clip Properties tool, 170–174
    defined, 130, 170
    and editing/production process, xi
    multiple clips, 176–178
    planning prior to, 171–172
    on Timeline, 175–178
tripods, 12, 19, 239
troubleshooting, 445–454
    analog capture, 449–450
    audio, 453–454
    distorted video, 448–450
    dropped frames, 451–452
    DV capture, 70, 448
    DV card/camera, 445–447
    FireWire cards, 447
Turbulence effect, 227
TV sets, aspect ratio for, 56, 60

U

UDMA, xi
Ulead Systems, 283, 286
Undo button/command, 31, 41
Unix, 416
USB ports, 68, 69

V

video. *See also* analog video; video clips
    adding logos to, 282–285
    archiving, 393
    creating watchable, 5. *See also* watchable video
    defined, 6
    displaying in Album, 122
    file size limitations, 75
    loading captured, 121
    playing, 123–124
    rescuing poorly shot, 241–242
    shooting, 5
    trimming. *See* trimming
    viewing captured, 83, 121–122
video backgrounds, 378
video buttons, 361
Video Capture Devices menu, 92
video clips. *See also* scenes
    applying color correction to, 235–237
    arranging on Timeline, 160
    deleting from Timeline, 164
    dragging
        to Storyboard, 150–151
        to Timeline, 157–158
    inserting between scenes, 152, 159
    previewing
        on Storyboard, 154
        on Timeline, 161
    trimming. *See* trimming
video distribution site. *See* StudioOnline
video editor, 3, 7
Video Feedback effect, 227
video flow, 344–346
video menus, 377–378
video production
    disk requirements, xii
    and Movie window, 145
    and Storyboard, 148
    terms, 6
video resolution, 405
Video Scenes tab, 32, 120
video thumbnails, 133, 386–389
Video toolbox, 34–35
Video track
    changing transitions on, 206
    dropping still images into, 190
    illustrated, 155
    placing title on, 260
    purpose of, 156
    synchronizing with Audio track, 148
VideoCD format, xi, 390
videotaping, 6
Visual QuickStart Guides, x
Voice-Over Narration tool, 315

467

Index

voice-over recording options, 308
Voice-Over tool, 305
Voice-Over track, 304
Volume Adjust control, 320
Volume Adjustment tool, 315
Volume Control dialog box, 98
Volume Control slider, 98–99, 335
volume fades. *See* audio fades
Volume Meter control, 320
Volume tool, 303, 305, 320–331
VST plug-in, 336, 337

W

watchable video, 3–28
    and camera settings, 10–16
    characteristics of, 4
    defined, 3
    guidelines for creating, 5
    and shot composition, 17–28
    and video editors, 7–9
Water Drop effect, 227
Water Wave effect, 227
Watercolor effect, 227
watermarks, 199
WAV files, 141, 305
Wave slider, 99
wedding effects, 220
white balance, 11
widescreen footage, 59
Windows
    Disk Defragmenter, 51–52
    Enable DMA option, 54
    file size limitations, 75
    Media Player, 422
    optimizing disk performance in, 54
    system requirements, xi–xii, 442
Windows Media files, 122, 141, 405, 422–424
Windows Metafile format, 111, 139
Wipe transitions, 198
WMF format, 139
word-wrapping controls, 272–273
writing to tape, 393–401
    controls for, 395–396
    multiple times, 401
    setting up hardware for, 394
    steps in process, 393

X

X icon, 45

Y

Y-connectors, 91

Z

zooming, 4, 13, 19